TAKE THE SLOW ROAD

SPAIN AND PORTUGAL

CONWAY
Bloomsbury Publishing Plc
50 Bedford Square, London, WC1B 3DP, UK
29 Earlsfort Terrace, Dublin 2, Ireland

BLOOMSBURY, CONWAY and the Conway logo are trademarks of Bloomsbury Publishing Plc

First published in 2023

A catalogue record for this book is available from the British Library

Library of Congress Cataloguing-in-Publication data has been applied for

ISBN: PB: 978-1-8448-6599-4
ePub: 978-1-8448-6595-6
ePDF: 978-1-8448-6596-3

10 9 8 7 6 5 4 3 2 1

Designed and typeset by Austin Taylor
Typeset in Catamaran, Janda and Raleway

Printed and bound in India by Replika Press Pvt. Ltd.

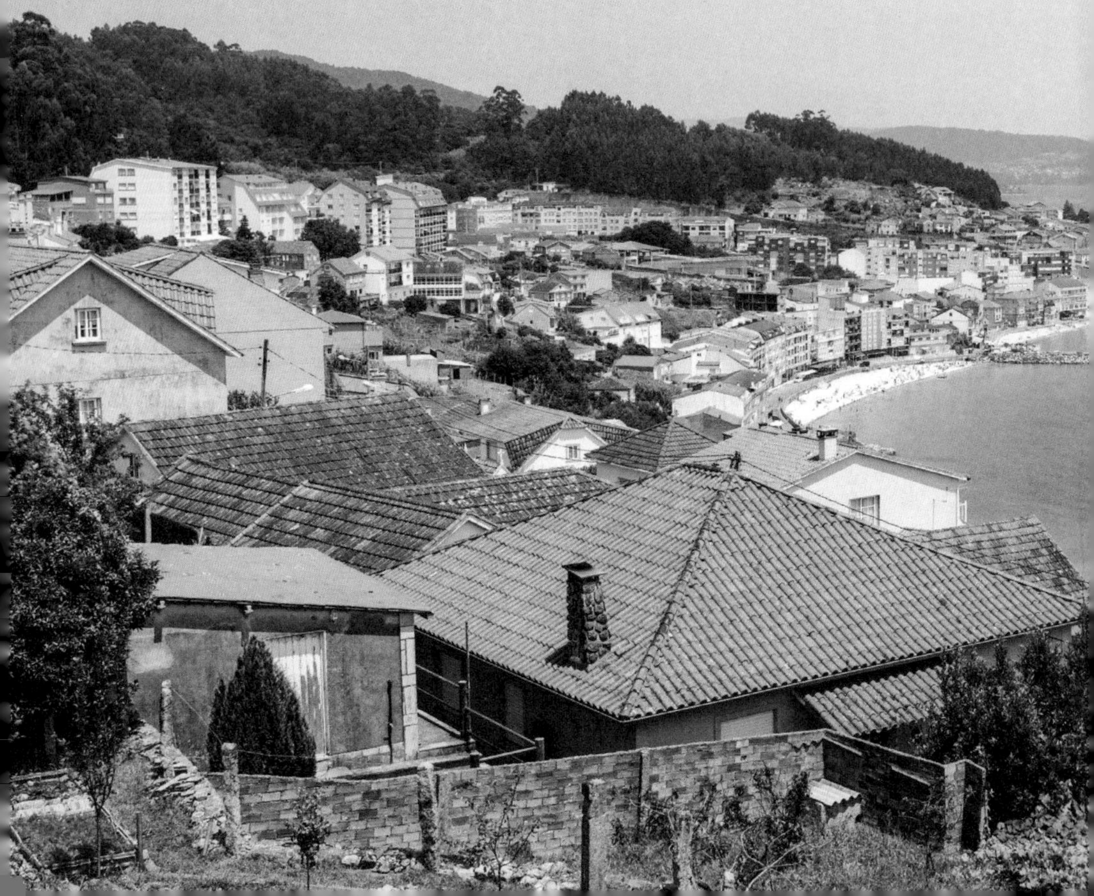

TAKE THE SLOW ROAD

SPAIN AND PORTUGAL

Inspirational Journeys Round Spain and Portugal by Camper Van and Motorhome

MARTIN DOREY

CONWAY

LONDON • OXFORD • NEW YORK • NEW DELHI • SYDNEY

CONTENTS

SPAIN 46

INTRODUCTION

¡Hola!

Welcome to another slow road adventure.

The idea with this book, and the *Take the Slow Road* series of books, is simple. Take your time. Explore. Have fun.

In the following pages, I will invite you to slow down and immerse yourself in the great driving, great places and great experiences you can find in Spain and Portugal. The information I have put together will help you plan and enjoy an exciting road trip where you get to take your time, explore slowly and gently, and properly get to know the Iberian Peninsula. There's far more to it than just the Costa del Sol or the Algarve!

Like the other titles in the *Take the Slow Road* series, this book is about making journeys by camper van and motorhome. Those that I have listed in this book have been put together for this project and are based on research, instinct, maps and lots of time exploring on the internet. Some follow existing routes, such as the N2 in Portugal. Many of the roads thread their way through gorges, over mountain passes and into the national parks. Others take the scenic route between Spain and Portugal's great cities and places of interest. Lots of them meander along the coast.

They all have several things in common: great roads, interesting scenery and stunning places to go and visit – because Spain and Portugal have those by the bucketload. From the Alhambra to Dalí's house in Portlligat, Madrid's art museums to the *pintxos* bars of the old quarter in San Sebastián, and

SA-201 outside La Alberca, Sierra de Francia

the beaches of Galicia to the cliffs and caves of the Algarve, there is always something to give you a glimpse of the real Spain and Portugal.

I don't expect you to follow the routes to the letter – although you can, of course – but rather use them as a starting point to write your own love story in Spain and Portugal. This book may not cover every inch of Iberia, but it will take you through a lot of its best bits as well as some of its quieter places. The coast of Asturias, for example, is stunningly beautiful. I could easily have spent months exploring its beaches. Inland lies a vast area of wilderness where relatively few visitors go and where Cantabrian bears roam free. This book will take you there, too. It will also take you to Benidorm and the Algarve, if you'd rather follow the well-worn path.

Of all the places I have travelled in my camper van, Spain and Portugal are my absolute favourites. I can safely say I have been at my happiest while travelling the backroads of the Iberian Peninsula while researching this book. The pace of life is relaxed, the roads are often empty, the places are beautiful and, on the whole, camper vans and motorhomes are welcomed with good campsites, a growing network of public and private stopovers and emptying points, and a relaxed attitude to free camping.

There's no need to rush. Taking the slow road is all about travelling at a pace that enables you to immerse yourself in the place, its people and customs. So, get off the *autovía* and meander a little. Take the old road, stop at a cafe, order a *café con leche* and meet the locals. It'll pay dividends.

My first experiences of Spain and Portugal were – like many Brits – on package holidays with my parents in the 1970s. They left an impression on me that I found hard to shift. However, some 20 years later, when I went to Málaga and Ronda to make a film,

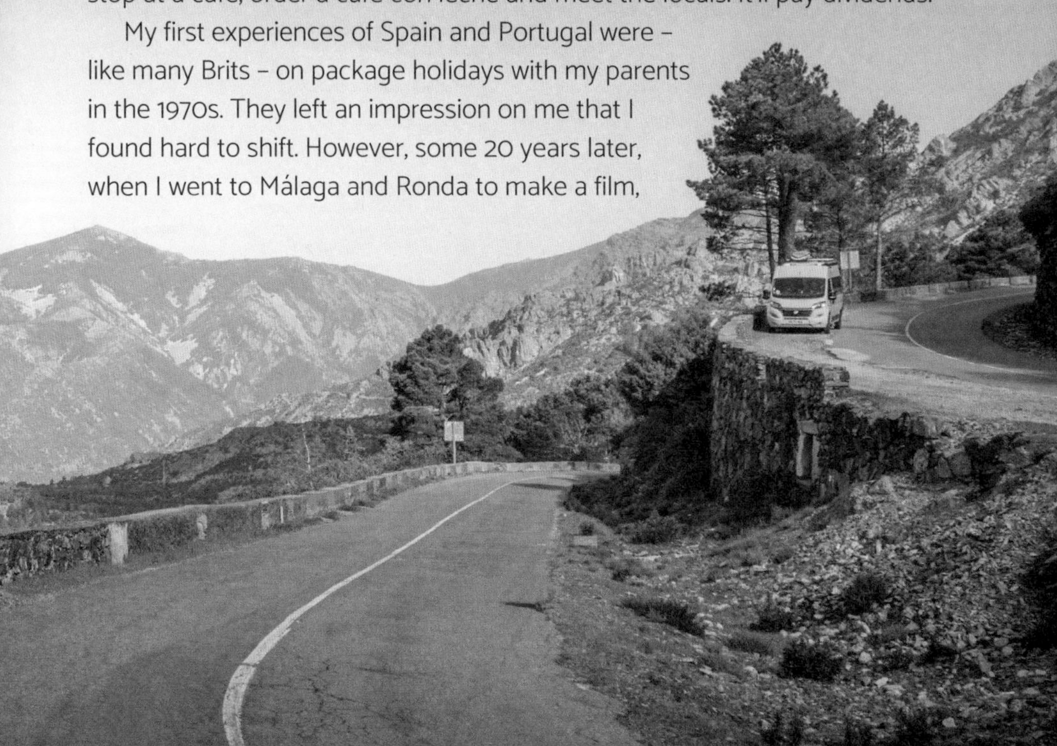

I discovered just how narrow-minded I had been. Oh Ronda! What an incredible, friendly, wonderful city.

Since then, I have been back a number of times, always by camper van and always to explore a little more of the places I have come to love: the Picos de Europa, Galicia, Asturias and the Basque coast. Portugal always seemed a little too far for the old cars and vans I took to Europe in my 20s, so getting there, finally, for this project, was a dream come true. Now that I have had the time to travel extensively through both countries, I am so very glad that I have. It's been an absolute blast and I wouldn't have missed it for the world. I hope that you will love it as much as I have.

¡Buen camino!

Be a conscious tourist (please)

As time goes on, it is becoming more and more obvious that we need to tread more lightly in all aspects of our lives. That includes our travels by camper van and motorhome. While motorhomes might produce fewer greenhouse gases than aeroplanes, they still produce emissions that are contributing to climate collapse.

With that in mind, I believe we can all do better, me included. We can become the type of 'conscious tourist' Spain and Portugal want by making a few urgent changes to the way we travel: we can contribute to the local economy, stay a little longer in one place, take care of the places we stay, walk or cycle more, shop local, pick up litter and contribute, where possible, to environmental projects.

During the research for this book, I met a captive wild Cantabrian bear on the Senda del Oso. The project that supports that bear is the Asturian Bear Foundation, a non-profit that aims to help support the continued recovery of the Cantabrian bear in northern Spain.

I donated the equivalent of my share of the first 200 sales of this book to the project.

• **www.osodeasturias.es**

HOW TO USE THIS BOOK

Praia do Tonel, Sagres, Portugal

Using this book is easy. The opening sections will help you with a little pre-trip planning, giving you an idea of what you might need to take, some things to organise in advance and a few bits of useful information. A lot of this has been learned the hard way so you don't have to find out for yourself!

After that, you'll see there are a number of routes. These routes are my suggestions of great roads to explore. I have researched, driven and explored these myself so the information contained within them is genuine. I rarely recommend anything I do not have first-hand experience of.

Each route has a different flavour and reason for doing it that I have chosen to make my theme for the time I was there. This could be obvious, like tasting sherry in the Sherry Triangle in Andalusia or it could be a little more offbeat, like searching for the best place to snorkel in the Algarve (and getting distracted by a cave).

Some of the journeys are inland, some in the mountains. Some follow rivers, while others follow the coast. Some will take you to ancient sites, moments in history or even, in the case of Seville, Madrid and San Sebastián, right into the heart of the city. Some routes may be good for cycling, surfing, swimming, snowboarding or sightseeing. All are good for seeing Spain and Portugal!

Please don't think that I have driven every road in Spain or Portugal for this book. I have not. My routes are based on research and the quality of the driving I hoped to discover. Failing that, they are designed to take

Albarracín near Cuenca

you to places of note in the most interesting way I can find. There are still thousands upon thousands of miles of roads that you can head off and explore for yourself. My routes are only a starting point.

Each route is separated into two sections. The first is my account of what happened when I was there. This will give you a taste of what you might expect and is meant to add colour to the route. While unique to my travels, I hope that these snippets of my travel experiences will inspire you to write your own story. These encounters are rarely planned unless I have needed to book an excursion or guide so they will give you an idea of what it's like to travel on that route in Spain or Portugal.

The second part of each route is the practical stuff, the A to B. It's written to help you follow the route and to explain what kind of driving

How Park4Night can save your world

I have travelled extensively with maps, books and now apps. Having once ridiculed the use of satnavs and apps to get around I will now admit to a complete U-turn, especially where apps are concerned. While the listings and comments on Park4Night are really useful to give you a feel for what a place will be like (although some reviews can be a bit ridiculous), the 'navigate' feature is by far the most useful. Why? Because it will save you having to try to navigate to places that are hard to get to or in the middle of cities.

I might be late to the party on this, but having Google help to guide you through a confusing one-way system to an *aire*, late at night and when you are tired, hungry and just want to get parked, is a revelation. It takes all the hard work out of it and brings back the joy because there is someone else to blame if it all goes wrong. Your navigator will be able to look out of the window and enjoy not having to get you there or suffer your frustration if you can't.

You can use the feature on your phone or integrated into your on-board system, if you are fancy like that. Either way, it will help enormously. Mobile signal in Spain and Portugal is, on the whole, excellent.

to expect along the way. By all means use it as a starting point if you want to meander and follow your nose or heart. There are no rules. I have been as detailed as I can be in these sections, but you will still need a good map to navigate your way around. The Park4Night navigation feature can also be a godsend at times – especially when navigating to overnights or car parks. It was for me.

The map pages, of course, will help you to find your way, but only up to a point. Please don't leave home hoping that they will suffice. I suggest using the *Michelin 1/200,000 Motoring and Touring Atlas* at the very least as my maps are pretty but might not be much use on the ground!

At the end of each route, I list a few places to stay and things to do in the area. These are based on my experience and are not the only things to do or see, by a long way, so please don't think that they are the be-all and end-all. I have not been to every tourist attraction or campsite.

See you on the road.

WHY SPAIN AND PORTUGAL FOR A SLOW ROAD ADVENTURE?

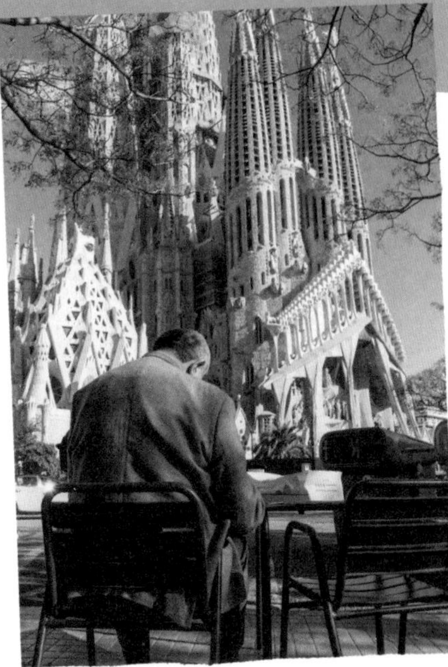

The *Take the Slow Road* series has now covered Scotland, England and Wales, Ireland and France.

When considering the next location, it wasn't hard to see that the Iberian Peninsula would be perfect. In fact, I could hardly wait to get started (once Covid restrictions allowed me to). Having travelled to northern Spain in a camper van a number of times between 2000 and 2016 I knew a little of what to expect. What I discovered along the way was even better.

Spain and Portugal are amazing countries to travel around in a camper van or motorhome. In fact, for many of us, they are just perfect, offering a heady mix of historical sites, great food, modern cities, interesting architecture, vibrant art and culture, vast areas of wilderness, incredible countryside and fabulous coastlines, with a good camping infrastructure to back it up and a generally relaxed attitude towards van travellers.

The way of life – laid-back and social – has made me think that the Spanish have got it right. Family and friends are important and life revolves around those, not work. The evening *paseo* – when everybody walks along an esplanade, beach or in the town – is a daily social event that keeps people healthy and happy. You'll really notice it when you go to the beach in high summer. Every town has some kind of social space – whether a *plaza mayor* or beachfront – where the community can meet and where events take place. People, as far as we can see, seem to value their community over anything else. That's to be admired, I think.

Spain has an incredible road network, too, which has been greatly

improved over the last few decades thanks to the EU, with *autovías*, tunnels and huge viaducts spanning mountain ranges, stretching across huge river valleys and joining up the conurbations. In many places, where local roads have been superseded by the need for speed, the local roads still exist, meaning it's possible to explore quiet, almost forgotten roads that are only used for local traffic these days.

Spain is one of Europe's most mountainous countries, with an average height above sea level of around 600m (1,969ft). What this means for us is that there are a lot of curvy roads to drive and plenty of jaw-dropping vistas to gawp at. These roads will lead you to high passes and isolated villages if you want them to. They will also take you to beaches, capes and lighthouses, into areas of wilderness and to pockets of the country where it seems nothing much has changed for decades.

Spain also welcomes motorhome and camper van drivers in their thousands each year from all over Europe. During our travels, we encountered a few Bits but not many. I hope this won't last too long as Spain and Portugal are amazing countries to travel in. They are, simply, incredible.

After Brexit

EU citizens can stay on the Iberian Peninsula as long as they like and there are no border checks between Spain and Portugal or Spain and France. The winter is mild and summer hot, with cooler temperatures in the mountains and to the north.

I don't know why we don't all just move there. Sorry, I forgot, we can't.

As a British passport holder, you are allowed 90 days in the Schengen area, on a rolling basis, without having to get a visa. Your passport will be stamped as you enter the EU. Once you have used up your 90 days' allocation you must spend 90 out of the area before you can return. Overstaying can lead to big fines, deportation and possibly a travel ban.

This is because we are a Third Country to Europe since

leaving the EU. This happened because, in my view, a cabal of liars and cheats decided Brexit would enable them to make the UK a deregulated, disaster capitalist paradise for bankers and billionaires and keep the population here to do their menial jobs for McJob wages. I have to say, I detest this, and it makes me so sad that our children will not be able to work and live in Europe as we did before Brexit. Frankly, it's deplorable. A great heist.

To calculate your allowable days in Europe, use the Visa Calculator: **www.schengenvisainfo.com/visa-calculator**

Language in Spain and Portugal

Spain and Portugal each have their own language, although they have similarities. However, Portuguese has a very different sound to Spanish, with greatly different – and difficult – pronunciation. This may be the reason why lots of Portuguese, especially in the tourist areas, speak English.

In Spain, a few people speak English, but this doesn't mean that you shouldn't at least try to speak Spanish. It is polite to have a go. And even if you make a hash of it (trust me, I have) people will appreciate that you have made an effort. The days of being a lazy English tourist are over. Besides, away from the major tourism areas (basically everywhere except the holiday enclaves of the Med), most people don't speak anything other than Spanish, or maybe even their regional language, such as Basque or Catalan, so to get by you will need at least a smattering.

Spanish is fun to learn and relatively easy to grasp so you can make yourself understood. I had a few hours of Spanish lessons before starting this book and it made all the difference.

YOUR ESSENTIAL CAMPING KIT LIST

Travelling with your own vehicle

Obviously, you'll need some kit. Bar the obvious like phone chargers, cables, Wi-Fi dongles, games and music, there are some essentials you have to take care of.

No doubt you've got your own list, but in case you haven't, here's mine.

Useful info

PORTUGAL TOLL ROAD PAYMENT: If you take a foreign-registered car into Portugal you will need to register a payment method to your number plate to pay tolls automatically: **www.portugaltolls.com**

LOW EMISSION ZONES: Spain is committed to creating hundreds of new low emission zones by 2023. At the time of writing, in 2022, only one was in permanent operation, in Barcelona, with others used on an emergency basis during pollution events. Information about LEZs, and who can and can't enter, plus how to get permission, is available at: **www.urbanaccessregulations.eu**

EMOVIS TAG: This will give you hassle-free motorway toll passage: **www.emovis-tag.co.uk**

ACSI CAMPING CARD: This card gives you a discount at hundreds of campsites in Spain and Portugal out of season: **www.campingcard.co.uk**

Camping de Comillas

Sort out your LPG connectors

If your motorhome or camper van has an onboard LPG tank or you use refillable bottles, then you'll need to fill up at some point. In Spain and Portugal, LPG is known as GLP or Autogas. UK motorhomes generally use a UK

bayonet type, which means you'll need an adaptor – either the DISH type or the Euroconnector – which you can get at **www.lpgshop.co.uk** if you are buying from the UK.

If you are unsure, check the information at **www.mylpg.eu**

Ensure your gas supply

UK propane gas bottles cannot be exchanged in Spain or Portugal, which means you will need to purchase a local gas bottle (and the appropriate adaptors for your motorhome's system) before you can swap an empty one for a full one. This can be expensive. Since Spanish residents use butane for cooking, and have to have an address to buy cylinders, you may also have to register yourself to buy one. Some forums suggest using a campsite address if you need to do this.

Campingaz is available in Europe and bottles can be swapped in the same way as in the UK at hardware stores (called *ferreterías* in Spanish and Portuguese).

Run a Gaslow system

The simple solution for many motorhomers seems to be changing gas over to a refillable system such as Gaslow. Having a refillable system means you can fill up at any time, at any service station that sells LPG. Motorhome dealers in the UK can do the necessary to change over from propane bottles for you, although it is possible to buy adaptor kits.

App to find LPG stations

All LPG stations in Spain and Portugal (or most of them) are marked on an interactive map from **www.mylpg.eu**. They also have an app, which is mighty useful if you need to cook your tea and need gas in a hurry.

Hoses and universal adaptors

Most Spanish and Portuguese water filling points (taps) have a screw fitting on them, which will fit to either a big or small Hozelock adaptor. So, it is essential to carry these if you use a hose to fill your tanks. In addition, it's very useful to carry a length of flexible hose and a universal tap adaptor in case of emergency, plus any specialist adaptors for your type of tank.

If you have a Porta Potti or onboard toilet, a short length of hose – to be kept separately from the freshwater hose – can help you to clean it out.

- 1 x 10m (33ft) of flexible freshwater fill-up hose
- 1 x set of universal tap-to-hose adaptors
- 1 x 1m (3.3ft) length of hose for slopping out toilets

Levelling blocks and spirit level

No doubt you already know that you can't sleep on a slope. So don't forget your levelling blocks (and chocks). It's a bit of an art getting vans level on some wonky surfaces, but it's worth the effort. If you forget your spirit level, a glass of water on the table will give you a good idea.

- 1 x set of Level Up levelling blocks (and chocks)
- 1 x spirit level

Electric cables and extensions

If you have electric hook-up then you'll need a C Form or 16 amp cable to go with it, plus a two-pin adaptor (lots of campsites use 16 amp but it's better be safe than sorry). About 25m (82ft) is usually enough to reach any pitch. It may also be a good idea to carry a 13 amp adaptor plug, as well as a 13 amp socket if your campsite doesn't have a 16 amp socket (but it should!).

- 1 x Euro two-pin to 16 amp adaptor
- 1 x 25m (82ft) 16 amp cable
- 1 x 16 amp to three-pin adaptor

Maps, maps, maps

I always carry a map for route planning, as well as large-scale maps of the specific areas I am visiting – so I can get into the heart of the landscape.

You can buy a whole set of 1/150,000-scale *Michelin Local* maps or you can buy the 1/200,000-scale *Michelin Tourist and Motoring Atlas* for a fraction of the price. It is this map that I use in the routes.

Apps and books

These days, you don't really need to carry books with you because everything can be found on an app, especially overnights.

Park4Night is universally used and is massively useful, especially as it will allow you to navigate to any destination.

However, books still have a place in my van and I still carry all the traditional guides to help with navigation and for finding surf or swim spots.

- *All the Aires*, plus map
- Campsite guides
  All of these are available from **www.vicarious-shop.com**

Specialist guides are also really useful, particularly if you have a specialist interest:

- *Alan Rogers* guides: **www.alanrogers.com**
- *Wild Swimming* guides: **www.wildswimming.co.uk**
- Low Pressure *Stormrider Surf Guides*: **www.lowpressure.co.uk**

Weather-appropriate kit

Do you need me to tell you this? It can get very hot in Spain and Portugal! It can also get very cold. And sometimes wet. Take rain gear, sunglasses, sun cream, hats etc, depending on the season in which you'll be visiting.

BBQs

Spain is hot and dry for much of the year. This means it could be extremely foolish to light fires and BBQs wherever you like. Many campsites will have designated BBQ places where you can light up, but lots of campsite simply ban it. If you want to light a fire, check with local rules and regulations, keep a bucket of water handy and don't take any risks.

If you want to BBQ, I recommend using a Cadac or similar.

Sites like **www.pitchup.com** will allow you to search for sites where fires are allowed.

Never use disposable BBQs. They are dangerous, give off huge amounts of carbon monoxide and are massively wasteful.

Toilet kit

If you have a loo, avoid blue chemicals as they are harmful. Use green stuff without formaldehyde.

- Green toilet liquid for the loo
- Trowel if you don't have a loo
- Cheap toilet paper (it tends to break down easier)

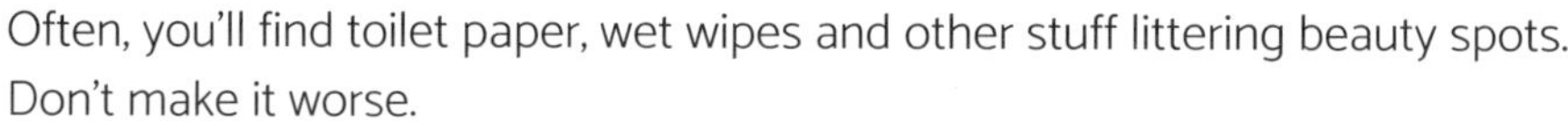

Often, you'll find toilet paper, wet wipes and other stuff littering beauty spots. Don't make it worse.

Do not urinate within 30m (98ft) of any open water, rivers or streams. If you do have to defecate, do it as far as possible from rivers, streams, buildings and animals. Dig a hole and bury it. Carry a trowel or folding spade.

Carry a universal sink plug as some sites may not have plugs.

Recycling

Most towns in Spain will have recycling bins at the side of the road. Look for yellow wheelie bins for plastic and tins, blue for paper and card, and standard green bottle banks for bottles.

Green living kit

You can easily reduce the waste you produce by taking a few essential bits of green living kit. Given what we now know about plastic waste and the destruction of the environment, it's the least we can do. Plus, it'll save you looking for bins.

- Green loo chemicals
- Reusable coffee cups: These may get you a discount as well as saving on plastic litter.
- Refillable bottle: don't squander cash on soft drinks and make waste when tap water is great. And free.

- Reusable shopping bags: Save waste by taking your own.
- Reusable veg bags: These save waste – when you buy loose veg – and are easy to store in the fridge. Spanish supermarkets often require you to weigh veg yourself, which means you have to use a bag. While the bags they provide are often not plastic, it pays to take your own mesh bags.
- Shampoo bars: These make no waste and can be kept in tins for ease of use and less mess. They last for ages and are smaller to pack than bottles.
- Tupperware containers: For taking to butchers, grocers and markets if you're shopping local, to save waste. Some supermarkets are getting wise to anti-plastic measures but not all. You may have a struggle if you take your own pots, but do persevere, it is possible.

If you are renting a van

A rental should include (whether as an optional extra or not) all you could need in terms of tables, chairs, safety stuff, gas, hoses and kitchen items and utensils but DO CHECK WITH THE SUPPLIER.

In theory, you should only need to take your clothes, towels and personal stuff, plus any toys.

Roof racks and straps are likely to be add-ons. Make sure you ask for them when you book!

Camping de Comillas

When you pick up the camper, check the kit list as supplied with your vehicle. Make sure you have the absolute essentials: green chemicals for the loo, hoses or a means to fill up with fresh water, gas to cook on.

If you are given a handover, make sure there are two of you present (unless you travel alone) as it can be daunting to take it all in during one session. IDEA: Take pictures on your phone of the important bits – better still, video the handover!

WHERE TO STAY IN SPAIN AND PORTUGAL

Spain and Portugal are incredible places to take a motorhome or camper van. There is plenty of space and, as a result, plenty of places to stay and a broad selection of options.

The locations in this book

In this book you'll find listed sites and places to stay. These are just suggestions and are based on my experience when I was travelling in that area. This isn't a campsite directory so don't expect it to be comprehensive. Also, while I choose places to stay very carefully, there is a chance that I have missed something, so please don't think that my places are THE BEST, because they may not be.

There are a lot of campsites and *aires* in Spain and Portugal. They vary in quality and size, with some run by corporations and others remaining independent. However, a lot of campsites tend to have a mix of touring pitches, tent pitches, seasonal pitches and, in more recent times, glamping pitches. On some sites you may find that the seasonal pitches are more like ramshackle villages with picket fences, add-ons and all kinds of semi-permanent features. This is because Spanish families will decamp en masse to their caravan to get away from excessive heat in the summer months. The rest of the time they remain empty and can end up looking very sad indeed.

Pantín, Galicia

Booking ahead?

If you are touring then it may not be possible to book ahead, especially if you don't know where you'll be. However, if you are travelling to a big four- or five-star site then it would be wise to book, especially in the summer months (July and August) as many sites can get full. At many places, such as camper parks, it may not be possible to book ahead.

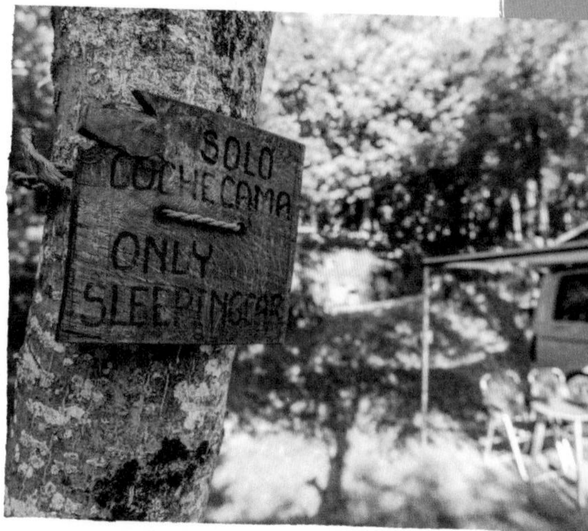

Áreas de servicio para autocaravanas (aires)

These are dedicated motorhome parking areas, often with emptying and filling facilities, but not always, which are provided by the local municipality to welcome us. They can often be free and can be in fantastic locations. However, it isn't always the case. Some may be little more than car parks in the centre of towns and have no facilities. However, the advantage is that they are useful if you haven't got anything else, want to save money or just like feeling free. Out of season, they may be the only option. You are expected to be self-contained to use an *aire*, which means you must have toilet facilities. You are not allowed to put out chairs and tables or set up camp with awnings and pup tents, although some do.

Some *aires* are privately run and are generally really great value, often with showers and toilets as well as emptying facilities.

Spain Discovery (España Discovery) locations

This is a member-only scheme whereby farmers, winegrowers, motorhome owners and artisans offer their land for you to park overnight for free in exchange for gratitude and politeness. It is expected that, as a guest, you'll say hello to the hosts and will, perhaps, spend a little money with them. That's it. There is no real obligation but if you happen to stay it might well be rude not to enjoy a meal... Membership costs around £27 per year, for which you get a guidebook to show your hosts to prove you are a member, and a QR code for each location to help you navigate.
Buy yours from **www.espana-discovery.es**

Campsites

Spain and Portugal operate an easy to understand grading system of campsites, which means you can always find something that suits.

Campsites are graded with stars ranging from two to five.

The more stars a campsite has, the more facilities you can expect, from pools to bars and restaurants. The thing to note here is that plots have a minimum size for different ratings, so the more stars it has, the bigger the plots. This is worth knowing if you drive a huge A-class. You might find that a 45m^2 (485ft^2) plot might be a bit tight.

All sites have to be inspected and rated with a star rating from two to five. Pitch size, facilities, languages spoken, whether a reception is open during the day, whether they are manned for 24 hours (three stars and upwards) or offer online booking all have a bearing on the star rating. Sites with pools and leisure facilities usually have higher ratings (there must be a pool or lake to qualify for five stars, for example) and all sites over two stars are expected to have Wi-Fi, unless they state otherwise.

Basically, the more you want, the higher the rating. However, all sites must have washing facilities, with sites over two stars requiring individual cabins for washing.

Municipal campsites

If you are looking for great value then a municipal campsite can be a good bet. They are run by the local authority and are often close to local facilities. They are often well signposted.

Wild motorhome camping in Spain and Portugal

Wild camping, unless you have the permission of the landowner, is not legal in Spain. However, it is not illegal to park a motorhome or camper van and it is legal to sleep in a vehicle. So, that means that if you park and don't camp, then you can stop over.

Camping, in the eyes of the law, is putting out tables and chairs, awnings or anything that extrudes beyond the perimeter of the vehicle. Levelling wedges are contentious, but may also be considered camping, not parking, because all four wheels must be on the ground.

Spanish law prevents camping in coastal areas, for the sake of the environment, so be wary of staying overnight in that beach car park.

In reality, wild camping (parking) is tolerated in a lot of places, with the exception of the busy resorts of the Mediterranean coasts and in National or Natural parks.

Portugal is slightly different. In 2021, after a clampdown on motorhomes (possibly because the pandemic brought lots of motorhomers and mess), the law was changed to make wild camping legal but only under certain circumstances. It was illegal prior to that but often tolerated. Since then, you may only stay for 48 hours in any municipality and you may not stay where there are signs (you'll see a lot of these) or in places that are on the Natura 2000 network, are protected areas or are covered by the Coastal Development Plans.

As always, if in doubt, don't.

Use Park4Night to find local *aires* or campsites or read their reviews to find out how others found areas.

Wild camping etiquette

- Ask permission from the landowner.
- Remember that wild camping is not a right.
- Tidy up when you arrive.
- Tidy up before you leave.
- Arrive late and leave early.
- Don't look as if you are setting up an encampment.
- Respect the locals, and if they ask you to leave, do it willingly.
- Ask locals, police, wardens or attendants if it's OK to park up overnight.
- Don't take the mick when it comes to goodwill. Be nice. Smile.
- Don't ignore 'no camping' signs.
- Do not allow any black waste to escape into the environment.
- Use eco liquids for washing up, washing and showering and don't let them escape into the environment.
- Do not litter.
- Pick up others' litter.
- Spend locally if you can.

HOW TO GET TO SPAIN AND PORTUGAL

Spain and Portugal are part of mainland Europe. Spain shares a border with Portugal and a land border with France and Andorra.

Spain has a coastline on the Bay of Biscay as well as on the Mediterranean. Portugal's coastline is entirely facing the Atlantic. Spain and Portugal are both members of the EU.

You can get to Spain from the UK and Ireland by ferry, overland via France, or by air.

Portugal can be reached by land via Spain, or by air.

If you are coming by camper van or motorhome

From the UK by ferry

Ferries from Channel coast ports Plymouth and Portsmouth arrive in Santander or Bilbao, taking around 24 hours to do so. They are expensive relative to ferries to France but will save around 1,000km (621 miles) of driving.

In addition, ferry services to Santander and Bilbao with Brittany Ferries can help to reduce driving if you're travelling to the Pyrenees or Atlantic coast of France. They are longer and cost significantly more but can save a lot of driving.

• **www.brittany-ferries.co.uk**

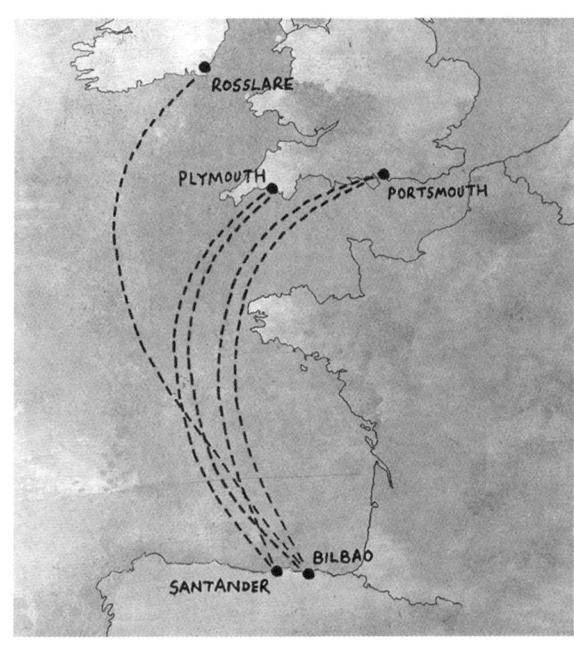

From Ireland by ferry

You can get to Spain from Ireland by ferry, either via the UK and then from Plymouth or Portsmouth to Santander, or direct from Rosslare to Bilbao.

From mainland Europe

You drive! It's a simple as that. The EU's marvellous freedom of movement policy means that if you come from within the EU you can travel to Spain from France or Andorra.

If you are hiring a van, it's simple to take a train.

By train

The Eurotunnel Le Shuttle (Channel Tunnel) can take motorhomes and camper vans from Ashford in Kent to Calais in a little over half an hour. Costs are comparable to some ferries. • **www.eurotunnel.com**

By train and renting a motorhome in Spain or Portugal

The Eurostar from London King's Cross St Pancras will whisk you through the Chunnel at reasonable rates (no, really) on certain trains to places as far afield as Barcelona or Madrid and even Seville and Lisbon. At the time of writing, fares from London to Barcelona were advertised for as little as £85.

If you are picking up a van then this is a feasible option, especially if you are taking your bike. Another advantage is being able to take more luggage than you might on a plane (and for free).

Flying and renting a motorhome

There are lots of viable and greener alternatives to flying these days. Train travel in Europe is easy and relatively cheap compared with the UK, which means taking a train to a motorhome rendezvous isn't out of the question. It makes sense from a planetary point of view, too.

If you do decide to fly, there are three international airports in Portugal: Lisbon, Porto and Faro.

Spain has over 30 airports, of which a number accept international flights.

DRIVING IN SPAIN AND PORTUGAL

First, and most importantly, you drive on the right in Spain and Portugal. You overtake on the left. In an emergency, call 112. These calls can be answered in Spanish, French or English. You must be over 18 and hold a full driving licence to drive in Spain and Portugal.

Before we get into the detail, let's have a word about what you can expect from driving in Spain.

On the whole, it can be a really pleasant experience, with little traffic (compared with the UK), good roads and a good standard of driving. However, as you will be driving a camper or motorhome, you may be the victim of impatience. This could mean people will try to overtake you, even when perhaps it's unnecessary or unsafe. Don't let it get to you.

SA-201 outside La Alberca, Sierra de Francia

Drive defensively and pull over safely to let others pass if they are in an obvious hurry.

You may find that some drivers have a liberal attitude towards traffic lights. Don't be tempted to do as they do. Only go on green, and stop on red. The rest is just bad manners. Do not jump the lights by going on the other carriageway's red.

Seat belts

If seat belts are fitted, *you must wear them.* The driver is responsible for everyone under 18 travelling in the car. Kids under the age of ten are not allowed to travel in the front, unless there are no back seats or there is no room. Kids under ten who weigh less than 15kg (33lb) must use an appropriate car seat.

Phones headsets

It is *illegal to use a mobile phone* (unless hands-free) while driving. Recent laws have made it possible to confiscate licences if you are caught. At least expect a fine.

You are *not allowed to wear headphones or headsets while driving* either and risk a fine and receiving points on your licence if you get caught, either in person or by radar.

Drinking

Drinking and driving is a strict NO in Spain and Portugal, as anywhere, with the maximum legal level of alcohol in the blood for private drivers set at 0.5 milligrams of alcohol per millilitre (mg/ml) of blood, with lower levels for some drivers. This is less than the UK's limit of 0.8mg/ml and represents a modest glass of wine. However, be warned: The penalties can be extremely severe if you cause an accident or get caught with over 0.5mg/ml, more over 0.8mg/ml, with huge fines and prison sentences for the worst offences.

Best advice? Don't drink and drive under any circumstances.

Random breath tests are legal and you can be tested if you cause a traffic offence such as failing to wear a seat belt.

Other rules

Tailgating and crossing a solid white line can also land you a fine.

In some cases, the authorities have the right to confiscate your vehicle: if you travel without insurance, at over 50km/h (31mph), or over the alcohol limit, for example.

Speed camera detectors are illegal in Spain and Portugal. It is also illegal to use satnav with speed cameras marked, so turn that feature off. It is also illegal to have any devices other than a satnav stuck to the windscreen.

It's worth noting that the Spanish and Portuguese authorities now have the power to track you down to your place of residence, wherever you live, through the EU Cross Border Enforcement Directive.

Items you must carry with you

- A valid driving licence covering you for the vehicle you are driving.
- An up-to-date passport for each occupant of the vehicle.
- Vehicle insurance documents, providing at least third-party cover.
- A valid MOT certificate if your vehicle is over three years old.
- V5 log book or a VE103 document for rented/hired vehicles.
- A warning triangle.
- Headlamp beam deflectors.
- It is illegal to drive with an important bulb not working. Having a spare bulb kit will help you to avoid this.
- A high-visibility vest for each occupant of the vehicle.
- Your vehicle should be displaying a UK sticker (unless you've rented one in Spain or Portugal).
- Snow chains are compulsory on some roads in winter.

Cuenca

Traffic lights

Spain and Portugal use the three-colour system of red, amber and green. However, unlike in the UK, they do not use an amber light after red and before green.

A flashing amber light means caution: Slow down and give way to vehicles coming from the right.

If a red light is accompanied by a yellow arrow, you may proceed in the direction indicated by the arrow. However, you must give way to any vehicles travelling in that direction, and pedestrians.

Motorways are sometimes operated by private companies, which means you'll pay tolls to use them. You can pass the booths seamlessly and without having to fumble with cards, cash and getting your passenger to do the work by using an Emovis Tag. These are linked to your bank account and debit each toll directly.

Low emission zones (LEZ)

These now operate in Madrid and Barcelona, with more planned. In order to be able to drive in Barcelona in the LEZ you need to register a foreign vehicle at **ajuntament.barcelona.cat/en/** at a cost of €7 (at time of writing). If your vehicle is permitted to enter, you may do so, for one year after registering. If not, you need to register, then buy daily passes to enter the city.

For Madrid, it is similar. See here for more **www.madrid.es**

Speed limits in Spain and Portugal

All speed limits are in kilometres per hour and all distances are in kilometres in Spain and Portugal. Limits are weather and condition dependent.

General speed limits

Type of road	Limit in km/h – Good visibility	Limit in km/h – Rain	Limit in km/h – Visibility less than 50m/55 yards
Motorway	130km/h (81mph)	110km/h (68mph)	50km/h (31mph)
Dual carriageway or priority roads	110km/h (68mph)	100km/h (62mph)	50km/h (31mph)
Other roads	80km/h (50mph)	70km/h (43mph)	50km/h (31mph)
Built-up areas	50km/h (31mph)	50km/h (31mph)	50km/h (31mph)

WARNING: Holders of EU driving licences exceeding the speed limit by more than 40km/h will have their licences confiscated on the spot by the police.

Motorhome speed limits

Type of road	Limit in km/h – 3.5 tonnes	Limit in km/h – Over 3.5 tonnes/under 3.7m (12ft)	Limit in km/h – Over 3.7m (12ft)
Motorways	130km/h (81mph)	110km/h (68mph)	90 (56mph)
Primary roads and dual carriageways	110km/h (68mph)	100km/h (62mph)	80km/h (50mph)
Other roads	80km/h (50mph)	80km/h (50mph)	80km/h (50mph)
Built-up areas	50km/h (31mph)	50km/h (31mph)	50km/h (31mph)

Road numbers and classifications

AP is an *autopista de peaje*: a toll motorway.
A is an *autovía*.

Junctions on the motorway are identified by their distance from the start of the road in kilometres. This makes it very easy to work out where you are or how long you have to go until a junction.

N is a national road.

Local roads are classified using a prefix of their local area, for example CA is Cantabria and AS is Asturias. In Spain, road names are hyphenated, whereas in Portugal they are not.

When you are map reading, you may find that road numbers can change without warning. This happens most often when roads cross the borders between departments or where another road scheme has joined the original road. Be aware.

Towing

It is against the law to tow a vehicle using an A-frame in Spain or Portugal. It's better to use a trailer (as long as it's not over 750kg/0.8 tons) for your runabout.

Any towing vehicle longer than 12m (39ft) must display red and yellow warning signs on the rear.

If you tow anything over 3,500kg (3.9 tons) then you'll need to register that trailer. • **www.gov.uk/register-trailer-to-take-abroad**

Bike racks

These are legal in Spain and Portugal, but you will need to carry a red and white-striped warning square.

Windmills at
Mota del Cuevo

Douro Valley

SPAIN AND PORTUGAL FOR NEWBIES

Spain, the basics

OK, here goes.

<table>
<tr><td>Spain is in mainland Europe.</td><td colspan="3" rowspan="2">The first language is Spanish, with 99 per cent of the population speaking it as a first or second language. Other than Spanish, the most commonly spoken languages at home are Catalan in 8 per cent, Valencian in 4 per cent, Galician in 3 per cent and Basque in 1 per cent.</td></tr>
<tr><td>The currency is euros.</td></tr>
<tr><td>The measurements are metric.</td><td colspan="3">Spain is one of Europe's most mountainous countries. It has an average height above sea level of 600m (1,969ft).</td></tr>
<tr><td>The population is around 47 million.</td><td colspan="2">Spain has an area of 505,000 sq km (194,982 sq miles).</td><td>About 36 per cent of Spain is forested.</td></tr>
<tr><td colspan="2" rowspan="2">Shops in Spain open at 9.00 a.m. until 2.00 p.m. and then close for the siesta until around 4.00 p.m. They often stay open until around 10.00 p.m. Supermarkets and shopping malls may stay open continuously from 9.00 a.m. until 10.00 p.m.</td><td colspan="2">Most museums and art galleries are closed on Mondays.</td></tr>
<tr><td colspan="2">Spain has 49 UNESCO World Heritage Sites.</td></tr>
</table>

Portugal, the basics

Portugal shares a land border with Spain.	The first **language** is Portuguese. Around 25 per cent of people speak English.	The **currency** is euros.
The **measurements** are metric.	Portugal **legalised drug use** in 2001. It now has among the lowest drug use in Europe.	The **population** is around 10 million.
Portugal has an **area** of 92,000 sq km (35,521 sq miles).	About **38 per cent** of Portugal is forested.	Portugal has 17 UNESCO **World Heritage** Sites.
Shops stay open from 9.00 a.m. or 10.00 a.m. until 7.00 p.m. Monday to Friday.	Portugal operates on **Greenwich Mean Time** and also utilises daylight saving time.	As with Spain, **museums** and **galleries** are usually closed on Mondays.

Seven Hanging Valleys walk, Algarve

SPAIN AND PORTUGAL HIGHLIGHTS

This is the difficult bit. Spain and Portugal are two remarkable countries where there's a lot to see and do. There is certainly more to Spain than the Costa del Sol or to Portugal than the Algarve. And the more you see, the more you will want to see. And then the more you will realise that there is to see. Here, I have listed my favourite experiences, places and things to do based on what I enjoyed most about being in Spain and Portugal. And there's still more!

1 Mud baths at San Pedro del Pinatar If ever there was a philosophy to help you enjoy Spain to the full it is this: get over yourself. You'll have to do this when you wade into the salt flats to grab handfuls of oozing, stinking black mud from the bottom. But once you have slathered it all over yourself and stood in the sun like a cormorant warming itself on a sunny morning, you'll realise that it was all worth it because you'll feel ... like you are covered in stinking estuarine mud (and it's brilliant). I loved doing this because it's not something you get to do every day. And it's free.

2 Surfing pedalos in Bendiorm Another good way of getting over yourself. Benidorm doesn't have to be crass. If you want, it can be fun and full of love and laughter. Our trip on the pedalos with the slides (it must have a slide) was such a lot of fun. Plus, if there is a little swell running you can pedal hard and catch a wave in. Sliding into the clear, warm sea on a hot day is something every child at heart should experience once in their life. There is much joy to be had from simple, silly things.

3 San Sebastián's old city

San Sebastián is one of my favourite Spanish cities. It is at once sophisticated and surfy, fun and foodie, with two divine beaches and an old city that sits between the two. Wander the narrow streets and sample *pintxos* – the Basque, at-the-bar-style tapas – at any number of down-to-earth bars. The best are to be found in Plaza de la Constitución, the colonnaded main square that once doubled as a bullring. Stroll up to the bar, order a few *pintxos* and take a seat. The magic happens when you start eating...

4 The Alhambra, Granada

This is one of Spain's most visited sites for a very good reason: it is simply magnificent. Never mind the other tourists, the selfie sticks and the tour guides leading tails of gawping clients, this is the real thing. The architecture is stunning, the craftsmanship otherworldly and the experience wholly wonderful. We booked early tickets for the Palacio Nazaríes and felt that we had really benefitted from it: It was less busy than later in the day and there were fewer people in the whole complex at that time. So that could be a tip. Even if you can't go early, it is an amazing place to visit – one for that bucket list.

5 Capela dos Ossos, Évora

It's small and a little bit macabre, but the Capela dos Ossos is worth a detour when you are touring Portugal. With bones from around 5,000 skeletons making up the fabric and decoration of the chapel, it's a weird place, designed to remind you that you are but a mere mortal. The display of Nativity scenes in the eaves of the church will bring you back to life if it's all too much.

6 La Alberca and Peña de Francia The little town of La Alberca is a delight in an often overlooked mountain range to the south-west of Salamanca. Overhanging, ramshackle, half-timbered buildings create an atmosphere that's straight out of the Brothers Grimm. You can buy local ham, honey and nuts in the Plaza Mayor or pop into a few little shops to get supplies, but the real hero is the village itself. The Peña de Francia is a mountain a few kilometres away with a monastery at the top. The drive is exhilarating, the views are sublime. Expect ibex.

7 Flamenco in Seville On a steamy night in Seville, we went off in search of flamenco. We found it in a tiny club down one of Seville's winding back streets. The whole experience, though largely executed in favour of the tourists, felt as authentic as we could expect. We ate tapas and drank beer and had a very hot, jolly time. Afterwards, we wandered the city streets until late, eating ice creams the size of houses and rubbernecking the magnificent cathedral.

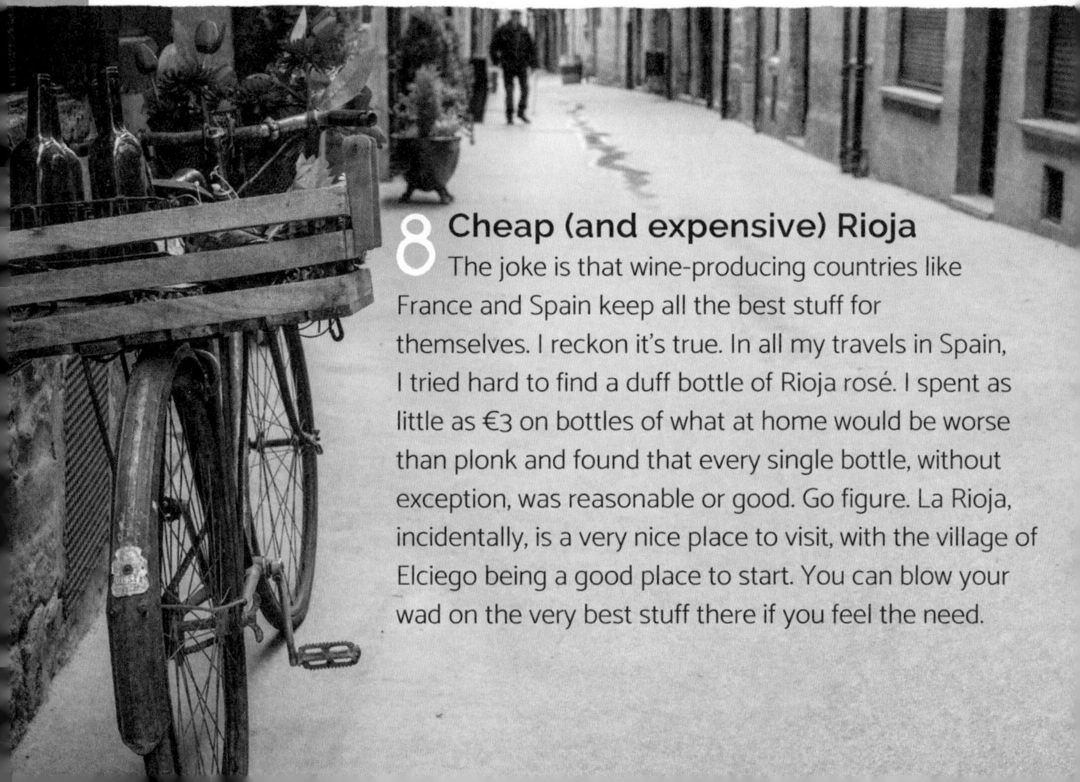

8 Cheap (and expensive) Rioja The joke is that wine-producing countries like France and Spain keep all the best stuff for themselves. I reckon it's true. In all my travels in Spain, I tried hard to find a duff bottle of Rioja rosé. I spent as little as €3 on bottles of what at home would be worse than plonk and found that every single bottle, without exception, was reasonable or good. Go figure. La Rioja, incidentally, is a very nice place to visit, with the village of Elciego being a good place to start. You can blow your wad on the very best stuff there if you feel the need.

9 Swimming wild in rivers, lakes and reservoirs Spain is a brilliant place for the wild swimmer. The country is full of reservoirs, rivers and lakes where you can swim safely. In lots of inland areas, local municipalities dam rivers to make pools, set up inland beaches on reservoirs or run municipal outdoor pools to allow people to cool off when it gets hot in the summer months. While you might not see many people swimming early in the year, and campsite pools don't open until June, once the summer months kick in, everyone is at it. During the course of writing this book, I have swum in waterfalls, rivers, lakes, pools and reservoirs. My favourite was a series of rivers cascading from the Sierra de Gredos that can be accessed along the EX-203 road that ends up in Plascencia.

10 Wild Asturias The coast of Asturias is fabulous. But head inland and you'll discover a world of wild peaks, wild roads and, if you are lucky, wild animals. Bears live in the woods in some of Europe's best-protected land. Follow the Senda del Oso into the mountains and keep your eyes peeled for bears in the woods. At the very least, you'll get to see a couple of orphaned (and unable to go back into the wild) bears that live in semi-captivity in a huge enclosure along the way. From there, you can go deeper into the Somiedo Natural Park with some wonderful mountain driving and the chance to take the sky-bound elevator road to Valle de Lago. The Muniellos reserve, to the south of Cangas del Narcea, only allows 20 people each day to walk among the protected oak forest.

11 Galician beaches Galicia is like Cornwall in the sun. Except more so. The beaches are glorious and the coastline is spectacular, with options for every day of the year. Surfing is popular here but unlike in other areas, has yet to reach saturation point. Free camping is tolerated and there is a good selection of *aires* and campsites, many of which are close to the beach, to choose from. The coast between Cedeira and Viveiro is wonderful, with remote villages and wild promontories creating a dramatic background to anyone's touring story.

12 Portugal's Route 66 The N2 crosses Portugal from border to border, starting in Chaves in the north and ending in Faro. It was devised and completed under the rule of dictator Salazar's New State in the 1940s to open up the centre of Portugal. It became an important trade route for Portugal's cork and wine industry. Today, the route has long been superseded by motorways and newer roads, but it is still possible to travel its entire length of 738km (459 miles). We drove it in sections for this book but would happily drive (or cycle) the whole lot, given enough time! It will take you through mountains, the Douro, to monuments and cities, to Portugal's heart and right into Faro and the Ria Formosa wetlands.

13 Córdoba's Mezquita-Catedral I couldn't help thinking that the Catholics had a nerve ripping the heart out of the mosque and plonking a cathedral in it. But they did and it provides an interesting contrast. The cool, calm, beautifully crafted arches and ceilings of the *mezquita* stand firm against the gaudy grandness of the *catedral*. Surrounding the whole thing are the narrow lanes of the Jewish quarter. Catch them in spring and you'll get the chance to visit the city's patio gardens in the Córdoba Courtyard Festival, when private courtyards are opened up to all.

14 Caves and cliffs of the Algarve

The Seven Hanging Valleys are – well – seven hanging valleys on the Algarve between Marinha Beach and Vale de Centeanes Beach. It's a walk that's just 6km (3.7 miles) end to end but that takes in some spectacular coastal scenery. Marinha is particularly wonderful for its caves, stacks and arches. The Benagil cave is the big-hitting feature that you can only visit from the sea, but there are plenty of other options to explore if you don't mind paddling in a kayak or on an SUP. Take a right out of Carvoeiro and there are plenty of quieter caves and arches to paddle through. Alternatively, head south of Lagos to Praia do Camilo for stacks and caves and lovely beaches.

15 The Pyrenees

The rack-and-pinion railway that takes you up to the 'resort' of Núria, a monastery in a beautiful valley at 2,000m (6,562ft), is one highlight of a trip across the Pyrenees. We did it in winter and linked all the major ski areas. Skiing in Spain is big news, but there are few resorts like those you'd find in the Alps. It's all a bit more low-key and very much cheaper. The scenery is great, the roads are relatively simple to navigate and the camping is easy at many of the resorts, although you may have to head down into the valleys for water and emptying. All in all, though, it's a great adventure.

16 The Picos de Europa

The diminutive mountain range is small but perfectly formed. The roads into the heart of it, at Fuente Dé, are great and the camping is brilliant. Walking is good, too, with an easy – and very swift – cable car whisking you up to the top of the magnificent cirque at 1,823m (5,981ft). The walk back down is fabulous, especially if the summer meadows are in bloom.

A much scarier prospect is the Cares Gorge, a walk that will take you through the heart of the Picos from Cain to Poncebos. It's a walk that's not for the faint-hearted as there are unprotected drops of hundreds of metres along the entire length. I have attempted it three times now and been pushed back by my vertigo on every occasion. Terrifying but amazingly beautiful. The road to Cain is fab.

MY TOP TEN SPANISH AND PORTUGUESE CAMPSITES

Spain and Portugal have a lot of campsites. Many of them tend to have a mix of seasonal pitches and touring pitches, with some having many more seasonal pitches than others, so making them seem more like high-density canvas villages. I tend to avoid those. But that still leaves a great many that are located in brilliant places, near beaches or high in the mountains that should not be missed. Of course, I haven't visited all of Spain and Portugal's campsites. But, for now, enjoy these cracking spots.

Best for the mountains

Camping el Redondo, Fuente Dé, Spain

This campsite in the Picos de Europa is relatively remote, simply because Fuente Dé is the end of the road. You have to drive down a steep, cobbled road to get to it, too, which makes it quite exciting and not for the larger moho or A-class. Once you are there, you'll enjoy sublime views of the mountains, a friendly bar serving cold Asturian cider and good showers. It's also a very handy two-minute walk from the cable car up into the high Picos.

• **www.campingfuentede.com**

2 Best for even more remote mountains

Camping Lagos de Somiedo, Asturias, Spain

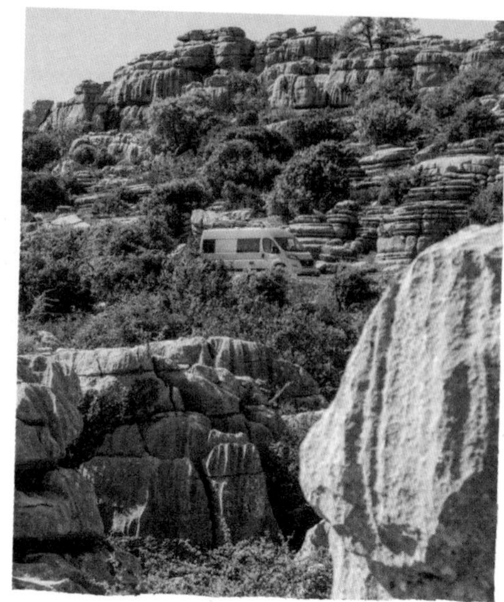

If you like your campsites rustic and simple then this is one for you. The only problem is that it's located 1,500m (4,921ft) above sea level, at the end of a steep winding road (with at least six hairpins) and the entrance is narrow. That said, your average 6m (20ft) Ducato will fit very nicely, thank you. The owners are lovely and very friendly. It's a tough 6km (3.7-mile) hike to the lake above the village from the campsite, but it'll take you through some sublime mountain scenery. Heavenly.
• **www.campinglagosdesomiedo.com**

3 Best for the ferry (and beach access)

Camping de Comillas, Comillas, Spain

The campsite at Comillas is just a short drive from Santander, which makes it a perfect stop for the night before the ferry or when you arrive. That said, it's worth a stop anyway. The campsite has a few pitches that are right on the cliff edge, giving great views over the beach at Comillas. At low tide, there is direct access to a tiny sandy cove. Really nice. Comillas is worth a stop, too. • **www.campingcomillas.com**

4 Best for birding

Camping El Burro Blanco, Miranda del Castañar, Spain

This site, high in the Sierra de Francia and not far from Salamanca, is a real gem. It's owned by a Dutch couple, Eddy and Vera, who go out of their way to make you feel welcome. We were given a glass of prosecco to enjoy on the terrace while they took down our passport details – a unique and very welcome experience. It's peaceful and full of wildlife, especially birds, which chatter away in the trees all day. The only downside is that there is no emptying of grey water (at the time of writing). But I can live with that.
• **www.elburroblanco.net**

5 Best for beach access

Camping and Glamping Muiñeira, O Grove, Spain

This small, family-run site has a fantastic position above the beach at Praia Raeiros and with direct access to it. In seconds, you can walk from your van to the sand and then plop into the sea. The sunsets are sublime and the beach is beautiful. The showers are good, too. What more could you ask for? • **www.campingmuineira.es**

6 Best for city access (Portugal)

Parque de Campismo Municipal de Faro, Faro, Portugal

Situated across the causeway from the airport, this is a nice municipal site. It is secure and perfect for visits to Faro, via the ferry, which runs from a jetty about 400m (437 yards) east. The beach is about 20m (22 yards) from the gates. Even if it's very busy, they are happy to accommodate. • **www.faro.pt/menu/1516/parque-de-campismo.aspx**

7 Best for city access (Spain)

Camping Osuna, Madrid, Spain

This place is friendly and a bit groovy, too, and is perfectly placed for a few days in Madrid. It has a bar and food and a very, very small pool, plus staff who are friendly and helpful. There's EHU if you need it, otherwise it's a free-for-all to get the shadiest spot.
• **www.campingosuna.com**

8 Best for birdwatching and the Doñana National Park

Camping La Aldea, El Rocío, Spain

El Rocío is an amazing place in an amazing, otherwise inaccessible national park. The town has streets of sand and sits next to a huge lagoon, where you can see spoonbills and flamingos, plus other wetland birds. Tours leave from the campsite, which has a great pool and nice pitches. There's a good restaurant next door. • **www.campinglaaldea.com**

9 Best for the Serra de Monchique

Camping Vale da Carrasqueira, Monchique, Portugal

A fabulous camper park with a pool high in the hills above Lagos and below Monchique. Its isolation makes it terrible for popping out but perfect for quiet and calm. The rates are reasonable and the showers are good. Pitches come with water waste and EHU. Perfect. • **www.campingvaledacarrasqueira.com**

10 Best for sundowners

Torre de la Peña, Tarifa, Spain

This site is right on the beach, with direct access and surf when conditions are right. The bar is great – a place to dip the toes while watching the sun go down. There are great views of Tangiers as the sun ignites the buildings and the lights twinkle in the twilight. Pitches by the beach are premium. • **www.campingtp.com**

SPAIN

From San Sebastián to the Sierra Nevada, Spain will be everything you hope it will be, and more. Yes, it has got beaches. Yes, it has mass tourism. But it also has amazing food, a long and fascinating history, Roman and Moorish relics, great cathedrals, world-beating art and isolated mountains. Its culture and way of life is vibrant, fun and beguiling. One visit will never be enough.

San Andrés de Teixido, Galicia

ROUTE 01

SANTANDER
RIBADESELLA
LIENCRES
CELORIO
SUANCES
PECHÓN
COMILLAS
MALIAÑO
CANGAS DE ONÍS
ANDRIN
A-67
UNQUERA
A-8
CELIS
CABEZÓN DE LA SAL
COVADONGA
DESFILADERO DE LA HERMIDA
TORRELAVEGA
N-625
POTES
OSEJA DE SAJAMBRE
N-621
LLÁNAVES DE LA REINA
BOCA DE HUÉRGANO

ROUTE 01

SANTANDER TO CANGAS DE ONÍS

UNFINISHED BUSINESS IN THE PICOS

The Picos de Europa is a relatively small mountain range in northern Spain. What the mountains lack in stature and area they more than make up for in spectacular views, plant life, birdwatching, crazy walking, wild swimming and brilliant mountain driving. Don't write them off because they aren't as big as the Alps or the Pyrenees. These little peaks are huge in every way imaginable (except perhaps their size)!

BEST FOR: Walking, cycling (if you like challenging hills), swimming and food

START: Santander

END: Cangas de Onís

MILEAGE: 300km (186 miles)

ALLOW: 7 days

MAP PAGES: 6, 7

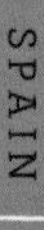

We disembark at Santander and within an hour or so are parked up at the campsite at Comillas. We grab a spot overlooking the beach, on the cliff edge, and go over our plans. The north coast of Spain is somewhere Lizzy and I have visited before, both separately and together, which means we have unfinished business here.

I have always loved travelling to this part of Spain as it's got everything I could possibly want: great food, great beaches, surf and interesting scenery. While many hit the motorway at Santander and head away over the huge viaducts and through the tunnels that straighten out the travel in this area, taking to the old roads brings us face to face with slow travel at its best. Plus, the views are amazing.

First up on the list of 'things we regret not doing when we were here before' is visiting El Capricho de Gaudí, a masterpiece of modernist architecture from Spain's most flamboyant creator, Antoni Gaudí. Handily, it's just a short walk from the campsite. We go on a bright, warm day and marvel at the craftsmanship and work involved in bringing this vision to life. It's a vibrant and vivacious piece of work that speaks volumes about a young, excited architect making his name with ironwork, hand-cast tiles and exquisite joinery. A taste of things to come.

Afterwards, I surf at Playa de Merón, finding a peak to myself that's about as fun as it gets. I take wave after wave, wondering all the while why no one else is surfing here. The water is warm and the sun is hot and I return to shore after an hour of almost constant paddling and surfing. I sleep well.

We visit the Museo de Altamira, too, another 'should have gone' location that went unvisited, more than likely because the waves at Playa de Merón called more loudly at the time. This time though, I slow down and we explore the museum and the *neocueva*, a replica of a local cave that was built after too many visitors started to cause the paintings to deteriorate in the original cave. It's truly remarkable. The cave is entirely believable. The paintings, like those in France's reproduction of Lascaux (see *TTSR: France*), provoke too many questions. They are truly beautiful, with perfect lines. If you were asked to draw a

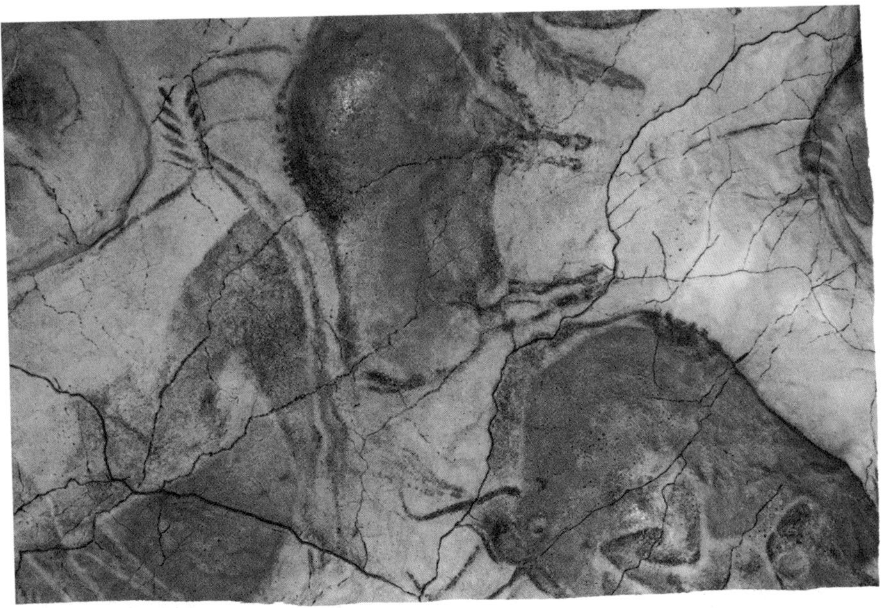

bison from memory, would you be able to? I doubt it. We have become so disconnected.

We head west, across the bridge at San Vicente de la Barquera and across the motorway into the hills. Almost immediately, the scenery changes and we follow the course of the Río Deva up the Desfiladero de la Hermida, a stunning gorge that twists and turns as it head towards Potes. The tiny town is the gateway to the eastern side of the Picos de Europa, a diminutive mountain range of sharp, stark limestone that rises sharply from the Bay of Biscay. When I say diminutive I mean in comparison to the Alps, not to Snowdonia. Some of the peaks are over 2,500m (8,200ft), which, if you use the Welsh scale of measurement, is nearly two and a half times the height of Yr Wyddfa.

The gorge brings us to Potes. We then follow the very curvaceous CA-185 to Fuente Dé, an enormous 'cirque' with a cable car that transports walkers and tourists up 750m (2,460ft) to the high plains and pastures of the Picos at 1,850m (6,070ft) above sea level. The cable itself is around 1.4km (0.87 miles) long. Details aside, it's dizzying to watch the tiny car, which carries 20 people almost vertically up the sheer faces, where choughs flap and water drips down the grey limestone.

This isn't my first visit. In 2012, during an extended tour in a 1979 VW Type 2, I took the cable car with the intention of walking back down. Despite the blue sky as we rocketed at 10m (33ft) per second up the cable,

San Vicente de la Barquera

the clouds closed in and gave us a whiteout at the top. My kids, grateful for the excuse to not have to walk, persuaded me to take the cable car down again. We headed back down the road as a huge, violent storm erupted around us. I was silently grateful.

This time, though, there will be no excuses. Lizzy, ever the curious botanist, is keen to explore the plant life of the high pasture. This is her unfinished business, too: she once cycled across the mountains as part of an extended tour of Spain and missed the chance to wander in the meadows and examine the flora and habitats properly.

We set off from the campsite (Camping El Redondo, see below) to buy our tickets for the 10 a.m. cable car. We stand in the small car, about 20 of us, jammed in like sardines, as the warning siren buzzes and we are whisked away from the base station swiftly, rising fast, but without any reference points to measure our speed. The cars and tour buses fade away swiftly, becoming dots in moments. I take a few photos and then I see that we are slowing and are about 1m (3.3ft) from the cliff face. There's a clunk and we stop. It's all over in less than four minutes.

We walk out of the car and to the viewing point, where we can look down – vertically – to the valley floor below. The view is really quite something: opposite us are the lower peaks of the Picos, which are green and tree-covered. To the left and right are the grey limestone edifices of the cirque. We can see a few walkers making their way up a steep path on some of the face's hundreds of metres below us. They look tiny.

Behind us is an open, seemingly barren plain between peaks with vegetation that's short and tufty. Gorse, growing low and stubby, is in flower, lending a yellow hue to the grey, rocky landscape.

We set off, walking on a well-worn path that heads into the interior and up and around a peak. When we reach the pass, around 1km (0.6 miles) later, we look down into another bowl-like valley where there are just two buildings, the Aliva Cantur refuge and a hotel, as well as cattle grazing and huge scree slopes. Below some of the peaks that rise vertically out of the scree there are patches of snow. The gentle clanking of cowbells drifts across the slopes.

We walk to the hotel and sit with a coffee as a chough glides past us, flapping its velvet-black and somewhat scrappy wings madly, its yellow beak in stark contrast. We rarely see choughs at home in Cornwall, but here they are plentiful. Above us, birds of prey soar against the blue sky. There are a handful of walkers on the track, as well as the occasional cyclist and one or

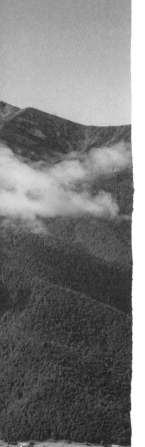

two 4x4s ferrying people on tours of the uplands.

We continue for another hour, following fingerposts back towards Fuente Dé. They lead us into a gully with a tiny stream running down it, towards a gap where the track changes into a concrete and stone roadway and descends sharply away down the mountainside. There is a cattle grid here and a wooden bridge over the stream, which leads us to a narrow rocky path that heads off across steep pasture and into the woods. This is the path we need to take. The difference between the pasture here and behind us among the peaks is stark. Where before the grass was heavily grazed, here plants thrive. There are butterflies and insects buzzing about and the gorse, through stunted on the other side of the cattle grid, is bushy and wild, the yellow flowers bright against the green grasses and young bracken. We stop for lunch and sit on a couple of boulders above the path looking at what's in front of us. The mountainside is a riot of colour, blue sea holly, yellow rattle, purple mallow, scabious, knapweeds and tiny purple *Pinguicula* (butterwort), its leaves dotted with trapped insects. A little further down, we find purple iris standing tall among the brackens as the path enters the woods.

We continue, walking through the forest on muddy tracks, descending all the time. We pass the occasional meadow where more grasses and flowers grow madly, untroubled by the hungry cow or horse. We pass through the forest of elder, ash, beech, hazel and holm oak, with each taking turns to dominate. I feel like I am at home in the Combes of North Devon or in the Chilterns where I grew up, except for the moments when the views over the valley, glimpsed every so often through a gap in the canopy, bring me back to Spain. It's cool and

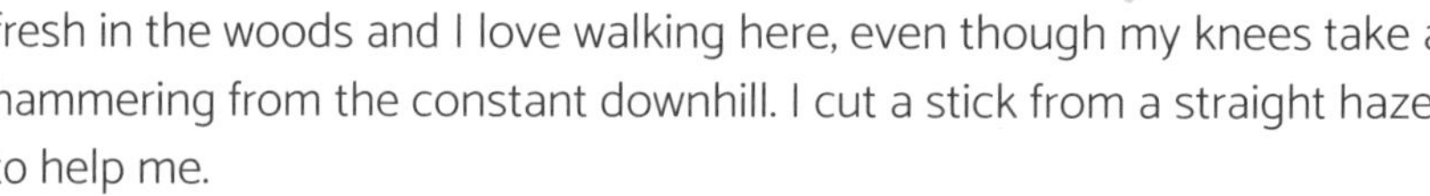

fresh in the woods and I love walking here, even though my knees take a hammering from the constant downhill. I cut a stick from a straight hazel to help me.

After about six hours of walking, ambling, lying in meadows, stopping for a drink, to look at flowers or to attempt to take photos of butterflies, we arrive back in Fuente Dé. It's been a very satisfying walk, both from a botanical point of view – Lizzy is happy she has seen at least some of the flowers the Picos are famous for – and also for dealing with my unfinished business. I feel glad of the clouds that thwarted my first visit, not only because my kids would never have made it off the mountain without cataclysmic complaining but also because to put them through such a long walk might have been bordering on abuse. They were eight and nine at the time.

We retreat to the campsite and reward ourselves with a bottle of Cantabrian cider, a local speciality that goes down too well.

Our final bit of unfinished business takes us into the very heart of the mountain range. The Picos are divided in two by a huge and very deep valley that carries the Río Cares to the coast. At Caín, the tiny village at the end of the road that descends into the valley, the river heads into a narrow gorge at a bottleneck. A track, cut into the side of the gorge by workers servicing a hydroelectric scheme, follows the gorge for 11km (6.8 miles) to Poncebos.

As the river falls in the bottom, the path stays at roughly the same height, meaning that the bottom gets further and further away the farther you walk. To make it worse for the vertigo-suffering camper (that's me), there are no guard rails or handrails and many of the drops are vertical, meaning one slip would see you plunging hundreds of metres to the river below.

I have tried walking the gorge on two occasions, from either end, and have had to give up twice, due to my vertigo. The furthest along I have managed was about a third of the way, to the second bridge from Caín.

I found it giddying to look up at the peaks and down at the river knowing that, at its deepest, the gorge is a mile from peak to river.

The idea to return to the Cares Gorge isn't to attempt to complete the walk but to see how far my limits have stretched, if at all, in the intervening years since Lizzy and I were last here. Plus, I want to get some photos. Also, despite the terror, it is beautiful in the extreme.

Lizzy and I leave the van at a new *aire* in Posada de Valdeón and jump on our bikes to ride down the valley to Caín. My memory of the road must have been absolutely obliterated by the horror of walking the gorge as I have no recollection of it. As we descend into the deep valley, we twist and turn around hairpins and past incredible viewpoints. The road is steep, with sections of at least 15%. The peaks, grey, sharp and sombre, loom above us as we hang on to the brakes. The road is difficult in places, passing through narrow gaps in the gorge, high above the river before we even get to Caín.

In 6km (3.7 miles) we lose 500m (1,640ft) of vertical height. It feels like we have descended into a big hole at the centre of the mountains into which the river will disappear.

We reach Caín and lock the bikes before setting off along the pathway to the neck of the gorge proper. I remember bits of it clearly now as we start to walk. The first section passes through a series of low, dripping tunnels where there are metal guard rails to protect you from the drop. At this point, it's only about 30m (98ft) down. When the guard rails fall away the drop is more like 50m (164ft). The vertigo comes over me like a wave of seasickness. I plod on, looking at my feet instead of at the drop. I get as far as I feel I need to, if only to confirm my fear, before turning back.

During the retreat, we pass a bridge over the gorge and a path that leads down to a small beach and a beautiful blue pool created by a tributary. We cross over and drop our bags at the pool before stripping off and swimming for a few moments in the cool, healing waters. It's typical of me to favour water over heights and it seems a fitting end to the adventure to stop it here with a skinny dip in a mountain stream. It feels a lot more positive than crawling along a pathway, at the edge of a terrifying precipice, blubbing with fear while people casually stroll by, wondering what the fuss is all about.

So, let's leave it at that.

The climb back up the hill on our bikes is a bastard, btw.

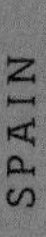

THE DRIVING

We began this route straight off the ferry at Santander, by picking up the N-611 from the junction where the A-67 from the port meets the S-20 (junction 199). Almost as soon as you leave the city, you'll find yourself in fabulous, rolling (and pitching) countryside, crossing the Río Pas on the way to Torrelavega. When you pass under the motorway, you'll take a sharp left, still on the N-611. In Barreda, after the huge factory, take the road on your right signposted to Comillas and go over the railway. This is the C-131 and it will take you to Santillana del Mar (if you follow signs for Comillas, it will take you on a detour/bypass on the C-137) and then on to Comillas through stunning scenery, small villages, churches on hillsides and pastures filled with wild flowers. Santillana is a quite special place and was once described by Jean-Paul Sartre as one of Spain's most beautiful villages. It most likely is, although plenty of tourists go there these days, making it a little hectic.

At Comillas (where you'll find the Capricho de Gaudí and the Palacio de Sobrellano, a neogothic masterpiece), you can carry on towards San Vicente de la Barquerra on the CA-131 and then the N-634 or follow the road to Oyambre for a fantastic ride down the estuary and along the coast to Playa Oyambre and Playa Merón. There are plenty of places to stop along here for a surf or swim. Some of the beach car parks will allow overnighting. San Vicente is a wonderful town, with two bridges and a stunning estuary. The setting, when seen from the beach at Merón, with the peaks of the Picos behind, is exceptional.

From San Vicente, take the road through town, across the bridge and out on the N-634. This will take you to a *mirador* (viewing point) with great views of the town and setting. Continue on until you reach the N-621 at junction 272 of the A-8 and then follow the signs for Potes. There is an *aire* a few miles along here – a good place to stop and fill up with water or empty tanks. There are only campsites from here to Fuente Dé.

The N-621, after Panes, enters the gorge, the Desfiladero de la Hermida. It is one of the highlights of this journey (among a few) and takes you through a narrow gorge carved through the limestone by the Río Deva. There are overhangs and tunnels and tight corners, plus dizzying heights if you look up, but most vans will make it with caution. Even the big fellas get down there, so don't worry. Unfortunately, there aren't any places to stop, but if you need to there are a few pull-ins where you can stop and admire the view.

The gorge ends at Castro Cillorigo, where it opens out to reveal meadows and villages. At Tama, there is an interpretation centre for the Picos that is worth a stop.

At Ojedo, take a right the roundabout (stay on the N-621) to go to Potes. Parking is free and easy behind the Lupo supermarket in Potes.

FOR FUENTE DÉ: Continue through the town and on to the CA-185. This will take you further up into the mountains on an excellent but winding road to Fuente Dé. Park for the cable car (go behind it for van parking) or continue up the lane for the campsite (vans over 7m/23ft beware).

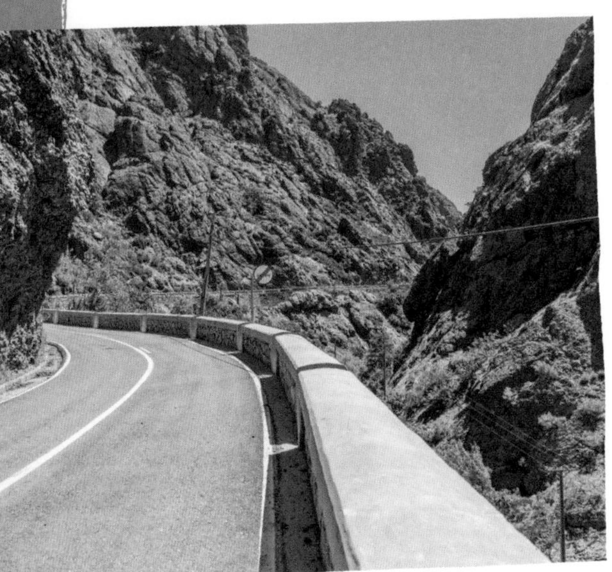

TO CONTINUE: In Potes, take the N-621 out of town towards Riaño. It is an unassuming turn (right turn after the bridge if you come from Fuente Dé) and easy to miss. This will lead you up and out of town to the south on a narrow road that soon gets wider. This is another brilliant

road that's very windy and steep in places. It passes through very pointy mountains through forests of oak, birch, beech, hazel and pine. The last section, which brings you on to rocky, scrubby hillsides of broom and gorse, has some fantastic hairpins, drops and curves. At the stunning Puerto de San Glorio you peak at 1,609m (5,279ft). Going over the top brings you into a different kind of scenery and feels like you have reached a plateau. The road will take you down a lovely valley and then into Llánaves de la Reina, after which you'll enter another brilliant and narrow gorge.

Turn right after the gorge at Portilla de la Reina on to the LE-243 (LE-2703) and into the village, where it's a bit of a squeeze. Once out the other side though, while a bit rough, the road is fine and takes you through some more fine scenery, forest and scrub.

Passing through the Puerto de Pandetrave will give you some fantastic views of the valley before you (you are still at around 1,000m/3,280ft here) and then a few curvy bits before you arrive in the tiny village of Posada de Valdeón at a little T-junction. Turn left here, on to the LE-244 (LE-2711), unless you intend to drive to Caín (not recommended for larger mohos but okay for sub-7m/23ft vans).

The road to Caín is small and difficult, with tight bends and narrow sections. If you intend to walk the gorge then this is the way to go. Parking is limited in the village, but plenty of locals give up their meadows to make a few euros in the season. Some allow overnighting (check on Park4Night – ask for Miguel!) The *aire* is in Posada de Valdeón.

Continuing on, follow the LE-2711 through the village and out the other side into the beautiful, lush green mountains, interspersed with meadows. The road follows the Río Cares to its source and then beyond to a couple of *miradors*. The Puerto de Panderrueda lies at 1,450m (4,757ft).

At the junction with the N-625, turn right to Cangas de Onís. This is a larger road but no less good for driving. It's curvaceous, with lots of tight bends, drop-offs and hairpins and takes you through steep, forested slopes, down gorges, and past waterfalls. Look out for pyramidal and butterfly orchids in the verges, along with wild strawberries! You'll drive through the stunning Desfiladero de los Beyos, another '100-times-better-than-Cheddar' gorge that's narrow, tall and, at times, with difficult overhangs and tunnels. Blimmin' excellent! Don't worry though – we passed lorries coming the other way and if they can do it, so can you. Just go slowly round the blind bends.

As you come out of the gorge, the scenery gets more open, with more of those pointy peaks around you, and more meadows. The road follows the Río Sella down to Cangas de Onís. Along this stretch, there are lots of white water kayaking operators and even a few sneaky riverside stopovers.

At Cangas, take the AS-262 for Covadonga and more Picos action, continue on the N-634 for Oviedo or the coast at Ribadesella.

WHERE TO STAY: CAMPING

Camping Comillas, Comillas
Calle de Manuel Noriega, C/ las Paserucas, 27, 39520 Comillas, Cantabria, Spain
Web: www.campingcomillas.com
Tel: +34 942 72 00 74

Stunning location overlooking the beach at Comillas and just about a ten-minute walk into the old city. Lots of pitches are a bit sloped so bring levelling wedges.

Camping El Redondo, Fuente Dé
39588 Fuente Dé, Camaleño, Spain
Web: www.campingfuentede.com
Tel: +34 942 73 66 99

A really lovely campsite in Fuente Dé that's behind the cable car base station. Great views of the peaks, with a bar and restaurant on site.

Camping La Viorna, Santo Toribio
Carretera de, 39586 Santo Toribio, Cantabria, Spain
Web: www.campinglaviorna.com
Tel: +34 942 73 20 21

The site is around 1km (0.6 miles) from Potes. It has a pool and bar. Great for kids.

Camping El Cares Picos de Europa, Santa Marina de Valdeón
Camino del Rejo, s/n, 24915 Santa Marina de Valdeón, León, Spain
Web: www.campingelcarespicosdeeuropa.com
Tel: +34 619 22 25 58

A great site in a natural setting not far from the Cares Gorge with lots of activities and a good bar.

WHERE TO STAY: *AIRES*

Santillana del Mar: There is an *aire* here as well as private car parks where you can stay overnight. Great location and easily walkable to the town.
Posada de Valdeón: The *aire* here, adjacent to the sports centre, is relatively new and is really well organised with separate plots and access to showers. €10 per night. One of the closest overnights you can get to the Cares Gorge walk.
Cangas de Onís: Space has been made available for motorhomes in the large car park that serves this bustling town. Not far from the Roman bridge that actually isn't Roman.

IN THE AREA

Cueva del Castillo, Puente Viesgo
Superb limestone caves outside Torrelavega with amazing formations as well as cave paintings, including hand prints. The caves were inhabited since 120,000 BC and are remarkable. A rare chance to see the real thing, if all you see is a fraction of the total. There are other caves in the vicinity to which visits can be arranged.
• **www.cuevas.culturadecantabria.com/el-castillo**

Museo de Altamira, Altamira This is the museum devoted to the (now closed) Altamira Caves. Don't be put off that the cave you get to visit is a replica because it is absolutely stunning. Once you are looking up at the beautifully decorated ceiling, you'll forget it's 100 per cent man-made. And it's really cheap entry at €3 per adult. • **www.culturaydeporte.gob.es/mnaltamira/home.html**

Santillana del Mar Described by Jean-Paul Sartre as 'the prettiest village in Spain', it's pretty good. In fact, it's almost perfect. Cobbled, virtually car-free streets, museums, a wonky church (check out the vaulted roof of the lovely Collegiate Church of Santa Juliana) and galleries as well as restaurants and shops make it more like a film set on its day off. Go visit. • **www.santillana-del-mar.com**

El Capricho de Gaudí, Comillas
The genius architect cut his teeth here in Comillas with a masterpiece of modernist design that includes all the things you come to expect of him: wrought iron, ceramics and natural iconography. The result is a bonkers but brilliant work of art that reeks of craftsmanship and care.
• **www.elcaprichodegaudi.com**

La Hermida 'spa' There is a hotel here where you can get a hot thermal spa treatment. Alternatively, you could clamber down by the bridge and get a free one in the river.

Fuente Dé cable car You can go up and walk down or you can get a return ticket. Singles from €11. Amazing views and the walk is excellent.
• www.cantur.com/instalaciones/5-teleferico-de-fuente-de

Cares Gorge This involves 11km (6.8 miles) of terror if you don't like heights, or 11km (6.8 miles) of beautiful walking if you do. Either way, it's one of Spain's most spectacular walks.

Covadonga and lakes Church in a cave, plus lakes, on the western side of the Picos. A side shoot from Cangas de Onís.

Olla de San Vicente Off the N-625 at Tornín, there is a walk to a spectacular swimming spot beneath a waterfall. It takes about 45 minutes but is worth it for the jumps and plunge pools. Gets busy on hot days.

Birdwatching There is all kinds of birdlife to be seen in the Picos, from the big stuff to the little, less showy stuff. We saw a nuthatch and a tree creeper in the campsite at Fuente Dé, as well as an Egyptian vulture and choughs in the *dehesa* below the cable car.

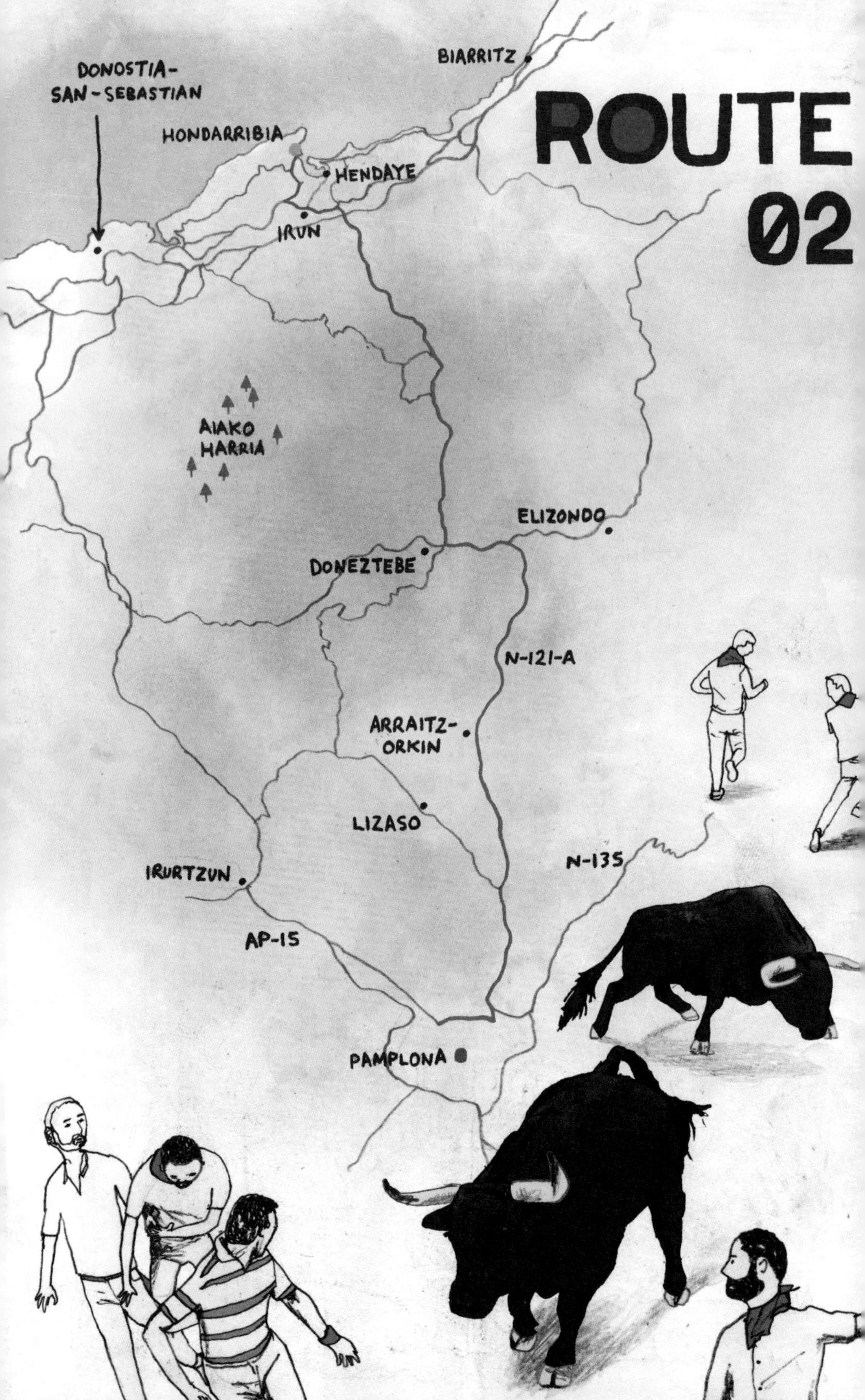
ROUTE
02
BIARRITZ
DONOSTIA-
SAN-SEBASTIAN
HONDARRIBIA
HENDAYE
IRUN
AIAKO
HARRIA
ELIZONDO
DONEZTEBE
N-121-A
ARRAITZ-
ORKIN
LIZASO
N-135
IRURTZUN
AP-15
PAMPLONA

ROUTE 02

HONDARRIBIA TO PAMPLONA

THE BULL RUNNINGS

This route will take you from Hondarribia in Spain's far north-west, along the border and into the ancient city of Pamplona. It's a route to get you into the very heart and soul of Spain in one easy, stunning drive along the French border and the edges of the Pyrenees. When you get there, you will be able to confront the spectre of bullfighting, if you want to. Or you could simply stroll around Pamplona's beautiful cobbled streets. Your call.

BEST FOR: Wandering city streets, bullfighting (if you must)

START: Hondarribia

END: Pamplona

MILEAGE: 110km (68 miles)

ALLOW: 1–2 days

MAP PAGES: 10, 11

I suppose, this being a book about Spain, that it was inevitable that I would have to confront Spain's national spectacle at some point or another. Bullfighting might be illegal in much of the world but – despite recent polls that showed just over half of Spanish people would like to see the 'sport' banned – it is still a relevant part of Spanish culture and to ignore it is to ignore Spain's history and culture. Also, as I find out while walking around Pamplona, it is impossible to ignore the concrete hulk of the Plaza de Toros.

The stadium holds almost 20,000 people and looms over a corner of the city just a short way from the city's main shopping street, its turrets like a sombre Wembley. A short walk away, on Pamplona's main shopping thoroughfare, Rafael Huerta's Monumento al Encierro (Bull Run Monument) shows 11 bulls running at a number of *mozos* (men and women who run with the bulls), with several of them falling, as they head towards the stadium.

Where better to look the beast in the eye than here, in Pamplona? It is the place where the bulls run free through the streets on their way to the ring every morning during the Festival of Saint Fermin in July. It's a unique spectacle, where bulls run a course of around 820m (897 yards) to the ring. The fiesta has drawn plenty of celebrity involvement over the years, and those who have taken part include Ernest Hemingway, who took to the ring as well as running with the

mozos. An old friend of mine, Vanessa, crossed the border from France to Pamplona to become a teenage *mozo* and went home with a scar on her forehead from being gored. For a Basque like her, it was a badge of honour, even though, at the end of the day, the bull never wins.

We find the bullring without trying while wandering the back streets of Pamplona's city centre. It's the third biggest arena of its type after those in Madrid and Mexico City and can be found on Paseo de Hemingway, of course. It's huge. The shuttered concrete terraces – the same brutalist construction technique used to make the Royal Festival Hall in London – rise above us. We walk down what looks like an entrance ramp to find out more. It's a natural way to enter the arena and, as it turns out, is the way the bulls are herded there too.

We find that it's closed. However, it will be open in the morning for tours (in English), so we decide to come back. But is it the right thing to do? I'm not sure. I am 100 per cent against any kind of cruelty to animals and am particularly against cruel sports. My face burns with indignation when I see huntsmen in their pompous red jackets, so why wouldn't I feel the same when men in red capes taunt bulls? I feel so torn because I think I need to see Spain as Spain is and not be judgemental, but I also feel that to tour the bullring is to contribute to the horror. The other thought that crosses my mind is to report on what I see in this book and to urge you to make up your own mind but tell you how I feel as honestly as I can. Then you can make up your own mind. I feel a little better when I read that all the money earned from the bullring goes to support the 580 elderly residents of a care home in the city. Is it a washing of the hands, I wonder?

We stroll around the city a little more before heading back to the *aire de autocaravanas*, a well-equipped and gated park that sits just below the city walls and adjacent to the river and a park with cherry trees in full pink blossom.

The next day, we head up to the city, arriving at the bullring just after it opens. We make fumbled enquiries in Spanish and are given handsets for a self-guided tour of the workings of the ring (in English, thankfully). We are led through the gate – where the bulls enter the ring during the festival – and are invited to watch a film about the running of the bulls. It's dramatic and tense and, from the number of people we see falling or being trampled, it's a very dangerous occupation being a *mozo*. The film shows a rocket being fired and six bulls being released. They charge off down the streets, where they are confronted by a crowd of men and women dressed all in white, with red neckerchiefs, wielding rolled-up newspapers as weapons (or a means of defence). Despite the recklessness, there are rules. The *mozos* must run with the bulls and not against them and they must not antagonise the bulls – as if they weren't antagonised enough – as they make their way along a fenced-off route towards the ring. We see more people falling and being trampled and we see bulls slipping over on the cobbles. It's chaotic, tragic and very upsetting.

Every year, between 50 and 100 people are injured during the run. It lasts on average three minutes, from the time when the bulls are released to when they arrive in the stadium. I don't feel sorry in the slightest for the trampled *mozos*, although it's hard to watch people being hurt. However, that is nothing compared to what is to come.

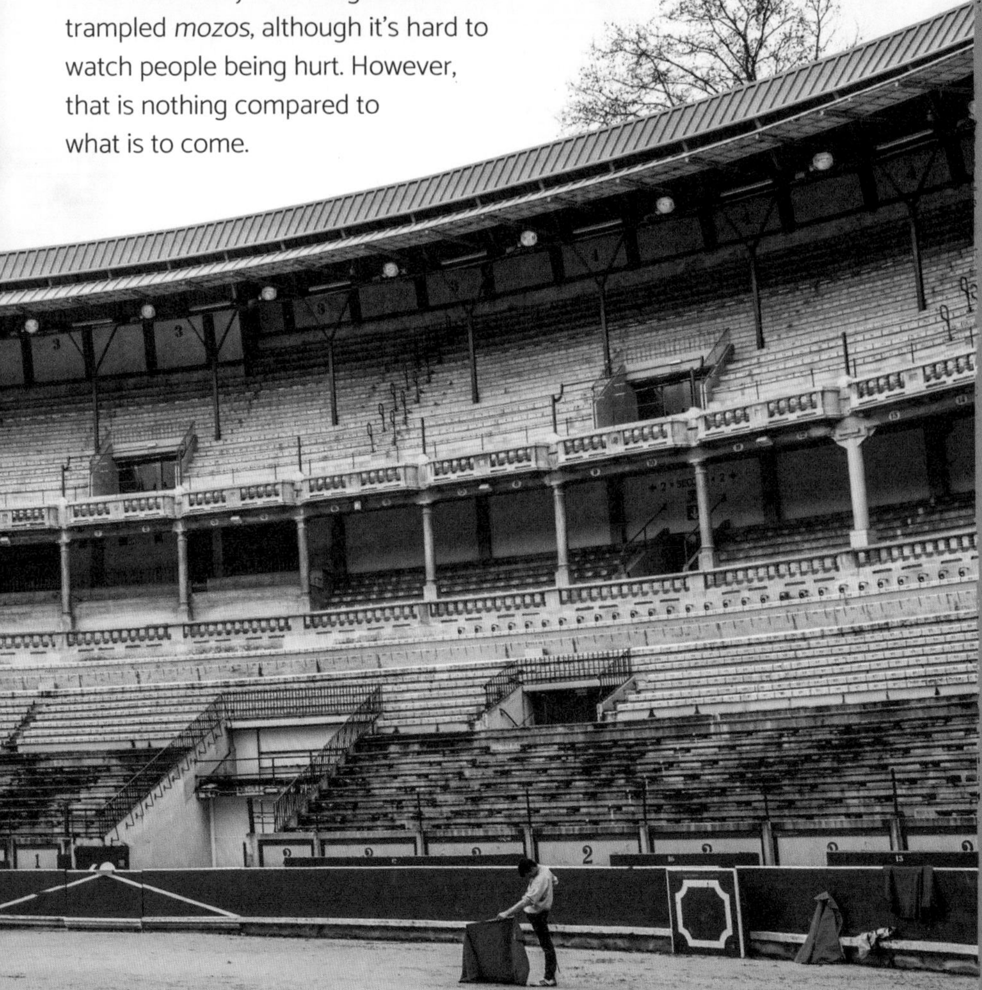

The film over, we are herded by our audio guides into the enclosures that surround the ring. Here, we get the first view of the stadium. We are at ring level, just one barrier away from the sand. The arena is enormous, with three tiers of seats above us. There are a few people in the ring: a young boy wielding a cape and an older man, presumably a coach, and what we assume is a parent. He stands back like a football dad, offering words of encouragement. A teenage boy is practising moves with a cape and a sword in another part of the arena.

We watch the little boy as he learns a few moves. Nearby, there is a bull's head attached to a kind of wheelbarrow with handles and a single wheel. We presume this is the practice bull, an altogether safer and less threatening foe than the real thing. The parent stands by, eager to see his boy get it right. I feel sorry for the young man as I imagine bullfighting may be illegal by the time he is old enough to enter the ring proper. I hope that he never has to face a bull. I hope, for his sake, that he doesn't get drawn into a world where machismo is mistaken for virtue.

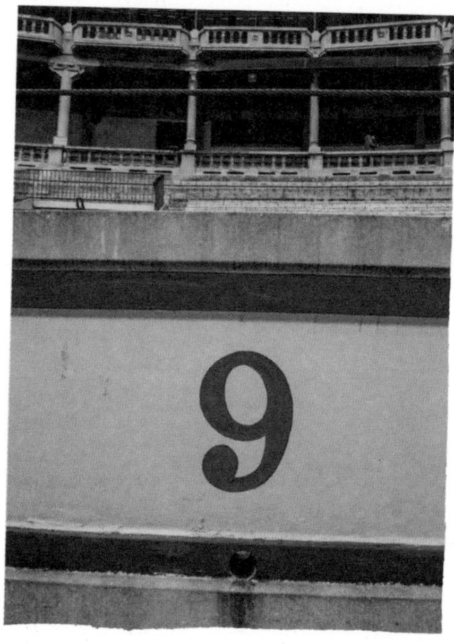

The teenager is a much more interesting prospect and is fascinating to watch. He lunges and twirls, making grunting noises as he does so. It's like a kind of ballet and he is graceful and elegant. He uses a cape and sword to deceive

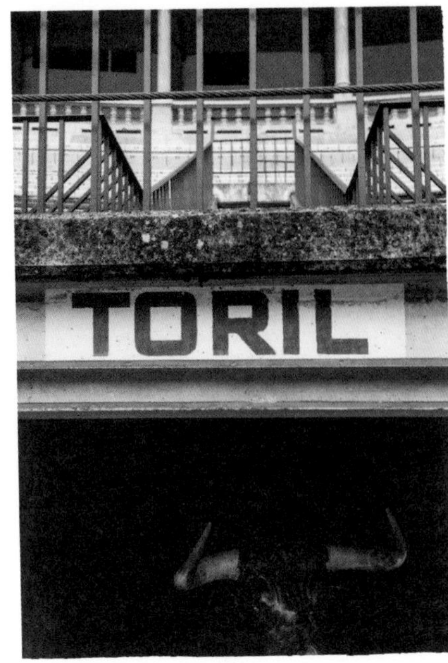

and plunge at an imaginary bull. I take pictures of him from close quarters and he seems completely oblivious. He's deeply into what he's doing. A young man on a pathway to something sinister and dark – murdering bulls for sport. He will be judged by the quality of his moves and the deftness of his sword. He may also be one to die in the ring, as others have.

We leave the ring and continue our tour, heading into the bowels of the stadium, where the bulls are separated and corralled before being forced out into the ring. It reminds me of the trenches we found in France, where slits in metal plates offered views of no man's land. Walkways and high walls allow those who handle the bulls to keep an eye on them and stay safe. It's all very ingenious and must have taken some planning and design. The things we do to amuse ourselves.

We enter the stable, which is now a room full of backlit panels showing the history of the bullring and photographs of bullfights. This is where it

WHERE TO STAY: CAMPING

Camping Faro de Higuer, Hondarribia
Ctra. del Faro, 58, 20280
Hondarribia, Gipuzkoa, Spain
Web: www.campingfarodehiguer.es
Tel: +34 943 64 10 08

This campsite is adjacent to the Higuer lighthouse above Hondarribia. It's in a great position and makes for a good start to any journey. However, beware, the campsite is enclosed by a wall, with an entrance that is 2.6m (8.5ft) high.

WHERE TO STAY: *AIRES*

Pamplona: Entry by barrier and ticket. €10 for 24 hours, with water, black and grey waste as well as EHU. Sitting just below the city walls, it's an easy walk into the old city and easy enough to get to. Recommended.

gets real and is the first time we see the blood. It's so very far from the small boy taking bullfighter lessons on a Saturday morning. The pictures show matadors standing in front of bulls that are bloodied, with iron *pujas* (a type of pike) hanging from their backs, their black hides made blacker by the dark, deep red of their own blood. The barbed pikes are designed to enrage the bull and make it fight more angrily. It almost brings me to tears to see it, but I feel I need to. The barbarism, the cheering crowds, the crowing, the pageantry and the death are all too real here. It belongs to an age of gladiators and fighting to the death, where a bull's owner prays his steeds put up a good fight or he will be shamed. However it fights, it still dies, so what does it matter?

We leave the room in silence, going into a room where there are artefacts. A cape. A matador's outfit. *Puja*s and swords. They are gruesome instruments and make me shudder. I am glad we are here now, in the winter, and not during the festival season.

The tour finishes at the ring, where it began and we watch the twirling young matador for a few minutes as he dances with an imaginary bull. It's beautiful, but still chilling. We walk through a small door and find ourselves on Paseo de Hemingway again, where life goes on. We wander back to the van through the back streets of this beautiful city, finding narrow cobbled streets filled with people drinking coffee, laughing and living. It seems strange to imagine them any other way.

I prefer not to.

THE DRIVING

Pamplona is a beautiful city, with a lovely cathedral, a huge 16th-century citadel, museum, countless bars and restaurants, vintage shops, music shops, a covered market and a huge park. So never mind the running of the bulls or the bullfighting if you don't want to; it's worth visiting anyway.

Anyhow, let's get on with the directions. This route is a good way to get to know Spain if you are coming from France. Hondarribia is right on the border, which is marked by the Bidasoa River. It's nothing to hop across the bridge from Hendaye, the French 'half' of the conurbation and start your Spanish adventure. If you are coming from the west then Hondarribia is the last junction on the AP-08 before it crosses the border at Irun.

Start by heading into Hondarribia and following signs for the centre of the town and then for the Faro de Higuer. The road to the lighthouse, the GI-3361, begins at the roundabout adjacent to the marina (before you get to the roundabout leading to the parking lot) and then heads out of the town and up on to the promontory that dominates the town. The road winds around the headland, giving magnificent views over the river, the marina and of France. The Pyrenees, dark, wooded peaks, lie beyond.

As you leave the lighthouse by the same road that brought you there (there is no other way), you will reach the river and then turn right. The one-way system will take you through the centre of town (very nice!) and out to the N-638, which is the main road in. With the airport on your left, follow the dual carriageway. At the

first big roundabout, follow the GI-2134 towards Baiona to the next roundabout. Here, follow the N-121-A for Pamplona. This will bring you on to the GI-636, a road that will take you to the river and along it until the next junction, a roundabout where you'll follow the N-121-A for Pamplona.

Stay on this road and it will take you out of the city and into the hills, following the course of the Río Bidasoa. The road criss-crosses the river a number of times as it heads to Pamplona. This is the new road. The old road, the N-1210, has been assimilated into this new road along much of its length. However, there are places where you can drive sections of the N-1210 that have been more or less abandoned, particularly where tunnels have straightened things out and, presumably, made things faster. In these places it's possible to pull off on to the old road and slow down to enjoy stretches of the river and the fabulous countryside. That said, the N-121-A is still very pretty. It's great countryside, with wooded peaks dominating and valley floors of agriculture sandwiched between, where the river allows.

The N-121-A hits the ring road, the PA-30, on the outskirts of the city. Take a left turn at the roundabout for the *aire* and it will bring you into another, final tunnel. When you emerge, you'll feel like you have arrived in a different place altogether. Pamplona lies before you, on the plain, surrounded by hills. The *aire* is just off Calle Biurdana, next to a pump track and just below the city walls, on the north-western side of the old city.

IN THE AREA

Pamplona Cathedral, Pamplona
An important cathedral in a country of important cathedrals. This is where the kings of Navarre were crowned. Interesting bell towers and museum exhibit:
• www.catedraldepamplona.com

Museum of Navarre, Pamplona
This historical museum is near the city walls in Pamplona in the old Hospital de Nuestra Señora de la Misericordia de Pamplona. • www.navarra.es

Pamplona bullring, Pamplona Guided tours in multiple languages are available and the cash goes to a good cause. Upsetting, in truth, but still a part of culture. • www.feriadeltoro.com

Citadel of Pamplona, Pamplona The city's 'new fort' is a public park to the south-west of the old city walls. Built in the 1570s, it's impressive enough and the enclosure is in a five-pointed star arrangement.
• www.visitnavarra.es/es/pamplona

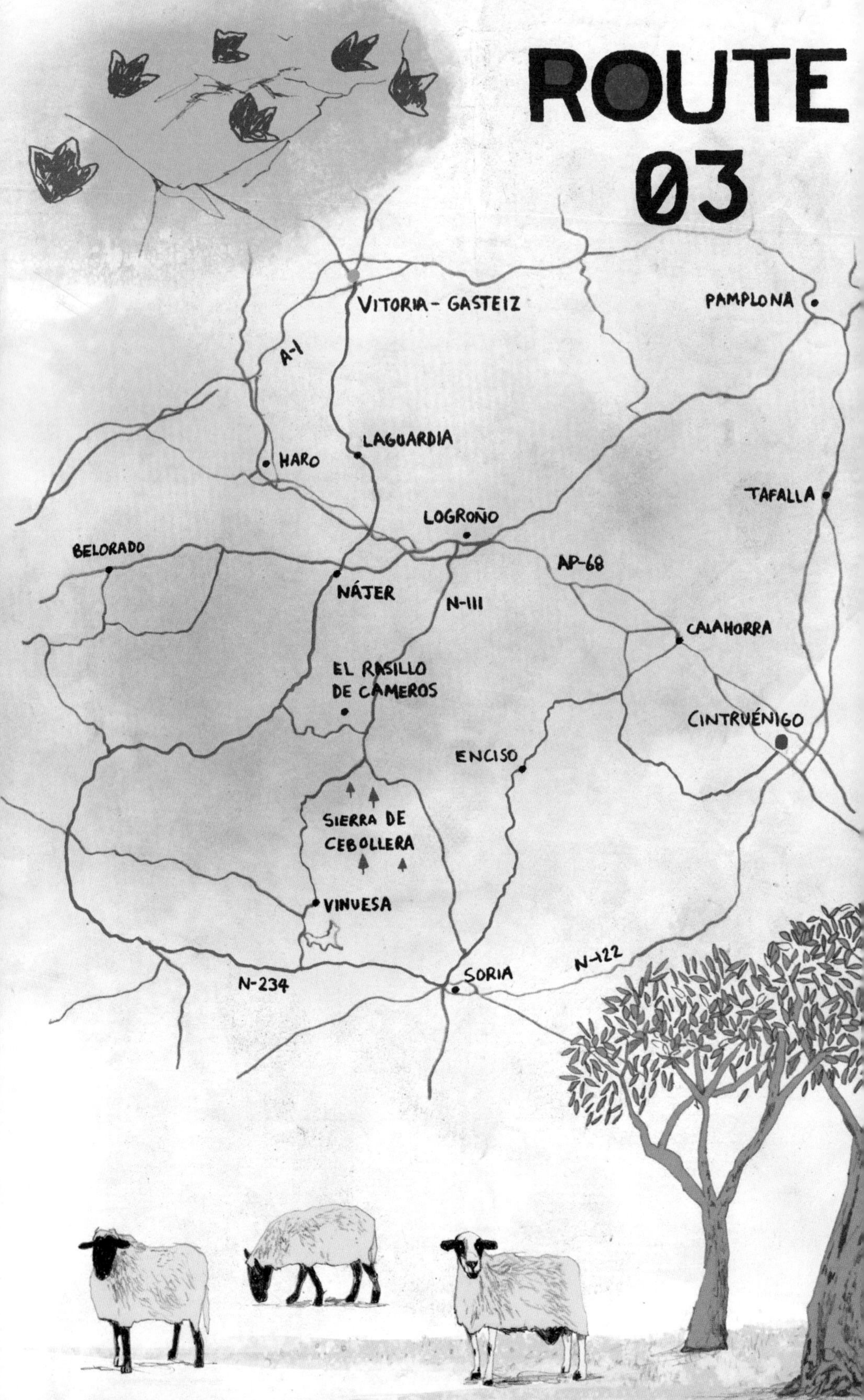
ROUTE
03
VITORIA-GASTEIZ
PAMPLONA
A-1
LAGUARDIA
HARO
TAFALLA
LOGROÑO
BELORADO
AP-68
NÁJER
N-111
CALAHORRA
EL RASILLO
DE CAMEROS
CINTRUÉNIGO
ENCISO
SIERRA DE
CEBOLLERA
VINUESA
N-122
SORIA
N-234

ROUTE 03

VITORIA-GASTEIZ TO CINTRUÉNIGO

THERMAL SPRINGS, WINE AND DINOSAURS

La Rioja surprised me. I expected rows and rows of vines growing on gentle slopes. I got that, even if they were leafless and stumpy (well, it was March). But I also got jaw-dropping gorges, mountain hideaways, views, dinosaurs and hot springs at the end of roads that oscillated like sine waves in three dimensions. So, it wasn't like any normal wine tour. I didn't even have that much wine. And the stuff I did have was only €1.50 and was amazing.

BEST FOR: Wine, gorges, dinosaurs, walking and hot springs

START: Vitoria-Gasteiz

END: Cintruénigo (for Tudela)

MILEAGE: 425km (263 miles)

ALLOW: 4–5 days

MAP PAGES: 18, 19, 32, 33, 34

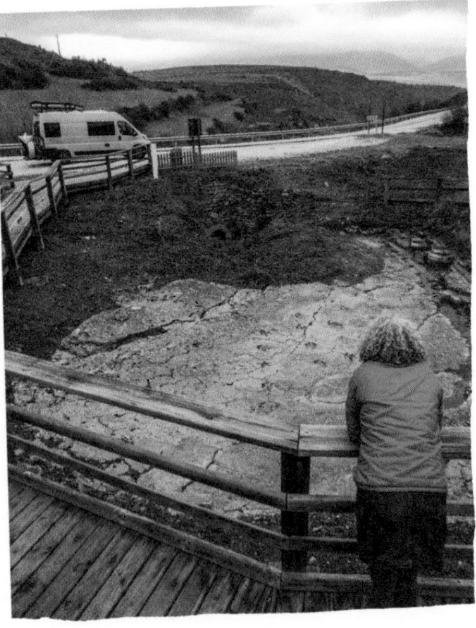

We are cruising down a beautiful road, the SO-615 from Soria to Arnedo. We passed the Puerto de Oncala, a pass that's 1,454m (4,770ft) above sea level, in heavy cloud cover and have descended enough to get below it again. The land is wild, scrubby and untamed, interspersed with rock and grassland. Some of the slopes have been terraced but look unkept, as if long forgotten. We turn a corner and there is a small brown tourist sign on the apex of the next bend. I pull in and we get out. The road drops away from us into a deep valley between rounded hills. In the distance, we can see more mountains. But for now, it's just us and the scrub. There is a small wooden walkway surrounding a patch of bare rock with a muddy stream running beside it into a culvert below the road. The rock is about 10m (32.8ft) square.

We head out over the walkway and stare at the ground. There, clearly for us to see in the rock (enhanced by a bit of paint I might add), are the prints of a theropod, a smallish dinosaur. The interpretation tells us they are 130 million years old, which I consider to be pretty impressive, to say the least. How they survived like that I cannot imagine. But there they are, in a landscape that feels suitably timeless, that's empty and cold and, apart from the odd flowering shrub, largely colourless, apart from the shades of khaki in the arid-loving plants.

We have stumbled upon the La Rioja Dinosaur Route and it's piqued our interest. As we descend into the valley, we see a huge, bright green, fibreglass dinosaur ahead of us at the paleontological park in Villar del Río, a tiny village that's all about the dinosaurs. Funny that it doesn't look out of place here at all in this huge landscape, even though it's the last thing you expect to see.

We are actually on our way to find something just as old, possibly, but much more visceral than prints that can't chase us or a fibreglass leviathan that's going nowhere. It's a hot spring at Arnedillo that's free to use and was built by the community for the community. Its presence on our map is marked by the icon of a fountain so tiny you'd almost miss it. Our travels are often marked by such things – the chance to slosh about in a geothermal spring is one of them – and so it was that we set off to find it on our slow road adventure in La Rioja.

The road to Arnedillo is remarkable, following a narrow gorge at river level as it bends around spurs in the rock. We stop at a waterfall and wander down to the riverbank, contemplating swimming. But it's cold and we have a mission. There is no one on the road and it's truly beautiful. Holm oaks populate the valley while bare rock hangs over us. Vultures spin in the skies above us, whirling around on the thermals. The road surface is a little rough – in fact it's pretty bad – but it improves as we approach the end of the gorge and the start of the Embalse (reservoir) Enciso, a reservoir that's not on any of our maps. This brings us down the valley to Enciso,

the home of a dinosaur-world theme park that looks decidedly extinct. It's probably the time of year. After Enciso, we come, after a few more bends in the road, to Arnedillo. Signposts direct us to motorhome parking as, apparently, we are banned from parking anywhere in town. It is high above the village in an area with toilets and power, surrounded by terraced olive groves and great views of the valley. On the other side of the river, we can see the glass-topped hulk of the Balneario Baños de Barro spa resort (**www.balnearioarnedillo.com**), where you can get treatments and relax in the hot spring water that's rich in sodium chloride, calcium sulphate, iron and magnesium.

But we aren't here for that. We're here for the free version where, we hope, we'll get the same water for nothing. We gather our kit and walk down the hill into the village. It's not hard to find the pools as they are well signed. We just follow the steady stream of wet-haired, bathrobed bathers walking away. We get our first glimpse from above, at the top of a set of steps leading down to the riverside.

There are three pools separated from each other and the river by low walls. The top pool, we assume to be the hottest, flows into the second and third and then into the river. There are five or six men and women lying motionless in the top pool. Some are on their backs, others crouch in the water, just their noses, ears and eyes visible. Some lie on their fronts, holding on to the wall, their legs splayed out behind them. The water, I can see from above, is clear and emerald-blue, despite the gloomy day. There are three young boys larking about in the shallows, making noise and splashes. No one seems to mind. Some young women are changing under a shelter.

We change, stash our stuff under a tree and step into the pool. I take my waterproof camera but feel reluctant to take photos with so many people here, so put it away quickly. It seems wrong to desecrate this sacred space with a photographic intrusion right now. I decide to wait.

I step into the third pool. It's as hot as a bath. I ease myself into the water and slowly immerse myself in the sulphurous water, sinking until my nose is just above the surface, like the other bathers. I look around at the people in the first pool. They are mostly in their sixties. Some of the men are balding, with wisps of white hair above their half-submerged ears. They remind me of a sculpture by Isaac Cordal entitled *Politicians discussing global warming*. They talk among themselves quietly, despite the raucous raptures from the boys.

I lie on my back and look up at the sky. It's cloudy and dull. Above me, I can see the catkin-filled branches of the tree our clothes are under and, beyond that, circling vultures. I hope they aren't coming for me. In my peripheral vision, I see the mountains and peaks above the village: they too are scrubby and scruffy with the lower slopes terraced for olives, above, bare rock. I recall the sheep wandering around the olive groves near our campsite.

Underwater, the sound of the boys turns into a dull, liquid roar, while the sound of my feet, toes curling into the pebbled bottom for grip, makes a higher tinkling not unlike a parrotfish eating chunks of coral on a tropical reef. I can just about make out, somewhere in the middle tones, the river gushing past on the other side of the retaining walls. The water feels soft on my skin as I float, my feet anchoring me to the spot. It's dreamy and makes me feel asleep, but also very alive.

Lizzy breaks the surface and rises, ready to step out of the warm water and down the steps into the river. I rise too. Ever cautious, I step into the warmer water that's flowing from the pools into the river. It soon cools down to the kind of temperature you'd expect from a mountain stream in March: flipping freezing. As I scoop up a few handfuls of water to splash on my chest like cheap aftershave, Lizzy immerses herself in the fast-running current and almost gets swept away, even though it's only a foot or so deep. We get out of the river and move up the heat-ranks to try the warmer pool.

As more people come and go, making space in the upper pool, we work our way up to the hottest part of the pools until we feel we've had enough and get out to change. I feel invigorated by the experience but perhaps not as much as I might have been if the water had been cold. The heat gives me torpor, the cold offers firing synapses and buzzing inner connections. There's something so real about immersion in cold water that hot springs can't match. But even so, it's truly magical.

The next day, we rise at first light for another dip and another crack at photographing them without worrying about taking shots of people in their smalls. There is a cool

wind blowing and it's chillier than yesterday. When we reach the baths, there are already four people in the hot pool. There is a man sitting, silently, with his face cupped in his hands like a great thinker. Unlike yesterday, it's almost silent, save for the rushing of the river and the chirping of the birds.

Lizzy and I start at the bottom and work our way up. I take a few snaps with my underwater camera but soon put it away when a man of about 30 arrives and strips naked before plunging in the middle pool. A few minutes later, my decision is ratified by the arrival of another naked dipper. This time, it's a man in his sixties. A woman arrives and gets in, removing her bikini as she enters the water. I feel we have intruded, perhaps, on a sacred time of the day, when nakedness is accepted. I feel dour and boring but keep my shorts on. I'm never one for shirking skinny dipping when the time is right – deserted beaches or night-time swims – but this kind of freedom is a little beyond my naked pay grade. I know it's my problem not theirs, but I still find it challenges me. I'm just not used to it and my reserve makes me uncomfortable. I stay in for a little longer, choosing to look to the sky again. When I have had my fill of quiet, up-looking contemplation, and the vultures have whirled away to another mountain, I take my leave and get out.

Lizzy follows and we change quietly, enjoying the afterglow of the heat and the cold river dips between. We walk back to the van and back to the reality of life on the road: We fill up with water, empty the loo and drain the waste tank before belting up and heading off down the road in search of something else we came here for – a really decent glass of hot-blooded Rioja.

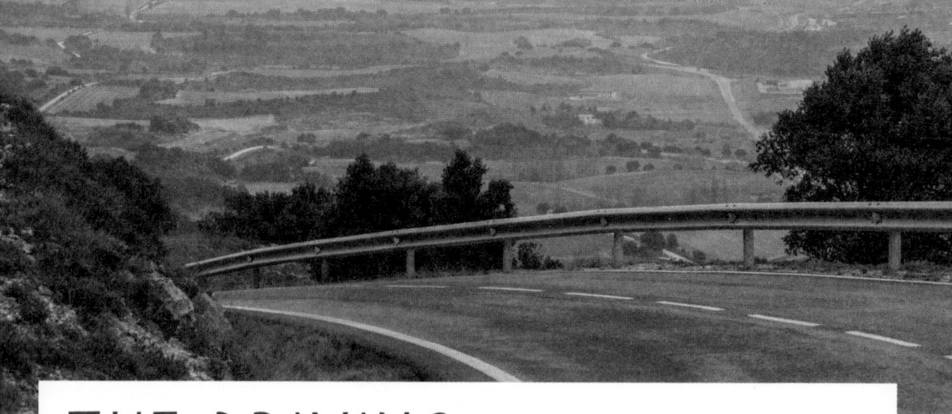

THE DRIVING

If I am honest, I will say that I didn't expect a lot from La Rioja. I have visited wine regions before, in and out of season, and they are usually very beautiful, very green and quite uniform: a hotchpotch of patchwork vineyards forming a green sea of ultra-cultivated green. Out of season, as it is now, it is just the same, only without leaves or tendrils: a sea of brown with nothing but potential for the harvest ahead.

So, as we took the A-2124 out of Vitoria-Gasteiz, I didn't expect too much. Don't listen to me.

The A-2124, a minor road by Spanish standards, climbs steadily away from Vitoria-Gasteiz through fields and scrub with deciduous trees and rocky hillocks. As you get higher, the scrub becomes mainly box and the occasional flowers in the verges. Eventually, after a little winding, you will reach the apex of a pass, the Puerto de Herrera, at 1,100m (3,609ft), and reach the Balcón de La Rioja, a lookout that will change everything you think you might expect from this journey. The views – even on a misty and overcast March day as it was for us – are stunning. Spread out before you is La Rioja and the Río Ebro, with the Sierra de la Demanda and Sierra de Urbión misty and tall in the distance. Creamy, terracotta-topped villages sit like islands in a sea of vines in the valley floor. Dusty roads snake between the vines and long strips of tarmac link the villages and towns like arteries feeding the *bodegas* (wineries) that are the life-giving organs of this valley of riches.

What you are looking at isn't just another wine region but one of the world's best, which has been producing its famous reds for more than a thousand years. It's a place where wealth and opulence sit side by side with gnarled, timeworn vines, dust and ancient stone. Here, you can taste wine all day long if you wish, and pay handsomely for it. On the other hand, you can also pop into your local Eroski supermarket and pick up a decent bottle for a couple of euros and it'll be better than anything you've had at home for less than 20 quid. In the bars, you'll find the same: no, they haven't forgotten to charge you for that second glass. It really is just €3 for a couple of glasses of *vino tinto* and it's actually flipping good.

Now that I have teed you up for what is to come, you'll need to get down off the Balcón and among it. The A-2124 tears down the escarpment in a series of loopy, curvaceous hairpins beneath the rocky peaks of the Cima Eskamelo, and deposits you in the valley floor. Outside Leza, you'll arrive at the N-232a, the road that will lead you to the vines. Your first stop on this road is Laguardia, a beautiful hilltop village with narrow, carless streets and lots of opportunities to taste wine at any number of *bodegas*. It's a classic cork-sniffer's stop-off and is a highlight on the La Rioja trail for those who want to slosh about here. Another nearby recommendation is Elciego, home of the magnificent Frank Gehry-designed hotel (the same architect who designed the Guggenheim) at the impossibly posh Bodegas Marqués de Riscal. If you can't get into the restaurant, don't panic, the Bodegas Valdelana does free tastings (at the time of writing) for those staying on the *aire de autocaravanas* just up the road.

For us though, we continue on the N-232a towards Logroño, the capital, as it were, of La Rioja, where there is a campsite near the city and an *aire*,

too, if you are stopping. However, this route isn't just about trotting about between wine tastings. We are here to see some of the countryside as well. So, it's off on the A-12 towards Burgos (take the N-232a into the city, then follow signs for Burgos via the A-13 and then the LO-20, which becomes the A-12). At junction 108, follow signs for Nájera and the LR-113, your tarmac roller coaster for the next section of this journey. This road will take you into the Sierra de la Demanda and dinosaur country, just in case you were getting weary of driving in a straight line.

The LR-113 is a magnificent road that just gets better and better the further you go. The vines will drop away, leaving space for fruit trees and big red sandstone cliffs, eventually taking you into a spectacular, steep-sided gorge that is, apparently, very popular with motorbikes. At Anguiano, you pass through a narrow section of the gorge and it feels like you are passing through a portal to somewhere truly wild. An old bridge spans the chasm. From here, it's proper stuff, with vultures circling overhead and dark, wooded slopes looming out of the mist (well, it was for us anyway).

The LR-113 winds its way up the river as far as the Embalse de Mansilla and then, all of a sudden, becomes a lost, locals-only road when the good tarmac runs out. The motorcyclists have long departed on another road but I want you to press on, despite the poorly surfaced, cupboard-rattling, egg-smasher of a road. It'll take you to the lovely village of Canales de la Sierra, a backcountry village if ever there was one. Expect crazy farm dogs to bite your tyres and for cows to wander freely on the carriageway, their bells clanking as they go. It's that kind of place. There is an excellent *aire* here and, actually, they do welcome visitors.

Beyond Canales, the road winds its way through scrubby, rough mountain scenery to the pass at the border with Castile y León at 1,240m (4,068ft) above sea level. The road is still pretty shocking and feels like it might run out at any moment, leaving you in a field. But hold fast. At the border, the road becomes the BU-825 and brings you to an upland plain of forest and pasture, with plenty of forestry and cattle raising, passing through a couple of villages before dropping down again to Salas de los Infantes, a town that's on the Dinosaur Route. There is a small-scale gorge here (just before Barbadillo del Pez), where we stopped to watch vultures circle above the road and perch on the rocks above. It's one of the best places I have been for seeing them close-up. There are plenty of places to stop and the river even looks a bit swimmy. You'll notice the trees dripping with lichens, an indicator that the air is ultra clean and fresh here. It's wild and wonderful. *Cytisus* (broom) lines the verges.

Outside Salas de los Infantes, take the N-234 towards Soria. This is a faster road (with a better surface) but it still passes through excellent scenery. You'll pass sawmills and through lovely pine forests with huge boulders of gritstone, eventually coming to the pass at Puerto Mojón Pardo, another high one, at 1,234m (4,049ft) above sea level. Hereafter, expect long straight roads on the run into Soria, one of the biggest cities in the area.

The N-234 meets the SO-20 outside Soria and goes north to meet the N-111 going north. We, of course, got horribly lost in Soria, which was fine as we ended up at the Ermita de San Saturio and the parking down by the river (use your Search4Sites app to find it). It's worth a stop. The N-111 will take you to Garray, where you'll need to take the SO-615 for the next part of this journey. There are remains of an Iron Age and Roman city here.

The SO-615 starts off pretty average as it heads across the plain, but it soon gathers pace as it starts to climb to another pass, the Puerto de Oncala. It does this very subtly, following the gentle contours of the rounded, scrubby hills until you realise you are actually quite high and it's really quite serious. By that time, you have rounded lots of bends, passed hundreds of snow poles and slid through acres of empty mountain grassland and reached the summit at 1,454m (4,770ft) above sea level. If I need to remind you, for scale, this average-height-pass is 100m (328ft) taller than the peak of the UK's biggest mountain, the diminutive (by comparison) Ben Nevis.

On the other side, you'll sweep down through epic bends and lovely, curvy hairpins, with nothing too alarming other than the odd drop-off. At the side of the road just outside the dinosaur-crazy village of Villar del Río you'll find some dinosaur footprints that are 130 million years old. That's something, and you can well believe it as you carry on down the hill and see Europe's largest dinosaur, in bright green, on the hillside opposite. There's a centre here and some more footprints, and a theme park, The Lost World, a little later at Enciso. In case you didn't realise, you are now on the Dinosaur Route (although you might not believe it since the signage is a little lacking) and it's a real cracker. After Yanguas (ruined castle), the road runs into the really quite exciting, this-is-what-we-came-here-for Río Cidacos gorge. It's scrubby, steep and small-scale, with the river running close to the road and a gushing, multi-stepped waterfall, the Cascada Barranco Sancabras, just off the road. The road surface isn't great, and it really does feel like a lost world with the gorge walls above you and the river rushing close by. The barriers aren't up to much either so thank your lucky stars the river isn't 100m (328ft) below you.

Sadly though, the gorge opens out at the Embalse de Enciso shortly after you cross the border back into La Rioja and the road name changes to become the LR-115. It's still a cracking ride down the valley past Enciso and Peroblasco to Arnedillo. Red sandstone cliffs overlook the road, peppered with olive groves on slim terraces. Before Arnedo, the valley opens out a little more into a wide river valley with mountains either side that heads towards the wider Ebro valley.

At Arnedo, we took the LR-123 back into the mountains in search of more dinosaur footprints at Igea and Cornago. The LR-387, which runs off from the LR-123 just after Grávalos, is another crockery-crashing cruise through scrub and rock, bringing you into Igea the hard way as a little side shoot to the amazing dinosaur prints and fossilised tree trunk. If you want to avoid it, take the LR-283 a little later.

Continue on the LR-123 to Baños de Fitero, which becomes the NA-160 as you pass back into La Rioja (and remember what you came here for – sorry about that if you thought this was just about wine) and hit the main roads passing through the valley, then Tudela, the gateway to the bizarre shapes of the Bardenas Reales. From here, you can explore the desert, head south to Zaragoza, north to Pamplona or head back up to Logroño for more of that fabulous, silky-smooth plonk they scoff the world over (and for cheap in the lovely, friendly Restaurante La Florida in Elciego).

N.B. I absolutely adored driving – and stopping – on this route, even though I didn't think I would, and I hope you will too. It's a real corker, with opportunities for all kinds of excitement, from glasses of splishy-splashy red to sophisticated wineries where you might have to dress up a bit, to dipping in hot pools with the nakeds, vultures sitting on rocks and dogs chasing cars. What's more to love about travel than all that? Enjoy, with love.

WHERE TO STAY: CAMPING

There are campsites in La Rioja, of course, but the area is also blessed with plenty of perfectly good *aires* in good places. We stayed on *aires* while exploring La Rioja.

Camping La Playa, Logroño
Av. de la Playa, 6, 26009 Logroño, La Rioja, Spain
Web: www.campinglaplaya.com
Tel: +34 941 25 22 53

A popular site in the middle of the city on the banks of the Ebro River.

WHERE TO STAY: *AIRES*

Elciego: A good, free *aire* with 14 places just down the road from the Frank Gehry-designed Hotel Marqués de Riscal if you want a night out and have deep pockets (I'm only bitter because we tried to book but it was full). Tokens for leccy are available from *bodegas* in the village.
Arnedillo: The *aire* is high up above the village among olive groves. Very steep walk into the village but only takes a few minutes. €10 per night plus tokens for leccy.
Canales de la Sierra: A fantastic *aire* above the Mansilla Reservoir on the LR-113 in a beautiful village where the dogs chase cars and the cows wander the streets freely. Free, but leccy tokens can be bought from the local bar.

IN THE AREA

Bodegas and wine tasting La Rioja is full of places where you can taste wine, go on tours of wineries and live the good life. Some charge for tours, others don't. Some have restaurants, some don't. It really is whatever you want it to be. Laguardia is a hotspot, as is Logroño and the area between. Elciego is another good option.

Bodegas Marqués de Riscal, Elciego The vineyard Elciego has a magnificent Frank Gehry-designed hotel and it's incredibly posh. The main restaurant offers Michelin-star-quality food, while their 1860 Tradition restaurant offers a more modest menu. Book online for tastings or dinner. • **www.marquesderiscal.com**

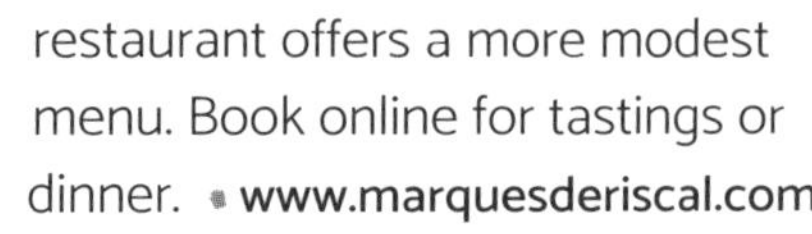

Bodegas Ysios, Araba Another inspiring monument to the riches in the wine world, this winery has a stunning building that's incredibly imposing when you walk up to it. It reeks of opulence and glamour. You can take a tour, taste the wines or pop in to gawp at the prices and the architecture from their terrace. • **www.bodegasysios.com**

Balcón de La Rioja, Álava You'll come across this viewpoint on your travels anyway if you follow this route, but if you don't it's well worth the drive just for the view of La Rioja spread out before you like a patchwork cliché. You might even see the odd vulture, too.

Hot springs/baths and spas
There are spas and bathhouses at Arnedillo and Baños de Fitero.
• www.balnearioarnedillo.com
• www.balneariodefitero.es

Ermita de San Saturio, Soria The Hermitage of San Saturio, who allegedly gave away all his money and lived in a cave here before it was built upon and turned into a church, is intriguing and very picturesque. • www.sorianitelaimaginas.com/monumentos/ermita-de-san-saturio

Bardenas Reales To the east of Tudela lies a difficult-to-access desert of strange shapes and water-carved peaks. It is possible to drive around the area, but only when access is permitted by the park authority. • www.visitnavarra.es/es/bardenas-reales

La Ruta de los Dinosaurios
There are various places where you can see dinosaur prints in La Rioja. They form the Dinosaur Route. There is also a popular walk from Enciso of 7km (4.3 miles) that takes in a number of sites. We found sites at Igea, Enciso and Cornago. More at • www.lariojaturismo.com

Via Verde Arnedillo
A greenway from Calahorra to Arnedillo. Spectacular scenery, suitable for bikes and hikes.
• www.lariojaturismo.com

ROUTE 04

SOPELANA
BAKIO
BERMEO
LEKEITIO
MUNGIA
ZUMAIA
SAN SEBASTIÁN
ONDARROA
DEBA
ZARAUTZ
GUERNICA
BILBAO
AP-8
N-634
ANDOAI

ROUTE 04

SAN SEBASTIÁN TO SOPELANA

IN SEARCH OF THE PERFECT BEACH

The Basque coast is convoluted and difficult and beaches are few and far between in places. But it makes for exciting travelling if you like taking your time to explore. Your rewards will be plentiful. San Sebastián is glorious while Bilbao is an industrial town turned to art with the building of the stunning Guggenheim Museum Bilbao. Between the two lie some of the wiggliest roads imaginable. And if you are peckish, there are *pintxos* to snack on at every stop. What more could you want?

BEST FOR: Amazing food, culture, art, beaches

START: San Sebastián

END: Sopelana (for Bilbao)

MILEAGE: 159km (99 miles)

ALLOW: 4–5 days

MAP PAGES: 8, 9

We arrive in Lekeitio on a sunny but windy afternoon. It's warm out of the breeze but when I am in it, I am reminded that it's still only March and perhaps it's too early for flip-flops. We stop at Karraspio Beach for lunch, taking a sharp turn off the tiny coastal road that's brought us from San Sebastián. It's a beautiful day and we think about swimming, but that cool wind is onshore so I'm not keen, even though we had swum at the glorious, ever-cool La Concha the day before. I sit on the step of the van sipping my tea, looking out over the beach, people watching. A few are sitting in the sun or walking down by the tideline, as they tend to do in Spain. To the west, there is a small offshore island, and beyond that lies the harbour and town of Lekeitio. Between us is a river and another beach, where I see a snorkeller surfacing from time to time. His long fins flap above the surface as he dives. A small swell laps on the shore.

I notice what looks like a sewer pipe on the far side of the river, between us and the diver. The waves slosh over it gently, revealing more as the time passes and the tide drops. I don't think much of it until the tide drops to the point where I can see it clearly. It runs from the beach to the offshore island. The snorkeller pulls himself up on to it, sitting to remove his mask before getting up, gathering his orange tow float and walking back to the beach. He appears to be walking on water. That's when I see that it is a causeway. With every slosh of the waves, it rises further from the sea, in a zigzag that leads from the town's beach to the bottom of the island. Intrigued, we decide to go

and look. We follow the usual routine to find parking, locate the *aire* in town and decide to have the rest of the day away from the wheel, with half an idea to walk to the island and half an idea to find somewhere sheltered to swim.

Half an hour later, we are cycling to the beach from the *aire*. We ride through the town, past its huge gothic church, through narrow streets by the marina and out to the gardens that back on to the town beach. We stop at the tourism office to pick up a token for the water at the *aire*. By this time, the causeway is fully uncovered and a few people are walking out to the island. We lock the bikes and set off. The causeway is about 1m (3.3ft) wide, 200m (656ft) long and with a couple of kinks in it. It is covered in bright green seaweed – gutweed – making it a little slippery. We pass a couple taking selfies. At the island, there is a set of steps cut into the limestone that lead us up, away from the water and on to a flat area about 20m (66ft) above the sea.

We turn and look back to where we have come. It takes my breath away. I can see the town, the marina, both beaches and the hills behind. It's like a layered *mise en scène* with each element resembling a glass painting

from old Hollywood. It's as if each part of the whole has been painted on a different plane. The further away the hills are, the further they retreat into the mist and their colour becomes milkier with the perspective. It's a huge, epic landscape, with lots of elements, perfectly placed, from the dark green wooded peaks to the golden sands and the blue sea, the whites of the apartment buildings and the terracotta roof tiles.

We shift our attention back to the island, following the path to its summit. We walk through a small wood of tall, straight Scots pines with scrub beneath. There are a few ruins here and there and piles of earth where it looks as if archaeological digs have taken place. I see a pile of broken clay roof tiles and the base of a stone wall.

As I follow the path upwards, I notice lizards scurrying away and into the bushes. They rustle in the undergrowth and catch my attention as they dart away. I pay more attention to what's beneath my feet, looking at the vegetation instead of the landscape in which it grows. Lizzy, who has scampered on ahead, is already bent double looking at a tiny flower in the scrub: a squill, she says excitedly. There are lots of other things here, too, almost hidden in the long grass and beneath the undergrowth: violets, scarlet pimpernel, a blue vetch and bird's-foot trefoil. Above them stand flowering yellow broom, tree heather and small holm oaks, and towering over them all the Scots pines. There is a world in miniature hidden here beneath the canopy, each element with its own plane. When we reach the top of the island, we hear gulls squawking above our heads, riding the breeze, squabbling. The wind is salty and the sun is bright, making me squint at the rounded limestone rocks I am taking care not to trip over. Here, at the summit, there are the remains of a lookout, protected on the seaward side by steep cliffs. Back towards the land, the view is even bigger from up here. It's like the view from Mount Igueldo in San Sebastián of La Concha, except better. It is so stunning, I feel that I am standing in front of the most beautiful painting. It seems to me that it is the most perfectly balanced location. I try to capture it in a photograph, but I feel that nothing will do it justice. It is my new favourite place. It transports me, in so many ways. I think about images and imagery, about describing and capturing the essence of this place: How will I do it? Will my words be enough? I hope so. I repeat the names of the flowers as I pick my way back to the causeway, taking photos of everything I see.

Along the causeway, we see hundreds of crabs. Some are inches across, some no more than a few centimetres. They scurry away and disappear into crevices as we walk. Even the tiny ones raise their claws towards us as they back into their dark hidey holes, in anticipation of some kind of battle, no matter their size. We let them be and walk back to the mainland.

That night, we cycle back into Lekeitio and sit in a bar on the harbourside. It's a Saturday so there are scores of people out and the bars

are full. More people walk along the harbour and through the lanes. Kids play on their bikes and parents chase them, generations together. Despite the cool evening, it's not windy and the air is dry so we sit sipping red wine for a couple of hours, taking it all in.

The following day, we leave early. I feel like we have reached a pinnacle in Lekeitio. We have seen a lot of beaches and a lot of places on this journey, but none has come close to the island and the views back to the mainland. A few miles up the road, however, we arrive at the beach at Laga. I pull in on a whim and we drive into the parking lot. We notice height barriers, but they are open, we assume because of the time of year, so we sail through and park.

We walk to the beach, past a cafe and on to glorious, golden sand. At one end, there is a huge cliff behind a typical Basque house. It's perfect. There is a small wave in the middle of the bay and the water is glassy smooth as there is no wind. It's perfect for a swim. We walk back to the van and notice that a beach tractor is pulling off the beach. He is taller than the 2.2m (7.2ft) it says on the parking sign and I suddenly have a horrible feeling we need to act fast. We walk briskly up the sand and see the tractor, now on the other side of the height barriers, which are closed. I shout at him

to catch his attention and run to the van. Lizzy runs towards him to try to delay his leaving.

When I get to the barriers with the van, he seems to twig the problem Lizzy has been trying to communicate. He says something to me in Spanish, which I don't understand. I say '*no comprende*' and he says that 'without me you are stuck!' '*Lo se,*' I say, '*todo el día! Muchas gracias!*' ('I know, all day! Many thanks!') He smiles, unlocks the gate and lets us through with a big wave, although I feel a little sad that we have to leave. It seems like a waste of time to continue on when we could have been held hostage by the barriers until the tractor's return the next day.

We'd have had 24 hours at the most perfect beach, stranded, with only our food, our wetsuits, a bar and ourselves for company. I kick myself as we pull away and continue on this winding, magical route through the Basque region.

N.B. There is very limited parking at Laga so beware. If you are low enough to get under the barriers, enjoy, but get there early. If you are too big, then there may be limited parking a little further up the road towards Bilbao.

Isla de San Nicolas, Lekeitio

THE DRIVING

Come with me on one of the highlights of my journeys across Spain. It's a journey I have taken a few times over the years and always loved. Sitting between two great cities and spanning just 100km (62 miles) or so, it's a journey that's fractal and long, winding and, at times, painful. Parking at remote beaches or in small beachside towns can be difficult and finding a place to stay sometimes fraught, especially out of season. However, it is and can be spectacular, simply because of the nature of the place. Each beach is a gem. Each town a wonder beneath wooded hills. And each stop-off brings something new each time.

San Sebastián and Bilbao are beautiful, regal cities, with lots to offer. Mundaka has world-class surfing and Gernika has a terrible story to tell. The Basques will tell you that their region is neither Spain nor France and it is different. The language is confusing but the cake is delicious.

San Sebastián is an obvious start point for this journey because it's the right place to set the mood for the Basque region. After a swim at La Concha and an evening spent strolling the old city or sampling *pintxos*, you'll be ready for more. But first, take a trip to the top of the town by following the road to Mount Igueldo, the Igeldo Pasealekua, a tiny road

that winds up to the theme park at the western end of La Concha beach. The views are stunning.

If you are small then you can carry on along this road, following it to the AP-8 motorway and the N-634. It's a narrow, winding route that will take you past the Igueldo campsite as well as farms and homes and then almost to the very top of the mountain before dropping back down into the valley via a couple of tight hairpins. Local restrictions ban motorhomes from this road, so it is small vans only. This will bring you to junction 33 of the AP-8, where you can jump on the N-634 and join up with the big boys in their big mohos for the rest of the trip (wasn't it worth it though?!).

If you are big then make your way out of the city on the AP-8 and rendezvous with the N-634 at junction 33, heading in the direction of Orio. Here, you'll get to meet up with the little guys again after they have descended from the heaven at the top of Mount Igueldo.

Righto. The N-634 will take you over a bridge on the river, to the right, past industrial buildings and then up a steep hill with a sharp hairpin and into open country. It's a good, fast road, if a little wiggly. There are great views

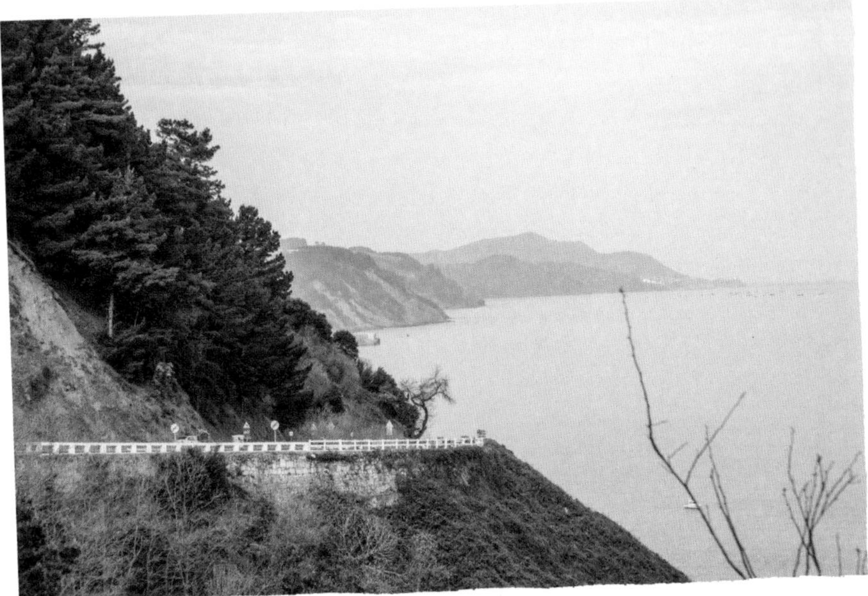

over the valley to your left as you pass over the AP-8 *autovía* and on to a roundabout. Keep following the N-634 into Zarautz and, if you don't want to stop, out the other side again. The road runs along the beach a couple of blocks back so a stop here might yield an ice cream or a swim, but we press on. The road leaves the town at the western end of the beach – you can look back at the beach – and then hugs the coast, giving views of the sea for the next few miles. This is a stunning section, with low cliffs on the landward side and nothing but the sea on your right. You'll pass the village of Getaria and continue along the coast. There are a few stopping places along here, and an *aire* overlooking Gaztetape beach at Getaria. You'll head around the headland, past the huge beach at Santiago opposite Zumaia.

Stay on the N-634 through Zumaia and out the other side into the countryside. It's curly and curvaceous and often forested with tall, mature eucalyptus, which isn't to Lizzy's exacting standards as it's imported and has run wild in this part of Spain. It's dense and dark and dominates the forest here. Despite this, it's a lovely section with lots of steep hills and curves, and it's great to hit the beach again at Deba, a few twisted miles later. You emerge from the forest at a viewpoint with Deba just around the headland. It's an easy pull-in to look at the sea below and to see the road snaking off in front of you.

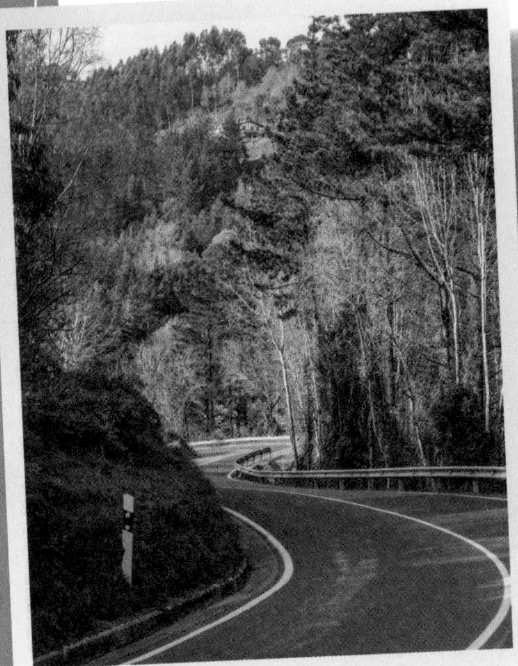

Deba beach, and its setting below steep hills, is lovely. There is a car park right on the beach (take a right in the park) that can accommodate vehicles up to 3.5m (11.5ft) in height. The road takes you through town and out the other side along the Deba River, a wide, tidal estuary. You'll come to a roundabout with a right turn over the river signposted for Mutriku on the GI-638. Take this road and follow it back up the river and out of town along the coast. It rises sharply after the harbour and takes you on another wild ride around the coast, high above the cliffs and down into Mutriku, another beach town. After Mutrika,

San Sebastián from Igeldo Mendiko Jolas-Parkea

the road rises again, heading into the hills of eucalyptus and pine. You'll come to a junction signposted for Saturrarán as you descend into Ondarroa. There is a campsite here and lovely beach with great geology and a huge car park. Recommended.

Keep on the GI-638 (it appears to change to the BI-638 at this point) and you'll arrive in Ondarroa, enjoying (I hope) great views of the tiny beach and harbour. In town, you'll come to a roundabout. Follow signs for the B-3438 Lekeitio. Go over the bridge and then take a left at the next roundabout through the town (there's a lovely sculpture of three women on the roundabout for reference!) around a sharp right, and out the other side of town up a narrow hill and eventually back on to the coast. For the next few miles, you are treated to another fine coastal road that lies high above the sea and goes in and out of the forest in a constant curve. Your next stop is Lekeitio.

From Lekeitio, take the BI-2238 signposted to Gernika. A little outside of Lekeitio, take a right turn towards Ispaster and Ea, going along another winding, small road that follows the curvy contours of the hills through forests of eucalyptus and pine. After Ea, you'll come to a junction signposted to Gernika. Take a right and continue on (it's the BI-2237 at this point) into Ibarranguela, following signs for Laga by taking a right turn at a junction that will bring you on to the BI-3234. This road will take you to Laga and then

Laida and eventually back into what feels like civilisation along the eastern shore of the Mundaka River.

Follow this road to the junction with the BI-2238 and turn right for Gernika, then, in the town, follow signs for the BI-2235 for Mundaka and Bermeo. It's a long, straight road with great views across the river. Mundaka is the home of one of the world's best surfing waves, so if there is swell, stop to look but don't go in unless you know what you are doing! There is a compact campsite here with a pool.

Continue on the BI-2235 until you get to a roundabout. Follow signs for Bakio and go through the tunnel following signs for Bakio on another winding road (BI-2101) through forests of endless eucalyptus high above the ocean. At Bakio, take the road out of town (BI-2101) and then take a right a little out of town signposted to Armintza (BI-3151), yet another winding road through green hills and forest that goes past a strange decommissioned nuclear power station and a reservoir with a huge dam right on the cliff edge. The BI-3151 will take you into Gorliz and Plentzia, nice beach towns of holiday apartments and bars on a river. Take the BI-2122 out of Plentzia and follow it up the hill to Barrika. This will lead you to Sopelana and the campsite.

WHERE TO STAY: CAMPING

Camping Sopelana, Sopelana
Avenida Atxabiribil Etorbidea, 30, 48600 Sopelana, Biscay, Spain
Web: www.campingsopelana.com
Tel: +34 946 76 19 81

If you want to visit Bilbao and stay by the coast there really is no other option. Camping Sopelana is small and compact (and tight in places) but that's by the by. The Metro is 20 minutes' walk away and the beach 5. Pool, bar, restaurant. Parking in Sopelana is difficult for anything over 5m (16.4ft).

Camping Igueldo, Donostia–San Sebastián
Padre Orkolaga Ibilbidea, 69, 20008 Donostia, Gipuzkoa, Spain
Web: www.campingigueldo.com
Tel: +34 972 83 77 53

This site is a little out of town, beyond Mount Igueldo, but it's the nearest option for the city if you want pools, bar, electricity etc.

Camping Igara, Donostia–San Sebastián
Camin o de Igara Bidea, 195, 20018 Donostia, Gipuzkoa, Spain
Web: www.campingigara.com
Tel: +34 943 35 88 12

This is a nice campsite, with a great pool and good plots, but it is a little out of town and can be hard to find. Don't trust the sat nav. Follow the website's instructions, especially in a big moho.

WHERE TO STAY: *AIRES*

San Sebastián: The *aire* is in a really good position and is a short cycle from La Concha, but it gets busy. Your best bet to find a spot would be to arrive in the morning after everyone has left and before the hordes descend.
Lekeitio: Brilliant *aire* that's just out of town and has lots of space. It gets busy. Get tokens for the water filling point from the tourist office in town. Other services are free.
Bakio: A good, paying *aire* that's close to the beach and that is almost the only option in town in which to park.
Bilbao: The *aire* above the city at Kobeta Bidea has amazing views. 20 minute walk into town.

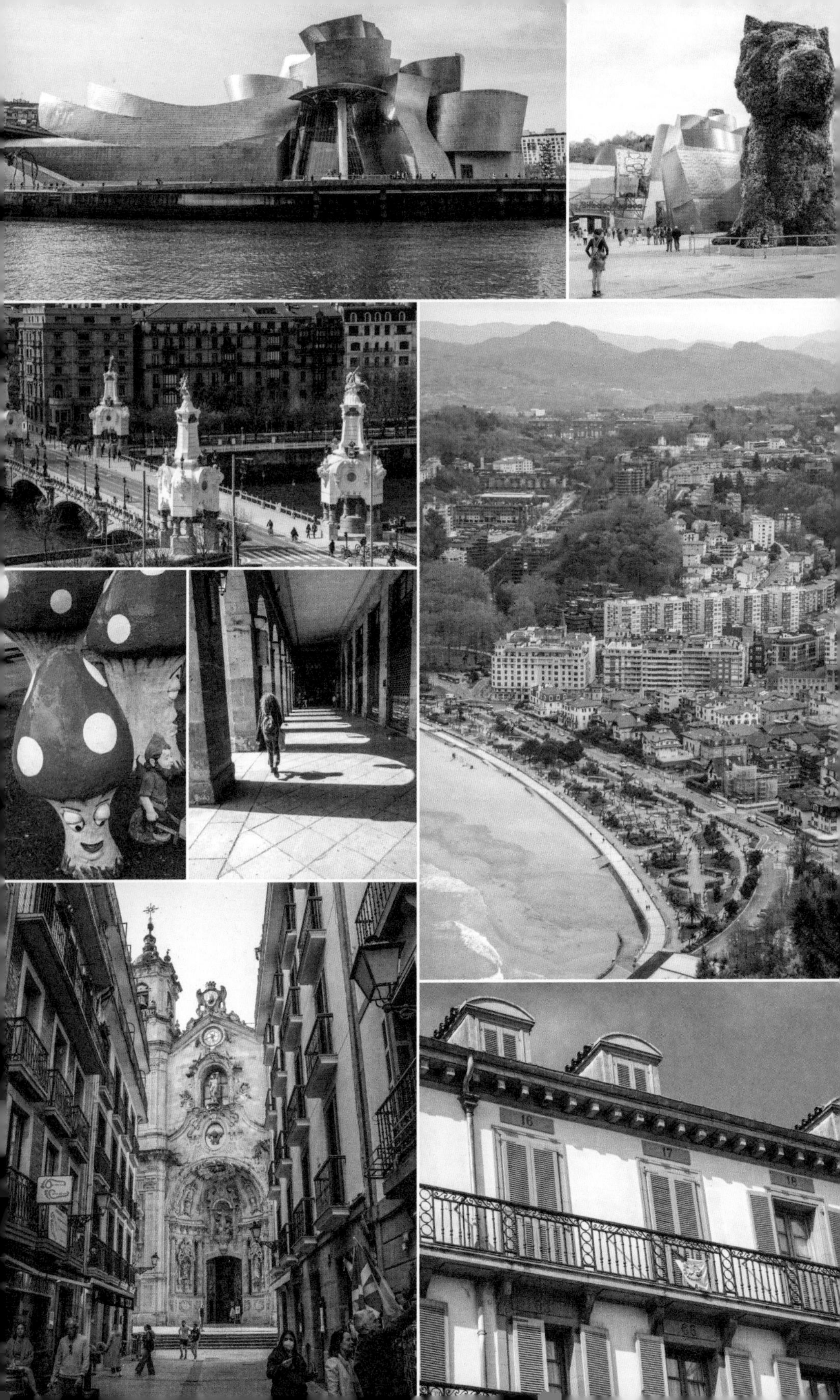
16
17
18
66

IN THE AREA

San Sebastián This wonderful city has a lot of attractions, including an aquarium (www.aquariumss.com) and the Miramar Palace, but the real stars of the show are the beaches of La Concha and Zurriola and the old town, where you can stroll the streets in search of the world's best *pintxos*.

La Concha, San Sebastián This is the main beach in San Sebastián. It's windy and sandy and great for swimming. A very popular place for people to hang out and the promenade is popular for the *paseo* (evening stroll). A cycle path will take you directly from the *aire*/university, all along La Concha.

Casco Viejo, San Sebastián San Sebastián's old city is wonderful, especially if you like tapas and *pintxos*. The Plaza de la Constitución is the beating heart of this area and is famed for once being a bullring.

Mount Igueldo, San Sebastián A theme park on top of the mountain looking over the city. Unsurpassed views. • **www.monteigueldo.es/home**

Guggenheim Bilbao Museum, Bilbao The city is defined by the Guggenheim, a glorious, shining beacon on the river. Fronted by Jeff Koons' flowered puppy and full to the brim with treasures and large-scale art, it's an absolute must. • **www.guggenheim-bilbao.eus/en**

Casco Viejo, Bilbao The old city is about a 1km (0.6-mile) walk from the Guggenheim. Like San Sebastián's old city, it has narrow streets and a main square that's chock full of *pintxos* bars. Great for a wander and a nibble.

Gaztelugatxe A castle on a rock not far from Bilbao that's been used as a *Game of Thrones* location, and is therefore popular. It was closed for maintenance when we visited but the setting is spectacular.

Gernika The town that was flattened by Franco and Hitler during the Spanish Civil War is a poignant place to think about where we are at, especially at the Peace Museum, a moving and fascinating space devoted to peace and the aftermath of the terrible bombing. • **www.museodelapaz.org**

ROUTE 05

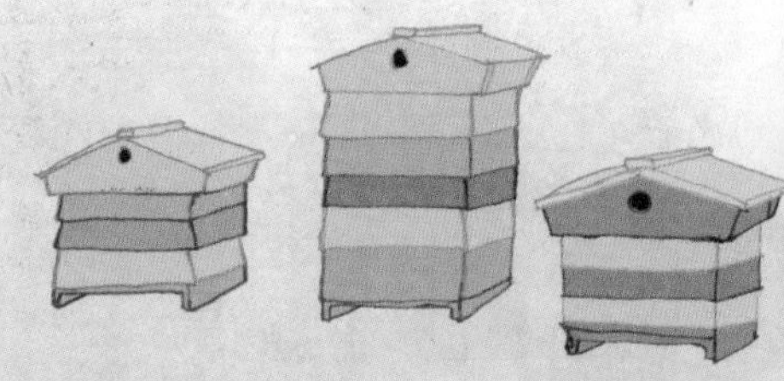

OVIÑANA
CUDILLERO
LUARCA
CADAVÉU
A-8
NAVIA
TREVÍAS
PRAVIA
N-634
CANDAMO
CORNELLANA
SALAS
GRADO
A-63
CASTRILLÓN
BORRES
ILLANO
POLA DE ALLANDE
BELMONTE
AS-15
AS-14
PROAZA
BERDUCEDO
GRANDAS
ENTRAGO
LIMÉS
AS-227
TORRESTÍO
VENTANUEVA
LA CUETA
CABRILLANES

ROUTE 05

CUDILLERO TO NAVIA

THE WILDER SIDE OF ASTURIAS

Most people come to Asturias for the beaches and coast, cheese, *fabada* (a classic Asturian stew) and cider. And they should, because they are excellent. But there is another side to Asturias that's isolated and untamed, where remote villages share the space with bears, pine martens, red squirrels, wolves and capercaillies. This journey will take you into the very heart of the Cantabrian mountains to search for the wilder side of Asturias. Here, you can be among the privileged few to walk in Spain's most protected biosphere reserve or cycle in search of brown bears. And the driving's not bad either, if you have a head for heights.

BEST FOR: Walking, wildlife, mountain passes, cycling

START: Cudillero

END: Navia

MILEAGE: 485km (300 miles)

ALLOW: 7 days

MAP PAGES: 4, 5

It seems fitting to start this journey at Cudillero. It's a very popular village on the Asturian coast that sits in a tiny crucible and faces out to sea, as if watching for the last of the boats to come home. It's one of those places that you'll think you recognise, even if you haven't ever been there. It is the village of dreams, with multicoloured houses, the smell of fish and garlic, just enough tourism infrastructure to keep you happy and a huge working port that adds grime to the glitter to make it feel like it retains its authenticity.

After walking around, taking photos and admiring the beautiful setting, we spend the night on the quayside, waking early to drive a few miles along the coast to find Playa de Silencio, another famous Asturian landmark. It's another of those places you'll know, even if you haven't been here, and is often cited as being Spain's most beautiful beach. We get there early and are the first to arrive and so get to see it by ourselves. We walk down the hill and peer over the edge at the *mirador* to assess the sweep of shingle that's backed by a semicircle of pine-covered cliffs. It's lovely, for sure, but the water doesn't look too swimmable and I don't fancy the walk down the zigzagging path. Instead, we follow an intriguing, overgrown path in the opposite direction. It takes us across a river on stepping stones and to an inlet to the east, where there is a double arch in the tiny rocky bay and another arch leading to another huge beach at the bottom of a difficult but low cliff. We decide this is a much better option than Playa de Silencio, so strip off and wade in. We swim through one arch and around it into a long cave that brings us, via a hole in the rock a few metres wide,

Cudillero

on to the second, larger beach. The water is dark and cool below me as I swim breaststroke under the arch. The small swell pulls me back and then releases me as I swim, allowing me to make two steps' progress forwards and then stealing one back from me. It's fantastic to swim to a beach that is quite difficult to get to without getting wet and I feel like I am pioneering something, even if I know thousands have been here before me. We haul out on the rocks and climb up the low cliff back to our clothes. It's a great, wild start to this journey.

We head south, away from the coast, following the Río Nalón into the mountains and to the start of the Senda del Oso ('Path of the Bear'), a cycle that will lead us further into the mountains, up a narrow pass and into 'bear country', one of the last strongholds of the Cantabrian brown bear. Conservation projects have seen numbers rise from critical levels in the 1970s to around 300 in recent years.

The ride, mostly uphill from the start of the trail, is stunning. The trail follows an old mining track as it winds its way up the valley, through villages

with ancient arched bridges, wash houses and *hórreos*, the stilted maize stores that are common here. It's sunny and we are in good spirits as we pedal along the track looking over the meadows, where farmers on tiny tractors, with help from family members with rakes, are gathering the first cut of hay. Cows, their bells clanking, graze on in other fields.

Our first stop is at the bear enclosure about 5km (3.1 miles) into the ride. Here, next to the path, there are a couple of female brown bears who cannot return to the wild. Paca, I read while researching this route, was orphaned as a cub, along with her sister, by a hunter in the late 1980s, while Molina was injured so badly that she was unable to return to a wild life.

The enclosures are big and I don't expect to see any sign of life, but, as we approach, I can see one of the bears walking around a pond right next to the path. She is pacing like a bear in a zoo while cyclists like us have stopped and are taking photos of her. She looks out at us as we stand and stare. She's about 16m (10ft) away from us and is absolutely beautiful. Her thick brown fur and small, round ears

Sablera la Barquera, near Playa de Silencio

makes her look like she'd be fun to play with, until you notice her claws. She is herbivorous, but I'm not sure I'd like to be so close to her if the 3m (10ft)-high fence wasn't there.

She walks away from the crowd, along the fence, and sits down facing me. She looks at me and scratches herself. She looks a little sad, I think. She's not in a zoo, but might as well be, because she can't be with her own kind, can't roam free and can't live the way her shy cousins do out in the mountains surrounding us. It makes me feel terribly sad, too, even though I am thrilled that I have been able to see her.

We cycle on, riding through dark, dripping tunnels, alongside a narrow gorge where climbers are scaling overhangs above us. The scenery is really incredible, with a fast-flowing river running on the valley bottom and peaks high above us. We jam on the brakes when we spot a red squirrel on one of the handrails that runs along the edge of the gorge. It scampers along the rail and then disappears up a tree before I can get my camera out.

We stop at San Martín, where we check out the *aire* before heading back down the path to the van. Some 20km (12.4 miles) goes in no time as we freewheel most of the way back to the van and then drive back up the gorge to stay overnight with a few of the other motorhomes who have made it this far into the mountains.

We get up early the next day and head further south, deeper into the mountains. We stop at the top of the Puerto de Ventana, a pass that's 1,587m (5,207ft) above sea level. We admire the views and take photos. There is a small herd of cows and horses grazing by the pass. Their bells clang as their herding dog, a huge, jowly Spanish mastiff, lolls about on the grass, doing its job keeping predators – presumably bears and wolves – away.

We roll down the other side of the pass, into the high meadows of Castile and León briefly before crossing the Puerto de Somiedo, another high pass with giddying drops and huge vistas. It brings us into the Parque Natural de Somiedo, a protected area that is home to many of Asturias's brown bears. It's a wild and rugged area of tiny villages and deep woods, topped by rocky heather- and bracken-clad peaks. We head for Valle de Lago, a dead end up an excruciating road with six hairpins that take us, like a lift, from the valley floor at 700m (2,297ft) to a tiny village that sits at 1,250m (4,101ft). We check into the small, rustic campsite and note the cider cooling in the fountain. The valley is long and narrow, with high rock faces on either side. At the head of the valley there is a lake, in a natural amphitheatre of mountains.

It's a tough 6km (3.7-mile) cycle from the campsite up a steep track, but the effort is well worth the reward. We leave the bikes and clamber down to a sandy beach on the far side of the lake, swimming briefly in the cool but incredibly clear water. Fish jump between the lilies as we swim. Above us, an Egyptian vulture swoops in circles, rising on the thermals. On the way back to the bikes, I almost step on a black snake. I scramble up the lake's bank very quickly while the snake disappears into a bushy willow that we had just been sitting next to. The ride back down to the campsite is wonderful, with views of the path stretching off into the misty beyond, peaks either side and meadows filled with flowers. Cowbells clang and farmers rake their hay in distant fields. It seems too good to be true and I am smiling to myself as I hare down the gravel track, stopping only to take photos when the enormity of the view hits me again. I get picky, but really, this is one of the most poetic, romantic places I have ever been. I feel incredibly happy as I ride my bike next to Lizzy, our hair still wet from the swim.

We leave Valle de Lago, reluctantly, and head north and west towards Cangas de Onís and the Muniellos Reserve, where we hope we'll be able

Lago del Valle, Valle de Lago, Somiedo

Parque Natural
de Somiedo

to get even further off the beaten track. We drive up another remote valley, though tiny villages and then take a small, steep road up to the interpretation centre for the reserve. We are met by a warden who seems surprised to see us. I get the impression that maybe they don't get many visitors up here. She turns on the lights for us and gives us a very brief introduction to the centre half in English and half in Spanish. She explains that the area is a UNESCO Biosphere Reserve and is the most protected place in Spain. Only 20 people are allowed in each day to walk the trails, where brown bear, capercaillies, wolves, pine martens, black woodpeckers and red squirrels roam, peck, fly and howl.

We walk to a viewing point behind the centre, where we are able to get a 360-degree view of the surrounding mountains. We look out at the steep wooded slopes of oak – it's the best-preserved sessile oak forest in Spain – and try to imagine a bear strolling into a clearing. But no bears appear, unsurprisingly, and all we can hear is the buzzing of insects. Other than that, it is completely silent. There are no cowbells or tractors, cars or aeroplanes, just the roar of nature's pollinators as they flit from wild flower to wild flower. I realise that I have been to few places as remote as this. It's incredible to think that, somewhere down below me, in the dark woods, there are some of Europe's most critically endangered

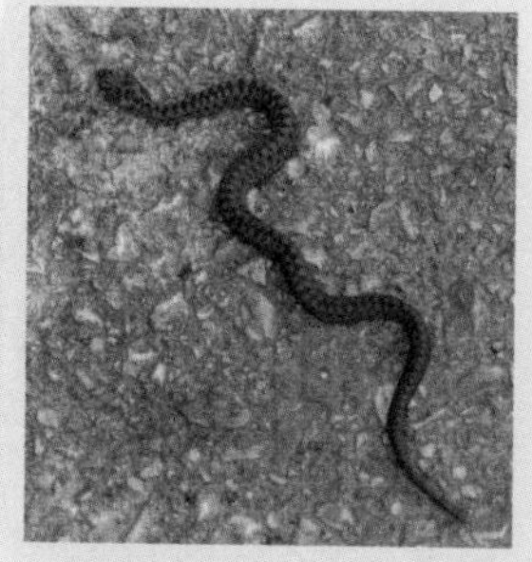

animals and birds living out their lives, safe for the moment, from progress. It's refreshing.

Our last act is to head down the hill and drive up a narrow, twisting lane to the gateway to the park, a small interpretation centre and sole point of entry into the wilderness. Here is the place where the lucky 20 each day are allowed to walk in the reserve. On the way, we pass a couple of stone-walled enclosures where farmers set up their beehives so that the bears can't raid them. It tickles me that bears, after all the hype, still love honey and will do almost anything to get it. We park and walk the last 100m (110 yards) – I almost step on another snake – up the lane to a bridge that crosses a small river. Here, a sign warns us that it is strictly forbidden to go any further. We don't have access so have to stop, looking into the forest for something, anything, in the great nothing that lies beyond.

No bears appear.

We wish them good luck and turn around, just as a warden comes out of the visitor centre to challenge us.

THE DRIVING

If you like going to wild, remote areas then this drive is for you. Some of the driving is a little wild, too, and will take you over high passes, along ridges and around steep mountains, relentlessly and without mercy. The point is to experience a little of rural, isolated Asturias away from the Instagram beaches and cutesy fishing village, although I think you should see those, too, because they are also special.

Tourism is relatively new here, so in some areas there is little infrastructure, few campsites and few places to overnight. That said, if you wanted to pull over and stay the night, I am sure no one will really mind as long as you are respectful, as usual. In the upper meadows and around the stone-built, slate-roofed hamlets, you'll see small-scale, traditional and subsistence farming, done in small fields, with small herds or in small orchards (cider is big news here) and vineyards. At times, you'll find yourself on roads that feel as if they touch the sky, whizzing past snow poles, trying not to look through the clouds down into the abyss – and the valley bottom – that lies many hundreds of metres below you.

We began our journey in Cudillero, heading south on the N-632 to Muros de Nalón and Soto del Barco, picking up the AS-16 to Pravia along the Río Nalón, then turning left on to the AS-236 towards Grado before the bridge

Valle de Lago, Somiedo

just outside Pravia, then following the AS-237 towards Grado. Before Grado, turn left on to the N-634 towards Oviedo. This road will take you under the A-63 and then start to climb into the lush green hills of inland Asturias. After a few miles, follow the AS-228 towards Trubia (it's more or less straight on in Udrión). This road will be your guiding light until you get to the pass at Puerto de Ventana, when it will shapeshift into the LE-481 at the border with the department of Castile and León.

Trubia is somewhat of an industrial town, with a history of arms making that continues today. You'll pass the factories as you head deeper into the mountains. After Trubia, the countryside starts to get more mountainous and more enjoyable, even a little gorge-like, although the road follows the bottom of the valley. At Tuñón, you'll arrive at the start of the Senda del Oso, where there is a large car park and bike hire/cafe.

After Proaza, the road starts to head into the spectacular Desfiladero Teverga, a narrow, steep-sided limestone gorge that twists and turns, going uphill all the way. Keep following the AS-228 here and take a right over the bridge at El Valle, which will take you into the deeper parts of the gorge. Once out of the gorge, you are in true mountain country and at the end of the Senda del Oso at San Martín. It is a good place to stay before heading further onwards. The road climbs steeply out of San Martín, reaching a massive gorge, which doesn't last long but acts as a portal to the next stage – high mountains, scary bends, huge drop-offs and massive vistas. Luckily for you, much of it is in the trees so you don't have to look at it as you drive. Here, the forests are native, with hazel and ash, oak and alder covering an understory of broom, heather and bracken. On the upper slopes, you'll see hay meadows, too. Closer to the top of the pass there are some beech stands, too, with the chance of seeing deer (and maybe even a bear). The pass itself is open, with lots of grazing and flowers to look at, as well as the view down the valley and also into the next valley. Here you'll be at 1,587m (5,207ft)... That's well high!

The landscape changes dramatically over the other side of the pass. It's less green and lush, with fewer trees and more scrub, and, thankfully for some, fewer steep drops. The road sweeps down from the pass into a wide plateau and the Parque Natural de Babia y Luna. Follow the road through a couple of small, high-altitude villages (note their slated roofs) to the CL-626, where you'll need to take a right turn and follow the valley for a few straight miles until the junction with the LE-495 in Piedrafita. The road then rises again, passing through the village of El Puerto at the pass (1,486m/4,875ft) and then through a small, boggy plateau before plunging down again on the lusher, greener side.

You have now entered the Parque Natural de Somiedo, the home of the bear, although it is unlikely you will see any. Still, road signs will warn you that they may be about. Time to sing the theme tune to the *Hair Bear Bunch* (if you're old enough to know what that is)...

The road heads down quickly in a series of sweeping bends, passing villages in high meadows before becoming rockier and more extreme as you slip down into the valley. Look out for the traditional thatched shepherd huts on the hillsides. You will reach Pola de Somiedo after passing through a few small villages.

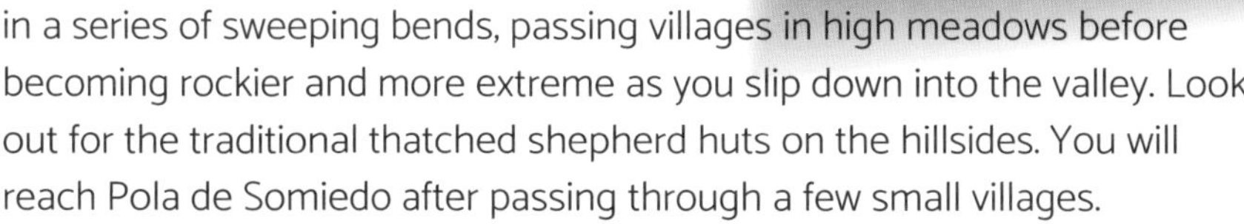

Turn right here for Valle de Lago, passing the campsite in town (this is the only real option for A-class mohos as the road up to Valle is narrow and steep and your moho probably won't fit into the campsite at the top – sorry) and then taking a left uphill on the unclassified road. It's steep and hairy, with six hairpins in a row that elevate you from the valley floor in no time. You'll run alongside the valley for a while, then turn into the Valle de Lago by a small *embalse* (reservoir). You have arrived in heaven...

Continuing on from Pola de Somiedo on the AS-227, you'll pass through more beautiful alpine scenery, with the road getting narrower as you pass through a gorge and past an *embalse* that will take you to the edge of the Parque Natural at Aguasmestas, where two rivers meet. From here, continue down the mountain until you reach the Río Narcea and its wide valley at the junction with the AS-15. Turn left here, in the direction of Cangas del Narcea. Enjoy the low-level, fast but bendy road for a while as you pass a couple of reservoirs and drive through a couple of tunnels. It's not the best part of the journey. However, it is taking you deeper into Asturias's hinterland.

If you want to visit the Biosphere Reserve (details below on how to book) then continue on to Cangas. If you don't, turn right on to the AS-14 after Tebongo – on which more later.

At Cangas, continue on the AS-15 until Ventanueva and then take a right on the AS-348, which is also signed with a brown tourism sign for the Reserva Natural Integral de Muniellos. Head up this road for the interpretation centre, which is high in the hills, 15km (9.3 miles) up the mountain (this is for the *mirador* of the reserve) or park in Moal and walk (if you are bigger than a small van) to the visitor centre at the edge of the reserve. To continue, head back up the AS-15 past Cangas and then take a left turn on to the AS-14 signed for Pola de Allende/Grandas de Salime.

The AS-14 is one of those roads that starts off quite unassuming but gets wilder and wilder the further you go. It wends its way around the mountainsides, getting higher and higher, constantly rising, relentlessly

WHERE TO STAY: CAMPING

As stated before, this area is remote and wild and there isn't a huge amount of tourism infrastructure away from the coast.

Camping Cudillero, Cudillero
Playa del Aguilar, Km 0800, 33150
Cudillero, Asturias, Spain
Web: www.cudillerocamping.com/en
Tel: +34 985 59 06 63

A very pleasant site above Cudillero with a pool. They will probably make you wear a swim hat.

Camping Lagos de Somiedo, Valle de Lago
33840 Valle de Lago, Asturias, Spain
Web: www.campinglagosde somiedo.com
Tel: +34 618 90 67 45

This is not a typical Spanish site. It's run by a lovely family and is high in the Valle de Lago. Big vans won't get in but anything around 6m (20ft) will be fine as long as you aren't too wide. Grass pitches, great views, incredible walks and cider available at the bar.

Camping la Pomarada de Somiedo, Pola de Somiedo
33840 Pola de Somiedo, Asturias, Spain
Web: www.lapomaradadesomiedo.es
Tel: +34 669 30 35 42

If you are in a big van then this may be your only option (apart from going wild) in the Somiedo.

WHERE TO STAY: *AIRES*

San Martín: A very pleasant parking area in the village with water and grey waste. Free and a great place to stop before heading over the Puerto de Ventana or making a stop after cycling the Senda del Oso.
Cangas del Narcea: A few dedicated places in the parking area next to the river in the centre of the town.
Pesoz: Just outside the village, on the AS-13, is a very pleasant car park with tables and benches and a fresh tap. Free. No other services.
Grandas de Salime: A few spaces in the back of the town car park. Handy for bars and food, if need be.
Cudillero: There is no official aire but vans do stay on the harbourside at the bottom of the relief road coming into town from the west.

offering you glimpses of the heights and bends ahead. Turn left at Pola de Allende (staying on the AS-14) and continue up through the oak forest, until you reach the treeline and enter a scrubbier landscape for the last two, huge bends between the snow poles that bring you to the peak of the pass, Puerto del Palo, at 1,146m (3,760ft). The views from up here are immense. Looking back down into the valleys from where you have just come and towards the ridge along which you must now drive is quite breathtaking. Everything, it seems, is below you. And all you have to do is get down!

Unfortunately, while the road drops initially in a hair-raising series of bends, it doesn't feel like you actually lose any altitude. The vistas are open and huge, with massive chasms below you and peaks level with you. You'll drive along a ridge where, at one point, there are huge drops either side of the road. This is when it really feels like you are driving along the sky road, at the very top of the world, among the highest meadows and the dizziest cattle.

You will, of course, lose altitude as you pass through dense forest, with views to the jagged peaks and into the deep valley of the Río Navia, rounding a reservoir and then driving over the dam. There are high meadows here and a little subsistence farming, the occasional small hamlets with dilapidated stone houses and orchards. It's remote and terrifyingly beautiful and makes you realise just how vast and empty much of Asturias is. The terrain is just too difficult for agriculture, but brilliant for bears, so they say. Even when you reach Grandas de Salime you're still well in the sticks. Here, follow the road to the right at the junction in the centre of the town, onto the AS-12 signposted for Navia. The road continues on, staying high above the Embalse de Doiras as it makes its way down the valley, slowly, torturously around bend after bend, through thick forest, past viewpoints and high meadows, isolated villages, and orchards. Then, finally, down to earth once you are almost in Navia and almost tripping over the A-8 *autovía*, which you will go under. From here, you can go right to go back along the Asturian coast or left for Tapia de Casariego and Galicia.

IN THE AREA

Senda del Oso A Y-shaped bike trail through the mountains of Asturias. Likelihood of seeing one of the bears, high. Seeing wild ones, less so. A great ride that's uphill from Tuñón to San Martín and downhill from San Martín. • **www.sendadelosoaventura.com**

Bears of Asturias Foundation, Proaza Housed in the old rectory in Proaza, the foundation provides education, environmental management, and protection of the landscapes in which the Cantabrian bear survives. They offer, from time to time, guided tours of the bear enclosures on the Senda del Oso. • **www.osodeasturias.es**

Somiedo Natural Park A protected area of mountains with amazing walking and the possibility of seeing bears. The walk to the Lago from Valle de Lago is beautiful (6km/3.7 miles either way) and will take you into beautiful alpine landscapes where traditional farming meet the wilds of the mountains. Like being in a dream. • **www.turismoasturias.es/en/descubre/naturaleza/reservas-de-la-biosfera/parque-natural-de-somiedo**

Muniellos Biosphere Reserve Limited entry to walk the 20km (12.4-mile) trail to 20 people per day. It is the home of bears, wolves, capercaillies and all kinds of other once-in-a-lifetime spots, as well as the chance to walk in one of Europe's most pristine oak forests and look over an empty, heavily protected wilderness. More information and booking here: • **www.muniellos.es**

Río Navia The valley is known as the Parque Histórico del Navia as it has been inhabited by Celts and Romans. There are a couple of sites where you can see excavated villages, one of which is at Coaña near Navia. It's an impressive place, with extensive ruins, both Celtic and Roman. • **www.castrosdeasturias.es/castros/46/15/el-castro-de-coaa**

ROUTE
06
SANTO
ESTEVO
DE LIRES
DUMBRÍA
ÉZARO
MAZARICOS
FISTERRA
OUTES
CARNOTA
LIRA
MUROS
LOURO
NOIA
ROIS
PADRÓN
PORTO DO
SON
CATOIRA
AG-11
BARRO
CAMBADOS
O GROVE
AP-9
PONTEVEDR
COMBARRO
PORTONOVO
MARÍN
VILABOA
ALDÁN
CANGAS
REDONDEL
VIGO

ROUTE 06

VIGO TO FISTERRA

THE WORLD'S BEST BEACH

Las Islas Cíes are often quoted – probably by those who sell tickets on the ferry – as being home to the world's most beautiful beach. Whether that's true is up for debate, of course, but there can be little doubt that Galicia has some, if not many, of the finest beaches to be found anywhere. This journey follows the coast from Vigo to Cape Finisterre to help you find a beach that really moves you. You'll be spoilt for choice. Put on your sunhat and go find it.

BEST FOR: Beaches, beaches, beaches

START: Vigo

END: Fisterra

MILEAGE: 338km (210 miles)

ALLOW: 7 days

MAP PAGES: 2, 12

It's a real kick, bollock and scramble to get the ferry to the Cíes Islands. There, we hope we'll find, if the PR is to be believed, the world's most beautiful beach. It was the *Guardian*, listing their Top 10 beaches, that declared the beach of Playa de Rodas the world's best in 2007. The Parque Natural Marítimo-Terrestre de las Islas Atlánticas de Galicia and the ferry companies have been dining out on it ever since it seems.

I wanted to go, not only because I felt I owed it to this book to see if it would live up to the hype, but also because I wanted to snorkel in clear water and the islands have, apparently, very clear seas. It seemed a no-brainer, so we set our sights on Vigo and made plans.

Islas Cíes

Getting to the Islas Cíes isn't quite as simple as it seemed it might be. First, we need to get authorisation from the park authority to visit. Because the Cíes is a 'pristine' natural environment only 2,000 visitors each day are allowed to disembark (the voice in my head says: ONLY 2,000?!). Once this online form has been completed, we then have two hours to book our ticket on the ferry with one of two companies allowed to operate. With a website that won't load properly, poor internet coverage and the time limit making me a little fractious, sorting out the booking becomes quite an 'exciting' event.

We stay overnight at the campsite on the beach at Praia de Samil, a long, white sandy beach to the west of Vigo where palm trees, a busy highway, basketball courts and a brilliant, golden sunset make it feel more Santa Monica than Galicia's most populous city. The campsite is small and cramped, with mobile homes that date back to the 1970s, but is the only option for the city, and the staff are very friendly, so we are happy. We wander along the esplanade and watch the Spanish at play. As night falls and the beach crowd is replaced by the night revellers, it seems everyone is dressed smartly for an evening out. I love that about Spain. Most people are very well dressed once they come off the beach.

In the morning, we leave with plenty of time to park and find the ferry terminal. It turns out to be a good move. There is precious little space anywhere near Vigo's huge, sprawling port – car parking, as is the case in

many Spanish cities, is underground with a height restriction – so we park half an hour's walk away, forgoing breakfast in the rush.

We aren't exactly sure where to find the terminal but spot a queue of people carrying umbrellas and beach chairs and guess that it's the place. A woman – possibly spotting the look of confusion on our faces – points us in the direction of the ticket office where we have to turn our email booking confirmation into a paper ticket. We join the queue and get on board the big Mar de Ons catamaran with minutes to spare.

The journey to the islands takes 40 minutes and is smooth and easy. We are among the first to disembark, so we head to the restaurant at the slipway and buy a cup of coffee and pastry each. We find a table on the terrace and take stock. The beach, Playa de Rodas, a gently curving crescent of sand backed by a tidal lagoon and with a rocky peak behind, is right in front of us. Our fellow passengers are making their way along it with their beach paraphernalia to find a spot. It looks pretty good as far as beaches go, I will admit, but I'm not sure how it'll fare once 2,000 people are plonked on it.

We finish our coffee and head off in the opposite direction, climbing to a viewpoint to look down at the lagoon and the beach at Playa de Rodas, and then finding a tiny cove at the north end of the smaller, less busy Playa de Figueiras. With eucalyptus forest behind, and sparkling, rounded granite rocks, white sand and water that looks like a perfect azure, it's pretty good, actually. Better than the best beach in the world? Possibly, because it's almost deserted and has interesting architecture: rocks, trees and paths snaking off along the cliff. We dump our stuff in a corner and pull on our wetsuits to snorkel but the water, disappointingly, has poor visibility, so we abandon our plans to explore the undersea kingdom. We take points off for that.

Later, we walk to the southern end of the island to find another beach, Playa de Nuestra Señora, another tiny cove with blue water and a thin slice of white sand above the high tide mark. It has hundreds of people packed on to it. They lie between the boulders and on the sand, some with their legs in the water. As if to remind us that we are in a national park and it is not ours, three seagull chicks wait on the sand for their parents to feed them, demanding their space. I imagine that this beach could be among the world's best, if only it were empty. It starts me thinking about what makes a perfect beach and why one beach should be better than any other. Surely, it's all about time, place, people, infrastructure, weather and how you feel at the time? My perfect beach wouldn't necessarily be somewhere to lay out a towel and snooze away the day. I like my beaches to be more active, with swimming, snorkelling, surfing or exploring on offer. I like them tiny, uncrowded, varied and interesting. When we walk back to the ferry and find

that four or five more boatloads of people have been deposited at Playa de Rodas, it is confirmed: this isn't my best beach at all, but I am very glad I came here to find out. The island, no matter how much I might find the company of 2,000 other people distasteful sometimes, is beautiful and well worth the trip.

We head north, out of the city, to continue this part of our journey. We are heading for Cape Finisterre, the cape at the western edge of Europe. The Romans thought of it as the end of the known world, the end of the land, the last place before nothing. Between Vigo and Cape Finisterre there are four of the 'Rías Baixas' (the low rivers) to negotiate. These are the estuaries of the rivers Vigo, Pontevedra, Arousa and Noia. Following the coast as much as we can, but without getting too widdly, we aim to amble up the coast, stopping to swim and check out the beaches to see if any of them can compete with Playa de Rodas.

Galicia's coastline is convoluted and fractal, with beaches that are estuarine, ocean facing, sheltered and wild. It means that there are almost any number of possibilities to find wind, tide, surf or calm to give you what you want. There are huge, open, dune-backed beaches as well as tiny coves. The rock, mostly, is a glistening granite, which means the sand is white and heavy, settling quickly to leave the water clear. With the Islas Cíes in our minds as a benchmark, we drive the coast, stopping to gape in awe at the mesmerising choice of beaches where we could make our dreams come true. But are they the best in the world?

At Balea Marítima, on the peninsula between Pontevedra and Padrón, we find a campsite on a rocky point with views to the west over Praia Raeiros, another white sand beach with outcrops at either

Playa de Figueiras, Islas Cies

end. We swim out to marker buoys in the bay and dry off on the rounded granite below the campsite. That evening, we sit on the still-hot rocks and watch the sun go down in a fiery sky of oranges and purples. Couples walk in the shallows as we watch, silhouetted by the vivid sky reflected in the water. It's perfect. And then a dolphin cruises across the bay, as if to make the point.

The next day, we explore the rest of the peninsula, finding tiny, deserted sands between rocky headlands and backed by native pine woods, before heading across the old bridge to the Illa da Toxa, a well-to-do spa town with more pristine forest, where women scrape the mudflats for cockles at low tide. At Illa de Arousa, another small island up the coast, we follow the road to find long, sandy beaches where Spanish tourists are making ready for a day on the sands. Small shacks sell drinks and tapas.

At Praia das Furnas, a long, open, west-facing beach between Noia and Santa Uxia de Ribeira, we turn up to watch perfect waves break on sand bars below a beach restaurant. We stop at a private *aire*, unload the boards and I hit the water, walking down the beach to surf away from the crowd. The water is warm and the waves are good, sparkling in the afternoon sun. The sea is opaque with froth where the waves break, but darker and clearer further out, where I sit and wait for the sets to arrive. It's hot and I am in heaven. For me, at that moment, this is the best beach in the world, bar none. When I get chatting to a local surfer, Lucas, and feel that

I am welcome here, the feeling is complete.

After surfing, Lizzy and I follow a wooden boardwalk that runs at the back of the beach across the dune slacks to a lagoon. The dunes are protected and support a wide range of plants that are flowering. We stop to photograph a fragrant sea daffodil, noticing the pinks, whites, yellows and purples of the littoral zone. Further back, gorses create dense bush while, further back still, pine colonise the dunes. It's really beautiful in its own way. Some might say it's barren and empty, but for me, it's a playground and place of fascination, always with something to look at, from waves to plants to people and the wind and weather. I could be happy here, I think.

We move on and find Praia Do Salto Abelleira, another tiny slice of white sand, reached by following a steep track down a muddy lane through mature pine forest. From where we park, we can see glimpses through the trees of the sparkling sea, but when we get there, we find the wind is onshore and the water quality is poor. Along with three noisy locals, we interrupt a woman who has had the place to herself. Protected from the

Praia das Furnas

breeze by a rock, she sunbathes alone. We feel bad for crashing the scene, thinking that this could be her best beach in the world, for as long as she has it to herself. We swim, briefly, and then retreat. Back at the van, we hear a kind of crack from above us. The heat of the day is making the pinecones open and release their seeds. The cones crackle as if they have been thrown into a fire and the kernels helicopter to the ground around us.

A trip to Praia de Carnota, a large, open beach with milky white water, reached by a long boardwalk over a salt marsh of sea purslane and purple sea lavender, gives us half an hour of bodysurfing at high tide. We laugh as the waves transport us right up the beach into the shallows. It takes an age to get the sand out of our swimmers when we wash the salt off at the beach shower. As we leave, in the late afternoon, locals are arriving to spend the evening with friends and family en masse after the heat of the day has subsided.

Finally, we arrive at Fisterra, parking up at the *aire* above the harbour. The view is magnificent, offering us the chance to look back at some of the coast we've covered to get here. We eat on the harbourside and wander around after, finding a tiny, east-facing cove, with water that screams at me to dip. It's the very last beach we'll get to before we arrive at the cape and Finisterre's lighthouse.

Will it turn out to be the best beach in the world? At the moment when I dive in and swim the first few strokes into the cold water, it doesn't really matter. But it could be.

Faro de Fisterra

THE DRIVING

As I have already stated, Galicia has hundreds, if not thousands, of beaches. Each one faces a different way and has different characteristics that will be affected by the tides and the winds in countless ways. What is perfect for me may not be perfect for you. And that's fine. This journey will give you a chance to decide for yourself. As usual, you don't have to follow my itinerary. In fact, I'd prefer it if you followed your own lines, explored for yourself, and found your own idea of perfect.

My journey is just the starting point. Even as I write this I am planning to return, at some point, to explore more of Galicia because I feel that I have only just begun to scratch the surface. It's as if all my favourite beaches in Ireland, Scotland, Wales and Cornwall were stolen and brought to Galicia to live out their days in the sunshine (although Galicia is often misty, so watch out for that).

Let's begin by heading out of Vigo on the AP-9 heading north in the direction of Pontevedra until junction 148. Come off and follow the N-552 towards Redondela, then take the N-550 (turn left in Redondela). This will take you along the edge of the Río Vigo through small towns and past salt marsh. Take the N-554 towards Vilaboa and Cangas (it's a tricky junction) and then continue on the PO-551 towards Moaña. Views of Vigo along this stretch are quite good.

The PO-551 will take you through Cangas, a small town with a marina, and on to the PO-315 to O Hío, on to Aldán and then on to Bueu, where you'll need to follow the PO-551 again, and then the VG-4.4, towards Pontevedra. It's a little tricky to get through Pontevedra – you can either take the *autovía* at junction 132 up to junction 129 for the PO-308 towards Sanxenxo or follow the PO-12/N-550 through the city and then cross the river to pick up the PO-308 through Poio and on to Sanxenxo. This road will take you along the north bank of the Ría de Pontevedra and around the peninsula to some really excellent beaches. Look out for the Isla de Ons offshore.

After Sanxenxo the coast is great, not too built-up and pretty wild with lots of campsites. It will bring you along the bottom corner of Praia da Lanzada (a surfing beach with dunes) before heading to the other side of the isthmus and over the dune slacks. Turn left on to the PO-317 (then the EP-9101) to circumnavigate the head of the peninsula and to reach the Illa da Toxa. There are some really great beaches on this headland, with lots of tiny roads to reach them. Go searching and you'll find it, I promise!

The PO-316 will bring you back to the junction with the PO-550 at the neck of the peninsula with the tidal flats on your left. Turn left on to the PO-550 and follow it to the north towards Cambados. You'll notice vineyards here. The town is nice, too. From Cambados, take the PO-549 and then the PO-307 over the bridge to get to the Illa de Arousa, where there are yet more beaches to explore. There is an *aire* after the bridge – a cycle track leads off to the beaches on the south side from here.

To continue north, take the bridge, turn left on to the PO-549 and then, in Vilagarcía de Arousa, on to the PO-548, which will take you through Bamio, Catoira and A Torre (among other villages) and on to the N-550 again just before the Río Ulla. Turn left here and cross the river, then turn on to the AG-11 in the direction of Ribeira. This is a section of *autovía* that runs along the coast (though not right next to it) and is your only real option

WHERE TO STAY: CAMPING

The coast of Galicia has hundreds of campsites, *aires* and places in which to overnight. So it's a really great place to explore by camper van or motorhome. Plenty do, of course, but it still feels empty and wild. Lots of campers stay overnight on out-of-the-way beaches and it seems to be accepted – as it is in much of Spain. In that respect, Galicia is something of a last frontier.

Camping Playa Samil, Vigo
Av. Samil, 71, 36212 Vigo, Pontevedra, Spain
Web: www.campingplayasamil.com
Tel: +34 986 24 02 10

It's jolly and friendly. Maybe a little outdated, but it's right on the beach and your best option for staying in Vigo.

Camping and Glamping Muiñeira, San Vicente do Mar
Ctra. de A Lanzada a, km 2, No 38, 36988 San Vicente do Mar, Pontevedra, Spain
Web: www.campingmuineira.es
Tel: +34 608 98 74 50

This site is in an absolutely wonderful position overlooking the beach at Praia Raeiros and with direct beach access.

Camping Ruta de Finisterre, Cee
Lugar Playa Estorde, 216, 15137 Cee, A Coruña, Spain
Web: www.rutafinisterre.com
Tel: +34 981 74 63 02

A small site that's set in the pines above the beach at Playa de Estorde, a few kilometres from Finisterre. The beach is opposite.

Camping Fraga Balada, Xuño
Carretera Playa das Furnas s/n, 15995 Xuño, A Coruña, Spain
Web: www.facebook.com/people/Camping-Fraga-Balada
Tel: +34 619 74 59 89

A pleasant site near Praia das Furnas with a pool and restaurant.

for doing this section, unless you want to navigate tiny local roads. Going off-piste will no doubt reward you with all kinds of beaches, if you have the time.

We took the AG-11 to Ribeira and then joined the AC-550 towards Noia. It crosses the peninsula and rejoins the coast at Praia das Furnas and Caamaño. Furnas is a surf beach and is absolutely lovely. In fact, the whole stretch to the south is lovely and is a protected zone. Tiny roads will lead you to beach car parks on near deserted sands. There is an *aire* at Furnas, as well as a campsite, but also opportunities for free camping.

Continue on the AC-550 north on one of the best stretches on this route. It follows the coast closely and passes through a few villages and towns, with lots of options for beaches and tiny roads to take you to viewpoints and more beaches.

As you approach Noia, take the AC-549 (unless you want to explore Noia) across the river and on to the next peninsula on the AC-550 and the AC-554 (cross over the Río Tambre) following signs for Muros. You'll go away from the coast a little here but will rejoin it around Freixo and follow

WHERE TO STAY: *AIRES*

Motorhome area Finisterre: The *aire* in Finisterre is really close to the town, harbour and beaches and is great value at €11 for a night plus EHU. Lovely people, too. **www.areascamper.com/ficha/area-de-autocaravanas-en-finisterre**
Furnas: A really relaxed private *aire* at Praia das Furnas, run by the laid-back Manuel. Perfect for surfing straight out of the van.
Sanxenxo: A private *aire* right on the beach at Sanxenxo, on the PO-308 just outside Portonovo. Direct access to the beach.
Illa de Arousa: Motorhome parking area just after the bridge. Handy for exploring the island and its nudist beaches.

it more closely. Again, there are lots of options for finding beaches here as the road passes through Muros and Louro and starts making its way up the north side of the peninsula, becoming more open and wilder. Carnota's beach is huge and wide open, with a long boardwalk across the salt flats. Once you round the estuary after Carnota, the landscape changes to be rockier, with huge granite boulders sitting between scrub. Houses and *hórreos* (grain stores) sometimes built on boulders stand out in the rough-and-ready – and hilly – landscape. It feels like an end-of-the-world place, like Cornwall, or Donegal or Harris. Mountains rise up quickly behind the road and the sea churns between the boulders on the rocky shore. The magic is soon broken at A Pontella when you pass a black and smelly factory.

At Cee, at the end of the main street, turn left on to the AC-445 for Corcubión and Fisterra and then, once past the great beach at Playa de Estorde (the campsite here is good) turn left on to the AC-445 for the final few miles into Fisterra on a long straight road of motels and hotels, garages and blocks. Continue through Fisterra for the road to the lighthouse. The *aire* is on the left as you enter the town.

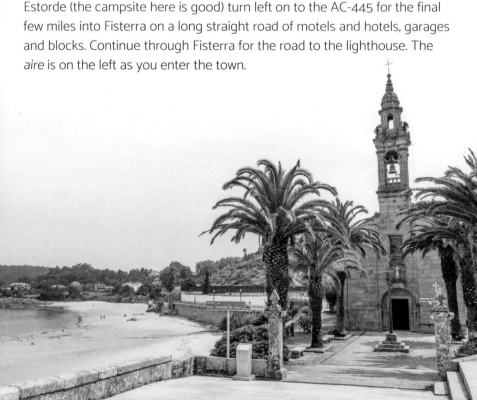

IN THE AREA

Islas Cíes The crowning glory of the National Park of the Atlantic Islands of Galicia is Cíes. Only 2,000 people are allowed on the island each day in the season and each one needs an authorisation from the park authority to go. Do it online at: • **www.lasislascies.com**

Hórreos, Lira and Carnota These drying huts are similar to those found in Asturias but are generally constructed of granite instead of wood. The two biggest are at Lira and Carnota, where, during the late 16th century, the two diocese had a competition to build the biggest and most magnificent. The example at Lira is on the east side of the road, at Carnota, the rival *hórreo* is near the beach.

Cape Finisterre (Cabo Finisterre) The final stop on the Camino de Santiago (Way of St James), Cape Finisterre is an emotional, emotive place. People arrive here on foot after leaving Santiago de Compostela. Many of them will have been walking relentlessly for weeks to get here. Some perform the ritual of burning their clothes in order to start their lives again, despite it not being encouraged. We watched as walkers of all nationalities, with beatific looks on their faces, arrived at the cape. Inspiring. Also, a lot of tourists...

Santiago de Compostela This is the final convergence on the Camino de Santiago. It's a lovely city, dominated by the cathedral. Worth a stop to eat seafood, wander the lanes of the old city or watch the walkers arrive after their epic pilgrimage.

Watersports Because Galicia has so many beaches it is inevitable that there should be access to lots of watersports, from diving and snorkelling to surfing, SUPing and kayaking. Many of the beach towns have rental places open in the summer – depending on their location – where you can get lessons or hire equipment.

ROUTE 07

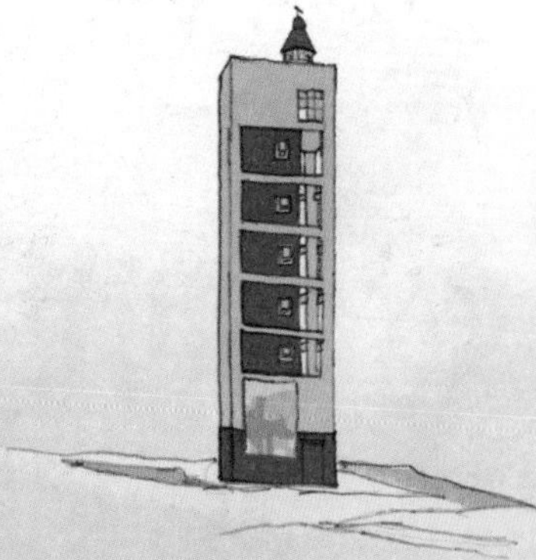

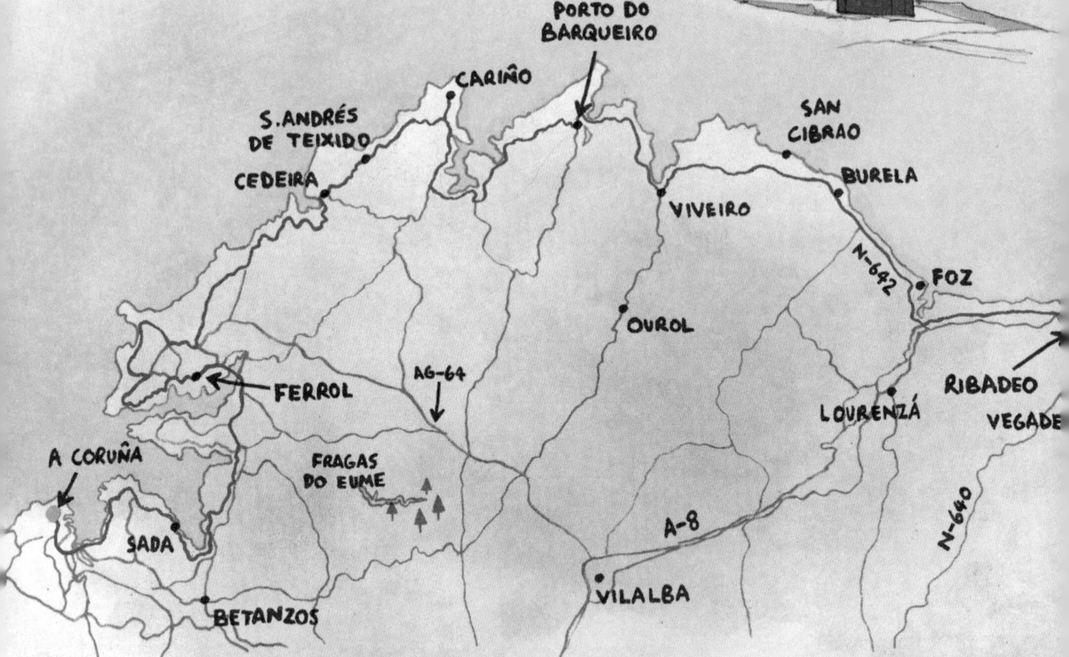

PORTO DO BARQUEIRO
CARIÑO
S. ANDRÉS DE TEIXIDO
CEDEIRA
SAN CIBRAO
BURELA
VIVEIRO
N-642
FOZ
OUROL
FERROL
AG-64
RIBADEO
LOURENZÁ
VEGADE
A CORUÑA
FRAGAS DO EUME
A-8
N-640
SADA
VILALBA
BETANZOS

ROUTE 07

Cabo Ortegal

A CORUÑA TO RIBADEO

LIGHTHOUSES AND A LIGHT LUNCH

The coast of Galicia is difficult and convoluted, with points and river estuaries making it beautiful and interesting to us, but dangerous to shipping. Around the coast, you'll find a number of lighthouses situated in the most desolate and beautiful spots, offering unrivalled views. Between are villages, beach towns, beaches, rivers and countryside. This route will take you around the coast, from A Coruña to Ribadeo via the lighthouses – and that means driving some of its more interesting roads.

BEST FOR: Lighthouses, beaches, countryside

START: A Coruña

END: Ribadeo

MILEAGE: 289km (180 miles)

ALLOW: 7 days

MAP PAGES: 3, 4

The Tower of Hercules is believed to be the world's oldest surviving lighthouse. It was built, originally, by the Romans in the 1st century AD but could have been built on the foundations of an earlier Phoenician tower. The design was based on the Lighthouse of Alexandria, one of the Seven Wonders of the Ancient World. There are many myths surrounding the lighthouse, one of which was that Ireland could be seen from the top, prompting the Celts to set sail there. Other legends say that Hercules slayed and buried his foe Geryon here, along with all his weapons, and thereafter commanded that a city be built on top. Building the tower was one of his trials.

Whatever you believe, the Tower of Hercules is a colossus that's 55m (180ft) high and still retains some of its Roman origins. It sits on a promontory in A Coruña, guarding the harbour and the busy city beaches, like a last outpost of Europe, shining its light to watch over sailors and swimmers in perilous seas.

Except today, the tower is shrouded in a thick, dazzling, backlit sea fret. Even though we can't quite see it in its entirety, it's still really impressive. We stand underneath it to look at its rough granite lines and classical windows that disappear into the mist above us. Below the light, closer to the edge of the cliff, is a giant mosaic decorated

with the points of the compass. Each arrows shows the direction of each of the Celtic nations. We find the finger that leads to Kernow and look out to sea in that direction: home.

The lighthouse sets off a chain reaction in my imagination. I love them, and always have, because they represent hope and light in the darkness. Here, on the Costa da Morte ('Coast of Death'), the beacon takes on a whole new depth of meaning and gives us a purpose for the continuation of the journey. Following the coast to join up the lighthouses – visiting as many as we can – will allow us to see its points and cliffs, outposts and lonely places: the fingers of rock, tallest cliffs and most remote corners. We figure we may be able to get to at least seven of them, following the coastline between.

I add an extra challenge: to try the Galician speciality *percebes*, or goose barnacles. This is a hugely expensive delicacy that is extremely dangerous to harvest and that has also taken on a mythical quality of its own. I have long wanted to try it. In the UK, we only ever see goose barnacles when they wash up attached to flotsam and jetsam. In Galicia, the barnacles grow on remote cliffs, below the tideline, where the seas are rough. They can only be gathered on the biggest spring tides at the very lowest part of the tide by the bravest of collectors, with ropes tied around their middles, using nets and knives on poles to harvest. The rewards are great, but the risks are great, too.

We leave A Coruña on a hot and clear day, getting a proper look at the Tower of Hercules before we leave. We head north to the next promontory, where we find the Faro de Mera and the Faro Pequeño. Here, the two lighthouses sit on top of a cliff with a beautiful beach resort, Playa Mera, to the left and open sea to the right. Across the bay there is a sight line to the Tower of Hercules, which we can see clearly now the sea mist has lifted. An interpretation centre and small museum in the old lighthouse keeper's house includes a full-scale model of a *percebes* gatherer on a rock above a tumultuous sea. The way the man is perched above the waves makes the whole scenario look like something from another legendary act of heroism. It doesn't look real.

We continue on, north towards Ferrol and the Cabo Prioriño Grande to see its light. It sits above the Puerto Exterior de Ferrol, a huge working port where wind turbine blades and aggregates await loading. A crane lifts heaps of coal out of the belly of a huge ship. The road winds its way through a forest of eucalyptus, arriving high above the light on a road that skirts the port. A barbed-wire fence runs along one side of the road with security cameras at intervals. Beyond the barbed wire is a drop of maybe 70m (230ft) to the port, which, it seems, has been carved out of the cliff. It's a weird, false environment and makes me feel uncomfortable. The light, when we get there, is unremarkable, sitting squatly and uninviting above an old battery. A visitor centre made of rusted steel and glass is closed and looks derelict. The views, however, are remarkable.

We arrive at our next stop, Cabo Prior, a lighthouse with a more classical and welcoming appearance, in the early evening and decide to stay for the night. There are a few other vans in the car park so we assume there will be safety in numbers. Below the lighthouse, a set of steps leads down a steep cliff to a lookout on a small rock platform high above the sea. Lizzy walks down to take photos looking back at the lighthouse. I follow, but the battery on my camera fails so I have an excuse not to follow her. The drops, where the steps turn at right angles to navigate the ridge, to the churning sea below, are huge.

I change the battery and wander off to explore one of the ruined buildings at the site. It is a gun emplacement – one of several here. It's ruined now, and it is spooky to amble around the narrow, graffiti-filled corridors. One leads

Faro de Cabo Prior

me out to the room where, I assume, the guns would have been sited. A narrow opening, like a horizontal arrow slit, offers a truly panoramic view over the ocean. There are pathways leading off through the gorse and heather, between granite boulders, to other emplacements nearby.

As the day goes on, the sea mist descends, rolling in from the water and down from the hills above us. When the light goes, at about 10.15 p.m., the beacon's Fresnel lenses light up, sending out beams into the night. Watching the light turning is mesmerising, especially in the mist. We can see its pattern clearly: there are two brighter beams with two less bright beams between each. It's like watching a searchlight illuminating the clouds, going around and around, a helicopter of light above the keeper's cottage, and, if we stand in the right place, the van, which is parked just 20m (22 yards) away.

In the morning, we drive down to the beach to the east of the point and are greeted by white sand and beautiful surf in the turquoise water. We park next to a couple of other vans, who have been here overnight, and scramble into our wetsuits. The beach, which arcs away from us towards the lighthouse, is about 1km (0.6 miles) long and backed by dunes flowering with fragrant white sea daffodils. There are maybe four people on the beach in total, plus a couple of people surfing. It's clean and the water is beautifully clear and we enjoy an entertaining surf under blue skies. As we leave, we talk about returning here at another time. It's one of those places.

Our next stop is at Punta Frouxeira a few miles up the coast. It sits on a low but rocky point, with cliffs of about 50m (164ft) high all around. The lighthouse is modern in design, striped blue and white, and is like nothing I have ever seen. There are some long tunnels below it that we explore, another battery from a bygone age, we presume.

I walk to the edge of the cliff to look at the drop and notice a rope knotted around a rocky outcrop. It falls down the cliff, over outcrops and slabs, to the rocks. Below, near its end, on the barnacled rocks below the high tide mark, I can see three or four people. One of them is waist deep in water, reaching down as far as he can to the waterline between waves. I work out that it's about low tide so figure that we have chanced upon *percebes* gatherers. I pick up my zoom lens and use it to watch them: they are dancing with the ocean, jumping from rock to rock, getting to the lowest exposed faces at the swell recedes, using their nets and knives on poles to prise the *percebes* from their holdfasts. I feel we have chanced upon something special.

The rope tightens and I look directly below me to see one of the hunters climbing back up the cliff. He's got a rucksack on his back and is wearing a thick divers' wetsuit with a beaver tail. The cliff face is near vertical in places and he needs the rope to haul himself up over ledges and steeper sections. When he scrambles over the last edge and stands on the clifftop I ask him if he has had much success. He pulls a plastic sack out of his bag and shows me. It's full of goose barnacles. He grabs a handful and holds it up so I can take a photo. The *percebes* have short and stubby, dark-coloured bases, with white, almost triangular heads and fiery orange mouths like a goose's beak. The fisherman tells me they are worth 80 euros per kg (per 2.2lb). I reckon he has about 10kg (22lb) in the bag, a haul of at least 800 euros that he has risked his life to get.

We drive on, with the light at Punta Candieira our next stop. The road, which drops down to the lighthouse in a series of unprotected harpins, is off-limits to all but the lighthouse keepers, so we park above it and walk part of the way down to take photos. The location is sublime, with cliffs of rough granite, heather and gorse stretching off in either direction. We head further east still, taking the Rota dos Miradouros ('Route of the Viewpoints') out of Cedeira towards the lighthouse at Cabo Ortegal. The countryside is stunning, and especially more so when we leave the eucalyptus plantations behind and drive into more natural grassland that's dotted with granite and

Faro de Punta Candieira

pines and where wild horses and cattle roam. The views of the huge cliffs are exceptional from the *miradors*.

About halfway along, we drop into San Andrés de Teixido, a tiny hamlet beneath some of the highest sea cliffs in Europe (600m/1,969ft) that's been a place of pilgrimage and death worship since the 12th century. It's a strange village, with just a few houses, a few shops selling trinkets and odd models made from unbaked bread that are offered to St Andrés. A few tourists mill about taking selfies of the view while some older locals work in the fields surrounding the hamlet. In the church, I find a few mildly disturbing offerings to St Andrew, some of which are items belonging to people who have died.

It feels right – for some reason – to sit down in a bar in this tiny village that's perched perilously between the cliffs and the raging sea and order some *percebes*. Maybe we are getting a uniquely Galician vibe from the village. Or maybe the signs on all the bars tell us that they have goose barnacles in stock (and they don't seem that expensive). We wander into the first bar and ask the young woman serving if we can try *percebes* and could she show us how to eat them. She obliges and invites us to sit down. A few minutes later, a bowl of steaming, ugly-looking barnacles is placed in front of us. The waitress patiently shows us how to open them – with a pinch and a twist – and leaves us to it. It takes a while to get the flesh out of the first one, but it is worth it. The meat inside the tough stem is soft and tender and absolutely delicious. We share the bowl and, once we have our hand in, devour it in minutes.

San Andrés de Teixido

As we leave San Andrés, the sun drops below the cloud and lights up the sea around the cliffs out in the bay, turning the water into hues of gold and purple. People stop and stare. Some gasp. If we were looking for meaning, we could find it here, among the pilgrims and offerings, sea-borne delicacies and ancient stone houses. We trudge up the hill and out of the village. We pick up the route again and make our way to the top of the Serra de Capelada crossing the peninsula to enjoy views of Ortigueira through a sea of wind turbines in the estuary many metres below us. We follow signs for the lighthouse and find ourselves on a narrow road traversing a steep wall of rock and heather with huge drops to the sea. It's a wheel-gripping ride down to the lighthouse, which sits on a narrow finger of rock. We park in a lay-by halfway down the steep road and walk the rest of the way in case turning is difficult at the bottom. We are shadowed by the huge cliff above us until we are almost at the lighthouse. Walking out from behind the shadows reveals the golden rays of the sunset. Together with the wind, it's like being hit by a blast of sunny, glowing ozone. A few vans are parked up in the small car park and people sit on the retaining wall looking at the sun as it descends. We take photos and hurry back up the hill so we can find somewhere to stay before it's dark.

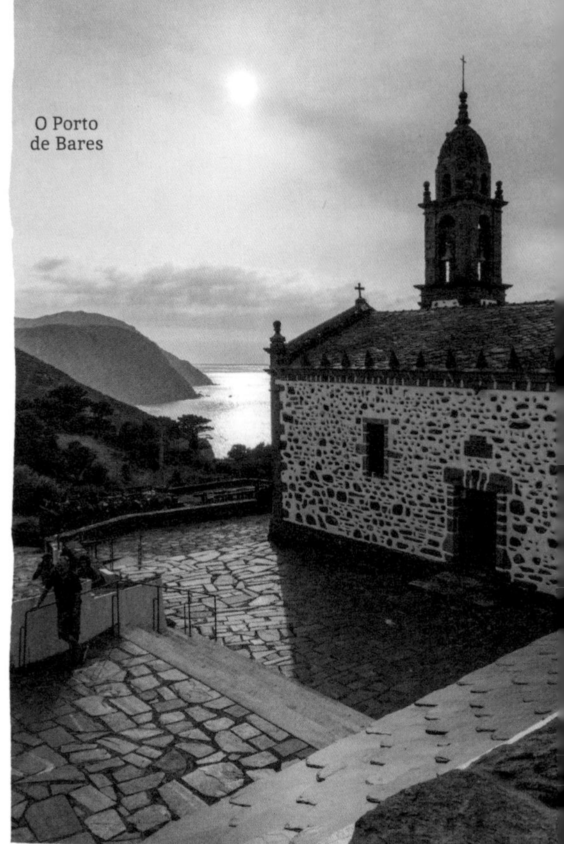
O Porto de Bares

We drive back along the peninsula and into the tiny town of Cariño, where we reject a couple of inappropriate overnights on Park4Night. Looking for a miracle, we drive out on to another slim finger of a peninsula that sticks out into the Río Santa Marta de Ortigueira, in the hope that there might be somewhere for us to stay. The narrow road leads us down the cliff and into a crucible of a bay surrounding a small beach with clear water. The road ends in a rough, grassy car park where a couple of other vans have parked up. It seems like such a gift. We set up and enjoy a beautiful, quiet night by the beach.

THE DRIVING

The basic premise of this route is to join up the lighthouses of Galicia. While it might sound straightforward, it does require some wiggling and creative joining up. The way that we drove it will take you along some incredible roads and out on to some of the wilder peninsulas, but it can, of course, be simplified. The AC-862 (then LU-862 and N-642) will lead you out of Ferrol and around the coast to Ribadeo in spectacular style offering opportunities to visit the lights you want to. Once it gets to Ortigueira, it is truly lovely.

However, if you want to join the dots, follow this:

From the motorhome parking in A Coruña, follow the coastal road through the city, past the Tower of Hercules, around the headland, through the port and out of the city on the AC-12 over the bridge in the direction of Ferrol and Perillo. After the bridge, take the AC-173 towards Santa Cruz and Mera. Keep following the AC-173 as it leads you out through the well-to-do suburbs, past the beaches at Praia de Bastiagueiro and Praia Grande de Porto Covo (Santa Cruz). (FYI: there is a place to fill up and empty black and grey waste on this road, just past the roundabout at Bastiagueiro.)

At Playa Mera, take a left turn at the end of the beach to the Faro de Mera. This road goes through a little of the urban area but eventually climbs away from the town and out on to the headland. The lighthouses and interpretation centre are here. On leaving the lighthouse, retrace your steps and follow the one-way system, then turn left at the AC-163 towards Sada. Follow the road through villages and hamlets with occasional views of the coast and wooded sections of eucalyptus to Sada, a small port town. Follow the road through the town as it becomes the AC-162. Turn left at the roundabout at San Cidre on to the AC-164 and over the little bridge, the Ponte do Pedrido, then turn left on to the AC-651 signposted to Ferrol and A Carreira. There are great views of beaches and the river here, even though it is estuarine. Follow the AC-651 over the next bridge, the Ponte do Porco, and towards Ferrol, over the next bridge, the Ponte de Pontedeume and on to Ferrol.

The next bit can be a little tricky and it may well be easier to go on to the A-9 at junction 27, then come off again at junction 34 for the FE-12 and then the N-655 for the Puerto Exterior de Ferrol, but we went the hard way and took the NC-651 and then the bridge on the FE-14 into Ferrol before making our way out of the city on the FE-12 and taking the N-655 for the port. Either way, the idea is to get on to the N-655 – a really good road towards the port. A few kilometres out of Ferrol, you'll come to a junction where non-port traffic must come off. At the roundabout on the slip road, take the first exit signed for Prioriño on the DP-3608 and then take the second exit at the next roundabout, and then the first left, which is signed for Cabo Prioriño. This is the tiny road that will take you to the Faro de Cabo Prioriño through the eucalyptus forest, past the port and out on to the cape. It's wild at times with some drops to the port, but it is well fenced. There is a little car park at the very end of the cape.

Retrace your steps from here, but at the first junction, turn right and follow the DP-3608 over the first roundabout, under the main road and on to the next roundabout. Take the fourth exit on to the DP-3607 and then DP-3606. This will take you past Praia de Doniños, on to Praia de San Xurxo and Ferrol. These are great beaches where you can (apparently) stay overnight without hassle. After San Xurxo, take a right at the T-junction and then a left at the next one, following signs for Cabo Prior on the DP-3603 (the road names aren't on the signposts though!). This will take you up to the cape, through some low-level housing and then on to a winding,

narrow road on to the headland, with great views over the beaches to the north. Eventually, after much winding and wiggling, the road ends up at the lighthouse. This is a really nice spot and is great for a sunset, with lots of derelict buildings to explore.

On the return journey, follow the road through the villages (follow signs for the beaches to go to the headland between Praia de Ponzos and Praia de Santa Comba. These are great beaches where vans park up happily.

Follow the DP-3606 back to the N-655 (the road to the port), but this time turn left towards Ferrol. Take it for just under 3km (1.9 miles) to the junction with the AC-116. It's a funny junction so it might take a bit of doing, but follow the AC-116 north towards Valdoviño. The road goes through the hinterland in a series of long straights. After the roundabout outside A Capela, turn left signposted for the Faro de Punta Frouxeira. This will take you out to the cape through low scrub and out to the sandy and rocky peninsula where you'll find the quite weird, blue-and-white-striped, ultra-modern lighthouse of Meiras.

Make your way back to the AC-116 and then turn left (third exit) at the roundabout junction with the AC-566 direction Valdoviño. This will take you past the beach at A Frouxeira, a really popular place, then on to Pantín, another surfers' favourite. Vans can stay here at Pantín. There are lots of surfers here.

Follow the AC-566 past Pantín and then along the southern edge of the beautiful estuary of the Río das Mestas and the Ría de Cedeira. This is a really beautiful part of Galicia, with lots of choice of beaches, surf and countryside and a feeling that it's free and easy to hang out here. Weekends get busy, but midweek, outside of the main holidays, it's quiet.

Follow the AC-566 into Cedeira and take a right turn after the bridge (go over it) for the Faro de Cedeira and the CP-2203. This is a great road that heads high into the slopes to the north of the town, out to a *mirador* and then through more eucalyptus plantations (it made Lizzy very annoyed as it's not native) until you come out above the lighthouse. There is a *mirador* on the top of the cape but to see the lighthouse you need to go past, park up at the parking area below and walk the last 500m (547 yards). It's worth it.

Back in Cedeira, cross the bridge again and take the second exit off the roundabout, followed by a quick left turn, following signs for San Andrés de Teixido on the DP-2204. Follow the road through villages along the river valley until you come to a right turn that's signposted to San Andrés and the Rota dos Miradoiros. Turn right here. This is the next stage of the journey and it's flipping good! As you head up towards some of Europe's highest cliffs, you'll pass through more eucalyptus forest until you hit a cattle grid after about 4km (2.5 miles). Then you enter another, wilder world of free-roaming horses and cattle, pine glades, open grassland, and

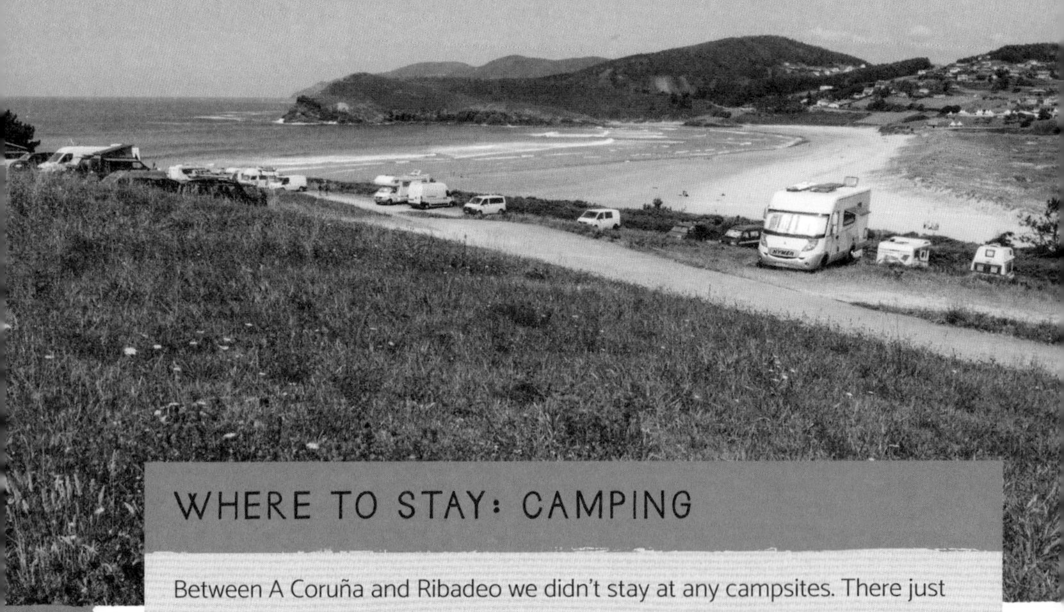

WHERE TO STAY: CAMPING

Between A Coruña and Ribadeo we didn't stay at any campsites. There just didn't seem to be any need. There are sites here of course but not many, and, besides, the opportunities for free camping are numerous. People were staying over at many of the lighthouses we visited too, and some beaches have facilities specifically aimed at motorhomes. A point to be reminded of is that many of the places *do not have emptying points* so it will be necessary to use Park4Night to empty and fill where you can: DO NOT EMPTY ANYWHERE YOU ARE NOT AUTHORISED TO DO SO.

Camping Playa Penarronda
Playa de Penarronda, s/n, 33794
Barres, Asturias, Spain
Web: www.campingplay apenarronda.com
Tel: +34 985 62 30 22

This campsite is at the end of the route, in Asturias, just beyond Ribadeo. It's about 100m (110 yards) from Penarronda Beach and is really, really nice. In fact, it's one of the best, with a cafe and restaurant on site and a bar next door.

WHERE TO STAY: *AIRES*

A Coruña: Parking spaces along the *paseo marítimo* (seafront) near the funicular and adjacent to the aquarium that are designated for motorhomes.
Praia do Esteiro: Designated places and facilities.
Praia de Doniños: Moho parking area.
Playa Rodo/Pantín: Motorhome parking at southern end of beach.
Santa Cruz: Emptying facilities on the AC-173.
Praia de Santa Comba, Praia de Ponzos: Free parking above beaches.
Praia de Fornos: Camper van parking, no facilities.

heather and gorse. And, of course, incredible views along the coast of some of Europe's highest sea cliffs. It's a great bit of driving, on narrow, winding roads. The first junction you'll come to will be the left turn to San Andrés. It's a dead end with a tight turn to get into the parking, but worth it.

If crazy religious villages with great views and lots of *percebes* aren't your thing then continue on, through the forest of wind turbines. About 8km (5 miles) out of San Andrés you'll come to a crossroads where you can turn left to go to Cabo Ortegal. This road is narrow and hairy and will bring you, eventually, to a *mirador* with amazing views of the Ria de Ortigueira and the towns below you. Follow the well-surfaced (though narrow) road and you'll drop down towards the estuary and on to the road to the lighthouse, which is at a T-junction. Turn left and you'll follow the (still narrow) road out to the cape. For the most part, the road is in the forest but eventually it comes out on the cliff, with scarily fantastic views down and out over the estuary and ocean. The first section is unguarded but don't worry – it gets easier. A wooden guard rail will see you all the way to the lighthouse as the road plunges, traversing the craggy cliff towards the final conclusion – the light. Vans park up here, seemingly without problems, mostly because of the remoteness and the sunsets.

(If you want to bypass the lighthouse, simply follow the Rota dos Miradoiros to the DP-6121 outside Cariño and turn right to continue).

From the lighthouse, retrace your steps but instead of turning back towards the Rota dos Miradoiros, head into Cariño (you'll have to take the right before the village as mohos aren't allowed through) and on to the DP-6121, another great, winding road with views over the river estuary. This will lead you to the AC-862, a road that will take you on to Ortigueira and along the next peninsula.

Next, take a left at the junction with the AC-100 just outside Porto do Barqueiro and head out to the *faro*. This is another lovely road (aren't they all) and will take you out to O Porto de Bares. Take the left for the lighthouse. Once you

Praia de Santa Comba

are here, you can walk through the lighthouse compound to reach the very tip of the point, which is the most northerly point of Spain!

O Porto de Bares is well worth a stop, both for the harbour and village and the beach, which is magnificent. While signs say no motorhomes, there were plenty staying on the day we went, on the ground adjacent to the beach.

From Bares, head back down the AC-100 to the AC-862 and head east towards Viveiro. As usual it winds its way around the estuary, through plantations of eucalyptus, through small villages and farmland – beautiful. In Viveiro, go over the bridge and head north to Ribadeo on the newly renamed LU-862. Outside Viveiro, once you have passed through Celeiro, take the left turn to the Faro Roncadoira, which is also signed for Praia da Area. This is the LU-P-2610 and it will lead you out past beaches and on to the Miradoiro de Monte Faro (a slight detour, follow the signs), which isn't a lighthouse but a lookout with a ruin of a house and fire pit where a light used to be lit. Great views back to Viveiro. From here, continue around the coast, through some really lovely villages and beaches (the beach at Esteiro is wonderful and has good moho facilities) and on to the last of the lighthouses, the Faro Roncadoira, which is an unremarkable light but sits in remarkable scenery of wind-sculpted granite tors, heather and gorse on the clifftops. There is a small car park at the end of the road. The views back to the west are incredible.

Take the LU-P-2601 to get back to the N-642 at Xove and head east again. This will take you along the coast in less interesting scenery but with lots of opportunity to head to the beaches. Skirt Foz on the N-642 and then join the A-8 for the last few miles into Ribadeo or take the N-634 closer to the coast, although it is a little unremarkable and will lead you through villages and past agricultural shops. It will, however, take you to the turn off-for the Praia das Catedrais (Cathedral Beach) which is well worth a look even if it is heavily subscribed and you need a pass to go on it! (More on that below.)

IN THE AREA

Océano Surf Museum, Valdoviño If you like surfing and the history of surfing then this is for you. Limited opening times. It's near Pantín, at Valdoviño. • **www.oceanosurfmuseo.com**

Picasso House, A Coruña Picasso lived in A Coruña for five yours in his youth. You can visit the apartment to which his family took him at the age of ten and where his artistic precociousness emerged. • **www.turismo.gal/recurso/-/detalle/31719/casa-museo-picasso**

Domus Science Museum, A Coruña A museum devoted to the human body in A Coruña. Fascinating. • **www.coruna.gal/mc2/es/domus**

Museum of Fine Arts, A Coruña A Coruña's arts museum is housed in a beautiful new building near the old city and houses a collection of paintings from the 17th to 20th centuries, plus temporary exhibitions. Excellently curated. • **www.museos.xunta.gal/en/belas-artes**

Banco De Mondo (Best Bank of the World), Bares Peninsula We thought we found it, but it turns out we hadn't. The best bank of the world is a bench overlooking the coastline on the Bares Peninsula near Ortigueira. It has become a viral sensation. • **www.artnaturagalicia.com/en/blog/the-best-bank-in-the-world**

Praia das Catedrais A beach with interesting rock formations, stacks, caves and arches that's a hugely popular draw. It is so popular that you have to book online at certain times of the year to go. Busy but nice. • **www.ascatedrais.gal**

Paseo marítimo,
A Coruña

ROUTE 08

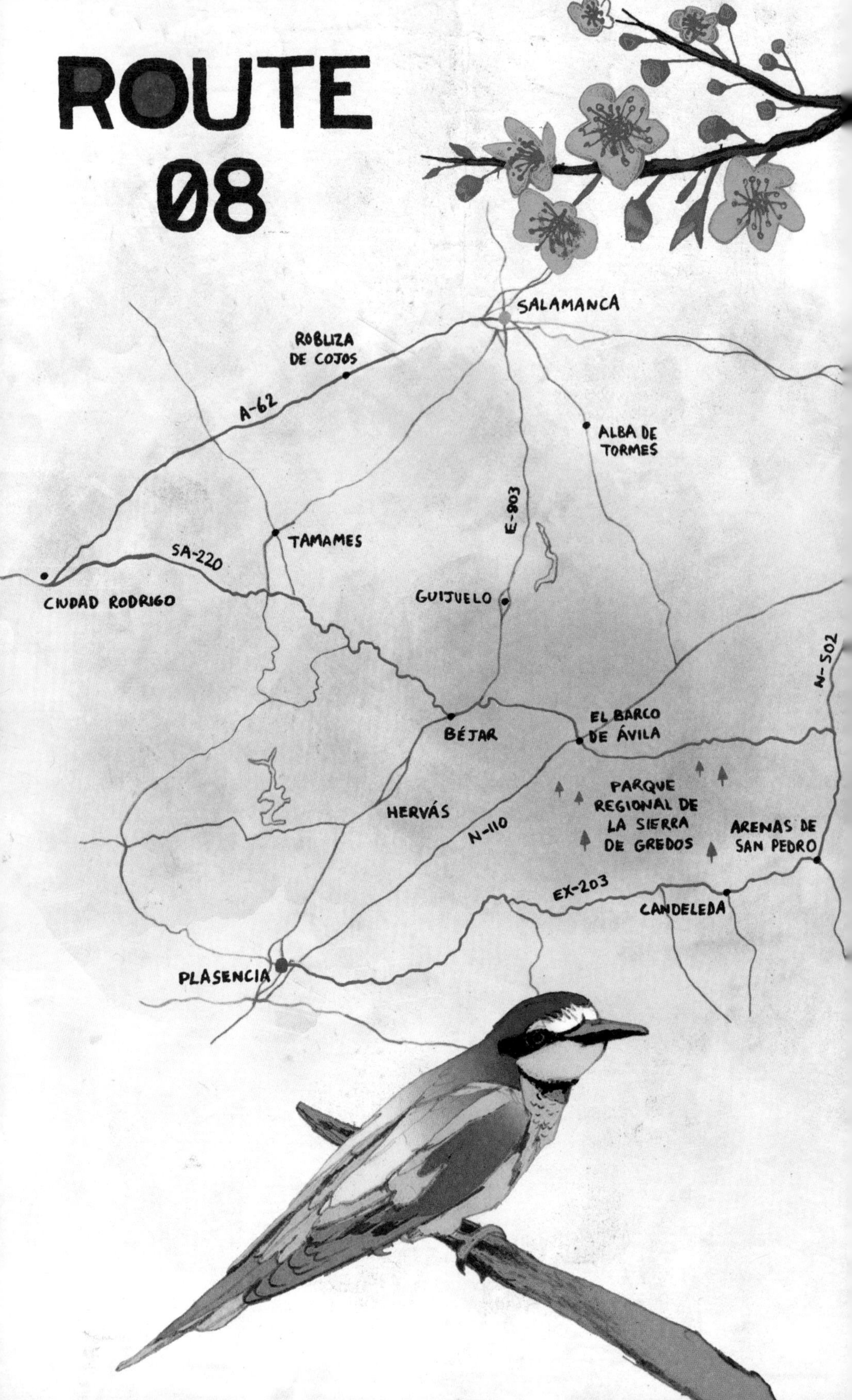

SALAMANCA
ROBLIZA DE COJOS
A-62
ALBA DE TORMES
E-803
TAMAMES
SA-220
CIUDAD RODRIGO
GUIJUELO
N-502
EL BARCO DE ÁVILA
BÉJAR
PARQUE REGIONAL DE LA SIERRA DE GREDOS
HERVÁS
N-110
ARENAS DE SAN PEDRO
EX-203
CANDELEDA
PLASENCIA

ROUTE 08

SALAMANCA TO PLASENCIA

BIRD LIFE

This route will take you through parts of Spain that the crowds rarely find, across precious habitats, into a secret valley in a national park and over some astonishing mountain ranges. This is the west of Spain, an area of wild beauty that offers great hiking and some of the best bird spotting in Western Europe. Take the opportunity to see exotic species you are unlikely find at home, get excited about birds and marvel in the variety of life in Spanish skies.

BEST FOR: Birdwatching, walking, cycling

START: Salamanca

END: Plasencia

MILEAGE: 415km (258 miles)

ALLOW: 4–5 days

MAP PAGES: 42, 43, 44, 56, 57

Something golden catches my eye. I'm driving through a pine forest on the lower slopes of Peña de Francia. It's native, natural forest, which means it's not dense like a plantation, and the understorey is alive with life. Young, bright green ferns unfold, while the last of the white asphodel flowers are dying back. The road is good but wound up like a spring, with tight turns and hairpins. I am feeling great after summitting the mountain, the highest point in the Sierra de Francia, at 1,728m (5,669ft) above sea level. The last 300–400m (984–1,312ft) took us out of the treeline and on to bare mountainside. At the top, the cold wind howled as we scampered around taking pictures. A pair of ibex sauntered past, grazing on the short stubby grass between the rocks.

I turn to look out of my side window. Flying beside me, a flash of bright yellow, is a bird I don't recognise. It flashes gold and black and then disappears into the forest as we motor past, descending all the time. I try to capture the memory so I can look it up later.

We arrive at La Alberca a little later and settle for the night in the *aire* after wandering around the quiet, narrow lanes of the medieval village. The half-timbered houses sit on top of each other, separated by narrow lanes, their overhanging roofs almost touching. It's old and, in places, feels abandoned, as if the population upped and left. We come to the square and find life. A few people sit outside a bar and a few shops are open and trading. We buy wine, ham and almonds. Huge storks make their nests on some of the higher buildings.

I wake in the morning to Lizzy whispering to me as she looks out of the window. A nuthatch is picking insects off the wall outside our van. I find

the bird book to identify it and look through its pages to find what I saw yesterday. I land on the golden oriole, a rarity in the UK but relatively common here. Even so, the memory of its bright yellow feathers stays with me. When we eat breakfast, we hear the sound of a cuckoo in the forest. Another rarity for us, but common here.

We leave La Alberca on the SA-201, climbing steeply to arrive at the Mirador del Portillo (1,240m/4,068ft) overlooking Las Batuecas valley. It's stunning. When we get out of the van to wander and take photos, we find tiny alpine daffodils (jonquils) flowering between the rocks. We descend into the valley and hit a series of seven or eight hairpins in the forest. The verges are busy with French lavender and sistus in bloom, along with santolina, lupins, gorse and broom, all in bloom too. The forest is made up of cork oaks and strawberry trees, along with pines. It's Mediterranean and alive with colour. I stop to take pictures of the hairpins as we navigate them, while Lizzy gets on her hands and knees to examine the flora.

Almost at the bottom of the valley, we stop to visit the

Monastery of San José de Batuecas and walk up the river valley. It's a hot afternoon so we pack swimming things, just in case we find anywhere along the way to swim. We walk alongside the river on a well-worn path past the monastery and into the forest in the steep-sided valley beyond. After about 1.5km (1 mile) we reach a set of steps in the valley side that leads us up on to a ridge below a cliff. Here, behind a set of railings are a series of Neolithic cave paintings that are believed to be between 5,000 and 7,000 years old. Despite being difficult to see, we can make out animals and numerical markings on the exposed rocks. They are remarkable.

We continue to walk upriver and pass a set of pools that look perfect for a swim, if difficult to reach. When the path becomes overgrown and unclear, we turn back in favour of a swim. It's hot and we are tired. We walk back to the pools and find a way down.

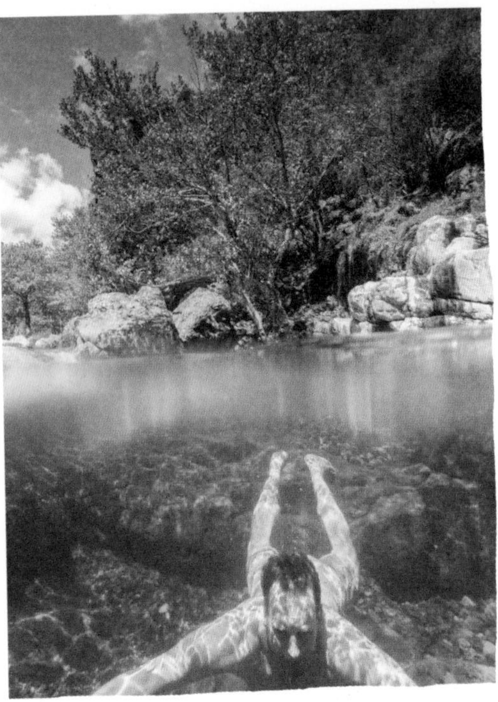

We strip in moments and get into the cool water from a slab of rock that's been warmed by the sun. The pool is fed by a small waterfall that drops on to a shallow ledge then into the deeper section of the pool. At its deepest, the pool is over 1.8m (6ft), with a boulder-covered bottom that leads to a shallow end where the water tips over another slab and then into a slide to another pool. Below that, the river runs shallow over boulders. Trees overhang the pools in places and, above, the valley sides rise steeply to a series of overhanging cliffs. Above that the sky is brilliant blue with wisps of bright white cloud and the occasional bird of prey soaring. Lizzy and I have swum in lots of places in our time together, but this is easily one of the best. It's like a painting, a romantic vision of perfection and we really can't quite believe we are here. Better still, we are alone – save for the birds and whatever is watching us – and haven't seen another soul for a couple of hours. We feel safe here in this steep, secret valley, surrounded by peaks and forest. I can see why Neolithic man came here.

Later that day, we arrive at Miranda del Castañar, another higgledy-piggledy medieval village. It sits on top of a ridge and is surrounded by peaks. The highest, Peña de Francia, can be seen in the distance. We settle into the marvellously wild Burro Blanco campsite and amble into the village, exploring the quiet, narrow streets. We settle in at a bar to watch the last of the light.

The campsite is awash with noise from cicadas when we return. It's deafening when we get close, but we can't find them in the undergrowth. They fade as we fall asleep and are replaced, at dawn, by the sound of birds.

The only call we recognise is the cuckoo, but it doesn't dampen our enthusiasm for twitching. We sit in the cool morning sun and watch birds flit about all over the campsite. They peck at the mossy grass, fly between boughs and call to each other across the forest. We see birds we don't recognise as well as some we do. Blackbirds, magpies, tits and finches dart between the trees. It's alive. We spot a hoopoe and a black redstart. I am excited to see the hoopoe as it means I have seen two of the three birds I have always wanted to see. The other bird I am keen to see, a European bee-eater, seems far too exotic and rarefied to make an appearance. When I flick through the bird book and look at its gold, black, blue and yellow markings it seems like an impossible dream.

Later, while looking for another swimming spot in the *gargantas* (gorges) of La Vera, we find ourselves lost up a narrow lane leading to the foothills of the Sierra de Gredos. It's a narrow road that winds its way up into the mountains. Suddenly, in a stand of oaks, we see flashes of yellow. I stop the van next to a meadow of yellow daisies and purple echiums and we get out. We walk back to the trees from which we'd seen the flashes. The birds are there still, plus black-headed azure-winged magpies, and they fly about in flashes of yellow, just beyond the speed with which we can train our binoculars.

We return to the van and turn around. While working our way down the road we see a flash of blue and gold pass in front of the van as it flies in front of us. I almost crash the van in astonishment. There's only one bird this can be: a European bee-eater.

We have twitched, entirely by accident, the triple.

THE DRIVING

You can get from Salamanca (amazing medieval city) to Ciudad Rodrigo (amazing medieval city) in a little over an hour if you want to. But why would you? There is a perfectly good way of getting there, on the old road, that will take you alongside the new *autovía*, at a pace that's much more suitable for immersion. You'll be able to stop to take photos, slow down to look at the countryside and wind down the windows to breathe in the fresh air while the rest of the world zooms by.

The A62-E80 runs in an almost straight line between Salamanca and Ciudad Rodrigo. Alongside it runs the old road. It's the N-620 and it's perfectly serviceable, with a decent surface and virtually no traffic. You can pick it up at the junction of the A-62 and the A-66 to the south-west of the city.

The N-620 passes through the *dehesa*, a habitat of grassland and forest of holm oak and cork that is used to raise cattle and for non-timber forest products such as mushrooms, game and pork. It's open and beautiful and, when we visited in May, was full of wild flowers, broom, gorse, fennel and French lavender. The cattle raised here have protected designation of origin (PDO) status. This is where Spain's fighting bulls come from, although it seems so very wrong to take animals out of this fabulous, pastoral landscape to make them fight. No wonder they are angry, taken from their peaceful life in the *dehesa*. Looking to the skies, you'll see storks sitting on their huge nests and kites patrolling.

Anyway, the N-620 gets hillier the closer you get to Ciudad Rodrigo.

As you approach the city there is an *aire*. There is a campsite to the south of the city (Camping La Pesquera). We crossed the Roman bridge and drove up the hill to the right to park outside the city walls for a few hours. There are great views of the surrounding countryside.

Leaving Ciudad Rodrigo on the SA-220, (pick it up to the north of the city or from junction 327 of the A-62) towards Béjar, the Sierra de Francia will loom ahead of you. The SA-220 will take you into low hills and more *dehesa*, and through Morasverdes and El Maílo. At El Cabaco, take the SA-201 towards La Alberca and head into the foothills. If you want to take a diversion to the top of Santuario de la Peña Francia, take the SA-203 2km (1.2 miles) outside of El Cabaco (it is clearly signed). The road is winding and a little tortuous but will take you into fantastic pine forest and up to the monastery at 1,748m (5,735ft). The last couple of miles are hairpin-rich and a little hairy, but if I can do it, you can too. It's exhilarating.

Coming down off the mountain the way you came will bring you back to the SA-201 via a little shortcut on the CV-134, and into La Alberca. The *aire* is at the top of the village and is clearly signed, just off the SA-201. The village is lovely and well preserved, with narrow streets and small squares hosting a few shops selling *jamón*, local produce and painted shoes (among other things). It's a bit of a tourist trap but still retains its charm, almost to the point of neglect in some of the back streets. We loved it.

Leaving La Alberca, turn right out of the SA-201 towards El Portillo, a high pass at 1,727 m (5,666 ft) that's among boulders and pine, with deciduous woodland at the lower levels. The views are great. The descent into the Las Batuecas valley from the Mirador del Portillo is fantastic, with eight tight hairpins in a row, incredible views over wooded slopes and a few heart-stopping drops.

A few kilometres after the last hairpin you'll find the parking area for the Monasterio Desierto de San José de Batuecas and the accessible trail that will lead you, eventually,

to the cave paintings and waterfall up the beautiful and isolated Las Batuecas River.

Continue on the SA-201. You'll pass into the region of Extremadura and the road name will change to the CC-167 until you get to La Mestas, where there is a large natural swimming pool (turn left at the junction and park immediately on the left). To continue on the route, turn left at the junction on to the CC-166 and follow it to the next T-junction with the EX-204. Turn left here towards Sotoserrano. This will take you up a beautiful river valley, with olive groves, more *dehesa* and views of the river until you reach Riomalo de Abajo (there is another natural swimming pool here) and the road name changes to the SA-225 and follows the Alagón River to Sotoserrano. There is a campsite here on the river just beyond the town on the DSA-280.

Continue through Sotoserrano on the SA-225 through vineyards, olive groves and fields of peach trees, along with deciduous forest, heading up all the time as you approach Miranda del Castañar, another beautiful village sitting on a ridge. The Burro Blanco campsite is here.

Continue on the SA-225 until the junction with the SA-220. Turn right here towards Cristóbal and Béjar. This will bring you into Béjar, once you have crossed the A-66 *autovía*, a town that's spread out along another ridge. Turn left in town and leave it on the AV-100 towards El Barco de Ávila. This road will take you up and into the Sierra de Candelario and the Puerto de La Hoya at 1,200m (3,937ft). At El Barco – where there is an impressive castle and Roman bridge – turn left on to the N-110 and follow it into town,

then, before leaving the town, turn right on to the AV-941, a road that will wind and weave its way above a high plain, with the Sierra de Gredos opposite. Eventually, you will come to the junction with the N-502. Turn right and follow it across the plain and then up a gentle incline of sweeping curves to the Puerto del Pico, a pass that's at 1,352m (4,436ft) above sea level. The views to the south are incredible and make you realise how high you've been for the last few miles. The valley bottom is way below you. Running alongside the new road is a section of Roman road (*calzada romana*) that you can see curving away down the mountain in a series of very steep, sharp turns.

The descent on the N-502 isn't quite as steep, but it is long and seems to go on forever as it whisks you through a few villages – and into a huge landscape – before bringing you to a roundabout at Ramacastañas. Follow the AV-P-708 (straight on) and then turn right onto the CL-501, which changes to the EX-203 at Madrigal de la Vera. You are on the southern slopes of the Sierra de Gredos here. The road follows the contours of the mountainside and crosses lots of *gargantas*. There are Roman bridges all along here, presumably because the *gargantas* provided narrow enough places for them to span with their high, arched stone constructions. The bridges are beautiful and often have swimming spots below them along with campsites and restaurants. It is a great place to explore if you like wild swimming!

The EX-203 gets better the closer you get to Plasencia and passes through Jarandilla de la Vera and Jaraíz de la Vera as the contours become steeper and the views get better to the south. Jarandilla and Jaraíz are famous for their cherry trees, and the blossom they produce in the early spring, which is supposed to be spectacular. Sadly, we arrived a little late.

The EX-203 arrives on the outskirts of Plasencia at the junction with the N-110. Turn right here for the campsite or continue straight on for the city.

WHERE TO STAY: CAMPING

As usual, there are plenty of campsites in this region and we only stayed at a handful along our route.

Camping Don Quijote, Cabrerizos
Ctra. Aldealengua, Km 1,930, 37193 Cabrerizos, Salamanca, Spain
Tel: +34 923 20 90 52

A great site with a popular bar and restaurant on site. There's a pool, too. You can cycle along the river, via the Via Verde, right into the city at the Roman bridge.

Camping La Pesquera, Ciudad Rodrigo
C. del Regato Cachón, 35, 37500 Ciudad Rodrigo, Salamanca, Spain
Web: www.campinglapesquera.es
Tel: +34 923 48 13 48

Opposite the city, not far from the Roman bridge, on the river, with good views of the city.

Camping el Burro Blanco, Miranda del Castañar
C. Corta, 0, 37660 Miranda del Castañar, Salamanca, Spain
Web: www.elburroblanco.net
Tel: +34 923 16 11 00

The best campsite you'll go to this year. Stunning birdlife, wonderful owners Eddy and Vera, and a really good welcome. N.B. Not great for big units.

WHERE TO STAY: *AIRES*

La Alberca:
A good, free *aire* just a five-minute walk from the village. Easy and free.

Swim spot on the EX-203

IN THE AREA

Salamanca A beautiful medieval city with one of the most impressive squares in Spain, plus a cathedral and impressive old quarter. The Plaza Mayor is huge and gets lit up like a birthday cake each night.

Casa Lis Art Nouveau and Art Deco Museum, Salamanca
A truly eclectic collection of art nouveau *objets d'art* including work by Fabergé and Lalique and a sinister collection of Victorian dolls housed in a former art nouveau mansion. • **www.museocasalis.org**

Ciudad Rodrigo Smaller than Salamanca but no less interesting, with city walls containing the whole place. The Correos (post office) is housed in an old convent and has lovely wooden ceilings, tiled walls and solid oak doors.

Peña de Francia Peak in the Sierra de Francia that's 1,748m (5,735ft). Hotel and café. • **www.hospederiapenadefrancia.com**

La Alberca A place that's lost in time (and all that). Really atmospheric village that belongs to another age with narrow alleys and stone houses on top of each other. It's impressive and well worth a stop. There are bars in the central square for people watching. Lots of shops selling local produce.

Plasencia Another impressive medieval city with a stunning aqueduct, though not a Roman one!

Miranda del Casteñar Another, slightly less well-kept, medieval village atop a ridge. Beautiful location and really great place to wander. The Plaza Mayor is a bullring and has features that allow matadors to escape the bull's horns.

Mountain bike routes There are several routes for mountain bikes based out of Cristobál from Centro BTT Entresierras.

Swimming in the garganta The EX-203 runs between Ramacastañas and Plasencia and offers lots of opportunities to explore the gorges and bridges that run down from the mountains. A great place for wild swimming or hiking. Amazing bird life, too. All *gargantas* are marked with road signs.

ROUTE
09
MÉRIDA
ALANGE
E-803
CAMPILLO
DE LLERENA
N-502
N-432
AZUAGA
LLERENA
BELMEZ
MONESTERIO
PARQUE NATURAL
SIERRA DE
HORNACHUELOS
CERRO
MURIANO
CÓRDOBA
CONSTANTINA
SIERRA
MORENA
PALMA DEL RIO
LORA DEL RIO
ÉCIJA
A-4
CARMONA
ARQUEOLÓGICO DE
ITÁLICA
SEVILLE

ROUTE 09

MÉRIDA TO ITALICA

HOW THEY LIVE

Spain's old cities and historical sites are wonderful. On this route you'll visit three of them, all of which are UNESCO World Heritage Sites and all of which will give you an insight into Spain's history. The driving to link them up isn't the most interesting, but it will take you across the plains, on roads through orange plantations and olive groves, and into the backcountry many never see. And if you are very lucky, you may see a lynx!

BEST FOR: Roman ruins, roman ruins and more roman ruins... and lynx (if you are lucky)

START: Embalse de Proserpina, Mérida

END: Italica, Santiponce

MILEAGE: 388km (241 miles)

ALLOW: 4–5 days

MAP PAGES: 67, 68, 80, 81, 91, 92

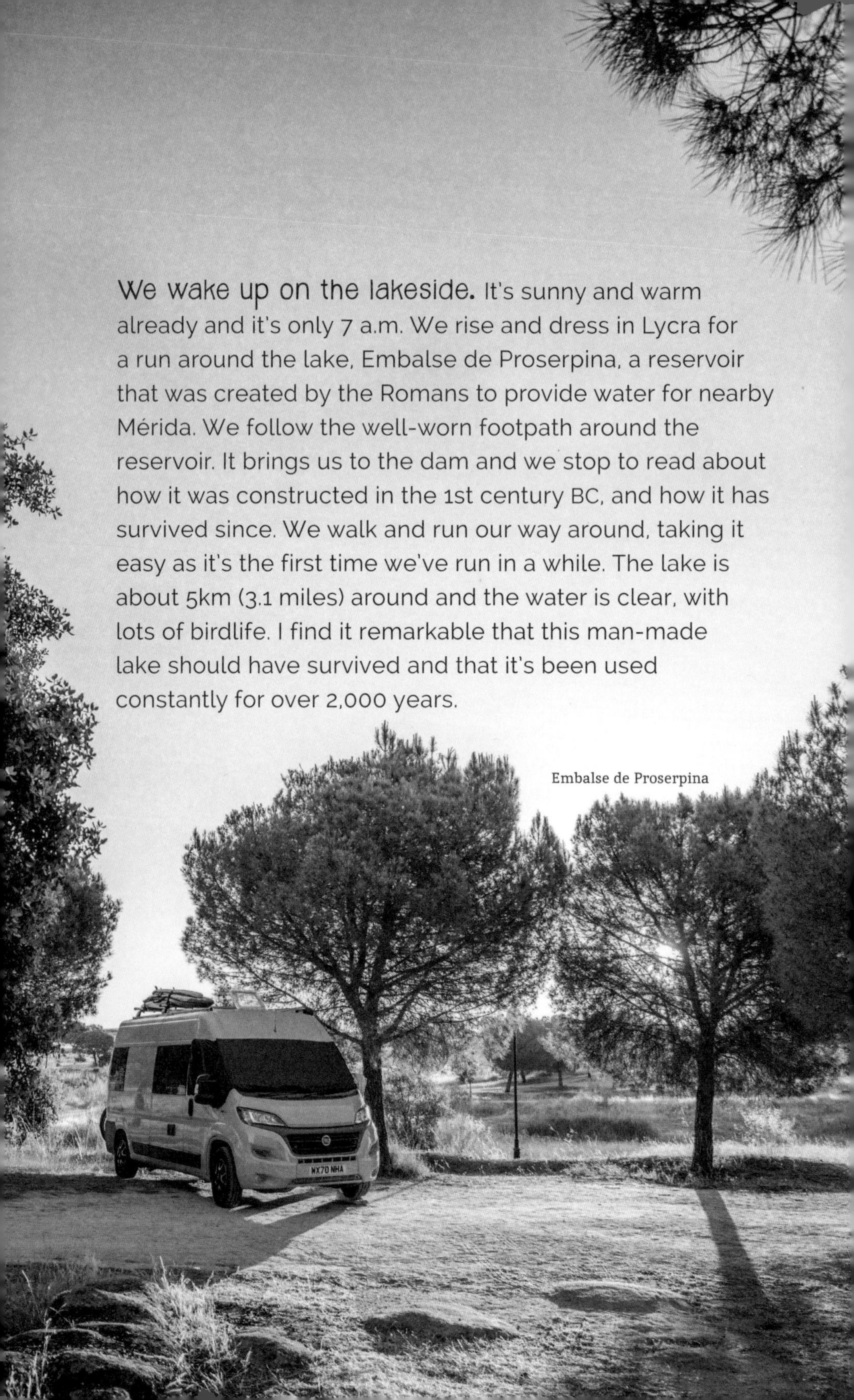

We wake up on the lakeside. It's sunny and warm already and it's only 7 a.m. We rise and dress in Lycra for a run around the lake, Embalse de Proserpina, a reservoir that was created by the Romans to provide water for nearby Mérida. We follow the well-worn footpath around the reservoir. It brings us to the dam and we stop to read about how it was constructed in the 1st century BC, and how it has survived since. We walk and run our way around, taking it easy as it's the first time we've run in a while. The lake is about 5km (3.1 miles) around and the water is clear, with lots of birdlife. I find it remarkable that this man-made lake should have survived and that it's been used constantly for over 2,000 years.

Embalse de Proserpina

We return to the van. It's parked in a scrub of low pines that offer us a little shade. There are a few flowers below the trees, in patches of grasses, but mostly it's tracks made by vehicles. We change into our swimming gear and swim in the clear, cool water. A few passing walkers and fishermen shout to us as we swim, surprised, we think, by the fact that we are swimming. Despite the air temperature being well into the 30s, it seems it's still too early in the year for the Spanish.

We head into Mérida, a little over 5km (3.1 miles) away, to take a look at the Roman ruins that I have heard described as 'the biggest collection of Roman remains in Spain'. Seeing as the Romans occupied Spain for over 700 years, I guess that's a big call, so we head into the city and park at the *aire*.

We walk to the main site, the theatre and amphitheatre, pay for a combined ticket with entry to all the Roman sites and wander through the shaded courtyard to follow the recommended itinerary around the ruins. I am not prepared for what we see as we walk through an archway of brick, stone and concrete into the gladiatorial arena. It is immense. Terraces at least 30m (98ft) high rise all around us, punctuated by gates and arched doorways. We walk to the western end of the arena, the area used to take the dead away, and look back. It's not hard to imagine the place full of baying crowds. It's chilling and wondrous all at the same time. The architecture – which uses cut stone, concrete and brick – is staggering. Below the terraces, huge corridors, with tall, arched ceilings, give us shade and a drop in temperature. When we emerge into the light, it's dazzling.

The theatre, next door, is equally impressive. Huge columns stand behind the stage and terraces, now restored so the theatre can be used for live performances, stand tall and bright in the sun. It is a glittering, shimmering symbol of the greatness of the Roman Empire and its power. It makes Hadrian's Wall look like a pile of stones.

We seek shade at another site, the mansion next door to the amphitheatre, which is covered with a roof to protect the intricate mosaics, bread ovens and bathhouses. It's a ruin but gives us enough of an idea to see the layout of the house, the functions of the rooms and the effort that went into creating this city. We view, through a crack in time, a little slice of how the Romans lived.

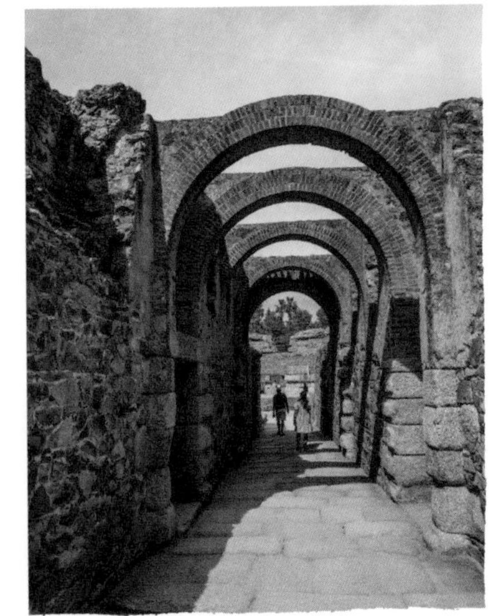

We overnight at the quiet *aire* in a tiny village called Alange that sits on the side of another reservoir. Adjacent to the *aire* is a hotel containing, so we read, an example of a Roman bath. After breakfast, we head over to see if we can get a look. The bathhouse, which is still in use as a health spa attached to the hotel, is like a sanatorium. White-coated therapists walk around while elderly ladies in bathrobes totter between treatments. Large pot plants tower

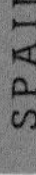

over the white-painted interior and the people sipping coffee in a huge palm house look at us. We do our best, in our broken Spanish, to ask if we can see the baths. After some misunderstandings and an attempt to get rid of us, we persist and are led, reluctantly, down a cool corridor to a domed room with a round pool. It's the original Roman bath. It's full of clear water, which steams gently in the humidity. A hole in the domed roof lets in a shaft of bright, sharp light. We feel transported, once again, to a place to which we don't belong. The spa is luxurious and expensive and the bath belongs to another age. As we walk out, we pass through the lush gardens where white-coated nurses watch us and robed patients shuffle. It really is another world from the van that's parked a few metres away in a free *aire*.

If Mérida was impressive, Córdoba is out of this world. It's busy and hot, although cooler in the narrow, whitewashed lanes that fan out from the Mezquita-Catedral, the former mosque now cathedral that's the heart of the city. Tour groups follow guides holding umbrellas above their heads

and snake around the lanes, criss-crossing each other as they tramp from site to site. We've so far been to places that have been quiet or deserted, at times of the day that haven't suited, so this is our first experience of mass tourism. There are French, American and Spanish tour groups, as well as gangs of excited school kids. It's a good chance to look into how honeypots work. All around the Mezquita, shops sell fans, leather wine flasks, straw hats, and ceramic tiles in a flourish of tat. It's intoxicating.

We head away from the cathedral in search of the city's courtyard gardens that are open to the public this week. They are defined by a pair of fir trees in red pots, and usually a queue outside to get in. We join a queue and wait for ten or so minutes for our chance to get our glimpse into how modern Córdobans live. We pass through a short, old wooden door and enter into a whitewashed courtyard that's probably no more than 5m (16.4ft) square. There is a well in one corner. The whitewashed walls

are covered in geraniums growing out of blue painted pots. A fig grows in a corner. Above us the blue sky. The courtyard is joyfully cool and dark and the cobbled floor is damp. It's an oasis and seems timeless, as if it's been here for centuries, which it probably has. Doors lead off into the house's dark interior but we are not able to look in any further. I take photos and gawp, enjoying the cool. Then our time is up and we step out again into the sunshine while another group enters. We repeat this throughout the morning before diving back into the throng at the Mezquita.

Inside the huge walls, behind the gilded doors, we find a palm-fringed garden filled with fragrant orange trees. Water channels feed them between the cobbles. We enter the mosque and are dazzled, not by the light, but by the beauty of the space. Huge double arches sit on top of marble and granite columns. Some are carved, others are plain. Much of it dates from the 7th century. Huge windows of fine filigree work provide a little daylight around the perimeter while the main space is lit by lamps hanging between the columns. The space is vast and yet intimate, simple and humble, beautiful and inspiring.

At the centre of the Mezquita we find the full-sized Roman Catholic cathedral. It's another vast space, but vertical, built with sky-piercing columns, pointed arches, gold-leafed icons and opulence. As a later addition, built in the 12th century after the Christians took over the city, it's brash and big and, while truly beautiful, feels tasteless next to the intricate carving and details of the former mosque around it. Both celebrate divine beings, and yet they feel so far apart: a reflection perhaps of the difference between Christianity and Islam.

The final stop on this journey brings us to a small town outside Seville. It's an unassuming place of whitewashed houses, a short way from a huge motorway flyover. It's also very hot. We pay a small fee at the entrance (non-EU citizens pay, EU citizens free) and wander into the compound. We are here because Italica, the Roman name for Santiponce, was the first Roman city in Spain. In front of us, we see the large, partly crumbling remains of an entrance. It's wide and paved with uneven marble slabs. We follow signs to a viewpoint up a dusty and steep path to the right. It takes us to the back of some more crumbling concrete and stone and then through a gap to a balcony. As we approach the railings, the scale of the site becomes apparent very quickly. We reach the barrier and look down on a huge amphitheatre. It is colossal, at least 100m (328ft) long, 50m (164ft) wide and 30m (98ft) high, easily the biggest structure we've seen. We read that it seated 25,000 in its day and was one of the biggest amphitheatres in the empire. Once again, we are blown away by the scale of the enterprise and we feel we're getting a glimpse into the might of Rome. It's more, much more than wandering about in a bunch of old ruins and I am so glad we decided to follow this route. We've seen inside Spain in more ways than one. It's stunning. Dazzling. Incredible.

THE DRIVING

I will be the first to admit that this route might not offer the very best in driving. However, it will give you a chance to see the plains and to smell orange groves as well as see signs that have lynx on them (if not the chance to see a lynx in real life), something you don't see very often. That said, it's not a route that takes you through ugly or unattractive countryside, just some that isn't as exciting as other routes.

OK, that's the caveat. Now let's drive. Leave Mérida on the A-5 heading south. Just outside the city, and once over the river, follow signs for Alange and the BA-089. This will take you out along the river and, eventually to the dam and then up the river valley up to the village. Take the BA-005 out of the village and then on to the EX-210 at Palomas heading south. This will take you through rolling hills, on straight, hot roads. This is an area that's

populated by lynx so look out for them and their rather beguiling road signs. Expect to see sunflowers, olives, *dehesa*s and oranges as well as wild flowers and broom, gorse, and oaks in the margins.

At the junction with the EX-103 turn right, then turn left on to the BA-016 after a few kilometres. Take this to the junction with the N-432. Follow the N-432 all the way to Córdoba. There are some sections of old road – the N-432A – that you can navigate that will take you through some nice countryside (instead of bypasses) but can be a little rough. When you come out of Cerro Muriano (if you take the old road), you'll get great views of the plains below as you descend into Córdoba.

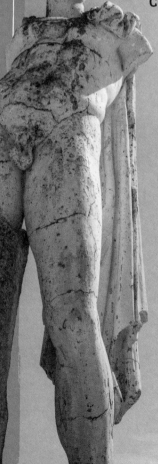

Leave Córdoba on the A-431, the road that runs out through the industrial suburbs and along the north bank of the Río Guadalquivir and south of the Sierra de Hornachuelos. Once you leave the industry behind, you'll pass through miles of sweet-smelling orange groves.

At Lora del Río, follow signs for the A-436 to head to the north of Seville. You'll pass the magnificent castle of Almódovar del Río as you climb above it. The A-436 will take you directly to Santiponce and Italica at junction 438 of the A-66 *autovía*.

IN THE AREA

Mérida Mérida has a dizzying collection of Roman ruins, including the amphitheatre and theatre, temple and lots of impressive houses and mosaics. It is a UNESCO-designated World Heritage Site. Tickets for entry into all the sites can be bought from any of the sites for €16 per adult.

Córdoba There is a lot to this fantastic city. Just to wander around the old city is wonderful. I have listed those we visited here:

MEZQUITA-CATEDRAL DE CÓRDOBA
Stunning part-mosque, part-cathedral. Immense and lovely, if a little too over-Christianised. Mesmerising.
• **www.mezquita-catedraldecordoba.es/en**

CÓRDOBA COURTYARDS FESTIVAL
This takes place in early May, when locals open up their courtyards to the public. Very colourful and popular. Be prepared to queue. Fantastic, especially for my tame botanist. • **www.turismodecordoba.org**

ARCHAEOLOGICAL MUSEUM OF CÓRDOBA
Fantastic artefacts from all periods, including Roman. • **www.museosdeandalucia.es/web/museoarqueologicodecordoba**

Santiponce Incredible ruins, mosaics and a huge amphitheatre and theatre.
• **www.sevillecityguide.com/italica.html**

WHERE TO STAY: CAMPING

As usual, there are plenty of campsites in this region and we only stayed at a handful along our route.

Campsite Lago de Proserpina, Mérida
Carretera. Proserpina. s, s/n, 6800 Mérida, Badajoz, Spain
Web: www.campings.net/en/camping-lago-de-proserpina-en-merida.htm
Tel: +34 924 12 30 55

A standard site near the lake at Proserpina, for if off-site parking is full or unavailable.

Camping Mérida, Mérida
Autovía de Extremadura, Km 336, 6800 Mérida, Badajoz, Spain
Web: https://camping-merida.negocio.site
Tel: +34 924 30 03 98

A site that's 2km (1.2 miles) outside of the city, with a pool.

WHERE TO STAY: *AIRES*

Mérida: A paying *aire* just a short walk from the ruins and city of Mérida. All facilities.
Alange: A nice *aire* (almost) overlooking the Embalse de Alange, with a friendly restaurant next door. It's 50m (55 yards) from the Roman baths and spa. Free.
Córdoba: Paying *aire* just outside the city walls. Some shade and lots of space. A five-minute walk into the old city. Very handy.
Umbrete: A free *aire* with all facilities but no EHU, about 20 minutes from Italica. Next to a sports centre with great outdoor pools.

WHERE TO STAY: OFF-SITE PARKING

There are several places around the Lago de Proserpina where it is possible to park a camper for the night, and we passed a very peaceful night there after picking up a lot of litter. Please treat this place with respect if you stay by clearing up some for yourself.

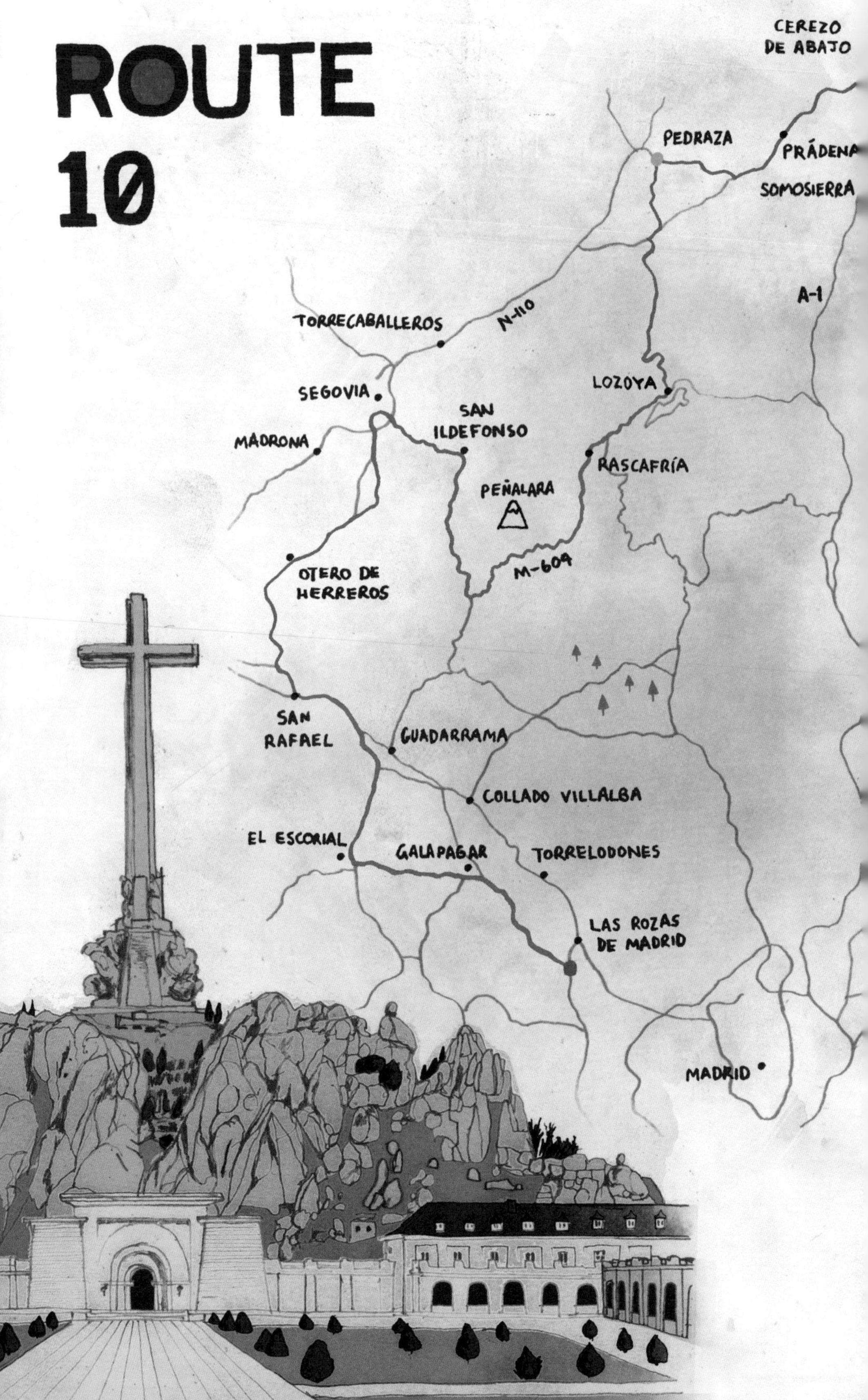
ROUTE 10
CEREZO DE ABAJO
PEDRAZA
PRÁDENA
SOMOSIERRA
A-1
N-110
TORRECABALLEROS
SEGOVIA
MADRONA
SAN ILDEFONSO
LOZOYA
RASCAFRÍA
PEÑALARA
M-604
OTERO DE HERREROS
SAN RAFAEL
GUADARRAMA
COLLADO VILLALBA
EL ESCORIAL
GALAPAGAR
TORRELODONES
LAS ROZAS DE MADRID
MADRID

ROUTE 10

PEDRAZA TO MADRID

VALLEY OF THE FALLEN

The Sierra de Guadarrama sits at the heart of Spain, to the north of Madrid. Its wooded slopes are popular with walkers, cyclists and, in winter, skiers. The mountains were a hiding place for the nobility during the hot summer months and they decamped from the city to be cooler in the vast palaces of El Escorial and La Granja and, at one time, at the Alcázar in Segovia. There is much history here – and not all of it is easy.

BEST FOR: Palaces, mountains, city life

START: Pedraza

END: Madrid

MILEAGE: 233km (144 miles)

ALLOW: 4 days

MAP PAGES: 45, 46

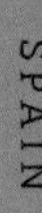

We stand at the edge of the huge, open square, looking out over the valley. It's hot and we squint into the sun as we survey the forest below us. It's a beautiful place, with pine and holm oaks making up a huge area of dense *dehesa* sheltering dry scrub and rough granite boulders beneath. In the distance, to the south-east, lies Madrid. Behind us, looming over us, stands the largest Christian cross ever made, a monolith of 150m (492ft) on top of a granite outcrop that's 950m (3,117ft) above sea level. Behind that lie the mountains of the Sierra de Guadarrama.

We turn and walk towards the crucifix, crossing the square's granite slabs in the bright sunshine, unable to step into the shade. Ahead of us, and directly below the cross, in a semicircle, there is a colonnade of 11 enormous granite arches, each backed with panels of plain, black, polished marble except the middle one, which houses a huge, studded wooden door. They make up the facade of the mausoleum of the Valle de los Caídos (Valley of the Fallen), Franco's mis-sold memorial to the fallen of the civil war and eventual one-time mausoleum. In any other mausoleum, we'd have expected to

see names of those fallen etched into the panels, but there are none here. The basilica (as it was classified by the Pope in 1960) is Franco's monument to a 'national act of atonement' and reconciliation. Built between 1940 and 1959, its outside is vast and faceless, built in a style I think of as modernist but that actually has been labelled as neo-Herrerian, after the master architect Juan de Herrera, whose basilica at the nearby palace of El Escorial we visit later and realise bears a more than striking resemblance. When I read about the Valley of the Fallen later, I discover that the style – blank, austere and overbearing – is also described as fascist classicism. Franco, I also read later, was interred here after his death in 1975, along with more than 34,000 dead from both sides of the civil war, and then exhumed in 2019 in an effort for Spain to distance itself from its grim past, to dissuade neo-fascists from coming here to pay homage to Franco and to somehow change the nature of the place.

As we cross the square, I know none of this yet, except I have a feeling in my stomach that this is a place of deeply significant meaning. I feel uncomfortable. There is no interpretation or guidebook to tell us what we need to know and yet we feel its weight and the darkness that lies behind it, despite the bright sunshine. Lizzy and I discuss it as we approach the huge doors leading to the basilica. We can't understand how this, a monument built by Franco, could possibly be a place of reconciliation, when what we know of his 35-year grip on Spain is that he crushed his enemies and removed all opposition during the civil war, and possibly after. To call it a national monument to atonement seems ironic and cruel.

We walk through a small opening in the huge arched wooden door, give up our bags to be scanned, and enter that vast chamber beneath the rock. A small glass box houses a gift shop that seems very out of place but is soon forgotten as we survey the basilica and step, open-mouthed, into the space. A set of marble steps lead us down into the main body, or nave, of the basilica, through a massive iron gate and past a pair of equally massive steel art deco angels that are holding swords with hooded and bowed heads. At this point, I should notice that these gigantic statues are symbols of fascism, but I don't.

The chamber is about 25m (82ft) wide and at least that high, with a barrel vaulted ceiling carved from the rock. Granite columns hold up the roof. The floor is black polished marble, a deep and dark pool, beneath which lies the crypt that's bigger than St Peter's in Rome. We head further into the basilica and down the nave towards the altar that's almost 100m (328ft) away. The lighting, in stark contrast to outside, is minimal. Signs implore us to be silent.

Mass is taking place and is being broadcast into the space through speakers hidden behind columns. As the priests say prayers and recite the service – I assume in Spanish but it could well be Latin for the feeling it gives me – their voices sound thin and ethereal, penetrating even. The choir sings in response, the notes resonating around the rock. The heavy notes of an organ dispense bass lines that linger. Burning incense hangs in the air. We sit at the side of the nave and wait for the service to finish so we can approach the altar and get a good look at the huge, domed, golden ceiling that we can just about see the edge of.

As I sit and listen, taking in as much of it as I can, I realise that I am witnessing high church *in extremis*. The actions of the priests taking mass are ritualistic and orchestrated, reminding me of the kind of rituals I watched as a child in 1970s horror films. It feels as if I have walked in on a cult. I look at the double-headed eagles holding up the lights on the walls and feel a chill. I don't know yet, because my naivety still believes the story, but I have walked into the belly of the fascist beast itself. It's no wonder I feel as if I am somewhere dark and restless, where the truth is disguised, glossed over and presented as reconciliation, because to do anything else would be to open painful, still-raw wounds.

The service finishes and the security guard allows us and others to pass into the body of the basilica. We walk between the rows of wooden pews and towards the Christ on the cross at the altar. The organ continues to play, getting louder as it brings the service to a final musical crescendo. I look at the cross and then up at the ceiling as the organ's sound and tone rise further, taking its exaltation to new keys and heights. As I walk, I allow my head and eyes to lift to the dome, craning my neck further and further back to take in the scene above me: at the centre is Jesus and around him, heading upwards, in a style reminiscent of a modernist Michelangelo, are people – the dead – transforming into angels as they rise to heaven. I feel like I am in a film, with myself as a camera making a long and revealing tracking shot, while the music reaches its peak and then stops, leaving me looking up at the ceiling in awe and wonder. The illusion is perfect: I have come from the darkness into the golden glow of the church. And yet I am a few hundred metres underground, below a vast outcrop of granite and the world's largest cross in Franco's love letter to fascism. I couldn't have felt heavier.

I notice, in a small side-chapel, an inscription that reads '*Caídos por Dios y*

por España' ('Fallen for God and for Spain'). It prompts me to think about which Spain this is really a monument to.

A few days later, I find myself sitting in the van reading all I can on the internet about the Valle de los Caídos. It chills me again. I find images of people making fascist salutes on the very spot on which I had stood and read about those who are interred there. I read about prisoners working to pay off their time building the Valle. Some paid with their lives. The bodies in the huge crypt below the basilica, I read, were exhumed from mass graves all over Spain. Some of them are known and some are not, but all of them are nameless, making it all the more difficult and painful for relatives of the disappeared to find their loved ones. For some, there can be no rest.

I read, too, about the exhumation of the body of Franco in 2019 and the legal battle to do it that entangled the Spanish government for almost 20 years. While other symbols of Franco's regime have been removed from public buildings, this monolithic mausoleum remains, a representation of the might, mood and power of fascism, but also of the collective memory loss of a time so troubling that many would prefer to forget.

As we return to the light – a pinpoint at the end of the huge nave – it's easy to forget what we have seen on this journey so far. Spain, as ever,

dazzles us with its beauty and its history and its magnificence, even if some of its history is hard to reconcile. At Segovia, we walk the length of the Roman aqueduct, slack-jawed and silent at engineering that's almost 2,000 years old. We tour the round-turreted Alcázar, the castle that was built on Roman foundations and was once served by the aqueduct. It was, so the story goes, the castle on which Walt Disney based the castle in his own magical kingdom.

We visit the summer palaces of La Granja de San Ildefonso and El Escorial, where the gilded cages of Spain's elite kept them insulated from the realities of life with incredible tapestries, drapery and art. The fountains, silent and dry, stretch off into the distance in the gardens of La Granja.

We drive over the high passes at Navacerrada, Cotos and Navafría, through the oak and Scots pine forests of the Sierra de Guadarrama, an area that Madrileños enjoy as their playground in summer and winter. They are beautiful and a further reminder of Spain's wonderful natural spaces.

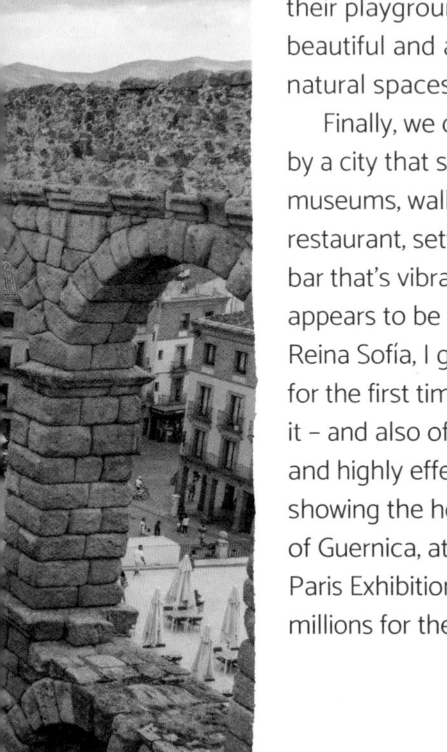

Finally, we drive into Madrid, where we are confronted by a city that seems to be really enjoying life. We visit art museums, walk the streets and eat tapas in a rooftop restaurant, settling in, on our last night, in a campsite bar that's vibrant and inviting. Spain, a country that appears to be moving forwards, delivers. In the Museo Reina Sofía, I gasp when I see Pablo Picasso's *Guernica* for the first time. I am in awe of the size and scale of it – and also of its power. It's a magnificent, terrifying and highly effective piece of Republican propaganda showing the horror and brutality of the Nazi bombing of Guernica, at Franco's request, in 1937. Displayed at the Paris Exhibition of 1937 in the Spanish Pavilion, it raised millions for the Republican's ill-fated cause.

THE DRIVING

The Sierra de Guadarrama is a protected area of immense beauty, so it's easy to understand why the elite of Spain built their palaces there. It lies to the north of Madrid, marking the boundary between north and south, Moor and Christian, Nationalist and Republican at various times in history.

This journey will take you from the north-east of the mountains into the foothills and over three high passes to the Valley of Lozoya and then to Segovia and over the range again to Madrid, Spain's vibrant capital.

Start at Junction 99 of the A1-E1, the north–south motorway from Burgos to Madrid. Follow signs for Segovia and the N-110, a road that runs parallel to the peaks in the foothills, through scrubby *dehesa*, with the mountains on the left and the plains on the right.

After about 15km (9.3 miles), turn right on to the tiny SGV-2512, heading in the direction of Pedraza through Arcones, a small village, and then out into more scrub of *dehesa* and rocky outcrops. Pedraza is worth a stop as it's really well preserved and has a few good restaurants.

From Pedraza, take the SGP-2322 back to the N-110. It's a great, if narrow, little road that winds at first but then leads you back to the plain, with fantastic views of the mountains in the background beyond the juniper, pines and Spanish broom.

Follow the N-110 for a short way and then turn left on to the SG-612, which is signed for Puerto de Navafría and Lozoya. This will take you up a fantastic, winding road for around 12km (7.5 miles) up to the pass at Navafría

(1,773m/5,816ft). It's a fantastic road that winds through the forests of pine, is quite narrow but not impassable, and is popular with cyclists. There aren't wonderful views from the top (there are lots of walking routes here), but as you descend, there are opportunities to look down into the Valle de Lozoya. At the top, you pass into the care of the Junta of Madrid and the road name changes to the M-637. This will bring you down the mountain into Lozoya. Turn right here on to the M-604 and follow the road along the valley, past the *embalse* and up its northern slopes to the Puerto de Cotos (1,830m/6,004ft) on another stunning road. From here, follow the M-604 to the junction with the M-601 at the Puerto de Navacerrada and then take a right down the mountain again towards Segovia. It's a busier road, but still a great drive and will bring you to Palacio Real de La Granja de San Ildefonso, then on to Segovia.

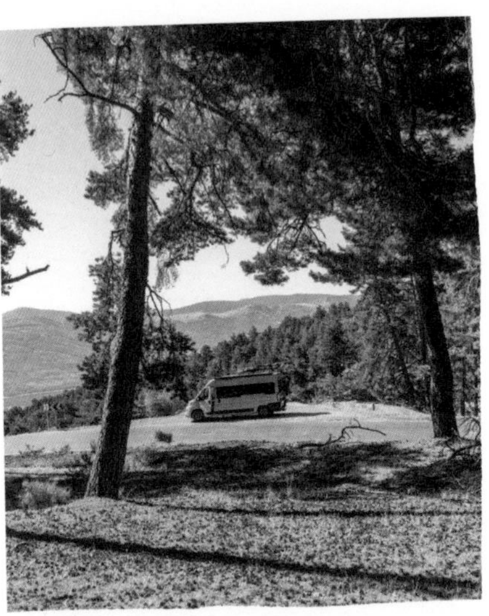

Leave Segovia on the N-603 and follow it to San Rafael, where

WHERE TO STAY: CAMPING

Camping Osuna, Madrid
C. Jardines de Aranjuez, s/n, 28042 Madrid, Spain
Web: www.campingosuna.com
Tel: +34 913 89 41 93

This is the nearest campsite to downtown Madrid. It's only about ten minutes' walk from the Metro so it's perfect for visiting the city centre. It's groovy and friendly and we loved it even though the pool is really, really small.

WHERE TO STAY: *AIRES*

Pedraza: We stayed at a small *aire* below the city walls and adjacent to the aqueduct at Pedraza.
Segovia: This popular *aire* has water, grey and black waste, and is just a 15-minute walk to the centre of the city.

it joins the N-VI at a set of lights in the town. Turn left and follow the road up the mountainside again, through Scots pine forest. It's a big road, often with two lanes, but it still winds up the mountain in a series of hairpins and steep curves. This will take you to the top of the Puerto de Guadarrama and then down the other side into Guadarrama.

Turn right in Guadarrama on to the M-600 towards Monasterio del Escorial. You'll find the Valle de los Caídos along this road and then after a further 15km (9.3 miles) you will come to the Monasterio del Escorial.

From here, take the M-505 towards (and through) Galapagar and on to Madrid on the A-50 ring road south or the A-6, then A-40 ring road north.

IN THE AREA

Pedraza This tiny walled medieval village has a lovely, if ramshackle, main square, a castle and narrow cobbled streets. It's well worth a wander and is full of evocative restaurants and bars specialising in lamb stew. One of Spain's most beautiful villages.

Segovia The Roman aqueduct is absolutely stunning. It spans the entire city, an incredible work of engineering that stands almost 2,000 years after it was built. According to World Monuments Fund, it is a unique structure. There is more to Segovia, though. The cathedral, built in the 1500s, is a masterpiece of late-Gothic flounce, with flying buttresses and pinnacles galore.

The Alcázar Segovia's crowning glory, the Alcázar is a rebuilt castle that was constructed on the site of a former Roman castle. Its turrets and pinnacles are said to have inspired Walt Disney when he designed the castle for *Cinderella*. Inside, it's got some great exhibits and is even homely in places. A proper castle, with an armoury and big wooden thrones. Marvellous! • www.alcazardesegovia.com

Palacio Real de La Granja de San Ildefonso Philip V spent part of his childhood in France at the court of Louis XIV and so, when he discovered the joy of hunting in the forests of the Sierra de Guadarrama, where the palace now stands, he decided he would recreate it here, and make it his summer residence. The palace is lavish, with fabulous gardens and fountains. The interior houses an incredible museum of huge tapestries and a number of royal suites decorated as they would have been. It's posh and crass and I loved it. A monument to the absolute wealth and vanity of the Spanish crown. • www.patrimonionacional.es/visita/palacio-real-de-la-granja-de-san-ildefonso

Monasterio del Escorial, San Lorenzo de El Escorial The biggest Renaissance building in the world, El Escorial is staggering. Once a monastery, basilica, royal palace, pantheon, library, museum, university, school and hospital, it still retains much of its glory. Kings, queens, princes and princesses of Spain are buried in the Pantheon of the Princes, some as recently as 1992. The basilica is huge and the library is divine, with wooden shelves holding gilded books by the thousand. Another magnificent ode to cash. • www.monasteriodelescorial.com

Sierra de Guadarrama The mountains are the playground for Madrid's everyday people as well as the kings and queens of old. Plenty of walking, biking and great driving.

Madrid As a capital city, Madrid has it all going on. There is so much to see and do that it can all be a bit baffling. So, pick and choose what to see and don't try to do it all – unless you have more than a couple of days.

MUSEO REINA SOFIA: This museum is devoted to modern art. It's vast and full of treasures, including its most famous resident, Picasso's *Guernica*. • **www.museoreinasofia.es**

CENTROCENTRO: A cultural space in the city centre that is home to cafes and exhibition spaces. A great building housing interesting stuff. • **www.centrocentro.org**

MUSEO NACIONAL DEL PRADO: One of the world's greatest art museums with the greatest collection of Spanish art anywhere. It is huge and wonderful and could take you a day or two to get around. • **www.museodelprado.es**

MERCADO DE SAN MIGUEL: An historic market building that survived and is now home to a whole host of gastronomic businesses selling food from all over Spain. Brilliant, lively and delicious. • **www.mercadodesanmiguel.es**

ROYAL PALACE OF MADRID: The official residence of the king and queen of Spain is open to visitors. It is one of the biggest palaces in Europe, if not the world. Another lavish and overwhelming hidey-hole. • **www.patrimonionacional.es/visita/palacio-real-de-madrid**

ROUTE 11

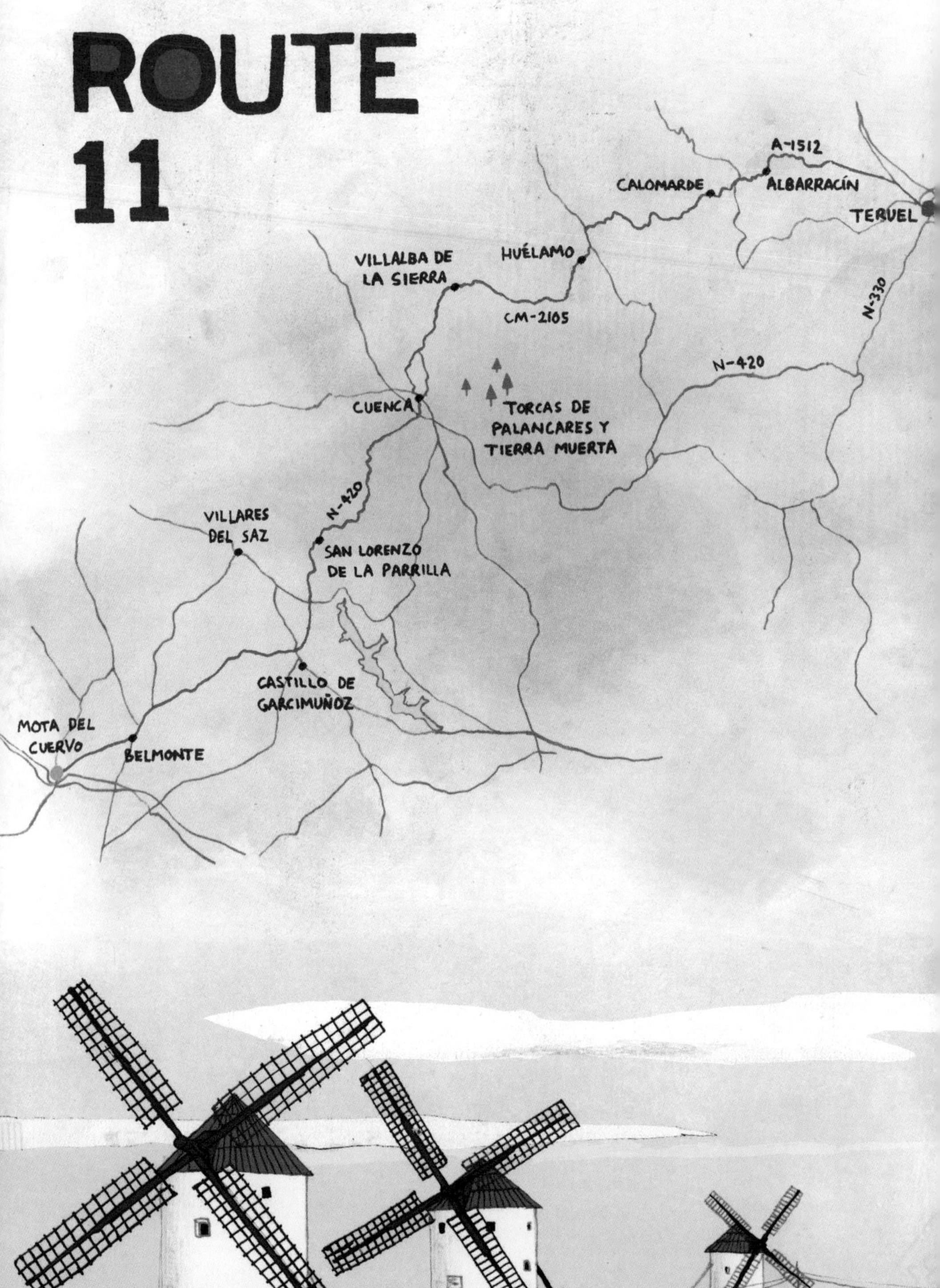
A-1512
CALOMARDE
ALBARRACÍN
TERUEL
VILLALBA DE
LA SIERRA
HUÉLAMO
CM-2105
N-330
N-420
CUENCA
TORCAS DE
PALANCARES Y
TIERRA MUERTA
N-420
VILLARES
DEL SAZ
SAN LORENZO
DE LA PARRILLA
CASTILLO DE
GARCIMUÑOZ
MOTA DEL
CUERVO
BELMONTE

MOTA DEL CUERVO TO TERUEL

THE SECRET MOUNTAINS

The Serranía de Cuenca, with its sinkholes, an enchanted city, a devil's window and gorge of arches, is a real find. It's only about 160km (100 miles) as the crow flies from Madrid, yet it's a world away. This journey, starting out at the Balcony of La Mancha province above Mota del Cuervo begins with windmills overlooking the plain and takes you through the heart of the mountains, over a pass of 1,617m (5,305ft), past the sources of two of Spain's great rivers and then back down to the plain again for the dead straight run into Teruel. A greater contrast would be hard to find!

BEST FOR: Walking, limestone gorges, exploring old cities

START: Mota del Cuervo

END: Teruel

MILEAGE: 363km (225 miles)

ALLOW: 4 days

MAP PAGES: 59, 60, 48

I wake with a start, blinded by the van's interior lights. I get used to the glare quickly to try to work out what's going on. I get a bit of a shock when I see Lizzy is standing over me holding the fly swatter above her head. She, too, has jumped out of bed, woken and angered by the buzzing of an insect in the van, and intent on revenge for whatever lump will appear somewhere on her body in a few hours' time. It's a terrifying sight to see her bearing down on me, about to swat a mosquito that's sitting, apparently, just above my head. It's made all the more confusing because she is stark naked.

Am I dreaming?

When I wake again, after sunrise, it's as if nothing has happened. Lizzy is none the wiser. I guess it was a dream.

I dress and ready the van to fill up with water. We arrived just after dark last night and were so tired we forgot to fill up before settling down. By the

Cañón de los Arcos

time we were ready to go to bed, no one wanted to break camp to fill up. Now we have to do it before we can even fill the kettle.

I step outside the van and look around. We are in a large parking lot, an *aire*, just outside the village of Calomarde, on the A-1704 in the Reserva Nacional de los Montes Universales, an area of mountains that celebrates a way of life that has been lost elsewhere. The mountains are considered common land, which means they are owned, grazed and cultivated by everyone for the benefit of everyone. The landscape is different from that of the Serranía de Cuenca, which we had travelled through last night, crossing the 1,617m (5,305ft)-high Puerto de El Cubillo at last light. There, we had encountered beautiful, replanted forests of Scots pine, while on this side of the pass the landscape is more cultivated but feels older – the result, we read, of continuous community ownership.

There is a low mist in the valley, but I can see that the tops of the mountains that surround us are bathed in orange sunlight. Beyond the mist there is blue sky. It is just a matter of time until it burns off. We are surrounded by fields and trees, the majority of which are poplars in their autumnal hues of glorious yellow. I wander over to the water filling point and notice that it's covered in a thin layer of ice. It's no wonder the mozzie wanted to seek shelter in the van last night. It must have been a stowaway.

As the mist lifts, we ready ourselves for a walk to the Cañón de los Arcos (Gorge of the Arches), a limestone gorge with bridges and walkways. I feel I have to make up for refusing to walk the Caminito del Rey (see page 308) or my half-hearted crawl along part of the way of the Cares Gorge (see page 65) so I am excited and a little nervous to begin.

We walk out of the *aire* and on to the road before turning off beside a couple of houses on a well-worn path between limestone peaks at the entrance to the canyon. It's wide here – around 50m (164ft) and the sun lights up the poplars in divine fiery yellows. Beyond that, the canyon is in shade, with a little mist hanging around. We are the only ones here.

We walk on and follow the shallow river as it meanders between the walls.

We come to a metal bridge that takes us over the river and beyond a section where the walls of the gorge converge, making it otherwise difficult to pass. It brings us to another section and then to another bridge and walkway and then another. The walkways are constructed to pass obstacles – a narrowing of the walls – and they allow us to pass. Where the path is narrow and slippery or high above the water, there are chains to hang on to. One section takes us up a steep overhang and over the top with sheer drops to the bottom of the canyon while another takes us just above water level and through a series of low arches where the river has punched through the limestone. I am reassured by the chains on the higher sections and make my way cautiously along, being careful not to trigger my fear of heights by looking down or up too much.

Eventually the path brings us into a dense forest of pine and then an open valley, where there is a ruined mill and pasture, some of which has been recently ploughed. We sit and eat our snacks overlooking the valley. To our left, above the river, there is dense pine forest. Along the river, a series of huge poplars marks the watercourse with a riotous show of autumnal yellow. On the side of the valley to our right, where the limestone is bare, the vegetation is Mediterranean scrub, with juniper, rosemary and low-growing bushes. The hillside rises quickly from river level.

We stay on the opposite side of the river to that which brought us here and follow a path along the valley bottom to a signpost that shows the way upwards, into the scrub and onwards to the top of a pass between two little peaks. We get to the top and then drop down into the gorge on its southern, sunnier side. We are out in the open and the gorge is wider here and the sides are steeply sloping as they lead down to the river. It's not an easy path as it follows the layers of limestone, dropping and climbing periodically from one layer to the next. Some bits require scrambling as we edge closer to what I know is coming: a section that sits high above the steeper, more vertical parts of the gorge we had just walked through. I can see it in front of me as it rounds the corner and disappears out of sight. I can also see a set of steep steps that bypass the tricky section and head back down to river level. As I become more and more anxious about the drop, I use the fact of the steps as my mental escape route if it gets too vertiginous for me.

Sure enough, when I get to the edge and look around the corner and down to the river some 30m (98ft) below, I get the wobbly legs and dizzy head that accompany me to cliff edges. I feel the panic rise and I know what to do, but I don't want to. I walk around the corner and push myself to look

at the drop. I can see that the path follows a ledge of limestone around a bend and above the drop for about 100m (109 yards) or so then disappears around another corner. There are no handrails or chains. I turn around and take the escape route, hating myself for doing so. I have wanted to conquer my fears for so long and wanted to push myself, but when it comes down to it I just can't. Lizzy follows me, reluctantly, down the slippery, crumbling steps to river level. I apologise.

We walk back along the gorge and soon come to a path that crosses the river and heads upwards. We figure it must be the end of the section we have just bypassed so I walk up it to see. It climbs sharply and then makes an acute turn around a little side valley before opening out on the sloping side of the gorge. At the other end, about 100m (109 yards) away, I can see the spot where I had bailed. I can also see that all I had to do was grit my teeth and walk and I would have completed the circuit. Lizzy looks at me like I have just had her dog put down. I apologise profusely for the next few hours, hating myself for being such a ... well you make up your mind on that one.

If you make it to the gorge, let me know how you get on.

Lago de Uña

THE DRIVING

This route begins at Mota del Cuervo, a town that sits below a ridge on the plains to the south-east of Madrid. It's easily accessible because it's on the AP-36 *autovía* that starts out from Madrid and leads to Murcia (on the A-30) and Valencia (on the A-3). The N-420 crosses the motorway and skirts the town to the south, heading north-east on to the plain. After a couple of miles, where there is a slight rise, there is a small turn-off to the left, where you can visit the windmills. This will give you some great views over the town and the plain. Continuing on the N-420 will take you on some long, straight stretches through a vast, open landscape of rough grassland, arable, almond groves, vineyards and patches of pines. You'll pass through Belmonte (castle, bullring and windmills) and then through La Almarcha, after which it starts to get a little more interesting, with low hills and holm oaks in Mediterranean scrub. It is getting hillier all the time.

After San Lorenzo de la Parrilla, you reach the Río Júcar and begin to follow it as it winds its way towards Cuenca through narrow gorge sections and out into wider sections, back out on to the rolling plain. You'll drop down towards Cuenca, meeting the N-320 at the first roundabout outside the city. Follow the N-400 and then the N-320A into the city, where you will pick up the CM-2105 to take you away to the north up the Río Júcar gorge. We stayed below the city in the *aire* at the underground car park on the CM-2104.

The CM-2105 will take you along the river – a beautiful valley with steep sides – until it widens out on to the plain again. Stay on the CM-2105 at the junction with the CM-2104 and then veer right at the junction with the CM-210, staying on the CM-2105. This will lead you through the plain and then up a steep escarpment with a couple of hairpins to the Ventano del Diablo, a cave and viewpoint all in one with fabulous views up the gorge. From here, you are in the Serranía de Cuenca, winding through mature pine forest. There is a right on to the CM-2104 signed for the Ciudad Encantada after a few miles. Turn here and follow signs to the Ciudad for about 6km (3.7 miles).

Returning to the CM-2105, follow the road towards Uña. This will take you through more of the same mountainous, pine-forested landscape, with the occasional limestone escarpments rising vertically from the valley floors. It's a great road that's safe but not without its moments of bendiness and grind. Enjoy it! You'll pass through the tiny but lovely village of Uña (it's worth a stop at the *mirador* to view the lake and valley on the left of the road just outside the town) and then on to the Embalse de la Toba, where the road winds around it, giving stunning views. You'll wend your way through the forested mountains until you come to a wide valley with fields surrounded by mountains and the junction with the CM-2106. Turn left. After a mile or so, the CM-2119 heads up the mountain to the right, but you can continue on to find the source of the Río Cuervo, where there is a beautiful waterfall and all the associated tourist bluster, including a couple of bars and restaurants. There are a lot of waterfalls and walking routes here in this beautiful valley, which is the watershed for the Tajo, the Cuervo and the Júcar rivers.

Back to the CM-2119. This is an absolutely fantastic stretch of road that follows the rocky edge of a steep, deep valley and will take you sharply up to the Puerto del Cubillo at 1,617m (5,305ft) above sea level and into the Department of Aragón. Once at the *puerto* (pass), the landscape changes as you enter an area that is famous for being 'commons' and belongs to the community. Here, there are small meadows and fields between the forests and pines. It is known as the Reserva Nacional de Montes Universales. Once over the pass and down into the next, wide valley, you meet the A-1704 at a monument to the national park. A left turn will take you to another *puerto*, at 1,790m (5,873ft), if you want to explore more of the mountains.

Turn right to continue, on to the A-1704 towards Teruel and Albarracín. A couple of miles after the turn you will pass the source of the Río Tajo, the Tagus, which empties into the sea at Lisbon. There is a monument. A little further along, there is a huge sinkhole that's marked – one of many in this region.

The A-1704 will bring you to Calomarde and the Ruta del Barranco de la Hoz, the gorge with the walkways. There is a fabulous *aire* here in the valley, just about 100m (109 yards) from the start of the gorge.

Continue on the A-1704 to a T-junction, where you will need to take the left turn on to the A-1703 towards Teruel. A few miles later, you'll arrive at another T-junction, where the A-1703 meets the A-1512. Turn sharp right towards Albarracín and Teruel. After 6km (3.7 miles), you'll enter Albarracín via a beautiful, wooded and narrow gorge, another remarkable place, with a huge castle on the hill above and a beautiful medieval centre with narrow, winding streets and lots of tourists. From here, the road begins to widen out and you leave the mountains behind as you re-join the plains on the long, very straight road into Teruel.

IN THE AREA

Windmills, Mota del Cuervo Seven windmills sit on the balcony above Mota del Cuervo to remind us of the apparitions of Don Quixote de La Mancha. Three of them can be visited. One is a visitor centre, the other two are occupied by artists. Great views.

Cuenca A fabulous medieval city that sits above two gorges. First inhabited by the Moors from 714, it has changed hands a few times over the years. It has a 12th-century cathedral and a few 'hanging houses' with wooden balconies that overhang the gorge. They were once very common, but few are left now. They are a popular draw.

Museo Paleontológico de Cuenca, Cuenca A really great museum with truly immersive exhibits. Lots of life-size models, fossilised bones and interpretation in a brilliant, modern building with amazing views of the old city. • **https://mupaclm.es**

Antonio Pérez Foundation Museum, Cuenca A 22-roomed contemporary art museum set in a medieval building in the old city of Cuenca that contains some real treasures from Spanish artists and also some international work from Warhol. Antonio Pérez was famous for collecting 'found objects' and there is a fascinating collection here. • **https://fundacionantonioperez.com**

Ventano del Diablo, Cuenca A viewpoint on the CM-2105. It's like a limestone cave with arches and two openings that give fantastic views over the Río Júcar gorge.

La Ciudad Encantada, Cuenca This is an area of limestone that has been eroded by millions of years of water to create odd shapes. Pay at the entrance and then follow the walk around the 'enchanted city' to find, perhaps predictably, formations named after the thing they sort of look a bit like. Even so, it's a great walk and well worth it. Some lovely geology going on.
• www.ciudadencantada.es

Barranco de la Hoz (Pasarelas de Calomarde) This is a lovely gorge with steep sides and a walkway that enables you to walk the whole length of the otherwise impassable gorge. It's a great walk that can be extended by continuing up the valley when it opens out. Some drops.

Albarracín A fabulous walled medieval town with more 'hanging houses' that sits atop a steep gorge and was once the capital city of a Moorish kingdom. Great wanderings and lovely narrow streets made of golden red sandstone. Amazing sunsets!

WHERE TO STAY: CAMPING

Camping Caravaning Cuenca, Cuenca
Ctra. Cuenca-Tragacete, km 8, 16147 Cuenca, Spain
Web: www.campingcuenca.com
Tel: +34 674 29 88 68

A huge campsite a few miles north of the city on the CM-2105.

WHERE TO STAY: *AIRES*

Cuenca: There are two *aires* in or near the city. The first is at the *playa fluvial* on the river at the gorge. The second is in the city on the above-ground section of an underground car park. Get a ticket from the barrier and pay on departure.
Calomarde: A really lovely large *aire* on the edge of the village. Scan the QR code, register and pay online for 24 hours. Cheap at €6 at the time of writing.

ROUTE 12

PYRÉNÉES
PAMPLONA
A-21
YESA
CANDANCHÚ
FORMIGAL
JACA
PUENTE LA REINA DE JACA
PARQUE NACIONAL DE ORDESA Y MONTE PERDIDO
FISCAL
AINSA
HUESCA
CAMPO
GRAUS
VIELHA
PARC NACIONAL D'AIGÜESTORTES I ESTANY DE SANT MAURICI
PORT AINÉ
SORT
BELLVER DE CERDANYA
BERGA

ROUTE 12

PAMPLONA TO RIPOLL

ACROSS THE PYRENEES

The Pyrenees are the great borderline between France and Spain. With peaks over 3,000m (9,843ft) and passes scraping the sky at over 2,000m (6,562ft) there's no easy, direct way to cross from the Atlantic to the Mediterranean through the mountains themselves. But it can be done. And there are a bunch of ski resorts to visit along the way, if you choose to do it in the winter. We packed our snowboards and took ourselves on a piste-seeking adventure in early spring. We found hidden valleys, high passes and fresh powder – all we could ask from a trans-Pyrenean epic.

BEST FOR: Snowboarding, skiing (winter), walking, biking (summer)

START: Pamplona

END: Ripoll

MILEAGE: 700km (435 miles)

ALLOW: 1–2 weeks

MAP PAGES: 20, 21, 22, 23, 24

It is what I believe skiers call a bluebird day. Last night was cold and it snowed a little. Yet this morning the sky is radiant blue and the wind has dropped to almost nothing. There is a chill in the air, but the day is absolutely, stunningly beautiful. There isn't a cloud in the sky and the snowboarding is good. It's mid-week, too, which means the slopes are quiet and the early-morning pistes are still groomed to perfection, with a dusting of fresh snow on top. The piste-bashers, those scary, Mad Max machines who tend the slopes when the lifts stop, have done a good job.

And yet, here I am, stuck in mid-air looking down on it all. I'm alone on a four-man chairlift because Lizzy has decided to stay at a lower altitude and also because no one wanted to share the chairlift with me (and why would they?), and the chairlift has stopped. It means someone has had a problem either getting on or off the lift and the operator has had to take emergency action. It happens, but leaves those of us in transit dangling over snowy drops. It doesn't help my state of mind, this dangling, partly because I'm never mad about heights but also because I am on the chairlift to make an effort to take my snowboarding up a level. After a few days of going green and finding my feet, I am going blue and it's a worry. I am entering an unknown world.

Lizzy and I are at Formigal, a smart ski resort just below the Col du Pourtalet, a high pass that links France and Spain at 1,794m (5,886ft) above sea level. We have been exploring the Pyrenees with a view to crossing from the Atlantic to the Med via some of Spain's ski resorts. So far, we've cut our teeth at Candanchú, spending a couple of days in a blizzard camped in the resort's parking lot (better than it sounds) and having lessons to get ourselves reacquainted with our latest sporting discovery. We have yet to need our snow chains or look into the kind of alpine abysses that I fear most. The journey has been excellent so far – we've driven up two lovely valleys, marvelled at snow-capped peaks and looked down on blue reservoirs – and it's only been marred by a minor problem with our electrics. This meant an unscheduled stopover and finding a local specialist to sort it for us, but all is good now.

As I swing gently in the air, I think about all these things. I also think about what is to come on the journey. We have yet to drive the terrifying road to Port Ainé ski station, a tiny road that climbs 1,000m (3,281ft) in 15km (9.3 miles). We haven't yet descended it in a snowstorm. We have yet

to cross the 2,000m (6,562ft) Port de la Bonaigua in another whiteout or encounter the amazing gorge at the Congosto de Ventamillo. And we've not travelled on the rack and pinion railway to the hidden, and otherwise inaccessible, Vall de Núria. All those pleasures are to come, and, of course, to be savoured. So why worry?

I feel the sun on my face and the breeze dry my lips a little. The sweat on the inside of my goggles cools as I sit there. It brings me right back down to earth, so to speak, and I remove myself from my inner world – where fear dwells – and I look around. Below me in the snow I can see the tracks of two cats weaving between the young trees. The footprints are clear and fresh and I assume they are those of a lynx as they are bigger than those of a domestic cat and definitely not those of a dog.

I look around at the mountains and at the blue sky and I decide, there and then, that this moment is something to savour, not to be afraid of.

In front of me, the cables of the chairlift ascend the mountainside steeply. Below me, there is snow. To my right, somewhere up the white valley, lies France. To my left and behind me, lies the village of Formigal. Above Formigal, there is a huge rocky crag piercing the blue. I am surrounded by beautiful, rocky mountains, snow-capped and glinting in the sun. Somewhere below me, Lizzy is practising her turns so that she'll be able to join me on the lifts and we can surf the mountain together.

I thank my lucky stars that I made it this far and take it all in, making a note to myself to remember it and to write it all down in this book. I love being here in the mountains, conquering fears, pushing my own limits, exploring new places, travelling with Lizzy and living my dreams and I sincerely hope that it inspires you to do the same, no matter your age, gender, capabilities or ambitions.

The journey here was fraught with difficulties, which makes being here all the sweeter, stuck on this lift, on this blue-sky day. We were postponed a year and a half by Covid, then halted by Macron's ban on UK travellers. We planned and packed, prepared kit and I worried. I fretted about driving mountain roads, about remembering how to snowboard, driving in snow, fitting chains to the van and being prepared in general. But here, soaring like a bird in the blue sky above the slopes, I realise it is all worth it, if only for this moment of quiet and reflection. I get to stop, for a moment, and breathe it all in. I get to fill my chest with clean, cold air, as if it's the first one after swimming underwater. It is glorious and refreshing, full of joy and promise, love and light.

The lift begins again. But the spell refuses to be broken. As my chairlift-for-one edges up the cable, I'm still in awe of where I am. Until, of course, I face my next challenge, and then look to the one after. I pull the safety bar over my head as the chair approaches the end of the lift and pull my board straight under my feet for the push-off. I slide away from the chair and on to the soft white snow of the upper station. I walk over to the run I am looking for – El Rio – and look at it. I can barely see over the edge. The slope is much, much steeper than I expected and it drops away from me sharply at

what looks like at least 45 degrees. Skiers drop into it as if they are dropping into a half pipe. I sit down. Think about what I have learned, clip into my bindings and go for it anyway.

This is what it's all about.

I think about this moment a few days later when Lizzy and I find ourselves in Port Ainé. We know that perhaps this day will be our last one spent snowboarding, so we jump on the lift and head up the mountain. Lizzy has progressed to the stage where she's linking turns and has got over her fear of lifts. It's a good day to do it. While there's no blue sky here, there is amazing snow. It's been snowing all morning and the wind is whipping around us as we climb ever higher in the lift. When we got here, the slopes were crowded and car parks full, but today, as it's Monday, there are very few other people skiing. Ski school instructors are having a day off in great conditions and we are the only ones using the lift. It's incredible.

The soft powder gives us confidence as we set off down the green run. I'm a little faster than Lizzy but wait for her after doing a few turns so that we can make it down the mountain together. It's all I ever wanted from a ski trip and I am so happy to be able to share the experience, from the stinging of the snow on my cheeks to the cooling sweat inside my goggles and the hairpins and mountain views. I feel sad when the last run ends and it's time to go before we get snowed in.

But now we know it's possible, I know we'll be back.

I hope you'll get here, too.

THE DRIVING

This adventure is epic. Take your time and enjoy it. Between Pamplona and Ripoll there are plenty of adventures to be had in the snow and off it. We went with snowboards looking for a few slides on easy green pistes, but there's no reason you couldn't do it for the walking or the biking, too. Or just to enjoy the incredible feeling of being in the mountains and looking over the edge at the world below.

There is, of course, a lot more to the Pyrenees than we were able to see. However, we planned this route to take in as many of Spain's ski resorts as we could. This meant taking offshoots up valleys that are not joined up by passes but often lead to routes into France.

Pamplona to Sabiñánigo

Leave Pamplona on the A-21 *autovía* (motorway) towards Jaca. It's the quick way to get into the mountains, but there is an alternative if you really want to dawdle. The A-21 runs alongside the old road, the N-240 for a lot of the way, apart from the odd place where the *autovía* is not yet finished and

you end up on it anyway. We came off at junction 47 and followed the old road around the remarkable reservoir Embalse de Yesa. Here, the road twists and turns around the grey shale landscape that often looks lunar where the waters have receded. The steep slopes are covered in all kinds of firs, juniper and birch. Once you reach Jaca, take the N-330 towards France and Candanchú. It's a main route into France but is no less beautiful despite being quick and reasonably busy. Once you pass the entrance to the Túnel de Somport (this is the quick way to France), the road continues up beyond the trees and takes a few sharp turns before delivering you at the small but pretty ski station at Candanchú (1,650m/5,413ft). If you need an unchallenging drive to get you in the mood for what comes later, this will do nicely.

Unfortunately, it's not possible to skip to the next valley so, to continue, head back down the valley on the N-330 and take the A-23 towards

staying and skiing at Candanchú

The parking lot at Candanchú is huge and sloping, so if you intend to stay over (we did for two nights) then you'll need chocks. There is no issue with parking overnight and lots of vans were doing it. There's not a lot there other than a couple of bars and restaurants, but it's got a nice vibe as a resort.

Ski passes were cheap (around €48). We had a private two-hour lesson (€80) to get us in the mood with an English-speaking instructor.

Sabiñánigo, then follow the A-136 towards Formigal along the Valle de Tena and the Col du Pourtalet. You'll head up the wide, pretty valley and rise up away from the floor to look down on the reservoir at Búbal and then the smaller but no less lovely reservoir of Lanuza. The road continues up, weaving around until you reach Formigal. For skiing, take the left at the roundabout and for the town, turn right.

From Formigal, it's only a few kilometres up the valley to the Col du Pourtalet, a high pass to France (1,794m/5,886ft) and it's worth it for the amazing views looking back down the valley as you return to Spain. With snow on the peaks and the village sitting on a ridge below dark crags, it's got a lot of atmosphere.

To continue onwards, it is necessary to head back down the wide valley to Sabiñánigo, where there is a good *aire* (€4 for 48 hours, including electricity), unless you intend to visit the Valle de Ordesa, the Pyrenees' most visited valley and one of Europe's first protected places.

Staying and skiing at Formigal

There is no *aire* at Formigal and motorhomes are not allowed to stay on the ski station lots. However, we parked up on the outskirts of the town, along with others, on the Calle Sallent opposite the town's main car park. There were no issues but beware anyway. Ski passes are around €50 for a full day's skiing. There are lots of green routes, easy lifts and magic carpets for beginners.

Sabiñánigo to Sort

From Sabiñánigo, take the N-260 towards Aínsa. This road is relatively unremarkable but gets better as it gets closer to Aínsa. The views improve after the tunnel at Fiscal, with a deep and narrow gorge on the Río Ara making for some curvy and quite lovely driving before Aínsa. At Boltaña, the valley opens out again with the river running wide and shallow towards Aínsa and the Embalse de Mediano. At Aínsa, cross over the river and follow the A-138 along the western shore of the reservoir. The landscape here is remarkable, with steep, water-worn shale gullies and creeks carrying rivulets towards the reservoir. It's another fast road that whizzes past creamy coloured hilltop villages and terraces of almond trees. At the bottom of the lake, take a left turn on to the A-2211. This will wiggle you beneath the dam and then take you up and into the hills in a curving, sweeping set of bends with just a few old concrete blocks on the road's margins between you and the fields below. Here, you'll find lots of pine and oak, but also terraces of almond and olive.

At the junction with the A-123a, follow signs for Campo and into more groves full

of gnarled, ancient almond and olive trees. Going higher, the vegetation changes to gorse, heather, pines, holm oaks and juniper, feeling more and more Mediterranean. Eventually, you'll reach the N-260 again. Turn right and follow the road into Campo.

After Campo, things get interesting as the road heads into a narrow gorge (Congosto de Ventamillo), where the road winds away around the cliff face. It's narrow and difficult and makes great driving but opens out before El Run and deposits you nicely in a wide valley with peaks either side. At Castejón de Sos, turn right at the roundabout (staying on the N-260) and follow the road as it heads uphill again to Coll de Fadas (1,470m/4,823ft)

Staying and skiing at Baqueira

There is a camper van park on an industrial estate just outside Vielha. Nice people and easy to book – just email. **www.valdarancamperpark.com**

There is a lovely campsite, Camping Era Yerla d'Arties, situated in the beautiful village of Salardú and right next to the river. **www.campingarties erayerla.com**

Otherwise, motorhomes are tolerated in the main car park of the resort, although there are no facilities.

The skiing is excellent in Baqueira, with telecabins taking you up from the village to a plateau where there are lots of green runs and magic carpets, plus chairlifts to lovely green runs. However, it is expensive: we paid €150 for two one-day ski passes. Buy online at **www.baqueira.es**

through woods and past meadows. You'll then reach another *coll* at Coll de Espina, which is slightly lower at 1,407m (4,616ft).

After this, you'll enjoy a weaving, bobbing, curving descent with great views as the road leads you down into the Val del Noguera Ribagorçana and the border with Catalonia. Here, you'll join the N-230 (turn left to go north), another good road that will lead you through deciduous woodland of poplar, willow and birch along the river and (if you were to carry on) to France. It heads uphill, gently at first and then starts to climb a little more steeply after a place called Bono, then enters a series of tunnels, past a lake (Embalse de Senet) and then into a 4km (2.5 mile)-long tunnel that descends. After the tunnel, the road continues to descend into Vielha, a beautiful town sitting in a crucible, surrounded by peaks. In Vielha, take the C-28 up the valley towards Sort and Baqueira-Beret, Spain's biggest and poshest ski resort.

After Baqueira, the road takes a rather exciting turn as you head up steeply to the Port de la Bonaigua in a series of sharp hairpins to 2,072m (6,798ft). It's an exposed, wild pass with a ski station at the top. When we passed, it was snowing heavily with deep banks of snow on either side of the road. After the pass, the road heads sharply downhill in a series of gentler, sweeping hairpins until you reach the treeline and the bottom of the valley. Here, you'll join the river valley of La Noguera Pallaresa, a wide valley surrounded by peaks, and the road will change to the C-13. Before you get to Rialp there is a left turn to Port Ainé, a small but amazing ski resort up a 15km (9.3 mile)-long mountain road. It's steep and narrow, with incredible, vertigo-inducing views when the trees allow you to see beyond the road's fringes.

After Rialp, continue to Sort on the C-13.

Skiing and staying at Port Ainé

Port Ainé is a tiny resort with a hotel and restaurant and a great selection of green runs. It's high (2,000m/6,562ft) so has great snow and lots of opportunities for going off-piste. We camped in the car park and it was no problem. There is an area devoted to motorhome parking and overnight parking is tolerated. Ski passes were the cheapest at around €25 for a debutante day pass with insurance.

There is also an *aire* at Rialp.

Sort to Ribes (Ripoll)

At Sort, follow signs for La Seu d'Urgell and the N-260. This will lead you steeply out of town to another pass on a series of gentle hairpins with views over Torreta de l'Orri (the back side of Port Ainé) to the Coll del Canto (1,725m/5,660ft) and down the other side. There are great views all along this section as you weave through wooded slopes with the occasional pasture. Finally, you come down into a wide, beautiful valley and a roundabout in the valley floor. Here, continue on the N-260 towards La Seu D'Urgell and beyond on the N-260. You'll drive through a wide valley with the Serra del Cadí to the south and Andorra to the north.

You can follow the N-260 north to Puigcerd or take the C-16 to the south if you intend to go to the ski resort at La Molina. Either way, if you go to La Molina (a busy, popular resort at around 2,445m/8,022ft) or stay on the N-260 you'll end up at the Collada de Toses, a pass among beautiful peaks of 1,800m (5,906ft). The drive down, although torturous, is brilliant, with incredible views, sharp bends and lots and lots of wiggly driving along steep-sided slopes, through forests of fir, with lots of vertigo-inducing drops. Lovely stuff, although I tend to over-grab the wheel.

At Ripoll, follow the N-260 through the volcano region and then on to the A-26 for Figueres and the coast. You'll miss the mountains almost immediately, but don't worry, there's plenty of hairpins left, especially on the Cap de Creus.

WHERE TO STAY: CAMPING

There are a lot of campsites and *aires* in this part of Spain. Many of the campsites were closed for the winter when we visited so choices were limited. However, we stayed at the following:

Camping Boltaña, Boltaña
N-260, km 442, 22340 Boltaña, Huesca, Spain
Web: www.campingboltana.com/en
Tel: +34 974 50 23 47

This campsite at Boltaña, just a short drive from the town, is a real gem with lovely staff. Great for families. Good showers and adjacent to one of the mountain biking routes.

Camping Era Yerla d'Arties, Salardú
Ctra. C-28 Vielha to Baqueira, 25599 Arties, Lleida, Spain
Web: www.campingartieserayerla.com
Tel: +34 973 64 16 02

Situated in the beautiful village of Salardú, a couple of kilometres from Baqueria and right next to the river.

WHERE TO STAY: *AIRES*

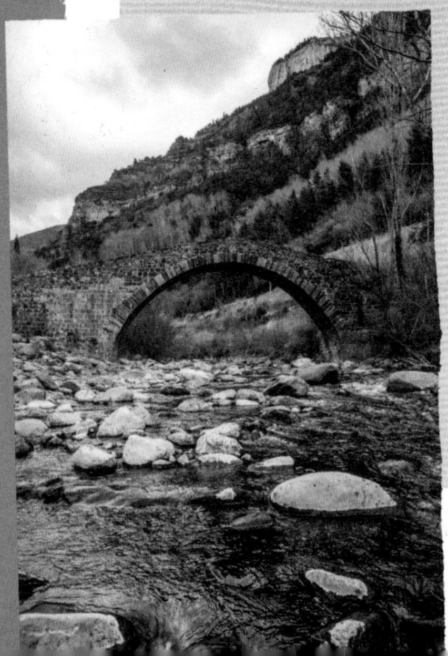

Sabiñánigo: Great *aire* on the edge of the town, run by the municipality. €4 for 48 hours.
Rialp: A free *aire* by the side of the river with water and chemical toilet disposal.
La Seu d'Urguell: Adjacent to the mediaeval city and free, with an easy walk into a beautiful colonnaded old quarter. Also here is the Olympic Park, site of the 1992 Barcelona Olympics, for kayaking and rowing.
Besalú: A free *aire* adjacent to a very impressive medieval bridge and village.

IN THE AREA

Walking in national parks The Ordesa National Park was Spain's first protected landscape and is often quoted as being a highlight of the Spanish Pyrenees. Hiking in the park is spectacular and popular. • **www.turismodearagon.com/en/ficha/ordesa-y-monte-perdido**

Vall de Núria by rack-and-pinion railway This was a serious highlight of our trip. The Vall de Núria is a secret valley that is only reachable on foot or by train. At the top is a hotel and lake, plus skiing and ski lifts. Amazing scenery and a railway that rises more than 1,000m (3,280ft) in just 12.5km (7.8 miles). • **www.valldenuria.cat**

Mountain biking in Aínsa Zona Zero is an impressive project with a great zero-impact philosophy based around Aínsa that provides routes and services for bike riders of all kinds. We tried out a blue route that took in Boltaña and Aínsa. It took us up some impressive (and very difficult) climbs with some epic sections of downhill. Pick up the route at Camping Boltaña. • **www.zonazeropirineos.com**

Whitewater rafting, Sort The Noguera Pallaresa river is famous for rafting. Find companies in Sort. • **www.reservesaiguadicciorialp.com**

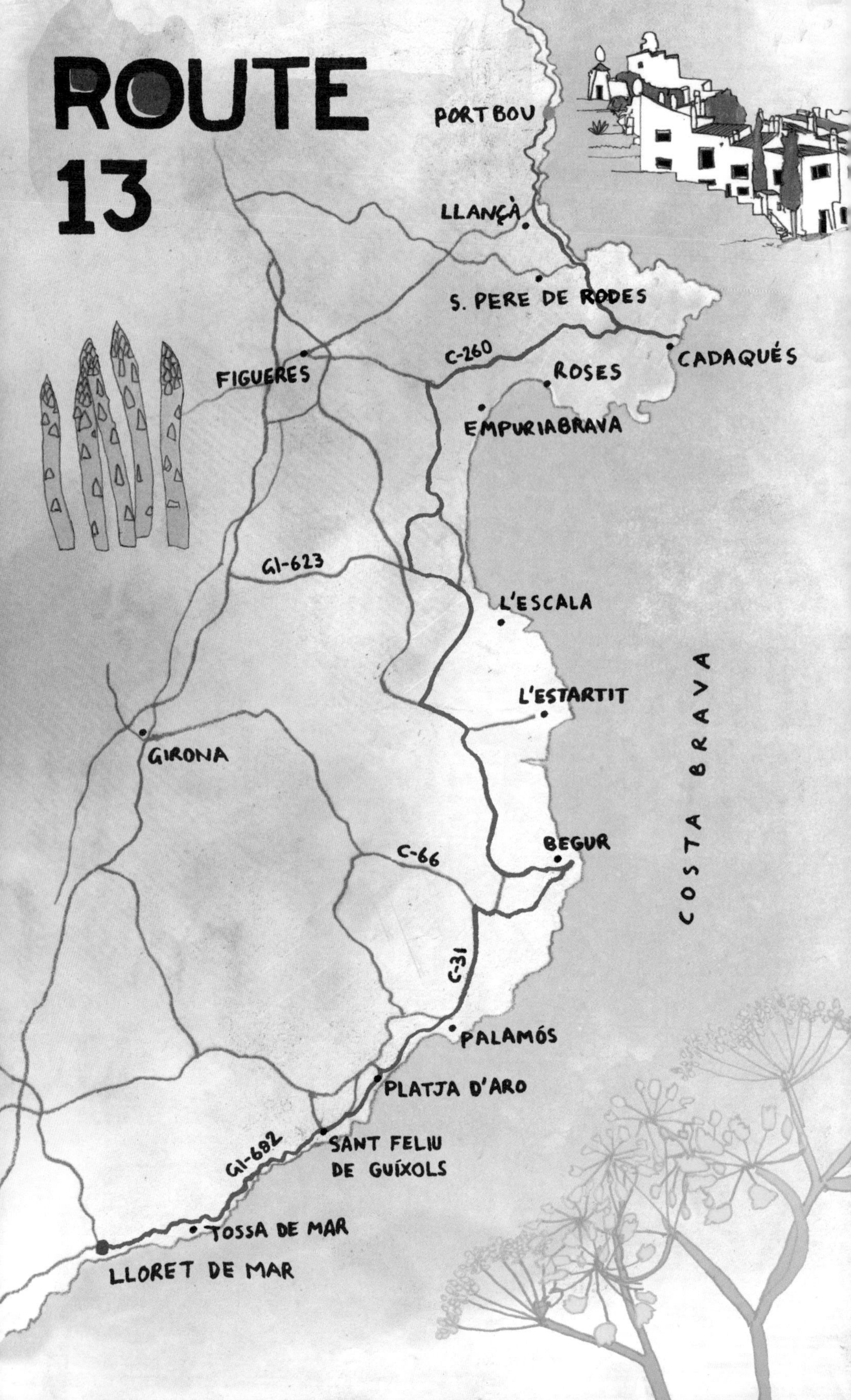
ROUTE 13
PORTBOU
LLANÇÀ
S. PERE DE RODES
CADAQUÉS
C-260
FIGUERES
ROSES
EMPURIABRAVA
GI-623
L'ESCALA
L'ESTARTIT
COSTA BRAVA
GIRONA
BEGUR
C-66
C-31
PALAMÓS
PLATJA D'ARO
GI-682
SANT FELIU
DE GUÍXOLS
TOSSA DE MAR
LLORET DE MAR

ROUTE 13

PORTBOU TO LLORET DE MAR

THE MASTER OF DECEPTION

This route follows the Costa Brava from the French border to Lloret de Mar at the end of a winding, spectacular drive. It takes in the Dalí triangle – Figueres, Portlligat and Púbol – and treats you to a chance to explore the wonderful weirdness, and breathtaking talent, that was Salvador Dalí. It's a surreal route that isn't always what you think it will be. But make no mistake, the artistry is there for you to find, if you look hard enough.

BEST FOR: Spectacular coastal driving, swimming

START: Portbou

END: Lloret de Mar

MILEAGE: 175km (108 miles)

ALLOW: 4–5 days

MAP PAGES: 25, 39

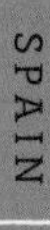

We wake up at the beachside campsite at El Port de la Selva. It's only been open for a few days and there is a flurry of activity. Owners of seasonal pitches are readying their caravans for the summer ahead after what must have been a harsh winter or a lot of time away. Like many Spanish campsites, it has a lot of pitches permanently occupied. After a winter of neglect, there are areas that look more like a camping jumble sale than a campsite, with kayaks, awnings, broken picket fences and all sorts of summer trappings lying about. On a sunny day, I'll bet it looks just like any other campsite, but today, our fourth day on the Costa Brava and our fourth day of rain, it just looks a mess. Still, the owners are working hard to make it better, so we remain positive and optimistic that all will be as expected. The campsite, we can't deny, is in a fantastic position right next to a small pebble beach at the northern foot of the Cap de Creus, a 'Parc Natural' reserve.

We rise early and get into some Lycra for a run along the footpath that runs around the coast. I find it hard to be enthusiastic about running under any circumstances but find it harder today. I'm fed up with rain. I feel like we've caught the Costa Brava with its pants down. It's as if, when you aren't looking, this area of mass tourism and sunshine puts on a glum face of mist and rain. As it's not the summer season yet (it's late March) it can't be bothered to be the someone else it has to be for the rest of the year. It's not what you think it is. It's wild, rugged, sour-faced and beautiful and that's the way it likes it.

We run, and despite the persistent rain, I notice small things in the landscape that make me stop and stare: the way the mist hangs on the hills above the beach; the terraces cut into the hillsides and the severely pollarded limes reaching out to each other across the campsite's pitches. I see the bright green needles of the umbrella pines and the tall Mediterranean cypress searching the sky. At ground level, I see prickly pears and purple mallow growing out of low cream-coloured stonework. On the open scrub, there are bright yellow gazania and pink stocks growing in clumps. French lavender, dark and mysterious, sprouts occasionally.

We run to the lighthouse at S'Arenella and shelter from the rain under its eaves. Despite the gloom, there is colour everywhere, from the pale greens of the cactus to the deep purple of the lavender and the bright pinks

of the mallows. The coast, while seemingly rough and tough, brutal and inhospitable, hides tiny coves and ways down to the sea that you'd easily jog past. There's a gentleness to it that's wonderful. You might spike yourself on a prickly pear, but spend enough time here and you'll find a shady cove or a finger of rock to fish from, a bay to snorkel in or a beach to laze on. Just be patient.

After our run, we swim, quickly, in the bay. The water is cold and dreary-looking but not as bad as I think it will be and I stay in longer than I expected. Lizzy stays in even longer.

I feel the same about Salvador Dalí's house at Portlligat when we finally get there. It's a masterpiece of deception, as you'd expect from the grand master of surrealism. Nothing is what it seems. The house, added to over the years, has a labyrinthine quality that draws you in and then entrances you with its wit and humour. There are areas for sitting and sleeping, a mirror reveals a view that would be otherwise unseeable, a narrow corridor leads to a bright

white garden, the long pool takes you to an outside seating area. It's surprisingly understated – unlike the clearly bonkers Salvador Dalí Theatre-Museum at Figueres – and shows that the Dalí you think you know may not be the real Dalí at all. What is truly remarkable is that Dalí left the house as it was following the death of his wife Gala, and never returned. It is as it was, untouched and unchanged by the years since, a testament to their love.

The drive to Portlligat is stunning and we love it. The road curls its way around the steep-sided valleys of the Cap de Creus offering views of vineyards in the valley bottoms and glimpses of waterfalls you can't quite get to. Here, we find more terraces and umbrella pines. When we stop, Lizzy is intrigued by the variety of plant life: there are Mediterranean herbs – thyme and rosemary – as well as olives, cork oaks, cistus, tree heather, euphorbias, broom, fennel and wild asparagus. It's a riot of greens with dots of colour exploding quietly, in its own time, of course, if you care to look.

The drive up to Portbou is similarly surreal. Here, the Pyrenees gasp their last before dropping steeply into the sea and the road complies by snaking around the hillsides in sharp hairpins on heart-stopping inclines. Below us, the towns, crammed into tight valleys, look like toytowns hemmed in by cartoon hills. We stop at the French border and make our way slowly back to Portbou, over the humps of the Cap de Creus to Roses on another twisting and turning mountain road before dropping down into the coastal plain and back roads that are straight and wide.

Later, when we drive the stretch between Sant Feliu and Lloret de Mar, we feel it all over again. It couldn't be more different from the Golf de Roses and its wide, long sandy beach: there are hidden coves between the deep gullies, pathways through the rock and pine, and fine villas sitting atop the precipices. The views from the road are breathtaking. It's harsh and gentle all at the same time: a coast of great beauty and softness. I find it deceptive. It reminds me of the peninsulas of Scotland, of Cape Cornwall, of the Côte d'Azur and yet it's unmistakeably Catalan because it's wild and free and refuses to be categorised the way I'd like it to be.

Because we are here just as the season starts, we are seeing it the way millions of others don't. It doesn't make it any clearer, rather it reveals the depth of its complexity: this place isn't what you think it might be. And yet it's everything and more.

As if the master – painter, artist, whatever – upped and left without looking back.

THE DRIVING

We began this journey in Figueres, at the Dalí Theatre-Museum. We took the C-260 out of the town heading west for the coast at Llançà. It's long and straight for a lot of it, but it does start to get interesting as you approach the Castell de Quermançó, where the plain gives way to the high land of the Cap de Creus and the dry Mediterranean scrub that covers the rounded sand and rock hillsides in the rich green of holm oaks, umbrella pines and olives. Approaching Llançà, the road skirts the southern edge of the upland before landing you at the coast.

From here, we continued on the N-260 to the French border beyond Portbou. The road follows the easier and flatter built-up coast for a few miles then starts to get more interesting again, following the contours around several small bays until Platja de Garbet, when it rises into the pines and goes all curvy on you, taking off into the hills and then descending quickly for stops at Colera and then Portbou. After Portbou, the road takes a couple of sharp hairpins upwards and inland to meet the border, clinging to the steep hillsides covered in gorse, broom, cistus, French lavender, rosemary, thyme and fennel. These slopes mark the dying heights of the mountains that have been the Pyrenees further inland. Views, as you'd expect, are wonderful.

Heading back the way you came, follow the N-260 again to Llançà and then take a left turn at the lights towards El Port de la Selva. This is the GI-612, a sprightly little road that weaves between the villas and the pines – with a few nice stops to take in the sea air – all the way to Selva and the long, flat beach. Take a right in the village before you get to the port. However, if you want to get out and explore, note that here, as with many places on the Costa Brava, you will need to make sure you aren't parking illegally – motorhomes are banned from some car parks and from on-street parking in many places.

The GI-612 becomes the GI-613 outside Selva. It rises quickly into the hills, following the tortuous contours of the hills as it rises steadily to meet the GI-614, the road to Cadaqués and Roses. It's a nice road to drive, if you don't mind corners and has a couple of interesting hairpins as it negotiates deep valleys and a pass that reaches a height of around 250m (820ft) above sea level. Some of the hillsides here are terraced with olive groves, but much of it is wild and free, fragrant and lovely. Lizzy, my semi-tame botanist, was in raptures every time we stopped to take photos (although there aren't that many safe places to stop).

At the roundabout junction where the GI-613 meets the GI-614 you can turn left for Cadaqués and Salvador Dalí's house at Portlligat or turn right for Roses. The road to Cadaqués is equally as twisty as the road up and offers amazing views of the town and the coastline below. As you'd expect, the road to Roses is just as curvy, taking you through more fantastic scrub, around some serious bends and past some stomach-churning drop-offs.

As with all good things, it soon comes to an end when it meets the flats suddenly and takes a straight-as-a-die course behind the

beach at Roses. Turn left on to the GI-610 at the first big roundabout for the campsites and beaches, or continue on to the C-260, the road that runs behind the beach and the huge marina at Empuriabrava.

Outside Castelló d'Empúries, we took a left turn at the roundabout junction with the GIV-6216 to stay close to the coast. This took us through flat lands and past resorts (with little beach access we could find) as far as Sant Pere Pescador, where we followed the GIV-6303 after crossing the river. This took us to L'Armentera, Viladamat on the GI-6301 and then to L'Escala and out the other side on the GI-623 then the GI-632 to meet the C-31. Turning left, we took the C-31 past Pals and Palafrugell, eventually coming off at the junction with the C-65, which took us into Sant Feliu de Guíxols in search of the road we were keen to drive, the tiny-yet-mighty GI-682. Follow signs in town for Tossa de Mar and take a right at the tourism office and before the history museum at the Plaça del Monestir.

This road will now take you all the way to Tossa de Mar and beyond into Lloret de Mar. It's a fabulous road – and what a slow road is supposed to be – and one of the best I have driven for a while. The surface isn't great and the barriers are largely made of wood and concrete, but it's got all the excitement of sharp bends, constantly, with the added threat of huge drops down to the sea or into steep wooded gullies to keep you on your toes. It's not particularly narrow so you don't have to worry about passing other vehicles but it's not easy for people to overtake. We pulled over as often as possible to let people pass as the van just wouldn't go around the bends any quicker. It's worth remembering that.

The carriageway is cut into steep-sided wooded hillsides so there is almost always rock on the landward side and trees or views on the seaward side. Umbrella pines, splashes of deep violet lavender, cork oaks and olives cover the hillsides. It's a magical place that feels wild and unpredictable. Along the way are a few holiday resorts and communities where access – it's really steep – is limited. In the distance, and far below you, you can catch glimpses of difficult-to-reach beaches. Rough tracks lead off into the scrub and down the cliffs. It would be a good place to explore, but from the road it seemed impenetrable and tricky to access, which kept us from doing what we'd normally do which is to chance our luck and have a little mooch around.

The views over Tossa de Mar, when you get there, are fabulous and I felt a little robbed as the road brought us back to the reality of a busy resort with limited parking where we'd have to scramble for a place. We stopped in Tossa – and absolutely loved it – and then continued on to Lloret de Mar to find a campsite.

The following day, we took the GI-681 towards Girona over the hills. It's a much bigger road but travels over the same hills so, while not as exciting, it has some good bits and a great view of the plain from the top. We followed this to the C-65, which we then took into Girona (via the N-11).

WHERE TO STAY: CAMPING

Camping Joncar Mar, Roses
Carrer Bernat Metge, 9–10, 17480 Roses, Girona, Spain
Web: www.campingjoncarmar.com
Tel: +34 972 25 67 02

A high-density campsite that's got the advantage of being one street away from the beach. Pool and restaurant. Nice staff.

Campsite Lloret Blau, Lloret de Mar
Carrer de l'Aiguaviva s/n, 17310 Lloret de Mar, Girona, Spain
Web: www.campinglloretblau.com
Tel: +34 972 36 54 83

Nice site in the city that's terraced and surprisingly green. Has a pool.

Camping Port de la Vall, El Port de la Selva
Carrer Port de la Selva, Km 6, 17489 La Selva de Mar, Girona, Spain
Web: www.campingportdelavall.com
Tel: +34 972 38 71 86

Site that's right on the sea but lacks a little something. Too many seasonal pitches perhaps? Great location.

WHERE TO STAY: *AIRES*

Púbol: You can stay overnight in Púbol, but for no more than 24 hours.
Autocaravaning Park at Roses: A private *aire* a little back from the beach but in nice surroundings. **www.autocaravaningparkroses.com/en**
Parking Vayreda Girona: A great *aire* in the city with all facilities. €13 per 24 hours. Close to a park with a twice-weekly market and pool. **www.empark.com/es/en/parking/girona/parking-vayreda-motorhomes**

IN THE AREA

Tossa de Mar This wonderful former fishing village and fort sits at the end of the crazy cliffside road from Sant Feliu de Guíxols. Its old city, a rambling collection of narrow streets within the castle walls, sits on top of a promontory at the southern end of the town. It was here that Ava Gardner came to film *Pandora and the Flying Dutchman* in 1951, and, if you believe it, started the Costa Brava's tourism boom. There is a beautiful statue to Ava in the old city.

Dalí Theatre-Museum, Figueres Dalí's great masterpiece, a former theatre stacked to the rafters with surrealism and artworks, will make you appreciate the sublime talent that was Dalí's. His talent and hard work bring this rambling building to life in the most incredible way. *Go* if you love art, even if you have yet to fall in love with Dalí. • **www.salvador-dali.org**

Dalí's house, Portlligat It's another work of art from the master, yet it's surprisingly calm and tasteful. It was completely the opposite of what I expected. Tours last for about 15 minutes, during which you'll barely have time to take it all in. A surreal experience in a sublime location. • **www.salvador-dali.org**

Gala-Dalí Castle, Púbol This is the castle that Dalí bought and renovated for his wife Gala. It houses her mausoleum and is the last place Dalí lived. It's a little calmer – and more sombre – than you'd expect but no less wonderful. • **www.salvador-dali.org**

Museum of Art Girona, Girona Girona's old city is mesmerising. Tiny lanes lead to the cathedral and its neighbour, the Art Museum. It's home to a collection of religious art and painting as well as some more modern works. Well worth a visit. • **www.museuart.cat**

Camí de Ronda Roses-Montjoi, Roses This is a path that runs around the Cap de Creus headland from Roses to Montjoi. It runs along the coast and will lead you to coves and out of the way beaches as well as villages. Pick it up in Roses and walk to the east.

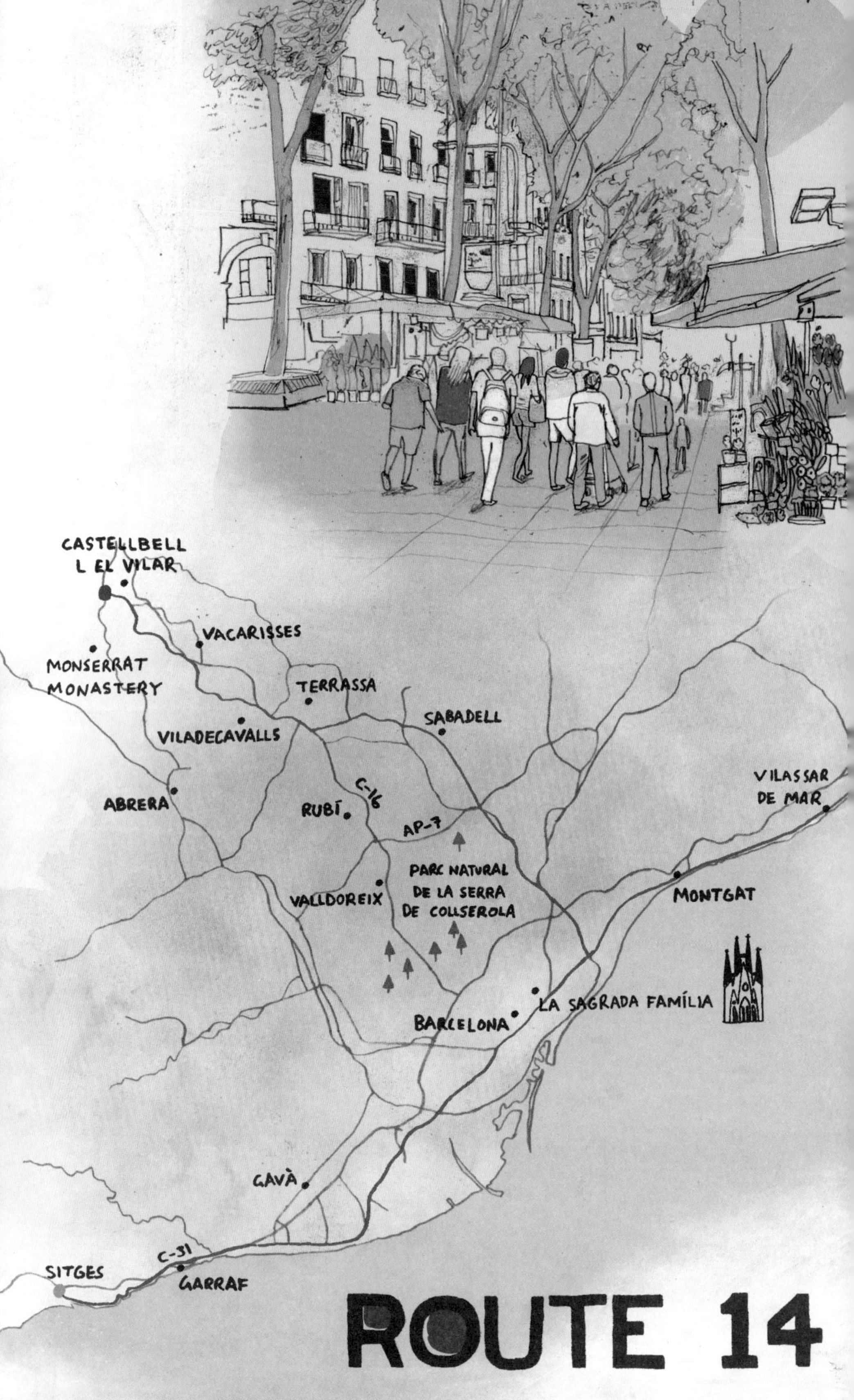

CASTELLBELL
L EL VILAR
VACARISSES
MONSERRAT
MONASTERY
TERRASSA
VILADECAVALLS
SABADELL
ABRERA
C-16
RUBÍ
AP-7
VILASSAR
DE MAR
PARC NATURAL
DE LA SERRA
DE COLLSEROLA
VALLDOREIX
MONTGAT
LA SAGRADA FAMÍLIA
BARCELONA
GAVÀ
C-31
SITGES
GARRAF

ROUTE 14

ROUTE 14

BARCELONA

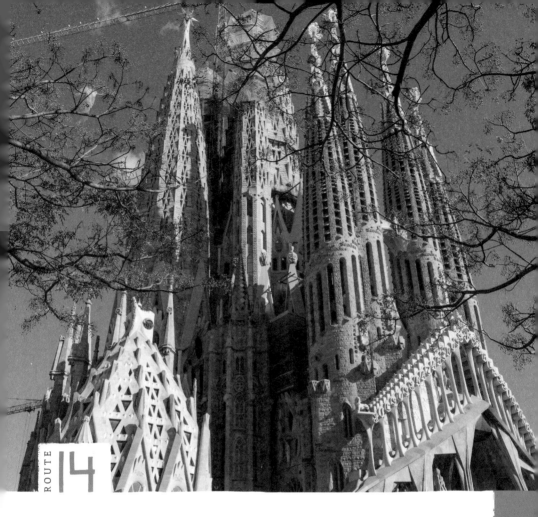

THE SAGRADA FAMÍLIA

Barcelona is one of the world's greatest cities, with a little of everything! While exploring it by van takes some work, because the nearest places to stay are a little way away and there is a sometimes confusing motorway network, it's hard to miss as a destination.

BEST FOR: City life, art, food

START/END: Barcelona

MILEAGE: 200km (120 miles)

ALLOW: 3–4 days

MAP PAGES: 38

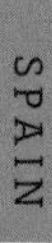

Time, as ever, while writing these *Take the Slow Road* books, is short. We have a lot of ground to cover and never enough time to do it in. Ironic, isn't it? That the work should be about taking time to see everything and slowing down, and yet the writing of the work demands exactly the opposite. Despite this, and the pressure it puts me under, I am determined to see one thing during the year I spend living and breathing Spain and Portugal, and that is to see Antoni Gaudí's unfinished cathedral in Barcelona. For me, it is the symbol of the Iberian Peninsula: creative, exuberant, life-affirming, colourful, exciting and still a work in progress. And that is before I have even seen it.

So, we head to Barcelona, though it's a mess of motorways and it seems impossible to find a route to accompany it. We approach from the south and arrive on the outskirts via the coast road out of Sitges. It's a winding, organic affair that hugs the cliffs. Huge concrete barriers separate us from a watery plunge as we wind around hairpins in the face of a constant stream of oncoming commuter traffic.

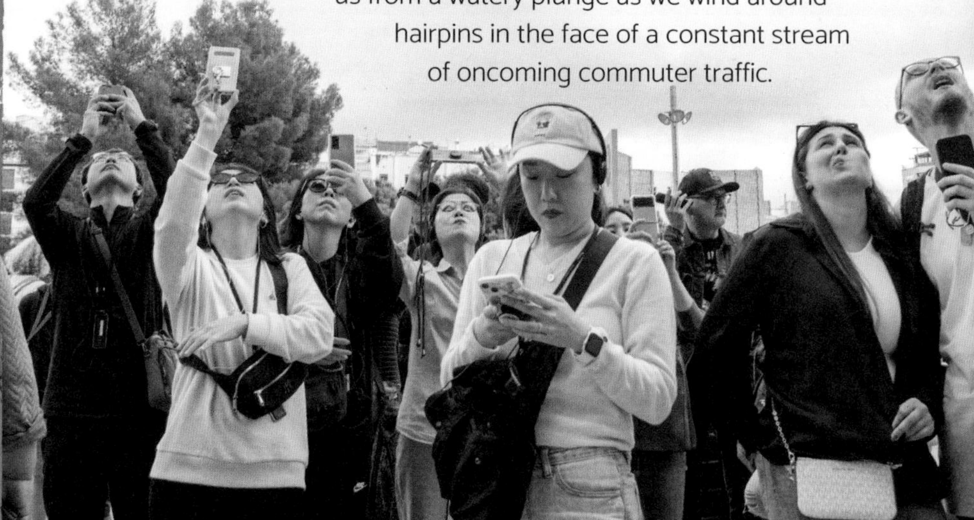

Barcelona at rush hour is a constant. There's no let-up from the noise, chaos and movement. It comes from all directions as we follow the satnav's instructions to change lanes and weave through the asphalt tangle. It only calms as we leave the city to the north and find the sedate suburb of Vilassar de Mar, where our *aire* is.

The train into the city is another rush of excited chaos the following morning. The ticket machine doesn't work so we can't buy tickets. A man advises us to take a photo of the machine and get on the train anyway, so we follow his advice and join the commuting crowds. The train runs along the coast, giving us views of the beach and the boardwalks that make it possible to cycle all the way in. We wonder why we didn't. Leaving the train station is hectic. We climb the steps and arrive, wide-eyed and blinking, into the late-autumn sunshine, at the huge Plaça de Catalunya. There are people, scooters, taxis and cyclists everywhere. It's a culture shock, as it is going into any new city, and we are beyond excited to feel it. We take direction from our phones and start walking towards the Sagrada.

I take a sharp breath when the cathedral appears between the trees at the edge of the Plaça de la Sagrada Família. Its unfinished bulk leaps into view as the leaves wave gently in the breeze. We reach the middle of the square, where we get a full view of its reaching spires and the cranes that seem to hang in the air above it. We join the throngs of others who have had the same idea as us. They stand, looking up, looking into their phones, which are pointed to the spires, or pose in front of phones pointed at them and the spires. Everyone is looking upwards and there's a carnival atmosphere with a hint of frenzy and excitement.

The Sagrada was begun in 1882 under an architect who then resigned a year later. Gaudí took over the project, redesigned it and made it his life's work to complete. When he died, in a tram accident in 1926, it was still less than a quarter finished. In the ensuing years, work was halted and delayed, most notably by the Spanish civil war when the crypt – and many of Gaudí's original drawings and plaster models – was bombed.

We buy tickets online, get our bags checked, pass through security and enter the building. Another intake of breath as we walk into the nave and look up. It is like every other cathedral I have ever been in, but so unlike any cathedral I have ever been in. The huge yet seemingly light columns lift up the roof like the trunks of a tree, spreading out at the top like branches. The stained-glass windows, lit up like neon by the sun, emit a rainbow of colour, splashing it over the floor, columns, walls and faces of the visitors. It's chaotic and wonderful, like life outside. Every element feels as if it has sprung from the earth of a faraway kingdom, where life is familiar but not the same. It's gothic but elven too, as if the great architects of the greatest cathedrals had all grown up in a parallel otherworld of great forests and glades with high, dense, comforting canopies.

I realise what Gaudí's work is all about as I notice spirals and details that can be found in nature. The way the roof hangs like the canopy of a forest, the way the stairs spiral like a shell or seed pod, the way the stonework has a natural geometry. It's astounding, heavenly, inspiring and beautiful and, for once, I am lost for words as I wander about taking photos and gaping, open-mouthed at the light, stonework, ironwork, glass and carvings.

As I stand there, I realise this is the moment I have been hurtling towards during the writing of this book. All the miles of driving and exploring, the churches, art museums, cathedrals and medieval villages, the planning, the days poring over maps and the nights developing my photos, they all converge here, at this modernist, gothic, otherworldly, art deco arts and crafts masterpiece. And it is just as good as I thought it would be. In fact, it's better.

I float down the nave, surfing the light, allowing my fingers to feel the lightest touch against the granite columns and my eyes to examine the curvaceous, extravagant detail of everything I can take in. And it's still not enough. There's more, everywhere, and it is fantastic.

No visit to a cathedral will ever be the same.

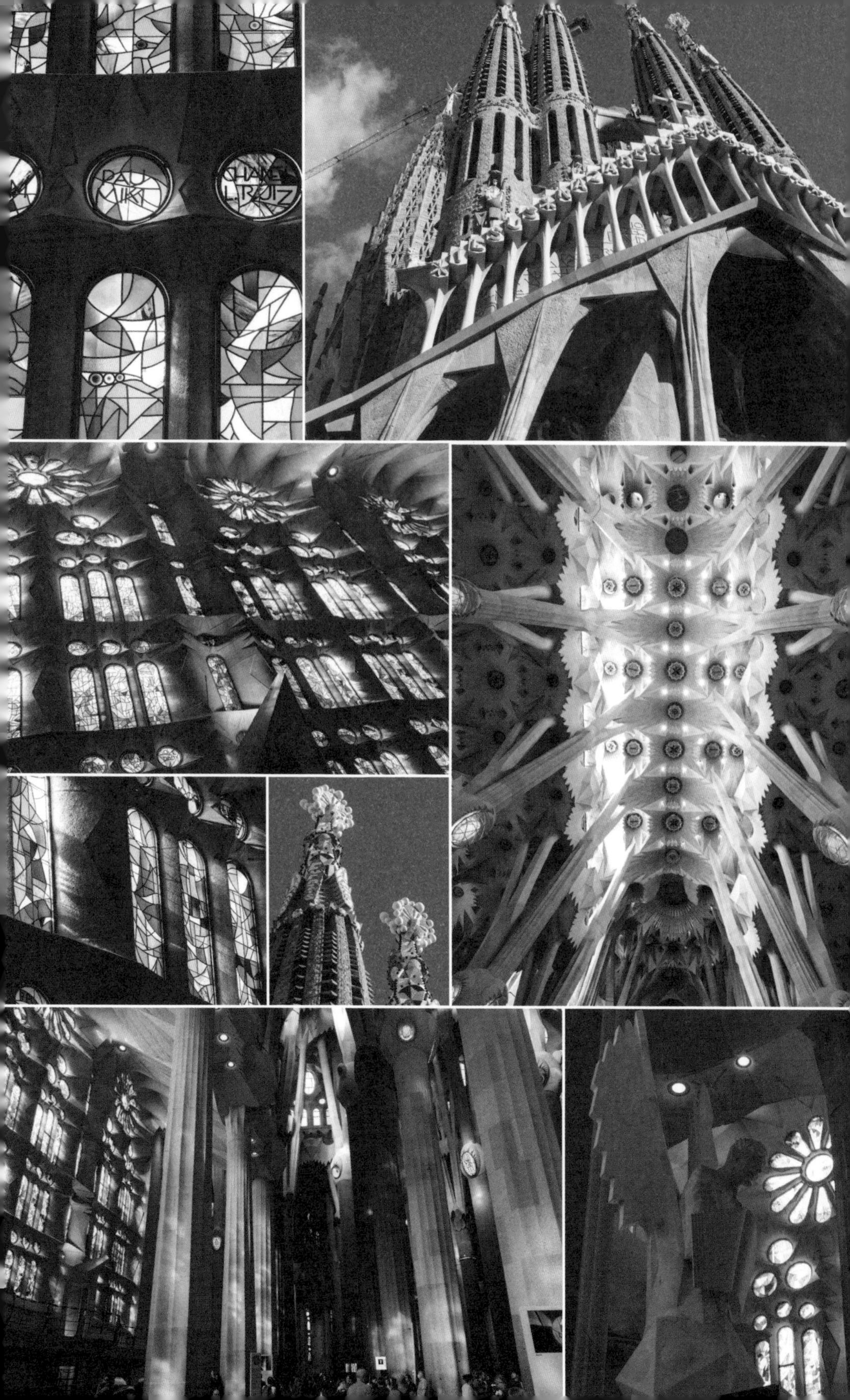
PAU
MIKI
CHANEL
L.RUIZ

THE DRIVING

This isn't a route. Rather it is a series of mishaps and efforts to see Barcelona. While not unsuccessful, it uncovered the risks and difficulties of visiting big cities in a van and left us without a route to draw on a map.

Tarragona was first: with no *aires* or campsites near to the city centre and terrible reviews for the few parking places shown on Park4Night, we spent a large part of a day trying to see the Roman ruins that Tarragona is famous for. None of the parking places felt safe enough for us to leave the van so we abandoned the city (sadly) in favour of continuing along the coast. The N-340 took us along the coast, with a stop at lovely La Mora. However, the road runs at a respectful distance from the coast due to the railway, which takes precedence here. Any hope of getting to the sea means finding tunnels that go under the railway. There are a few campsites that are on the seaward side, but, since we were travelling in November, they were already closed. It is a seasonal coast. At Cunit, we picked up the C-31, which runs along the coast, but always behind the railway, and often through suburban coastal sprawl.

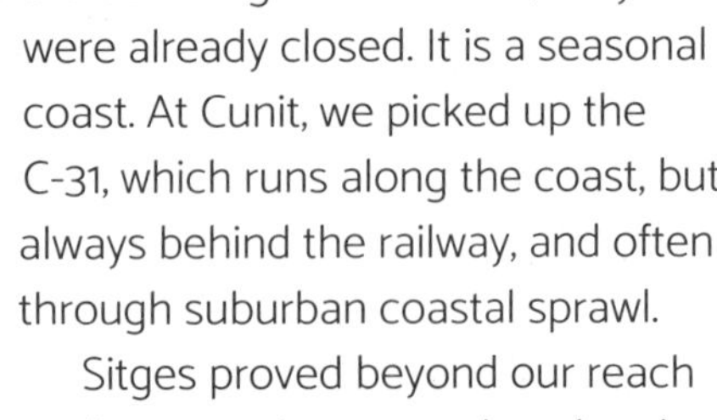

Sitges proved beyond our reach as the campsites were closed and the *aire* is well outside the town. That was truly disappointing, but it did lead us to the section of road between Sitges and Barcelona. Here, the C-31 twists and turns, bucks and rears up like a horse wanting to throw you off as it winds along the cliffs. There are few places to stop, too, so you just have to take it easy, grit your teeth around each hairpin, try not to look down and ignore the gathering queue behind you. There are a few tiny resorts below the road at small harbours along this section.

The C-31 brought us into the outskirts of Barcelona, where it changes to become an *autovía*. There are a couple of campsite options here, but the reviews weren't great so we, stupidly, opted to try the new *aire* on the opposite side of the city. This meant taking the B-10 along the waterside right through the city and then picking up the C-31 again out of the other side to Vilassar de Mar. That was interesting, and it was great to actually see the city.

We enjoyed Vilassar de Mar's old town and seaside feel but, as with all towns along the coast, it is cut off from the beach by the railway. That said, the railway whisked us into the city in about 50 minutes from here and was relatively easy.

After visiting the city, we drove out of Vilassar along the coast road N-11 and picked up the motorway to Montserrat, with the help of our satnav. If I am honest, it would have been very difficult without the satnav, so I am readily admitting defeat. At Montserrat, we parked at the bottom of the 1930 cable car and took the quick way up the mountain.

WHERE TO STAY: CAMPING

There are plenty of campsites around Barcelona, but many of them were closed when we visited, so I cannot say what they are like. We found those that were open all year had poor reviews and were just as far from the city as the Camper park, which is why we didn't stay at them.

WHERE TO STAY: *AIRES*

Area Camper Barcelona Beach: This is about the only option for Barcelona if you don't want to risk car parks. There is very little else apart from campsites to get you closer. That said, this is a good *aire* in a very nice area that's just a 15-minute walk from the railway into Barcelona. www.areacamperbarcelonabeach.com

IN THE AREA

Barcelona Barcelona has so much to see and do that I could never do it justice in the time I had. There are entire books devoted to the city, and rightly so, which means there's not much point in me trying to outdo them. However, my experiences covered the following:

THE WATERFRONT AREA AND BEACH AT LA BARCELONETA: La Barceloneta's beachfront is lively and exciting, with bars, restaurants and shops. The beach is fabulous and you can even get a mojito from a street vendor! The harbour is equally interesting with the huge superyachts on their moorings.

LA SAGRADA FAMÍLIA: Gaudí's unfinished masterpiece is just one of many reasons to visit Barcelona. I loved it because it's like no other building I have ever been into. • **https://sagradafamilia.org**

LA RAMBLA/LAS RAMBLAS: This street is the most visited in Barcelona. It's a bit like a leafy Oxford Street in London, with lots of street food, cafes, artists and, apparently, pickpockets.

SEX MUSEUM: The museum houses a huge collection of historical erotica, objects and costumes relating to sex. So, expect lots of phalluses and vulvas and a bit of the *Kama Sutra* and Victorian porn and you won't be shocked. Interesting. • **www.erotica-museum.com**

LA BOQUERIA MARKET, LA RAMBLA: A fabulous food market with just about everything your could ever wish for. Great stalls selling everything. Good place to pick up a snack. • **www.boqueria.barcelona**

GOTHIC QUARTER: On the eastern side of La Rambla you'll find the maze of streets, squares and shopping areas that make up the Gothic Quarter. The cathedral is here.

Montserrat Monastery, Montserrat Built high up in the Montserrat mountains, some 40km (25 miles) north of Barcelona, this monastery houses the black, 12th-century statue of Our Lady of Montserrat with Jesus. The story goes that in 800, some shepherds saw a vision in a cave in the mountains that was repeated for all who came to see it. To cut a long story short, they built a monastery... The abbey can be reached by road, cable car or rack-and-pinion railway. The cable car and the railways connect with services from Barcelona. • **https://abadiamontserrat.cat**

Museum of Fine Art, Montserrat The museum, which is contained in a series of underground rooms at the abbey, houses a remarkable collection of art – from antiquity to modern art and sculpture – that reads like an alternative history of art as we see it. It includes work from Picasso, Pissarro, Monet, Dalí and Caravaggio. A really great surprise to see it in such an unexpected place. • **www.museudemontserrat.com**

The Stairway to Heaven, Montserrat

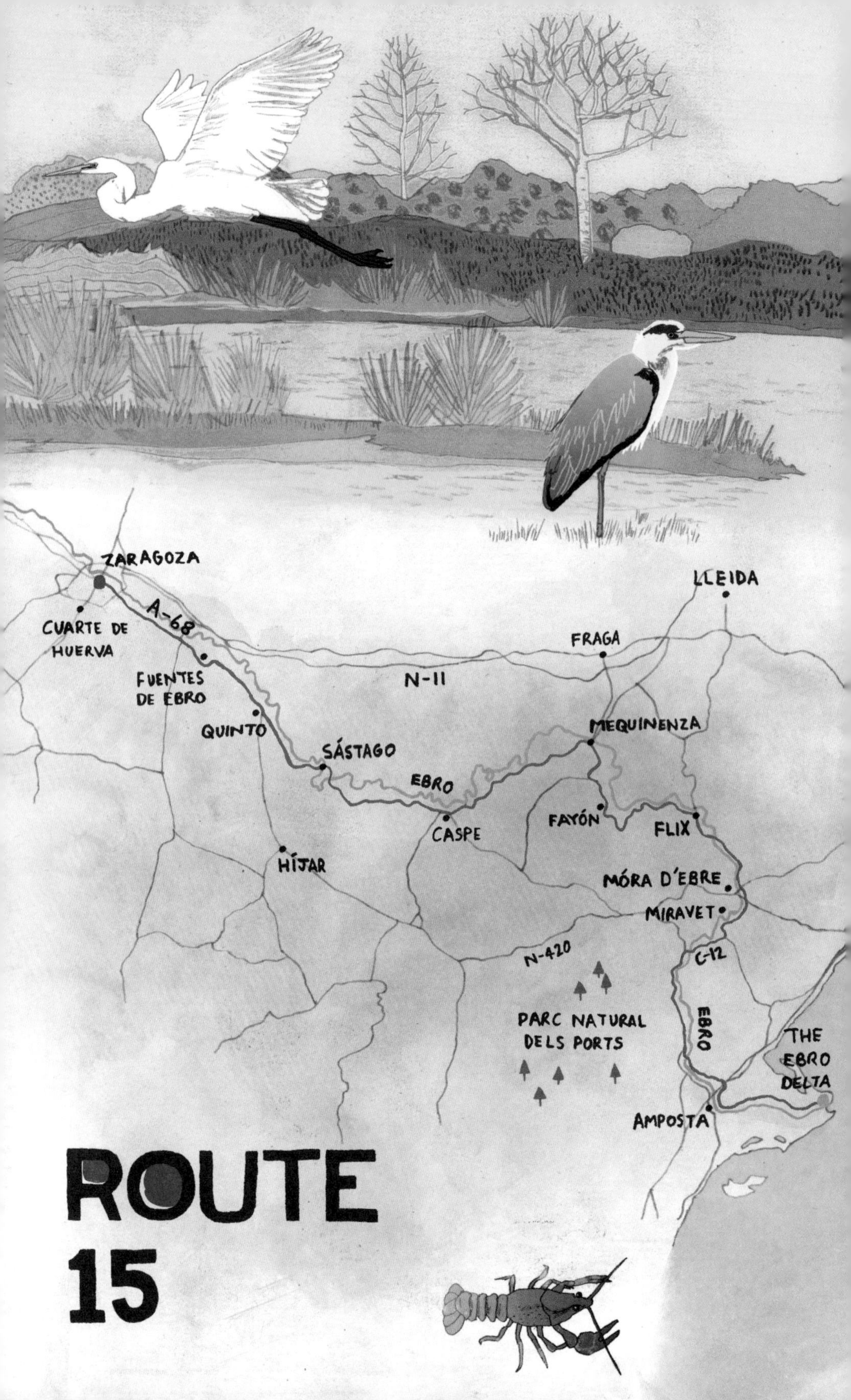
ZARAGOZA
LLEIDA
CUARTE DE HUERVA
A-68
FRAGA
FUENTES DE EBRO
N-II
QUINTO
MEQUINENZA
SÁSTAGO
EBRO
FAYÓN
FLIX
CASPE
HÍJAR
MÓRA D'EBRE
MIRAVET
N-420
C-12
PARC NATURAL DELS PORTS
EBRO
THE EBRO DELTA
AMPOSTA
ROUTE 15

ROUTE 15

EBRO DELTA TO ZARAGOZA

CYCLING ON THE EBRO

The Ebro is the longest river that runs entirely in Spain, flowing from near the Cantabrian coast all the way to the Mediterranean at its delta, a protected landscape that's a haven for thousands of wetland birds, between Barcelona and Alicante. Its tributaries bring almost all the water running off the Spanish Pyrenees. This journey begins at the delta and follows the river upstream as far as Zaragoza. Both ends of it are perfect for cycling – and so very different.

BEST FOR: Twitching, cycling, walking

START: The Ebro Delta

END: Zaragoza

MILEAGE: 360km (224 miles)

ALLOW: 2–4 days

MAP PAGES: 35, 36, 50, 51

We arrive at the campsite at Playa de l'Ampolla late in the evening, getting there thanks to the help of Park4Night, so we have no idea where we are, really. We know where we are on the map, of course, but our surroundings elude us – it's pitch-dark.

The morning brings a clear day with light cloud and a cool breeze coming from the east, which, when we wander out of the site and across the road to the beach to look to see if it the sea is swimmable, means the water is flat calm. It's a surprise to see the beach so close to the campsite. To the left, and inland, we can see the town of L'Ampolla across the bay, with the mountains behind. To our right is the Ebro Delta. The road outside the campsite runs along the beach for another 200m (218 yards) or so along the shore, then heads in to the delta's interior, but there is a sandy path that heads off along the shore. We decide to explore on our bikes instead of walking.

The Ebro Delta is the most important wetland area of the Western Mediterranean, with much of it designated a natural reserve by the Spanish government. It is important for migratory birds as well as its resident populations of waders, raptors and gulls. Among those who use the delta's important wetlands are glossy ibis, egrets, herons, marsh harriers and flamingos. As well as being home to diverse wildlife, the delta is the place where some of Spain's best rice is grown, mussels are harvested and seafood is caught. The Ebro itself is a remarkable river. Not only does it give the Iberian Peninsula its name, but it is also the longest river that

runs its entirety in Spain, at 933km (580 miles) long, and has a catchment area that covers about a quarter of the Iberian land mass, draining much of the Spanish Pyrenees and Andorra.

We ready the bikes and head off along the sandy path that follows the beach. We bump along, rolling over tree roots and through deeper patches of sand beside a few scrubby pine trees, until we reach the Bassa de les Olles, a lake where there is an observation platform. We stop and take a look.

As I walk up to the highest level it seems I am making too much noise. Tens of white egrets rise from the dense reeds at the edges of the lake, flying away from the noise I have created. Ducks, unbothered by me, cruise about on the water. From the top, I can get some idea of where we are on the delta. The land is absolutely flat, with canals and fields in systems, interspersed with small lagoons and inlets. At the centre there are a few buildings and the whole area is backed by the mountains, which rise to as much as 1,500m (4,921ft). It's a multi-layered landscape with pale browns of

the reeds contrasting with the light green pines, the dark mountains and the deeper browns of the paddy fields. The sea, reflecting grey skies, is blue-grey.

We ride on, with the aim of looking for a beach to swim at. Across the water, we can see the Punta del Fangar, a sandspit that sticks out into the basin, and the white Far del Fangar (lighthouse) with its single red stripe. In the middle of the bay there are huts on stilts that, we assume, are where mussels are harvested and gathered. One of the stilted platforms has a caravan perched on it, making it look like it was somehow washed up there after a terrible storm during a particularly bad holiday.

We follow the coast as much as possible and come to a small, rickety bridge over a creek. As I wheel the bike over, I notice a small red swamp crayfish in the water. When I move closer for a better look it raises its pincers at me, so I feel it's probably ready to take me on. It wouldn't be the first time: the red swamp crayfish is an invader from the southern states of the USA, introduced, so I read later, in 1973 and causing problems by burrowing into the dykes that protect the paddy fields, eating rice plants and outcompeting the perhaps more placid and peaceful natives.

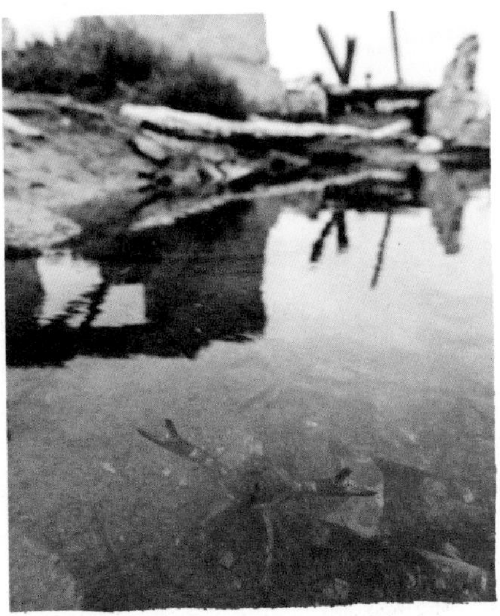

The more I find out about the Ebro, the more I realise what a fragile, fascinating place it is. Humans, sea life and birds live side by side in a dynamic environment that changes all the time due to the effects of the river, waves and weather. The only problem is that dams further upstream have halted the flow of water, and along with it the flow of silt and nutrients, so the delta isn't continuing to build up the way it should be and has been for centuries. What should be feeding the rice paddies and the birds is being held back upstream by hydroelectric plants, while the sea is taking it away with winter storms.

We visit the Eco-Museum in Deltebre, the town at the centre of the delta that sits on the Ebro. The museum is small, friendly and with what seem like frenetic opening hours. It costs €2 to enter. Here, there are displays, and even a small aquarium, detailing the history of the delta and how it's been used by man. We learn more about the wildlife and find out about the plight of the glossy ibis, a bird that was in sharp decline until the 1990s. Now there are a few thousand individuals recorded on the delta. They thrive because they are able to feed on the flooded rice paddies in the winter.

Our cycle brings us to Platja de la Marquesa, a beach on the seaward side of the delta. We try to get to one of the bigger lagoons to look for more birds, but we are unable to do so due to environmental protections. We cycle back on a more inland route, through clouds of midges that get in our eyes and mouths, passing a field where hundreds of dark, long-legged wading birds with long, curved beaks are grazing, along with a spotting of stark white egrets. As we cycle alongside, they begin to rise off the fields and fly together in a giant murmuration, tumbling and circling until they come to rest again in the next field. These are the glossy ibis. It's amazing to see them so close up, and, once again, we are happy to have made the effort to get out and explore the delta by bike. It's easy cycling and, apart from the midges, is a great way to get closer to the birds than we might have been able to in the van. I am a bit miffed not to have seen any flamingos, but we get to see them the next day when we explore the southern half of the delta in the van before heading upstream to our final destination, Zaragoza.

We arrive at the campsite, Zaragoza's municipal site, around six in the evening and it is already dark. We have no food so we decide to head into the city to find some tapas, which the city is famous for. It's only 7km (4.3 miles) so we decide to cycle. We see there are cycle paths throughout the city – how hard could it be?

Beginning by going along an unlit canal-side path, we cycle into the darkness, passing walkers and joggers as we go. It's cold and dark but still and dry and there are a few people about, but not many. It seems like folly to be cycling along a gravel path alongside a quiet canal in a strange city, in a foreign country, but actually, it makes perfect sense: We have never, at any point, felt threatened in Spain. Even here, as we ride our bikes through a dark grove of huge beech trees while a motorway rumbles nearby, we feel safe. We have each other and we have the bike lights. The only thing that would be a disaster is a puncture. Spain has always felt safe to me so I can't see why this wouldn't be either. Besides, it's a great thrill to get up some speed and ride in the dark, the canal glinting orange with the sodium lights from the road on the opposite bank.

We reach a bridge, go under it and ride up the bank to the carriageway. There is a cycle path painted green running alongside the road, so we head off. We are under the streetlights now, among traffic but safely separated from it. We reach one of the city's main thoroughfares, where trams, cars,

pedestrians and bikes share the space. Traffic lights for the bike lanes let us know when we can go across big junctions, making it feel completely safe. We ride fast, side by side, grinning at the city. The cycle track takes us on to a wide street with two sets of carriageways, tram lines and a bike path running right down the centre beside a footpath and beneath huge pollarded plane trees. It's flat and fast and really fun to ride here. It's really busy, despite the cool night, and everyone seems to be on a bike, an e-scooter or walking and, during the moments when we have to ride on a shared path with cars (where bikes get priority), we still feel OK. I doubt I'd feel like that in London. Even at home, in Bude, a small town in Cornwall, it feels like cars and bikes are enemies. Zaragoza feels the opposite.

It's thrilling to be moving under our own steam, exploring, gawping at the lights, watching the people doing their evening *paseo* (the Spanish like to walk – *el paseo* – you'll see it on beaches, esplanades and in large open spaces in cities). We arrive

at the Plaza de España, lock up the bikes and head into the throng that is walking towards the pedestrianised old city and cathedral to find some of Zaragoza's famous tapas. We feel swept up by the atmosphere: it's that time when Spanish people walk and talk, drink and socialise before settling down to a late dinner. The people we encounter are smartly dressed, walking in large family groups, chattering and drifting. It's wonderful to be among it and we feel truly blessed to be able to be here, at the end of a long trip, making an adventure out of something as simple as finding our dinner.

We settle into a couple of high stools in the window of a bar on the Plaza de Nuestra Señora del Pilar. Out of the window, we can see the magnificent cathedral, a 17th-century baroque basilica with elaborate, domed towers, that was built on the same site as, it is believed, a small chapel built by St James to the Virgin Mary in 40AD. Behind the cathedral lies the Ebro, the Bridge of Lions and Spain's greatest waterway.

We order and drink a toast to cycling in Spain.

THE DRIVING

This is a journey of great contrasts. From the flat wetlands and dead flat, dead straight roads of the Ebro Delta to the sinuous, winding mountain roads of the Ebro and on to the plains of Zaragoza, it will take you on a journey through Spain's heartlands. You could use it to take you back to the north coast for a ferry or simply as a way to get closer to Madrid. Then again, it could be a destination in itself.

Leaving from Deltebre, the town at the heart of the Ebro Delta, take the main road out of the town on the north side of the Ebro. This is the TV-3454. It will take you to Amposta, where you will need to take a left on to the N-340a to go into the town and over the bridge. Follow signs for Tortosa C-12 until you get to the C-12 and then follow it north, away from the delta and along the southern bank of the Ebro. This is a good road that follows the wide valley upstream. Expect orange groves and small villages in the bottom of the valley. The first stop is Tortosa, an interesting town with Roman history and a museum housed in an old, nicely decorated slaughterhouse.

Continue following the C-12. After Xerta, the valley narrows and the river flows out of a gorge, the road taking you into more mountainous scenery as it begins to wind a little more. Stay on the C-12 and cross the river at Benifallet. You'll head up again, between rocky slopes covered in pine, while the river winds away below. There are some great views of the river and olive terraces on this stretch. Around Móra, the valley widens again and there is more agriculture. But it won't last. After Garcia, you enter a narrow gorge, then rise above it before dropping down to river level again before Flix. At Flix, take the T-741 left just before the bridge.

WARNING: This is a tiny road that will take you high into the hills and around some really winding roads. You will need to pass under a bridge that is 3.5m (11.5ft) high. If you are taller then you'll have to continue on the C-12 then the C-45 to Fraga, then pick up the N-211 from there.

The T-471 is the start of a really excellent stretch and will lead you to some really good driving. After Riba-roja d'Ebre, you will arrive at a roundabout. Take the second turn for the TV-7411 and follow it along the river. It will give you some good views of the river and, when you get to it, the dam (Pantà de Riba-roja) itself. You'll rise up to the level of the top of the dam and then veer off left up a tributary/side valley of the reservoir. Climbing almost constantly, you'll wind your way around the pristine, pine-clad, sandstone hills in a never-ending series of hairpins, dips, curls, drops and sharp turns until you reach the top. Once up here, you'll notice that all the surrounding mountains are the same height and the valleys have been caused by millions of years of erosion from rivers, carving steep-sided, winding valleys leading down towards the Ebro. It is really something.

Turn right on to the TV-7231 towards Fayón (it will change to the CV-103 when you cross the river again into Aragón), a road that will take you down to river level and a bridge across it that will soon rise again. Just as you thought the twisty bit was over! Not yet! You'll head back up to the high level and pass through fruit trees and agriculture on the plain.

The CV-103 will bring you to a T-junction with the A-1411. Turn right towards Mequinenza and follow the road across the plain. It will drop sharply at a series of hairpins just before Mequinenza. There are great views of the river from here.

Take a left before the bridge on to the N-211, another lovely road that will lead you through pine and agriculture, olive groves and almonds on the southern side of the reservoir as it makes a large loop to the north. Once you meet the reservoir again, the road will sweep you past on a lovely curving road without too many sharp turns. When you reach Caspe, allow the N-211 to take you around the town and then follow the A-221 on to the flat plains. It will take you past huge solar farms and on long, straight stretches – a complete contrast with what you've just been through.

In Escatrón, take a right-hand turn after the skatepark to stay on the A-221 towards Sástago. You'll cross the river and more scrubby, rocky semi-mountainous country until you get to Sástago and drop down and go around a sharp right-hand bend to cross the Ebro on the narrow bridge. The view of it as you round the bend is great! Stay on the A-221 and let it roll you on along the river until you get to the N-232 just outside Quinto, where you'll need to turn right for the final, quite busy stretch into Zaragoza.

IN THE AREA

Eco-Museum, Deltebre A really nice museum and information centre for the delta. Go here to find out about cycle routes, walks and places to watch wildlife. • **https://parcsnaturals.gencat.cat**

Cathedral, Zaragoza This is one of the true holy of holies. It's ornate and gregarious, in the baroque style, with elaborately tiled towers and a flamboyant central dome, but inside it's serious, dark and sombre. • **https://catedraldezaragoza.es**

Goya Museum, Zaragoza I never knew I loved Goya until I went to this museum. His sketches are incredible, offering a visual history that's as stark and telling as Dickens. Visiting shows add something extra, along with painters working before, during and after Goya's time. • **https://museogoya.ibercaja.es**

Belchite The village of Belchite was the scene of a battle during the Spanish Civil War. After a bloody 15-day siege, the town was almost completely destroyed. Following the battle, Franco ordered that the town should be left as it was as a testament to his power. A new town was built ten years later next to the ruins, which you can tour. However, it is also still possible to walk around the perimeter fence and see the destruction. In fact, in some places it will feel like a war zone, even today. Haunting. • **https://belchite.es/entradas**

Roman Zaragoza The city was occupied by the Romans (where wasn't in Spain?) and it was on exactly the same site as the city today. There are walls, a forum, theatre and baths, all in the city centre. Find the forum and museum near the cathedral.
• www.zaragoza.es

WHERE TO STAY: CAMPING

As usual, there are plenty of campsites on the Ebro, especially on the delta. However, there is only one option for Zaragoza (apart from an *aire*, which is 3km/1.9 miles north of the city centre).

Camping Ampolla Playa, Tarragona
Passeig Platja Arenal, 30, 43895, Tarragona, Spain
Web: www.campingampolla.es
Tel: +34 977 46 05 35

A large and very well-presented campsite on the northern side of the Ebro Delta, at Ampolla Playa. Good restaurant and lots of facilities. Right opposite the beach.

Camping Ciudad De Zaragoza, Zaragoza
C. de San Juan Bautista de la Salle, s/n, 50012 Zaragoza, Spain
Web: www.campingzaragoza.com
Tel: +34 876 24 14 95

A nice campsite with good facilities and a pool that's the best option for Zaragoza. Cycle lanes go straight into the city. Cycling takes about 30 minutes.

WHERE TO STAY: *AIRES*

Ebro Delta: There are three *aires* on the delta: one by the beach at Riumar, another large open *aire* at Deltebre and another at Amposta on the southern side of the delta. Good for watching flamingos.
La Campaneta: This is a relatively new *aire* that's just off the Ebro, near Móra d'Ebre. With showers, loos and emptying facilities, it's a great stop run by a nice family, on their family farm.

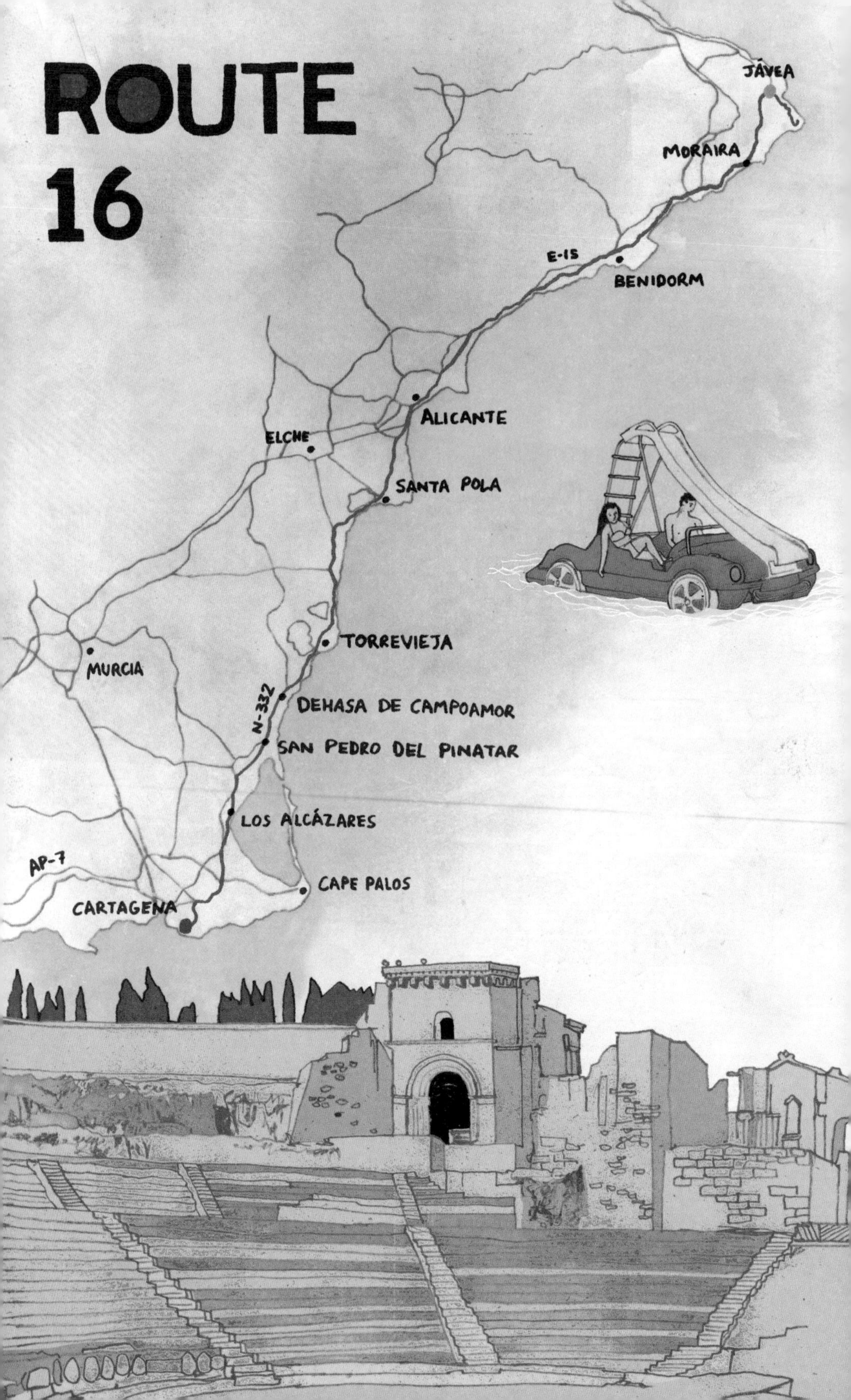
ROUTE
16
JÁVEA
MORAIRA
E-15
BENIDORM
ALICANTE
ELCHE
SANTA POLA
TORREVIEJA
MURCIA
N-332
DEHASA DE CAMPOAMOR
SAN PEDRO DEL PINATAR
LOS ALCÁZARES
AP-7
CAPE PALOS
CARTAGENA

ROUTE 16

JÁVEA TO CARTAGENA

THIRTY-SIX HOURS ON THE COSTA BLANCA

The Costa Blanca has been synonymous with mass tourism, cheap package holidays and overdevelopment since it first became a marketing thing in the 1950s. Its skyline is wide and tall, but it sits in some amazing countryside with opportunities galore for fun and exploration. We went, and had an absolutely brilliant time, proving, once again, that there is more to Spain than just Benidorm. And even that can be fun, if you can get over yourself.

BEST FOR: Sun-soaked beach hols

START: Jávea

END: Cartagena

MILEAGE: 237km (147 miles)

ALLOW: 3 days

MAP PAGES: 74, 85, 86

We have a little trouble finding somewhere to stay in the vast, urban, high-rise sprawl that spreads out behind three of the Costa Blanca's best beaches. We drive through the city, following our satnav to dead ends and to out-of-the-way campsites through the narrow streets and out on to the wide, roundabout-heavy outer roads. Eventually, we find the Sunbeach Campark, a really nice, privately run *aire* about 800m (½ mile) from Playa de la Cala de Finestrat, a small beach surrounded by cafes and high-rises.

We are here, in Benidorm, because I want to see what I have been avoiding for most of my adult life. Until I went to Ronda in my 30s and discovered how beautiful and elegant Spain can be, Benidorm was shorthand for all I saw that was wrong with Spain: Brits abroad and all-day English breakfasts in the sun. Mass tourism, typified by the package holiday to Benidorm, was anathema to me and I wanted to avoid it at all costs.

Benidorm was developed as a resort for mass tourism in the 1950s following the decline of the fishing industry and the opening up of the country by Franco's government. The Costa Blanca, a name given by marketing people, was the first area in Spain to be developed and parts of it have since been used as an example of what uncontrolled development looks like: other places have tried to avoid falling into the same trap.

Once safely installed in the *aire*, we set off to explore. We cycle to the beach to find some food on wide roads lined with restaurants, fast food joints and shops selling blow-up beach goods, sun hats and beach chairs. When we get to the small, palm-backed beach it is really busy, with umbrellas lining the shore to make an almost constant line of shade. It's about 7 p.m. and we are surprised by how many people are still in the sea or lying on the sand. More people mill about at the beachfront, looking for food or just walking. Some are sitting outside bars. On the whole, Spanish is being spoken, with the odd snippet of English from families whom we pass as we push our bikes. It's a great holiday atmosphere – totally the opposite to what I have expected.

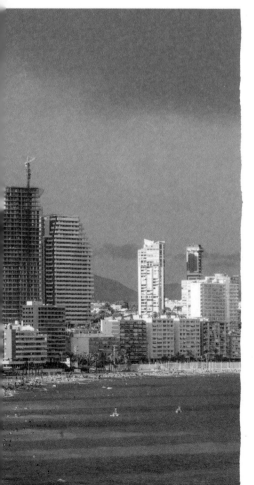

We cycle over the promontory that separates Playa de la Cala de Finestrat from Benidorm's other beaches, ending up at the south end of Playa de Poniente, a huge arc of white sand beneath an impressive skyline of high-rise apartments and hotels. The Gran

Hotel Bali, a 186m (610ft)-tall hotel, dominates. Some high-rises are unfinished, which gives me a twinge of sad satisfaction that I was right in expecting it, thanks in part to years of gaslighting by the UK media.

We cycle along the esplanade enjoying the warm night. Scooters overtake us while elderly Spaniards take their evening *paseo* in the golden sun. It's a really great atmosphere, despite the cruising Black Marias that pass by from time to time.

We eat pizza at an Italian restaurant overlooking the beach, which enables us to watch the people go by. There is a broad mix, mostly Spanish, but also a few Brits, Russians and Germans. Most of them are in family groups or couples.

We cycle back to the little cove as the sun goes down and the lights of the high-rises begin to flicker in a fantastic golden hour light show. Despite myself, I am really enjoying it here and love the skyline and the warmth. By the time we reach the little cove, it's dark. The beach is lit up by the street lights and the neons from bars and cafes. A few people are still in the water. We decide to strip off and swim. The water is really warm and the white

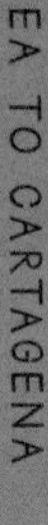

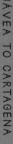

sand soft beneath our feet as the small waves slosh on the shore. We swim out into the bay a little and look back towards the land. I can't help smiling. It's absolutely brilliant to be here watching the happy people drinking outside bars, eating in open air restaurants or just strolling along the short beach front. I feel free.

As we get out of the water, I notice there are pedalos locked up on the sand. Unlike normal pedalos, these have water slides attached to them, with a ladder up the back and another, retractable ladder that drops into the sea. They are shaped a bit like the new Beetle car and have cute faces with eyes on the front. I've always thought pedalos would be a bit dull – and typify the kind of holiday I would normally deride – but these look FUN. We set our sights on trying them the following morning.

We rise early and get down to the beach at 9 a.m. We are surprised to find that it's already really busy with umbrellas and beach chairs. The pedalo operators haven't yet arrived so we muck about in the sea until they turn up. It costs us €20 for an hour on the water. We help push a big green pedalo into the surf and then jump in and pedal it beyond the surf and swim zone and into the deeper water.

Lizzy goes down the slide first while I jump into the water with my camera. The sea is choppy, which makes the climb up the ladder a little wobbly. Once at the top, Lizzy sits on the slide before letting go and slipping into the sea with a plop, her arms wide and a big smile on her face. The force of Lizzy's momentum sends the pedalo backwards and we have to swim after it. We remount and pedal it into position so we face the chop.

I climb the ladder while Lizzy gets into the sea with the camera. I slip down the slide and drop into the clear water. I come up with a grin on my face. I realise then that this is what fun is all about: losing yourself in silliness and simple things. We take ourselves too seriously sometimes, I think. The sea is a perfect temperature, the sun is hot and the beach is gorgeous. Despite it being busy, it's a great atmosphere and we love it. We even manage to surf in on a wave when our time is up, lining ourselves up with the boat landing area, waiting for a decent wave and then pedalling hard to catch it. Momentarily, we experience the weightlessness you feel when you get picked up by the surf. It dumps us neatly on the beach. The man hiring the pedalos says '*Perfecto*!' as we cruise in.

Once again, Spain has managed to surprise and delight me in ways I never thought it would. We were reluctant to come to Benidorm because of its reputation, but all we have found here is fun and good times.

Later, we make our way down the coast to San Pedro del Pinatar, where, we have discovered, there are free natural mud baths in the salt flats. We park and walk along the busy town beach looking for the baths. It's only when we see people wandering around coated in mud from head to toe that we know we've found it. The baths are in a salt flat that's separated from a coastal lagoon by a causeway. To one side is a beach and on the other there are four or five wooden pontoons with steps leading to the water. On each pontoon, there are people standing in the sun, making themselves as

wide as possible to get as much heat as possible, with their legs slightly apart and their arms raised. They are waiting for the mud, which they have gathered from the bottom of the pool and smothered on themselves, to dry off. They look like marionettes waiting for the show to begin. In the water, there are people in the earlier stages of the process, scooping mud from the bottom to smear all over each other.

We waste no time and get in the salty water, grabbing handfuls of the oozing, slimy, black mud from the bottom. We gather a bucket load and stand on the pontoon, rubbing it into each other's backs, legs and arms until we are black with it, just our eyes and mouths the colour they should be. I feel like a naughty child making mud pies, almost expecting to be told off for mucking up my clothes. But the chiding never comes and Lizzy and I laugh at each other as we splat the mud on our bodies, take selfies and make the most of the experience.

We stand like everyone else, facing the sun, willing the mud to dry quickly. It feels good and unlike any other spa treatment I have ever had. As the mud dries, it begins to tighten the skin and crack like a dried-up river bed. The warm wind dries my front while the sun warms my back. When we get to the point when we think it's time to rinse off, we wade out into the water and cleanse ourselves, rubbing the mud away with handfuls of the warm, brackish water. It takes longer than expected, partly because my shorts are full of mud, as is Lizzy's bikini. The mud comes off easily but is harder to get out of the crevices. Nevertheless, it leaves us feeling salty and fresh, even if our skin smells of sulphur.

We sit on the sea wall eating ice creams and talking over our 36 hours on the Costa Blanca. While we haven't explored all of it, we will be able to drive away feeling really positive, despite our skin smelling a bit. It is what it is and we are grateful for that. The Mediterranean was warm, the people we met friendly, the beaches excellent, the food good and the atmosphere jolly and relaxed. The verdict? Come and see it for yourself.

THE DRIVING

Start at Dénia and Jávea – small, well-to-do port towns on the Cap de la Nau. Latterly, they have become swish resorts for the summer exiles from Madrid and Valencia. As such, they make a perfect start to this journey because, whatever you might have thought about the Costa Blanca, they are not it. The countryside is lush and green, with a lot of forest where wild boar roam.

We began this journey on the AP-7 at junction 62, where we took the CV-725 into Dénia, following signs for the port. At the port, take a right on to the CV-736 signposted to Jávea, which will take you along the coast, below the castle and around an outcrop of rock. You'll head out of the village into terraced scrub of pine, juniper and carob and wind your way up a rocky hillside. At the top, there is a *mirador* at the Cap de Sant Antoni on a slight detour that will give you great views of Jávea and the port below. The road winds back down the hill and you'll have to stay on the CV-736 as motorhomes are not allowed into the village. Stay on the CV-736 until the junction with the CV-734, which is signed to Alicante/Gata and will take you through the outskirts. At the roundabout junction with the CV-740, follow the CV-736 to Benitachell, then pick up the CV-737 towards Moraira. There are great views over the valley here with lots of terraced fields, olive groves and villas on the hillsides. Follow the CV-743 to Moraira, then the

CV-746 to Calpe. This will bring you alongside a lake, where there may be flamingos!

The CV-746 will bring you to the N-332, which will be your guiding light for the rest of the journey, although, as usual, I want you to veer off course and do some exploring of your own. The section around Jávea, Calp and Dénia has lots of difficult-to-get-to beaches that are stunning but tricky. So, if you have time, go and find them.

The N-332 will take you along the coast to Altea and then into Benidorm. It's the old road but has some stunning sections, with the sea to your left and mountains, scrub and forest to your right. You'll go through a few tunnels and along a rocky gorge that is absolutely lovely. This is when you get your first views of Benidorm's crazy skyline. The N-322 will take you through Benidorm and south in the direction of Alicante through a hilly, desert-like landscape that's dotted with palms, cypress, pines and olive groves, and is often terraced. These terraces may have been shaped by the Moors when they ruled this part of Spain more than 1,000 years ago. Aside from the modern developments and motorways, they are the ones who shaped this landscape.

The N-322 will take you alongside the AP-7 motorway, through La Vila Joiosa and on to El Campello then right into the heart of Alicante on palm-lined roads, rushing you along as you pass by the port and the docks and, eventually, out the other side right by the sea. You'll enter a wetland area next, where you are likely to see more flamingos in the salt marsh and in the lakes created by the salt industry. You'll pass the airport and head further south towards Torrevieja. By now, you'll notice that the mountains are a way off inland and there are resorts on the seaward side.

The N-322 will take you through Torrevieja and then on to Cartagena and the Mar Menor (little sea) – a huge inlet with a series of high-rise developments on the sea-facing side. San Pedro del Pinatar (and the mud baths) is at the top end of the Mar Menor. Take the road off the roundabout where the N-332 crosses the AP-7.

Continue on the N-322 around the Mar Menor and into the heart of Cartagena, the port that was once the heart of Roman Spain.

WHERE TO STAY: CAMPING

Camping Jávea, Jávea
Camino Fontana 10, 03730, Jávea, Spain
Tel: +34 965 79 10 70
Web: www.campingjavea.es

Good, friendly campsite with bar, pool, tennis and shaded pitches. Well recommended.

WHERE TO STAY: *AIRES*

Sunbeach Campark, Benidorm: This is a really nice *aire* that's within an easy cycle or ten-minute walk from Playa de la Cala de Finestrat, one of Benidorm's nicest beaches. Grey and black waste, plus showers, washing machines and loos. www.facebook.com/profile.php?id=100075839592684

IN THE AREA

Benidorm The town has a bad reputation but beautiful beaches, a great seafront and a good selection of restaurants from which to watch the evening strollers. The sea is warm and clear and the place has a good vibe, although we didn't sample much of the nightlife...

Roman Theatre of Cartagena, Cartagena The theatre here is splendid. Having been dug out of the old city as recently as 2003, it's remarkably intact and very evocative. The current museum opened in 2008. **https://teatroromano.cartagena.es**

Baños de lodo, San Pedro del Pinatar Free mud baths in the saline mud that's supposed to be good for arthritis and skin conditions. Take a bucket to gather the mud, slap it all over and then let it dry. Rinse off. Feel great!

Alicante This town has a lot going for it – including castles, marinas and beaches – and it is possibly one of the best places in Spain to take part in the *paseo*, the tradition of taking walks in the evening, on the fabulous Explanada de España.

ROUTE 17

HUÉRCAL-
OVERA
ÁGUILAS
LOS LOBOS
GRANADA
A-92
SORBAS
MOJÂCAR
DÚRCAL
SIERRA NAVADA
OHANES
TABERNAS
DÉ MESA
ROLDÁN
CÁDIAR
UGÍJAR
NÍJAR
ALHAMA
DE ALMERÍA
ÓRGIVA
LAS NEGRAS
ALMERÍA
MOTRIL
ADRA
SAN JOSÉ

PALACE

ROUTE 17

ÁGUILAS TO GRANADA

FORT WORTH TO THE ALHAMBRA

This journey takes us along the coast of the Costa de Almería via a swish, off-the-map Spanish hideout, to the home of the Spaghetti Western in the Spanish Wild West near Tabernas, across the southern slopes of the Sierra Nevada mountains and into Granada to visit Spain's premier attraction and the pinnacle of Moorish architecture in Europe, the Alhambra and the Generalife gardens. A drive into the Sierra Nevada from Granada also reveals incredible views, skiing in season and walking and biking in the summer.

BEST FOR: Wildness and high culture

START: Águilas

END: Granada

MILEAGE: 391km (243 miles)

ALLOW: 5 days

MAP PAGES: 94, 95, 96

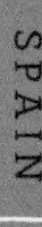

We drive through the desert from the coast, taking the small road from the beautiful and unspoiled beach town of Agua Amarga through the *parque natural* and into the deserts of Almería, arriving at Fort Bravo outside Tabernas along the dried-up Rambla de Tabernas on the Via Augusta, a Roman road that is now known as the N-340. We stop beneath a huge hoarding on a rough and dusty lot and look across the desiccated river at a collection of buildings, a wooden fort, some tepees and a sign that says 'TEXAS HOLLYWOOD' in huge white lettering. We are here to visit the old movie sets of the Spaghetti Westerns, but Fort Bravo Texas Hollywood isn't on the radar.

We carry on and, a few kilometres down the road, turn into the parking area of Oasys MiniHollywood, the place we had planned to visit. We sit in the van and google the two places. Both claim to be original lots of films made from the 1960s until the present day and both have slick websites. Oasys, though, takes the edge when it comes to professionalism on the basis that it is really busy, has a few coaches outside, has a tarmacked car park and also houses an animal park on site. It seems to me that this is the slicker of the two, so, always in favour of the underdog, the hokey and the home-made, we decide to give our day to Fort Bravo, whatever that means. We turn the van around and head back.

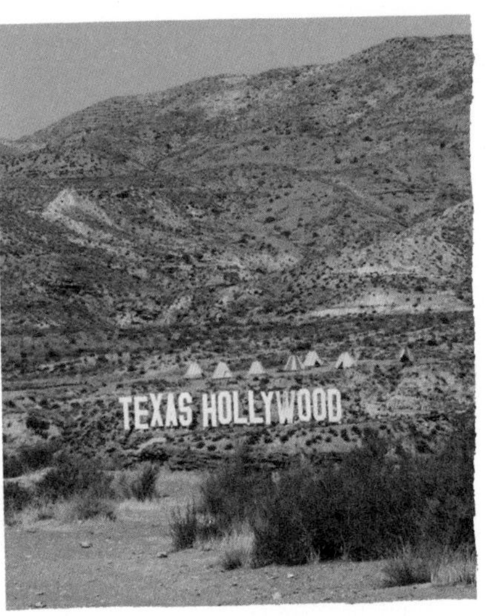

Almost immediately, it seems that we have made the right choice if we are looking for something different. The road to the fort takes us under an old bridge, along the river bed and into the desert of scrub and dust along a rough, unmade track to a rickety shack where we are relieved of €17 each. We get two vouchers for a horse cart ride and are informed there will be a free bank robbery at 2.00 p.m. and a can-can dance at 4.00 p.m. in the saloon.

We park, open all the hatches on the van (it's really hot!) and wander into the collection of wooden buildings that were built to double for the Wild West after film director Sergio Leone came here looking for cheaper places to film his Spaghetti Westerns. The lot at Fort Bravo was bought by a stuntman in the 1970s to increase his chances of getting work if Hollywood chose to film here. It has since become a theme park with pool, camping, lodges and even a camper van *aire*.

We realise, soon enough, that this probably isn't the place where *The Good, The Bad and The Ugly* was shot, or indeed any of the actual Leone Spaghetti Westerns, although it has been used for episodes of *Doctor Who, The Young Indiana Jones Chronicles* and a whole lot of Westerns in the 1960s and 1970s. From that point of view, it is authentic, of course, but it's obvious from the moment we walk towards the main street of the Western town that it's a little lacklustre these days.

We amble past a building with 'Lumber Yard' painted on its faded and dusty facade and realise that it's nothing more than a frontage. Behind it lie stables. Beside it there is a collapsing wooden water tower. Beyond, the rest of the town, featuring drugstores, hotels, saloons, a bank and even a little ramshackle church. We wander into a *cantina* and what is like a museum of dusty saddles,

stagecoaches and assorted Western regalia, presumably which were once used for filming but that now sit here waiting for their latest commission. It is fascinating to peruse this Wild West prop store to see lines of saddles with notes saying what films they were used for but I can't get over the dust. It is everywhere and covers everything in a film of what I see as neglect.

We drift into a few more buildings. They are, on the whole, just carcasses, sometimes filled with props, at other times locked up or just nothing more than frontages. The effect, when I look through the lens of my camera, is authentic, if you can ignore the other tourists strolling around in cowboy hats they have borrowed from the wardrobe department for the day. The town really looks like it has been transplanted from the wild frontier and the surrounding *campo* (countryside) is as good as it gets. In fact, it's around 40°C (104°F), dry, hot and sandy, much like you'd expect to find in the real Wild West.

The thing I can't get over is that the notion of the Old West – one of the foundation stones of American mythology – was a golden period that lasted no more than 25 years and probably wasn't even real. Before that, the dime novel had exaggerated and simplified the frontier into a world of goodies and baddies, Indians and cowboys, violence and heroism. So, it's basically a construct, which was picked up by Hollywood and turned into what we know today. This place, this film set, as with all film sets and theme parks, is a fabrication of a fabrication. Fort Bravo is a facade that's not real. Look behind it and you see the grubby, dusty business of fakery.

The more time I spend here, the more I realise that Fort Bravo is just like the botched-together theme parks of Devon and Cornwall where diversification has changed into a business: a working farm becomes a petting zoo and then adds a few slides, a cafe and, eventually, a crap roller coaster. By the time I get there it's all a bit forgotten and neglected, smelling of chips and exuding a sad, out-of-season melancholy.

We settle in for the free bank robbery as 2.00 p.m. comes around, finding a seat outside the bank along with the rest of the paying visitors. There are maybe 50 of us clustered around the main square, cameras at the ready to capture what is about to happen. Music of the old Westerns blasts out of some speakers on the wooden balcony above the saloon, followed by a long speech – we assume it is a scene-setter – about – we assume – the Wild West. Five cowboys ride into the square and are applauded before they disappear again and we are treated to some music you might have heard in a Western. It's all very familiar.

What unfolds next is a story of three cowboys who are driven out of town by the sheriff and his mate at the bank but who return, go for a drink in the saloon and start a fight before being driven out of town again. They then return with bandanas on their faces to rob the bank, shoot a few times

at the sheriff and then ride off. The sheriff then gets together a posse of him and his mate at the bank and they ride off in pursuit. Somehow the five of them end up back in the square (after some more music) with one of them dragged behind a horse, for a shoot-out. One of them tumbles from a balcony on to a mat in front of a horse trough while the other gets gunned down outside the bank. Finally, in a *High Noon* moment, the last of the gunslingers faces the sheriff in a duel, which, of course the sheriff wins, but not without some seriously hammy death acting from the baddie.

I might mock, but it's only with fondness. Some of the stunts are quite good, a little of the shooting takes us by surprise and the fight is well rehearsed, even if the acting is a little ham-fistful of dollars. The horses are magnificent though and the crowd really seem to enjoy the spectacle that's created: a section of them put their hands up as one of the baddies points his six-shooter in their direction. Once the show is over, the cowboys take a bow in the middle of the square and the crowd mob them to get selfies and high fives. It's all high camp at high noon and I actually enjoy the whole thing a lot more than I thought I would.

We don't bother to stay for the free can-can in the saloon at 4.00 p.m.

As we drive towards Granada through the desert, we wonder what the other theme park would have been like. A little slicker perhaps? Less dust? More corporate? Probably. And would it have been better for it or just a little more fake? Who knows. But we stand by our decision.

We roll on, passing the old Moorish pueblos of the Sierra Nevada until we arrive in Granada. We drive up to the ski station to marvel at the view from 2,100m (6,890ft) and cycle in the forest. It's hot and deserted at the ski station

– a little like an abandoned theme park – in that unique way ski resorts can seem without snow.

The climax to our journey – a visit to the Alhambra – comes after a night in the car park beyond the city walls. We rise early because we have tickets booked for the first timed session to the Palacios Nazaríes at 8.30 a.m. We have to be there at 8.15 a.m. to have our tickets and passports checked before strolling with the rest of the early birds to the entrance, which is a ten-minute walk into the Alhambra complex itself.

The Palacios Nazaríes is considered to be the pinnacle of Islamic art in Europe and is one of Spain's most visited attractions. It was begun in the 13th century and was the seat of power for the Nasrid kings until the Christian Reconquista in 1492, after which it was the royal court of Ferdinand and Isabella. The whole site housed a city with everything needed by Muslim kings, including a hammam, flowing water, gardens, workshops and a tannery.

Stepping into the Palacios Nazaríes is like stepping into another world. Outside, the walls are plain and austere while inside, it is highly decorated and absolutely beautiful, with slim marble columns, filigree work and intricate carvings, coloured tiles and carved wooden ceilings. Water flows everywhere throughout the palace, in marble channels that help to keep the atmosphere cool. The centrepiece, a courtyard with a fountain of six lions (the Patio de los Leones), the most private part of the palace, is wonderful. It seems so light and golden compared with the austere, solid

The Alhambra

walls that contain it. Compared with some of the Christian castles and palaces we have visited in Spain it exudes a different kind of opulence and wealth. I feel the lightness and promise of this heavenly place on earth and love the humble scale and modest reverence for brilliant detail and craftsmanship. It is simply magnificent. I wander, slack-jawed, with my rucksack on my front (rules, I am afraid) snapping away at the details, the ceilings and the spaces. It is mesmerising.

Outside, we wander through the palace gardens. The hedges are myrtle and privet with spaces of flowers between and water flowing everywhere. Pools reflect palm trees and the towers of the Alcazaba. It is heavenly and cool.

As the time passes, we notice that the palaces become busier and busier. Large tour groups bustle their way through the gardens, dominating the spaces and intruding on the relative quiet of the early shift. By the time we get to the Generalife, the summer palace and its gardens, we seem to be in a constant queue, shuffling from one photo opportunity to another while selfies are taken. I seem to be a target for people wanting to have their photos taken because I have my camera on me. I take pictures with phones of couples against windows, with pools of water in the background and beside fountains.

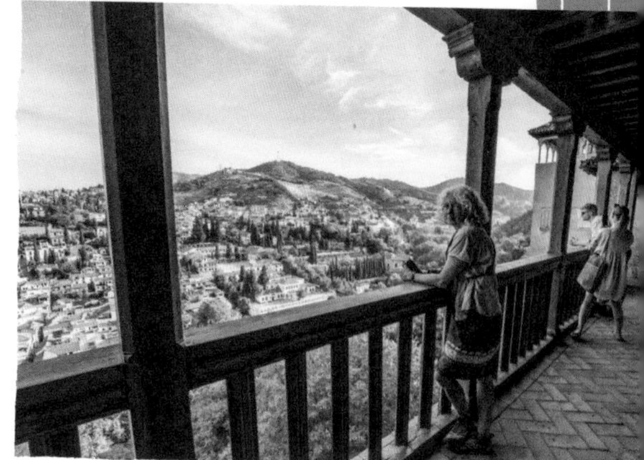

By the time we leave the city it is well into lunch time and the place is heaving with visitors from all over the world taking tours in French, Spanish and English or just wandering about taking selfies. We stop for a coffee at a cafe just outside the city walls and take it all in.

The Alhambra – and the Palacios Nazaríes particularly – is an illusion just like Fort Bravo or the ski station without snow. It's the realm of kings where craftsmanship and faith came together to create an idea of heaven and perfection that few would ever see in their true splendour. We feel blessed that it survives and that we can see it. It might have been a gilded cage for those who lived at the court, but what a cage it was.

We rumble off down the road in our own little palace on wheels (it is to us, anyway) towards our next adventure.

THE DRIVING

We began this journey by climbing to the top of the promontory that bisects Águilas so we could get an idea for the road ahead. Below us lay the town and its palm-fringed beaches and busy marinas and in the distance, the deserts of Almería and the Sierra Nevada. We left town on the RM-333 south, heading out along the coast as closely as possible and then following signs to San Juan de los Terreros (this is the A-332). The landscape was of fossilised sand dunes, low hills and cliffs, with plenty of opportunities to park up next to the sea. Outside San Juan, take the AL-7107 along the coast to more scrubby countryside, a few villas and lots of opportunities to park by the sea. There are great views, too, and, as you get closer to Garrucha, a few old mine workings and grey scrubby hillsides. This turns to holiday sprawl as you get to Garrucha, with a few theme parks, villa complexes and beaches. Take the AL-5107 at Garrucha to stay on the coast and make your way slowly through the holiday complexes of Urbanización Los Ángeles and Mojácar.

After Mojácar, the road goes inland a little and takes you over the pass by the Mirador de la Granatilla, where the views to the south are incredible. There's a great winding mountain road, too, which leads you into Carboneras. Follow the coast still and then take the road south (N-341) for a while before turning off along the coast, past the port and on to the AL-5106 to Agua Amarga, where you will enter the *parque natural*. This road does a loop to the south via Agua Amarga and joins the N-341 further on into the desert. You'll start to see large-scale agriculture here in the form of plastic-clad greenhouses that will be a feature for some time since the area around Almería is famous for growing a lot of the fruit and veg we rely on. The N-341 brings you out at the A-7 *autovía* at junction 494.

Head north on the A-7 one junction and come off at 504 on to the A-1102 heading north to Los Molinos de Río Aguas, on another great mountain road through the desert of Almería. It's dry, scrubby and hot, with a few olive terraces and deep, dry canyons. You will reach the N-340. Turn left towards Almería and cruise on this easy, straight road along the valley that was once the Roman road serving this area. You'll pass through seas of olives, factories and solar farms, with the ever-present greenhouses. Ahead of you is the Sierra Nevada and either side of you there are more mountains. You'll pass the turn-off for Tabernas and before too long will arrive at Fort Bravo and then Oasys MiniHollywood a few miles later. The N-340 then hits the A-92 *autovía*. Here, the N-340 continues alongside it, taking you through a few forgotten towns that don't look so very different from the Wild West film sets.

Just after Rioja, in the village of Benahadux, you'll come to a roundabout. Turn right here on to the A-348 – the road that will take you along the southern slopes of the Sierra Nevada. This is a magnificent road, with incredible views, more greenhouses, olive groves, scrub and desert, and deep ravines. The region is called Las Alpujarras and was the last stronghold of the Moors who were pushed out of Spain in the 1490s, settling here before finally leaving. The architecture that remains in a lot of the villages is typical of the Moors and similar to that found today in North Africa. To find a lot of them, you will need to head north on to the A-4130, a road that will take you into the high and wild mountains and that runs parallel (sort of) to the A-348. You can turn off at Cherín and Narila to reach it.

You'll pass through Órgiva and Lanjarón on the A-348 before it brings you to junction 164 of the A-44 motorway. There is no realistic choice other than to join it in the direction of Granada, which is fine for a few junctions. Take the GR-30 for the Alhambra.

The Alhambra is signposted clearly from the GR-30 and then the A-395, as is the Sierra Nevada, which is on the A-395, the road that will transport you straight up into the mountains and up to over 2,000m (6,562ft).

WHERE TO STAY: CAMPING

Camping Las Lomas, Güejar Sierra
Carretera de Güejar Sierra km 6.5, 18160
Güejar Sierra, Granada, Spain
Tel: +34 958 48 47 42
Web: www.campinglaslomas.com

A great campsite with a pool and very nice staff, plus a fantastic restaurant overlooking the mountains, not far from Granada

WHERE TO STAY: *AIRES*

Agua Amarga Camper Park: A great *aire* in Agua Amarga, a tiny enclave on the Cabo de Gata.
Alhambra: It is possible to stay at the Alhambra overnight. No facilities. A little expensive.

IN THE AREA

The Alhambra, Granada If you only go and see one thing when you visit Spain, make it the Alhambra, the finest example of Islamic architecture in Europe. It is exquisite, in the finest sense of the word. However, it's busy. So, book tickets online and book them for early in the day. The Alhambra opens at 8.15 a.m. and the Palacios Nazaríes opens at 8.30 a.m. for the first visit. Book online and take your passport. Tickets include access to the palace, Alcazaba and Generalife, a summer palace and gardens that is incredible. • **www.alhambra.org**

Fort Bravo, Almería An original set for shooting Westerns that was bought by a stuntman to improve his chances of getting work, this theme park is fascinating, if not a little run-down (which is what makes it brilliant). There are shows every day and an *aire* for campers and mohos. • **www.fortbravo.org**

Oasys MiniHollywood, Almería The other original Hollywood theme park, with real sets used in Spaghetti Westerns of the 1970s. Perhaps swisher and slicker than Fort Bravo and with an animal park and aquatic zone. Also offers free Western shows daily. You decide which you'd rather visit. • **www.oasysparquetematico.com**

Sierra Nevada There's skiing in the winter and biking in the summer at this small, purpose-built resort at 2,000m (6,562ft). • **www.sierranevada.es**

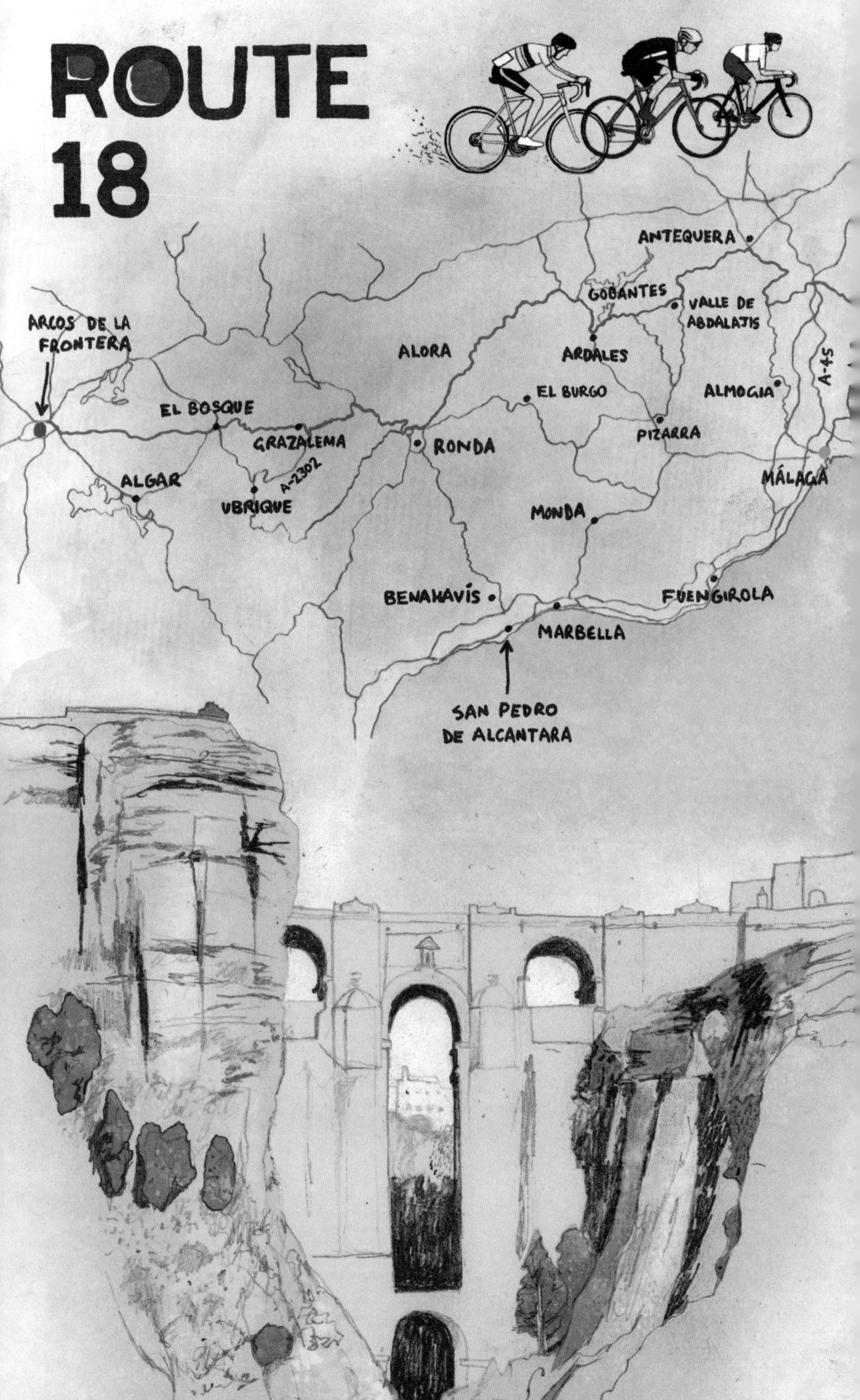

ROUTE
18
ANTEQUERA
GOBANTES
VALLE DE
ABDALAJIS
ARCOS DE LA
FRONTERA
ALORA
ARDALES
A-45
EL BURGO
ALMOGIA
EL BOSQUE
GRAZALEMA
RONDA
PIZARRA
A-2302
ALGAR
UBRIQUE
MÁLAGA
MONDA
BENAHAVÍS
FUENGIROLA
MARBELLA
SAN PEDRO
DE ALCANTARA

ROUTE 18

MÁLAGA TO ARCOS DE LA FRONTERA

THE BIG RACE

Andalusia is famous for its *pueblos blancos* or 'white villages'. While travelling between them, the camper van adventurer will find some excellent and intensely dramatic driving. Passing through a number of *parques naturales* you'll find a couple of good swimming spots, a crazy gorge walk, some tough cycling and great hiking as well as rare habitats where you can see bee orchids by the side of the road and fantastical limestone landscapes that look like nothing you've ever seen before. At the heart of it is Ronda, a busy, beautiful *pueblo blanco* that's one of the best.

BEST FOR: White villages, walking, cycling and swimming

START: Málaga

END: Arcos de la Frontera

MILEAGE: 281km (174 miles)

ALLOW: 7 days

MAP PAGES: 92, 93

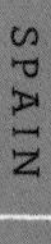

We park up at the campsite a little way out of Ronda and climb aboard our e-bikes for a quick trip into town to do some sightseeing, have a meal and enjoy the atmosphere. Ronda is one of the major players in the *pueblo blanco* market and we want to soak it all up.

I'm not expecting a big welcome in Ronda if I am honest. The last time I was here, sometime in the late 1990s, nothing remarkable happened. I stayed for a few days and then left. I expect to be able to slip into the town unnoticed. Just another tourist, which I am.

We cruise down the hill and arrive at a roadblock at the foot of the road leading to the old town. I ask a policeman if it's OK for us to pass and he says yes, it is, but go slowly. I had heard from the receptionist at the campsite that the roads were closed because of a big event so I think nothing of it as we climb the hill. Something is a bit odd though. There

are people lining the road on either side and some of them are clapping and cheering as we pass. We cruise up the hill, coming up fast behind some panting cyclists (who don't have the luxury of e-bikes) and who have numbers on their bikes. More cheering. The further we go, the more people there are, the more clapping greets us.

It takes us a few moments to realise that we have crashed the final stages of a bicycle race. At this rate, it seems, we might even be in with a chance of a medal.

More cyclists come up the hill behind us, all of them in team jerseys and all of them looking absolutely pooped. We pull off the road and head off down a side alley to get away from the crowds. Lizzy is mortified. I find it funnier than she does. We look for a way through to Ronda's famous bridge, but when we find ourselves in a dead end with no way back but to head down the main road again – the route of the race – I am all for it.

Ronda

We join the race again, freewheeling down the last little hill towards Ronda's famous Puente Nuevo, the huge bridge that was built over the town's gigantic chasm, as people cheer us. More often than not they clock that we aren't in the race – probably something to do with the way we are dressed for a night out rather than a bicycle race – once we get close, then they laugh. I shrug my shoulders as we cruise to the bridge and stop. We can't keep this up. We walk the last section, doing our best to blend in with the crowd, fully undeserving of any welcome, accolades or cheering.

Still, that's the way to arrive in town, I think.

The 101km (62.8-mile) Ronda race, a gruelling stretch of off-road biking and running, is run by the army and is famous throughout Spain. Eight thousand (plus two) people enter each year and it is a huge spectacle, drawing big crowds and filling the town.

We lock the bikes and lose our bike helmets. The town is thronged with people who cheer each competitor over the line. On the bridge, the police blow their whistles to warn of incoming competitors as the crowds wait to cross the road. The sun is hot and it's busy on the main thoroughfare so we walk to a viewpoint for a good look at the gorge and the countryside below. We gaze down at the chasm and see the river 120m (394ft) below us. Where the gorge opens out, we see a road snaking its way up the hill towards the town. It looks dusty and steep and stands out from the lush green fields either side. There is a steady stream of cyclists making their way up

the road. Most of them are pushing their bikes up the steep hill. It looks excruciating and we wonder how the cyclists are feeling after having done almost 100km (62 miles) of rising to suddenly encounter this hill. It must be torture. We feel more than a little humbled – and foolish – seeing this.

We walk around the old quarter, check out the views, the old bridges and a beautiful garden that's been built into the side of the gorge. Ronda is truly lovely and we are enchanted by it. It's the king of all the *pueblos blancos* and we can see why. Narrow cobbled streets full of bars, with tables and chairs on the street, give the place a carnival atmosphere. And all the while, the cyclists are limping up the hill and freewheeling down the straight to a rapturous welcome. When we settle down to eat at an open-air restaurant adjacent to Ronda's famous bullring we can see the competitors as they pass, just 50m (55 yards) from the finish. The clanging of cowbells and the cheering and clapping lends a surreal soundtrack to our meal as we eat and drink like champions.

The next day, we climb aboard the bikes again to go for a proper ride in the hills around Ronda. Our mission is to cycle to the Cueva del Gato ('Cave of the Cat'), a local beauty spot and place to swim where, we understand, water comes out of the mouth of the cave that looks a bit like the face of a cat. Armed with a map of local cycle routes, some of which make up part of the race, we set off, choosing a route to get there that includes some of those ridden yesterday by the peloton of 8,000 riders. We are immediately astounded by the steepness of the climbs. Even on e-bikes, we have to engage turbo and granny gear to get up some of them. We are further humbled by the achievements of the riders who competed yesterday and feel more than a little foolish for being so blasé about crashing their race. Still, we try to make up for it by not getting off to push at any point and by being brave.

It's an exhilarating ride on dusty back roads, through meadows filled with pink sweet peas, bright red poppies, pink alliums, blue echiums, white wild roses full of bees and waves of wheat and oat grass swaying in the breeze. We pass soldiers clearing up the debris of the race: plastic tape and gel sachets. All around us there are steep hills and deep valleys, and above that, rocky limestone peaks. It's a beautiful landscape of olive groves, meadows and peaks.

We arrive at the Cuevo del Gato to find it deserted. We lock our bikes and wade across

the river to a walkway beneath a railway that takes us to the pool at the foot of the cave. It is huge, a massive crack in a near-vertical slab, and towers over us as we stand in the shaded glade at the side of the river. A waterfall rushes out of the mouth of the cave and plunges a few metres into a bright blue pool, which, unlike the banks, is blessed with bright sunshine. The water is deep and clear and frothing with bubbles. Either side of the waterfall there are bushes with huge pink flowers – like a giant fuchsia – dripping over the surface of the pool. It looks tropical.

Cuevo del Gato

Sadly, when I strip off and enter the water, I find out that it isn't quite as tropical as I had hoped. The water, coming from deep inside the cave system that lies behind the Cuevo del Gato, is cool and more than a little refreshing. As Lizzy and I frolic and swim against the current, people arrive with dogs, which dive into the water and dash around barking. The spell is broken. More people arrive, some with picnics and blankets, but none swim. It's too cold for most.

We dress and make our excuses. We decide to wend our way home on another path that heads into Ronda from the next valley and then picks up the last few miles of the race – the bit that the cyclists had to endure before we joined them.

We follow the road up into a village and then cut out across more meadows, taking a path that rises steeply in a series of sharp hairpins and brings us to the top of the slab above the Cuevo del Gato. The views are stunning, but the path that runs away from us is narrow, with a near-vertical drop of about 100m (328ft) to the cave below if we were to fall. We push the bikes down the path, using the brakes to steady ourselves on difficult sections. I focus on the path and try not to look down at the cave below us. Eventually, the path levels out enough to remount and we freewheel down

the narrow, flower-lined single track to a meadow at the bottom of the valley, where we eat our lunch in the shade of an olive tree.

The last section brings us on to the final few miles of the race. After a climb through a pine forest to a gap in a bluff, we get views of Ronda across the river valley. Seeing the white houses atop the huge sandstone cliff and the gash that cuts the town in half makes us gasp with astonishment. The structure of the Puente Nuevo stands tall, like Samson pushing against the columns of the temple. It's on an epic scale and exactly what we came here for – to experience the *pueblos blancos* of Andalusia in all their forms.

The ride into the valley and up the dusty track on the other side is tough. Yesterday, when we had looked over the edge of the bridge into the valley below, we had seen competitors pushing their bikes up this same stretch of road like tiny ants struggling with their finds. Once again, we are put to shame and feel like cheats as we engage turbo and inch up it ourselves. But at least we don't push. It's not much of a victory to be honest, but it's all we've got.

When we arrive in Ronda and freewheel down the road to the bridge, crossing it in beads of sweat, there is no one cheering.

THE DRIVING

Ronda is the middle point of this journey, and it makes up a small section of it. From the start in Málaga to the final descent from the Sierra de Grazalema it's a bumpy, undulating, exhilarating ride (whether you get on your bike or not). The scenery is second to none and the roads are, for the most part excellent. There are also some useful diversions to take that will get you to some of the more popular *pueblos blancos* and I have listed them here. All in all, I loved finding and driving this route. We did it in May, when the meadows were filled with flowers and the hillsides covered with the exuberant shoots of spring.

Starting in Målaga, on the A-7, come off at junction 243. The road you are looking for, the A-7000, begins in a steep neighbourhood above the city but then soon winds its way out of the smog and into the hills – very sharply – and back over the A-7. As you progress, you'll pass a *mirador* (viewpoint) that's worth a stop for the views back towards the Med, then through a couple of tunnels that makes it feel as if you are actually corkscrewing up the mountain.

Now you're in forested mountain, a national park, with broom, pines, cistus and gorse on the roadsides. You'll reach the Puerto de León, which at 900m (2,953ft) is way above where you started only a few kilometres

El Torcal de Antequera

away. Keep going straight on towards Colmenar as you descend and pass through high meadows and olive groves. At Colmenar, take the A-7204, following it under the A-45 motorway and then take the first left to Villanueva de la Concepción on a small white road that will lead you into the neat village and then out again on the very steep A-7075 towards Antequera. A little outside the village, you'll see signs for El Torcal. This is a Parque Natural and is well worth taking a detour up the (very steep) road to the Parque centre (ignore the first two car parks and take a sharp left). Even if you don't take this little detour, you'll realise that the landscape here is massive and very impressive. Strange-shaped limestone crags – a bit like weathered tors but much, much bigger – hang above the road on the north side while the valley drops away dramatically on the south side. It's all rather excellent. After the turn-off to El Torcal, the road slides through a gap in the mountains and descends towards Antequera among high meadows and the back of the limestone peaks on your left, with plenty of silver broom and gorse on the roadsides.

Before Antequera, take the A-343 towards Álora, another stunning road that runs alongside the Sierra de Chimenea and through extensive olive groves and grassy meadows with peaks above. It's a landscape of pointy lumps rather than rolling hills, and the road curves and bucks as it negotiates them, going around, below and over. It's narrow in places but a great drive all the same. It will bring you under a railway viaduct at the valley bottom then into Álora, a place of lemon and lime trees.

Follow signs for Álora and El Chorro through the outskirts over the river and railway line. At the roundabout, turn right, following signs for El Chorro on the MA-5403 up the Garganta del Chorro, a narrow valley lined by lemon trees. When you come to the dam, go over it and park if you intend to walk the Caminito del Rey (walkway). Alternatively, you can park at the other end and bus it back. If you don't fancy it, follow the road past the dam and up the side of the reservoir (great views of the Caminito del Rey as you go). This road is a real smasher and will take you through some extraordinary sandstone rock formations in the pine forest. Take a right when you reach the Embalse del Conde de Guadalhorce if you want to swim or camp at the brilliantly situated Camping Parque Ardales right on the lakeside. This road also takes you to the start point of the Caminito del Rey and gets busy with traffic, especially at the weekend.

Carrying on the MA-5403 will bring you along the reservoir (great views and places to stop) to the junction with the A-357 close to Ardales. Turn right here towards Ronda and then, soon after, take the right slip road on to the A-367, which will take you through the Sierra de los Merinos towards Ronda. The campsite is on the south side of the town, on the A-369.

Leave Ronda on the A-374, the main road to Seville. It's a biggun, but it's worth a look because it's got two big switchbacks and passes through some excellent countryside. First, you'll pass through some excellent *dehesa* as you drop out of the town, then up a gorge with huge trees. As you exit the gorge, take the left-hand turn for the A-372 on a sharp bend. This is signposted for Grazalema and will take you into the Parque Natural Sierra de Grazalema on an exciting, winding road through the forest that's very alpine and makes you want to yodel.

Eventually, after 15km (10 miles) or so, you'll descend into a wide valley with the *pueblo blanco* of Grazalema on the opposite mountainside. The road will take you into the village and through it, but do stop (the car park at the far end of the village is best for mohos) because it's lovely. Great views.

Continue out of Grazalema up and into the mountains again, this time up to 1,103m (3,619ft) at the Puerto del Boyar, where the views down into the valleys below are astounding. We found orchids, including bee orchids, growing by the side of the road here. The descent, on to the plains on the way to Arcos de la Frontera, will take you along the side of the mountains, around a few tight bends and through more olive plantations and forest of pines. Great views all the way. Didn't I say it would be a good one?

Cruise into Arcos de La Frontera through the plains and park up for your final wander through one of the best-placed *pueblos blancos*.

WHERE TO STAY: CAMPING

Área El Hornillo camper park, El Hornillo
Diseminado el Hornillo, 70, 29749 El Hornillo, Málaga, Spain
Web: Find it on Park4Night
Tel: +34 659 96 52 95

This is a camper park that's just short of Torre del Mar to the east of Málaga. It's right on the beach and has half-decent facilities if you don't want to go into a campsite.

Camping Parque Ardales, Málaga
Carretera de los Embalses, Km. 7, 29550 Ardales, Málaga, Spain
Web: www.parqueardales.com
Tel: +34 951 26 49 24

A great place to get an early start on a walk along the Caminito del Rey. Adjacent to the river and with its own beach and water sports.

Camping Tajo Rodillo, El Bosque
Carretera de El Bosque-Grazalema, Km 47, 11610 El Bosque, Cádiz, Spain
Web: www.campingtajorodillo.es
Tel: +34 670 40 79 40

Situated in the forest above Grazalema, this is a great site at which to immerse yourself in the Parque Natural that is famous for birding and rare species of flora.

Camping El Sur, Ronda
Km 1.5, Ronda-Algeciras Road, 29400 Ronda, Málaga, Spain
Web: www.campingelsur.com
Tel: +34 952 87 59 39

A great site with lovely people and a pool. If it's busy, you can stay on the aire next door, which has good showers and all facilities.

Camping El Nogalejo, Setenil de las Bodegas
Carretera de Setenil Alcala, 11692 Setenil de las Bodegas, Cádiz, Spain
Web: www.campingelnogalejo.es
Tel: +34 623 39 28 63

The place to stay if you want to visit this lovely pueblo blanco.

WHERE TO STAY: *AIRES*

Ronda: A paying *aire* in the northern section of the city. All facilities.
Antequera: A free *aire* (dusty car park) overlooking the town and castle. Stunning views. No facilities.

IN THE AREA

Casa Museo Don Bosco, Ronda A mansion on the edge of the gorge with a fabulous interior and tiled gardens. In summer, they put on regular Spanish guitar concerts. • **www.casadonbosco.es**

Hiking and mountain biking around Ronda The tourist office is between the town's bullring and the Puente Nuevo. For €5, they will sell you a detailed map of hiking and mountain biking routes in the area.

El Torcal de Antequera An absolutely incredible area of limestone tors near Antequera. There is a restaurant and interpretation centre at the end of a long and winding road off the A-7075 between Antequera and Villanueva de la Concepción. There are plenty of signposted walks into the area to explore the rocks and see the rare plants, animals and birds. • **www.torcaldeantequera.com**

El Caminito del Rey The 'Little Walk of the King', which runs at 100m (328ft) above the Desfiladero de los Gaitanes, used to be known as the world's most dangerous path following a number of deaths, but today

it's a major attraction, having been updated. In case you were wondering, I didn't do it because I am afraid of heights but it was very busy. Tickets are available in El Churro or from the western end.
• **www.caminitodelrey.info**

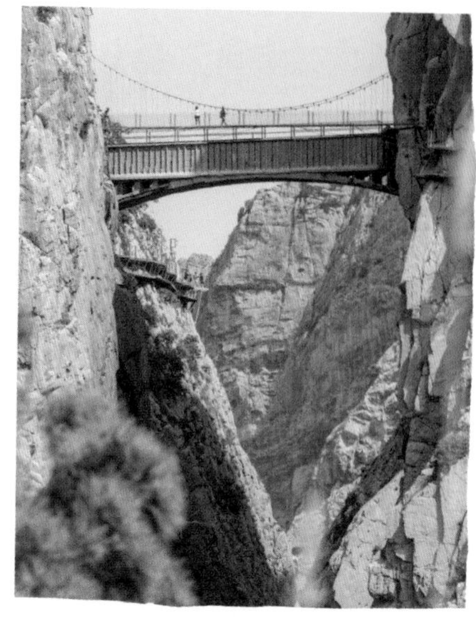

Ronda A marvel of a place, with an astounding gorge separating the town. The Puente Nuevo is huge, while the older two bridges are less impressive but still worth seeing. The bullring, dating back to 1784, is one of the oldest in Spain. There is a great restaurant scene in Ronda, with lots of options. Lots to see and do in the area, including cycling, hiking and sightseeing (see above).

Setenil de las Bodegas This is one of the most famous of all the *pueblos blancos* because it sits in a deep and beautiful gorge. Some of the cliffs overhang the streets. Parking is difficult in the village and the main car park is inaccessible for anything over 2.05m (6.7ft). If you want to visit, and you do, stay at the lovely, newly opened Camping Nogalejo, which is slightly out of town but will enable you to park!
• **www.campingelnogalejo.es**

Cuevo del Gato The 'Cave of the Cat' is so called because it looks a bit like a cat, but not much. It's a popular spot, so get there early. At the time of writing, the bridge across the river was out of commission so it was necessary to wade across the river.
• **www.andalucia.org/en/benaojan-natural-spaces-cueva-del-gato**

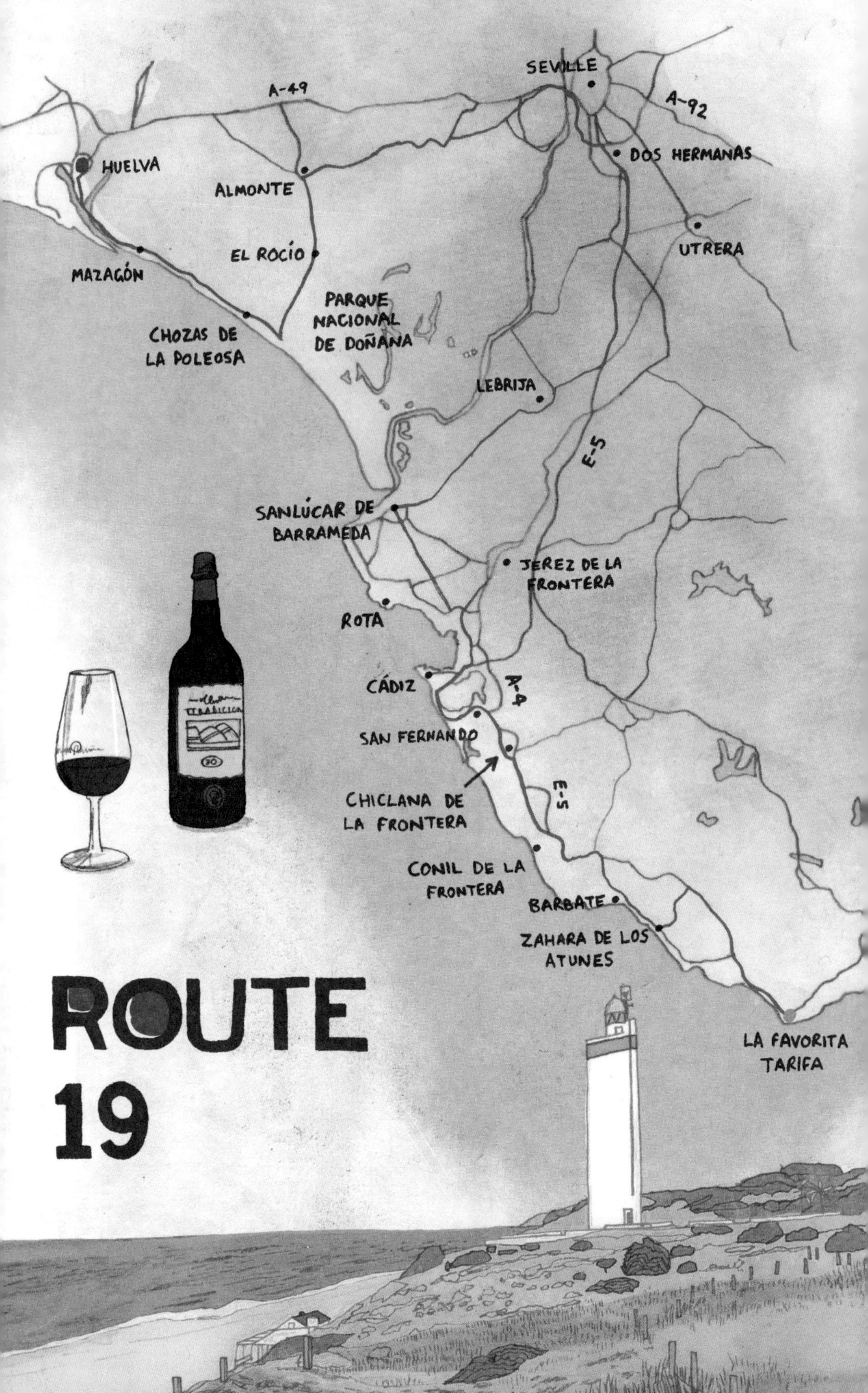
SEVILLE
A-49
A-92
HUELVA
ALMONTE
DOS HERMANAS
UTRERA
EL ROCÍO
MAZAGÓN
PARQUE NACIONAL DE DOÑANA
CHOZAS DE LA POLEOSA
LEBRIJA
E-5
SANLÚCAR DE BARRAMEDA
JEREZ DE LA FRONTERA
ROTA
CÁDIZ
A-4
SAN FERNANDO
CHICLANA DE LA FRONTERA
E-5
CONIL DE LA FRONTERA
BARBATE
ZAHARA DE LOS ATUNES
LA FAVORITA TARIFA
ROUTE 19

ROUTE 19

TARIFA TO HUELVA (VIA THE SHERRY TRIANGLE)

FLAMENCO TO FLAMINGOS

Some things are just about as Spanish as it gets. Sherry and flamenco are two of those things. This journey will take you from a hip beach town at the southernmost tip of Europe, through the Sherry Triangle to taste a drop and then on to Seville and the national park. So, it's got everything. Flamenco, flamingos and maybe even the chance to see an Iberian lynx.

BEST FOR: Flamenco, sherry, flamingos

START: Tarifa

END: Huelva

MILEAGE: 418km (260 miles)

ALLOW: 4–5 days

MAP PAGES: 90, 91, 98, 99

We wake on the quayside in Cádiz. It's a beautiful, warm day and we are slow to get going. Our aim, today, is to drive the Sherry Triangle between Sanlúcar de Barrameda, Jerez de la Frontera and El Puerto de Santa María with the sole purpose of going on a tasting tour in a *bodega*. The driving isn't great because we have little choice but to take *autovías* out of Cádiz. That leaves us free to think about sherry. Our first stop, a few kilometres over the huge, 3km (1.86 miles)-long 'La Pepa' bridge, is El Puerto de Santa María, once an important port for the wine trade.

We drive into the town and park on one of the long, straight roads near to a number of *bodegas*. One of them is the Bodega Osborne, a winery that was set up by an Englishman, Osborne, in 1872 when his family bought all the shares of an existing company, which had operated since 1772. You will know the Osborne brand even if you don't know their name. Their huge, black, bull-shaped Toro Negro (black bull) advertising billboards have been part of the Spanish landscape for decades. They are a big deal in sherry. We decide to give them a miss this time, in favour of one of the smaller *bodegas*, Gutiérrez Colosia, a couple of streets away. A quick Google confirms to us that they offer English language tours in ten minutes. We are in luck but have to hurry.

We arrive at the *bodegas* at 11 a.m. sharp, pay for the tour and a tasting and are duly introduced to Paloma, our Spanish guide. She tells us she has been learning English for three months, which is remarkable as it's very good indeed. Paloma leads us into the warehouse, where hundreds

of dark, time-honoured American oak barrels are stacked up three high. Compared with the outside, it's cool inside at just 23°C (73.4°F), the optimum for the fortification process. It's also dark, with illumination coming from a few lights and some partially covered windows. The huge arches of the warehouse are dark with mould – a result of the humidity and temperature that the casks need to turn the wine into the PDO-status Jerez-Xérès-Sherry that is famous throughout the world.

We walk around the *bodegas* and take in the smells and atmosphere. It feels like a very hallowed place that must be respected for the time, craftsmanship and skill that exist here. We hear a little about the history of the company and the way their wines are made, why they taste the way they do and what makes them different from each other. We see barrels that have been in use for at least 50 years, signed by Spanish celebrities, visitors from afar and the father of Spain's current king, Juan Carlos I. The proof of the pudding, of course, comes later when we are invited to a large

refectory to taste their different sherries. I sit down in front of six partially filled glasses with colours ranging from pale yellow to a deep, chocolatey brown. Paloma talks us through each one as we sip away, taking our time to appreciate the flavours and the story of each. The lightest, the Fino, is a surprise to me. I love its dry, salty taste that's a direct result of the Palomino grapes that are grown by the sea. At the other end of the scale, the Pedro Ximénez, a dark, molasses-coloured sherry that's made with sun-dried grapes, is sweet and rich, with a taste that reminds me of dates and chocolate. Unlike the Cream, a lighter, but sweet sherry that's based on the kind of stuff we like in England, it's too sweet and deep for me, but it still reminds me of Christmas and my grandmother. To break the spell of musty old memories, I go back to the Fino and sip it again, savouring the light and dry almond flavour. It's even better after the sugary sweetness of the Pedro Ximénez. For me, that's what I wanted from this visit – to find something out I didn't know or had assumed already about a drink I often associate with fustiness and tradition. We buy a bottle of Fino and a bottle of Moscatel, a sherry that's somewhere between the Cream and the Pedro Ximénez, intensely flavoured and with a hint of orange blossom and honeysuckle.

Shopping completed, we step out into bright sunshine from the cool of the *bodegas* and are struck by the temperature. It's now midday and it's warming up. We set off to explore the rest of the route.

When we approach Seville from the south, I have the air conditioning on in the van. I usually try to live without it as I feel it gives us a false sense of where we are, especially when it's hot. But today, I feel that we deserve a little treat. It's glorious to feel the cool air on my hands as I hold them over the vents. I look down at the instrument panel and notice that the temperature has hit a new high – it reads 40°C (104°F).

I turn off the aircon and wind down my window to feel the temperature. Can it really be that hot? The simple answer is yes. The air is hot and dry, as if I'd just turned a hairdryer on myself. It's the kind of temperature that's hard to imagine. You might be mistaken for thinking it would be too stuffy to breathe. Thankfully, I don't die of exhaustion or exposure or heat stroke or any other heat-caused condition and we are able to continue on, hoping that, eventually, it will cool down or we'll get used to it. We find the *aire* closest to the city, a secure compound run by a car valeting and delivery company. It's perfect, but very, very warm.

We set out in the early evening to find somewhere to have food and watch flamenco. We have a recommendation from one of Lizzy's gardening clients, a bon viveur, designer and gentleman in his eighties. When we mentioned we might be in Seville he gave us the name of a club that he had visited so this is our homage to him. We get very lost trying to navigate our way around the old city. Unlike Cádiz, which is laid out on a grid system, Seville's heart is an intoxicating and confusing maze of tiny cobbled alleyways, lanes, blind alleys and *callejones*. The heat isn't helping as we push our bikes down lanes thronged with people, but every so often, we make a turn and find a dark, cool alley. The drop in temperature between places is remarkable.

Eventually, down a hot, narrow lane we find the place, or at least we think we do. A small red door in a larger door is ajar. Inside, we can just about make out that the alley continues on. The walls are painted blue and white and there are pot plants lining the way. Lizzy walks in to check it out. She comes back and says she thinks it is the place so we lock the bikes,

have a bit of a freshen up (I take off my sweaty T-shirt and replace it with a Hawaiian for coolness) and walk through the door.

We reach a courtyard. It's about 20m (66ft) square and completely enclosed by buildings at least four storeys high. There are tables and chairs and a sun canopy over part of it. The rest of the courtyard is taken over by palms in pots, geraniums and a huge tree with a vine growing up and around it. The lush greenery makes it feel cooler, and yet more humid than the street outside. Along one side of the courtyard there is a roof that leads to a large, open bar with a raised platform along the back wall.

I walk in. There are a few people sitting on benches at long, well-worn refectory tables and a bar down one side. The floor is concrete. Around the walls there are posters. Ceiling fans keep the hot air moving – just. Opposite the bar, a woman prepares food in a tiny kitchen, handing out the dishes on paper plates: tacos, guacamole, tortilla, *ensalada*. As I stand at the bar waiting to be served, I catch snippets of accents: there are Americans, Germans and French here as well as Spanish. The atmosphere is excited. People are eating and drinking, waiting for the show. Some people fan themselves. It's hot and reminds me of bars I have been to in Central America rather than anything I have visited here in Spain: it's a little ramshackle, a little home-made, a little out of time and a little down-at-heel but feels welcoming all the same. The bar staff are friendly. It's cash only for jugs of sangria. I wanted the real deal and hope that this is it.

I buy a couple of drinks at the bar and step outside but almost as soon as Lizzy and I sit down a group of people arrive so we decide to claim a seat for ourselves inside before it gets too late. We sit, order some tortilla and *jamón y queso* (ham and cheese). The place fills up and gets hotter.

I really want this experience to be 'authentic' (whatever that means) and am really happy that the atmosphere appears genuine, but I realise that the large majority of the audience are non-Spanish. Behind me, a young American tells a Spanish couple about his travels in a loud, somewhat stereotypically brash voice. I let it drift over me and continue to ease myself into the spirit of the evening: we are here to see and listen to flamenco, an art form associated with Andalusian gypsies that's full of love, anger and grief. The heat is in the emotion, as well as the air. Even if we've come to a flamenco pastiche, I will rest assured that at least we came at a time when the temperature was right. I sweat into my Hawaiian shirt.

The lights dim and three figures – a woman with tied-back black hair, wearing a black shawl over a black-and-white dress, a man, and a young woman with a Spanish guitar – step out from behind a red curtain. There's no stage and they take seats in the corner of the bar next to the kitchen. The man stands up and makes a quick speech in Spanish then sits down between the two women. The guitarist begins to pluck at the strings of her guitar. It's unamplified but it resonates beautifully throughout, its bass notes reverberating around the room. The man starts to sing and the woman, claps her hands and stamps her feet, flamenco style, as she begins to join in and add the colour and harmony.

I don't understand the lyrics but I can feel the rhythm, mood and texture of the music. It seems to soar and then plummet, like a high-flying bird. It dives and swoops, at once mournful and joyful, angry and soulful. Despite having heard flamenco many times during my life on the media – or snippets of it – it's nothing like I expect. All the cues are there but this is different, like someone getting up to do a turn because they want to. It's a little like a trad session in an Irish bar.

The second piece of music sees

the woman take to her feet and begin dancing. She stamps her feet and swirls the skirt of her dress. Her face is serious and focused, her arms expressive and precise, her feet strong and rhythmic. The crowd is as engaged as she is with the music, leaning forwards on their chairs and benches and crowding the intimate performance space eagerly. A few of them clap along. It feels real, hot and sensuous, emotions perfectly conveyed, and controlled and released as the bird of the music soars and swoops, dives and crashes.

The crowd erupts as the song comes to an end and the lights go up. The dancer is sweating and panting as she takes the applause and sits down, picking up a fan to cool herself. The crowd begins to disperse and we sit in the room as it empties, doing our best to take it all in. It feels tropical, like a hot night in Panama or Barbados. The lush garden makes it feel more so as we walk out into the courtyard and then through the little red door and out into the heat of the night, where the streets are thronging with people.

Seville Cathedral

A few roads away we find the cathedral. Lit by orange sodium lights, it looks vast against the deep blue of the night sky. It's still incredibly hot.

We cycle back to the van, cooling off with the breeze our momentum gives us, and sleep on top of the covers.

Tarifa

THE DRIVING

As I stated earlier, the Sherry Triangle doesn't make particularly brilliant driving, so a lot of this route is not about that. It's about the experiences to be found along the way. From flamenco to flamingos in the Parque Nacional de Doñana, there is a lot to be savoured and enjoyed.

We began our journey in Tarifa, on Spain's southern tip. It's the most southerly point in mainland Europe and is just under 15km (9 miles) from Africa. The town is surfy and cool, with great bars and an old town that oozes hip, along with the promise of a good night out.

Heading west out of Tarifa on the N-340 you'll pass along the back of the huge beach at Tarifa. There are campsites and stops along the way here and it's where a lot of van people, surfers and kite surfers hang out.

As you head north-west, you'll notice a huge dune ahead of you. If you want to visit it then take the road to Punta Paloma (A-2325). If the wind has been blowing, you might just get to see what I consider to be the pinnacle of human futility as diggers and bulldozers struggle to keep the road open despite the sands of the dune threatening to engulf it. The views back to Tarifa are great.

Continuing on the N-340, the next left turn (CA-8202) will take you to the ruins at Baelo Claudia. It's a nice drive over a small pass and through pasture and below a couple of rocky hills in the Parque Natural del Estrecho. At the end of the road – it's another dead end – the Roman ruins are amazing.

Back on the N-340, you'll pass through fields of wind turbines and agriculture with distant hills. It feels remote and wild – just farm land and *dehesa*.

Take a left towards Zahara to get back to the coast. This is the A-2227 and it will take you to Zahara, a swanky but incongruous resort in the middle of nowhere. Follow the A-2231 for Barbate next. This is a road that runs along the coast with lots of opportunity to get out and swim. Barbate is a big port town and is close to Cape Trafalgar. When you arrive in town, you'll go over a bridge, then take a left at the roundabout in town to follow the A-2233, which will take you out past the port and into the Parque Natural Cabo de Trafalgar – consisting of scrub and pine forest.

You'll get great views down the hill to Los Caños de Meca as you descend the cape and head into another lovely stretch of coast, where there are a few surf towns (El Palmar and Zahora) and lots of opportunities to get wet. At El Palmar, take the left turn on to the CA-215 in the direction of Conil de la Frontera. This will take you along the coast again to Conil, a place with an open sea front (although mohos aren't allowed in many of the car parks – beware). In Conil, take the CA-3208 out of town and then take another left turn towards Cabo Roche on the CA-4202. This will lead you to the lighthouse and then a section of coast with a number of tiny coves. The sandstone here is like crumble and is filled with shells and fossils. The beaches are popular but well worth a walk down the cliffs. Head through Roche (a community in the middle of nowhere) and into and through Novo Sancti Petri, which appears to be a series of high-end gated communities catering to golfers.

Once here, the mission is to find your way to the A-48 for Cádiz. There are plenty of signs showing you the way so follow them on to the *autovía* and out through the salt pans and marshlands around Cádiz. Follow the CA-33 if you want to see Cádiz. If not, follow the A-4 and then the AP-4 and then the CA-32 to El Puerto de Santa María.

You can drive the Sherry Triangle but it's not that interesting. Motorways make up two side of it. The other side, the A-2001 between Sanlúcar de Barrameda and El Puerto de Santa María, is long and straight and passes through arable land, with the occasional vineyard. So don't sweat it. The most important part is the sherry.

Once you have had your fill, the next stop on this journey is Seville, which sits at the top of the Parque Nacional de Doñana and gets in the way if you want to follow the coast. However, Seville is a wonderful, chaotic, hot and sultry city that somehow manages to keep its linen pressed and its denizens cool, calm and collected.

From the Sherry Triangle, take the AP-4-E-5 *autovía*. Follow your app for *aires* mentioned below – it's much easier than me explaining!

When it comes to leaving Seville, take the A-49 *autovía* for Huelva, then come off at junction 11 for Bollullos de la Mitación on the A-8059. Follow signs for Aznalcázar and Pilas and join the A-474. Follow the A-474 around Pilas (the ring road goes to the south), then take the A-8060. This will lead

you into the national park, but also alongside plenty of polytunnels and agriculture first. You'll pass through Villamanrique de la Condesa and then hit a long, straight stretch (at least 20km/12.4 miles) which runs you through the park – the downside is that there are lots of speed bumps. But that's good because you'll get to slow down!

The A-8060 joins the A-483 just outside El Rocío, the weirdest town I have ever been to. It sits on a lagoon and has sandy streets that make it feel more like the Midwest than Spain. The church is huge, with a huge, gilded and ornate apse. There is also a campsite and a 1,000-year-old olive tree.

From El Rocío, take the A-483 south to Matalascañas, where you'll meet the coast. Turn right and take the A-494 towards Huelva. This road will carry you along the coast but with no views of it, though it does run behind the dune system, and there are several points where it is possible to walk to the beach. The A-494 turns into the N-442 for the final few kilometres into Huelva, which goes straight through the middle of the oil refineries here. If you take the A-494 towards Moguer you can visit the Monasterio de La Rábida, a 14th-century monastery at which Christopher Columbus prayed (presumably that his smallpox would clear up before he landed in the New World – sorry, bad-taste joke).

The church (*top image*) and 1,000-year-old olive tree at El Rocío

WHERE TO STAY: CAMPING

Torre de la Peña, Tarifa
km 78, N-340, 11380 Tarifa, Cádiz, Spain
Web: www.campingtp.com/en
Tel: +34 956 68 49 03

A nice site on the road out of Tarifa with a pleasant seawater pool. It straddles the main road so the beach side (with a great beach bar) is the one to pitch up on if possible. Waterside pitches go early.

Camping la Aldea, El Rocío
Carretera de El Rocío, Km 25,
21750 El Rocío, Spain
Web: www.campinglaaldea.com
Tel: +34 959 44 26 77

A really nice campsite that's well laid out, has good-sized plots and a great pool. Perfect for visiting the national park.

WHERE TO STAY: *AIRES*

Seville, Gelves: A paying *aire* in the port area of Seville. Safe and secure in a compound devoted to valeting cars. Nice people and all facilities. It's a 10-minute cycle into the historic centre.

Cádiz: At the farthest end of the island there is a secure car park that will allow you to overnight (paying). There are no services but it's a great location near the old city and adjacent to the Castillo de Santa Catalina.

IN THE AREA

Tarifa The old town of Tarifa is small and perfectly formed, with alleys and squares and lots of places to get your espadrilles and surf gear. Great pastries, too. Lots of kitesurfing to see on the town beaches when the wind is right. Great sand, blue sea. Loved it.

Roman ruins, Baelo The ruins here are really spectacular and have an impressive seaside location. There are bathhouses, a forum and a theatre as well as a great museum. Free. **www.museosdeandalucia.es/web/conjuntoarqueologicobaeloclaudia**

Seville Seville is a great city with lots of atmosphere and style. It's hot in summer, but the narrow, winding lanes will keep you cool. The area around the cathedral is fantastic and filled with bars and restaurants.

Seville Cathedral, Seville A gothic masterpiece and the largest of its type in the world. It's immense and dominates the old city. Tours and tower visits daily. **www.catedraldesevilla.es**

El Rocío

Flamenco There are lots of places to see flamenco in Seville, and also in the other towns of the Sherry Triangle. We went to:

LA CARBONERÍA SEVILLA
A tavern and tapas bar with free live music and flamenco. Worth it for the atmosphere. • **www.lacarbonerialevies.blogspot.com**

Sherry Triangle There are plenty of *bodegas* in and around the Sherry Triangle, including the famous Osborne, of the silhouetted bulls on hillsides fame. We went to:

BODEGAS GUTIÉRREZ COLOSÍA, EL PUERTO DE SANTA MARÍA
One of the smaller *bodegas* in El Puerto de Santa María. Friendly, and delicious sherry. Daily tours in English at 11 a.m. Check for details: • **www.gutierrezcolosia.com**

Parque Nacional de Doñana A huge national park and important wetland area for birds and animals. Vast and unpopulated, with few roads. Visitor centres at El Acebrón, La Rocina and El Acebuche. You can take tours in huge 4WD trucks if you want or ride horses around El Rocío. Alternatively, get up early and watch the roost take off from the *paseo* (walkway) overlooking the lagoon and El Rocío. • **www.miteco.gob.es/es/red-parques-nacionales/nuestros-parques/donana/#section**

PORTUGAL

From Porto to Faro, Portugal is exciting, lively and interesting. It has great museums, fabulous food and drink, heavenly beaches and beautiful mountains. The surf is awesome and the people friendly. With lots of really good campsites and a growing network of aires, it is a brilliant place to take a camper van or motorhome. You won't want to come home!

Praia do Zavial

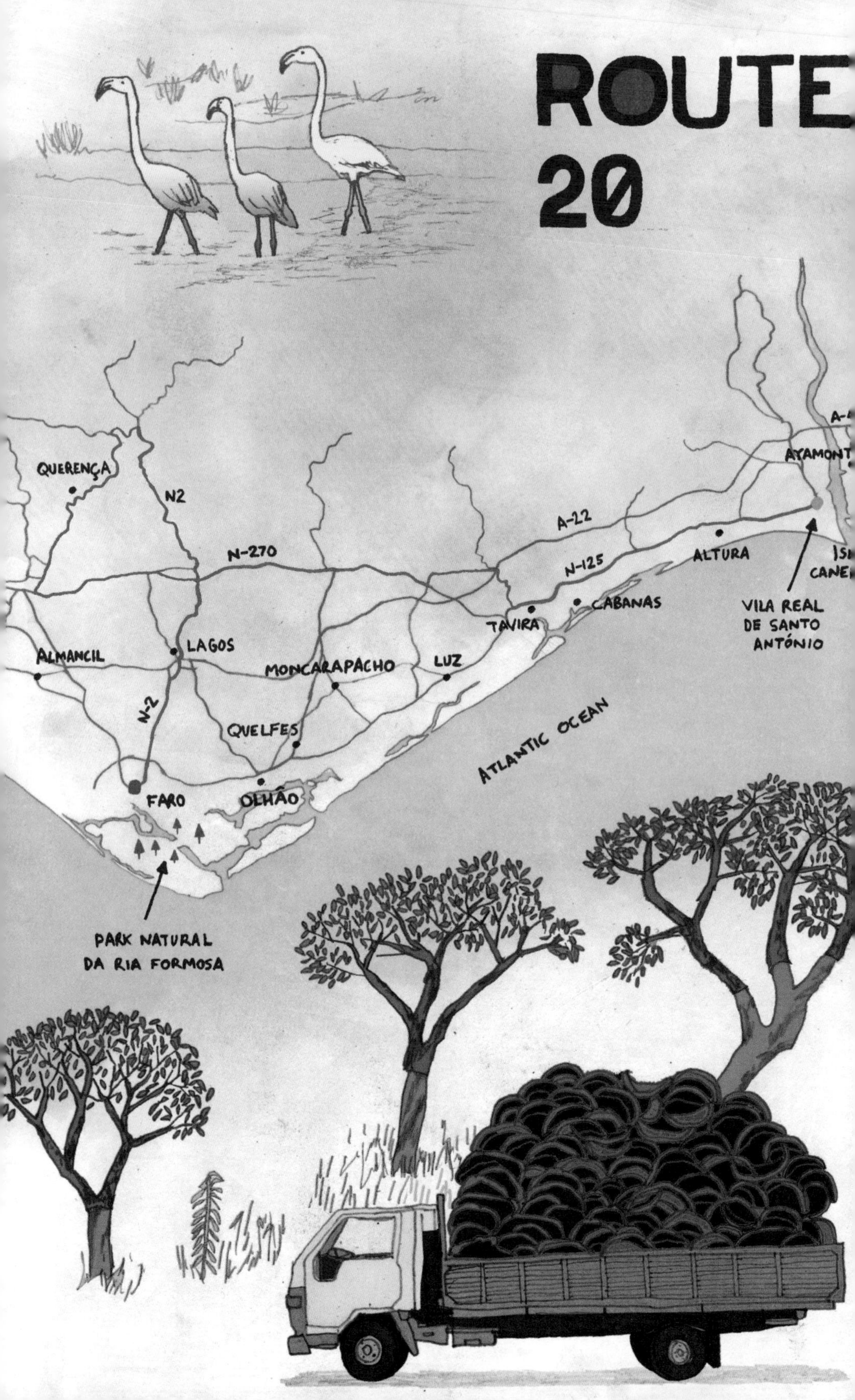

ROUTE
20
QUERENÇA
N2
N-270
A-22
N-125
ALTURA
CABANAS
TAVIRA
VILA REAL
DE SANTO
ANTÓNIO
LAGOS
ALMANCIL
MONCARAPACHO
LUZ
N-2
QUELFES
ATLANTIC OCEAN
FARO
OLHÃO
PARK NATURAL
DA RIA FORMOSA

ROUTE 20

VILA REAL TO FARO

A JOURNEY OF DISCOVERY

Once you cross the Guadiana River you enter Portugal. Here, you can almost immediately hit the beach. Within a few miles, you'll arrive in the Parque National da Ria Formosa, a huge area of wetland and islands that stretches 60km (37 miles) from Manta Rota to Garrão beyond Faro. Behind it, snaking off into the Serra do Caldeirão, is a fantastic route of that's sometimes called Portugal's Route 66. And almost nobody has heard of it.

BEST FOR: Beaches, kayaking, cycling, driving

START: Vila Real

END: Faro

MILEAGE: 181km (112 miles)

ALLOW: 4–5 days

MAP PAGES: 89, 90

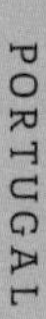

Occasionally, I meet people who throw me off course, even if they don't mean to. Bruno is one of those people. He runs the new *aire* at São Brás de Alportel, a small town just north of Faro. We meet him when we are packing up to leave after a night at the *aire* and pop into the office to say goodbye.

We are here because we wanted to drive the N2 north out of Faro. I wanted to include this section of the road because it would enable us to do a loop to visit Loulé, swim in a waterfall and cycle a part of the Via Algarviana, a long-distance footpath and MTB trail that crosses the bottom of Portugal from Alcoutim to Cabo de São Vicente. As usual, we wanted to get a flavour of what it's like to be here, in the hills of the eastern Algarve.

We had begun at the border, stopping at Tavira and taking the ferry across to Tavira Island, a fabulous islet that's part of the chain of the Ria Formosa archipelago and home to chameleons and lizards and all kinds of littoral flora, including the yellow broomrape orchid. There we swam in the sea, walked through the bush and explored the island. From Tavira, we took a tiny road out of the town to find the waterfall, and then ended up on the N2 heading north with the intention of using our legs on the hills of the Serra do Caldeirão.

We had set off on our ride, only to have a spoke break on the very first descent. This took us into Loulé, a tidy town with a great vibe and a lively market, to find a bike shop. By the time the bike was fixed we had decided to stay the night at the *aire*. So that's how we come to meet Bruno.

With trees giving shade, an area for pétanque, a BBQ area, electricity, Wi-Fi, showers and washing machines, it is easily the nicest *aire* we have stayed on. And yet we are the only ones here, which I find baffling. It should be full. I wander into the small reception and thank Bruno for the *aire* and tell him how nice I think it is. He tells me, in his soft Portuguese accent, that it's new and not very busy. But he believes it will get busier because it's on the Estrada Nacional 2, a recent tourism route that he hopes will bring more visitors to São Brás de Alportel. I ask him more about the N2 and he hands me a leaflet for a small museum that's in the town devoted to the workers who maintained the roads during the time of the Estado Novo (New State), the regime created by Portuguese dictator António de Oliveira Salazar in the 1930s.

This little bit of information changes everything. We had intended to drive the N2 because of its beauty but had little understanding of its significance until now. We head into town and, after taking an age to park, we find the Casa Memória EN2. It's a tiny white building with blue windows and doors on the old N2 in the middle of the town. It looks closed but a sign on the door says it's open so we knock gently, hoping to be able to get in to have a look. Sophie, immaculately dressed in white jeans and a frilled blouse, answers and lets us in. She apologises for her English (we also apologise for our Portuguese) and begins to tell us the story of the museum and the N2.

The house is just one of its kind remaining in Portugal, and is where the local governing office of the road workers was housed during the Estado Novo after the creation of the Estrada Nacional 2 – the first road to cross the country – in 1945. The local workers – the *camareros* – were housed in unique-style buildings situated every 16km (10 miles) along the road. They lived and worked from these buildings, with each man

responsible for 8km (5 miles) of roadway. In the museum, the tools of the trade are on display along with images of the road from shortly after it was completed. Sophie explains the significance of the N2 to Portugal and to those living near it. Until then, all routes radiated out of Lisbon so it became vitally important for trade to the cork and wine growers of the region.

Today, the road has been superseded by motorways and aeroplanes, so people no longer need to travel the N2 to get from the north of Portugal to the south and vice versa. While the road has been assimilated in places, or downgraded in others, it is still possible to travel its entire length. In 2015, so I understand, local councils along the route got together to bring the N2 back to significance, this time as a tourism route, to try to lure a little of Portugal's lucrative tourism industry away from the beaches.

The museum displays images of the roadhouses where the roadworkers lived, as well as petrol stations that were once controlled by the state. Each was identical and some still stand today. The pizzeria we passed on our way to the museum was once a weighbridge and police HQ where trade could be controlled.

At the end of the mini tour, we are given 'passports' that we can get stamped at various places along the 738km (459 miles) of the road. I promise to do my best to drive the whole length of the route, even if I have to do it at intervals. That's the change this discovery brings: sending me off in a different direction, all from a simple conversation. It's what travelling these slow roads is all about for me.

We set off – on the N2 of course – to get to Barranco do Velho, the point where the Via Algarviana crosses the N2. As we climb away from the coast, we see the road in a new light. We see the tiled, hand-painted waymarkers on the sides of the few workers' houses that remain. Each one, like the petrol stations of the day, are identical and housed two workers. Each would be responsible for their 8km (5 miles) either side of the house. We find a few. Mostly they are empty, abandoned and looking a bit sad, but in other places they have become homes or official buildings.

The thing that strikes me most about the drive is that it's absolutely brilliant. The road twists and turns as it rises and falls, following the contours of the steep hillsides and ridges and passing through tiny villages with streets of cobbles where men and women sit outside bars drinking and talking, watching us as we pass by. Perhaps, I think, we've found the real Portugal here in the hills.

We leave the van at the crossroads in Barranco de Vielha and find the course of the Via Algarviana on our pushbikes. As soon as we leave the road, the path drops quickly into one of the deep valleys between the soft peaks of the mountains. The route is well marked and we find it easy to follow as it winds its way around the mountains. The descents are steep and the ascents hard, even on an e-bike. We reach a tiny hamlet and stop to have our lunch in a bus stop. It's hot and dry and the countryside, though stunning – with cork oaks, eucalyptus and pine and a lively understorey of flowers and grasses – is wearing. We vote to make it to the next hamlet and then take the N124 back to the van. By the time we reach the road we've covered 16km (10 miles) of difficult terrain, which makes riding on the smooth, hot tarmac even sweeter. It's another brilliant road, with sharp bends and great views. We cover 10km (6.2 miles) quickly, and with time enough to enjoy the mountain views.

Back at the van, we head off north to drive as much of the N2 as possible before we head back towards Faro. It gets better and better the further we go. We pass more tiny villages and more beautiful countryside as we sweep around the bends and brake for the corners. The road is virtually empty, with just a few cars using it. We pass a group of touring cyclists.

It's mid-afternoon and we are getting hot in the van. We pass through Ameixial and then, on a bend below the road, we spot the Fonte da Seiceira, a pool with a grassy sunbathing area. We decide, there and then, that we'll cut short the day's exploring and take a dip. I turn the van around and park. We are out of the van and in our swimming togs within a few minutes. The pool is about 20m (66ft) wide and about 10m (33ft) across. Its walls are made of slate and it has a sloping beach of concrete. Next to it there is a pond by a spring where water pours from a tap. A few small groups of people lying on towels on the grass beside the pool watch us as we enter the water. Disappointingly, the water is chlorinated, even though it looks as if it comes from a spring. Even so, it's a great way to wash off the sweat from the ride and the grime from the road.

Afterwards, we spread out our towels on the grass and lie in the sun. We've covered about 50km (31 miles) of the N2 so far and it's been wonderful. We plot to drive the rest of it during the writing of this book – somehow. I have no idea how it'll fit in to our plans, but that's not important. We will do it. But it won't be today.

We head back to Faro to kayak the Ria Formosa delta and swim, again, this time in Praia de Faro, the small beach resort opposite the city. Portugal is turning out to be everything I had hoped for – and more.

THE DRIVING

This route began, for us, in Spain. We crossed the border on the A-49-E-1 – the main route from Seville – across the Ponte Internacional do Guadiana.*

Take the first exit, number 18, off the motorway, then the N122 to Vila Real and then the N125 to Tavira. On leaving Tavira, take the N125 towards Faro and then, straight after crossing over the Gilão River, take the slip road on the left (M514-2) and follow it under the flyover and along the river. This is a great little road – a little narrow in places – that will take you through plantations of carob and orange trees, olives and figs. After about 6km (3.7 miles) you'll come to a right turn. This will take you to the Pego do Inferno waterfall, a local beauty and swim spot.

Continue on the back road until it reaches the N270. Turn right. This road is really nice, passing more lemon groves and olive groves until it meets the N2 on the ring road around São Brás de Alportel at the third roundabout. Take the N2 north towards Alportel. Once out of São Brás de Alportel, the road winds its way up into the mountains, passing through a few villages as it goes. It's fantastic, passing through great scenery and an area that once relied heavily on the cork trade. Look out for trucks piled high with raw cork and freshly cut cork oaks.

Continue on the N2 to Barranco do Velho. This is the point where the Via Algarviana crosses it.

**N.B. Here, we were required to complete a toll prepayment at a booth just off the main road. Our cards wouldn't work at the toll booth so we retreated to the Spanish side and completed the form online at www.portugaltolls.com. This enabled us to pass any tolls and the payment would be deducted automatically from that card.*

SIDE SHOOT: At Barranco do Velho, you can continue on the N2 for about 600km (373 miles) if you fancy. Or you can take it as far as Ameixial if you fancy a dip in the pool there. It's spectacular driving and a real pleasure – a true slow road. Before Ameixial, there is a lookout with a swing that's great for photos.

SIDE SHOOT 2: The N124 is another road that's a great drive for the hell of it. Take a right to Cachopo, a typical Algarvian village.

TO CONTINUE: At Barranco do Velho, take a left on the N124, then take a left after about 3km (1.9 miles) on to the N396. This is another great road that will take you to Loulé. Along here, you'll find the circular Seven Springs Walk, as well as a walk to the Fonte da Benémola, a natural spring off the M524 (it is well signed). This road is another delight and will take you through more natural scrub and cork oak and then into Loulé through the Portuguese version of *dehesa*, which is known as Montado, a protected cork oak ecosystem. Continue on the N124 into Loulé and then take the N270 back to São Brás de Alportel.

On the ring road, take the N2 south towards Faro, the end of this journey. The N2 dissolves into a strip of car dealerships, restaurants and supermarkets as it enters Faro. For Praia de Faro and the campsite, take the N125 towards, and past, the airport and then on to the island via the narrow causeway.

WHERE TO STAY: CAMPING

Camping Ria Formosa, Cabanas de Tavira
Parque de Campismo Ria Formosa, Lda.
Quinta da Gomeira, Cabanas de Tavira
Web: www.campingriaformosa.com
Tel: +351 281 328 887

A really nice campsite about 6km (3.7 miles) from Tavira in the village of Cabanas. It's easy to get to Tavira by bike on the Ecovia do Litoral (coastal cycle route). Nice pool and generous pitches.

Parque de Campismo Municipal de Faro, Faro
Av. Nascente, 8005-520 Faro
Web: www.faro.pt/menu/1516/parque-de-campismo.aspx
Tel: +351 289 870 805

Across the causeway from the airport, this is a nice municipal site. It is secure and perfect for visits to Faro, via the ferry, which runs from a jetty about 400m (440 yards) east. The beach is about 20m (66ft) from the gates.

WHERE TO STAY: *AIRES*

Tavira: There is a nice *aire* with good facilities (showers/washing machines) in Tavira adjacent to the salt flats. Handy for the town.
São Brás de Alportel: The *aire* here is excellent and, to us, underused. Nice people and all facilities.

IN THE AREA

The Ecovia do Litoral This cycle route runs along the whole coast of the Algarve. Use it to get around safely from campsite to town and beaches.
• www.ecoviadolitoralalgarve.com

Tavira A really nice city on the Gilão River with a castle. Catch a boat from here to Tavira Island, where there is a great beach (with a seasonal campsite) and lots of wild places to explore, including an anchor graveyard at Praia do Barril.

The Via Algarviana A long-distance path that runs from Alcoutim to Cabo de São Vicente. You can pick up the path from the N2 at Barranco de Vielha and walk east or west. There is also a short, circular walk in Barranco that aims to show you the area's vast biodiversity.
• www.viaalgarviana.org/en

Parque Nacional da Ria Formosa Stretching 60km (37 miles) either side of Faro, the Ria Formosa is a protected habitat. You can visit it by taking a boat charter from the marina in Faro. There are lots of operators so choose one that feels good. We hired kayaks from an outdoor adventure company, Lands, on the marina. It was really windy for us so I'd recommend going on a calm day or it'll be a slog. They speak English and have an online booking system.
• www.lands.pt

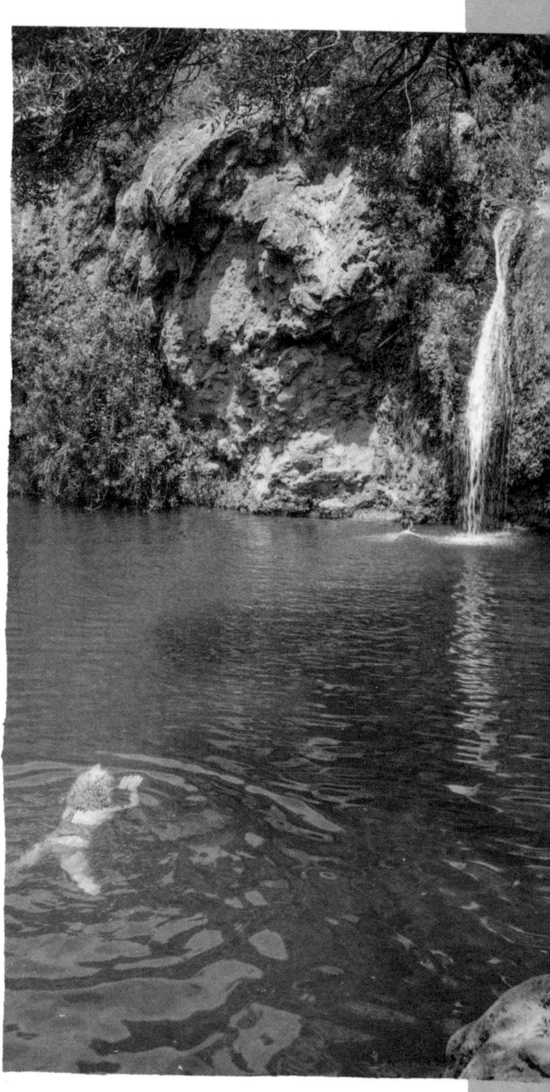

Faro The old city is really lovely and has a lot of bars and restaurants, galleries and places of interest. We dropped into a pop-up art exhibition from the University of the Algarve and the Palace of Tiles, a former residence of cardinals (although I'd recommend that you don't go if you are the kind of person who believes the clergy should lead austere and humble, pious lives).

Fonte da Seiceira A lovely swimming spot just north of Ameixial.

Cascata do Pego do Inferno A small waterfall and lake just north of Tavira. There's parking followed by a short walk through rushes to get to the pool. Great for a dip.

ROUTE 21

A22
N264
ALGOZ
N268
SÃO SEBASTIÃO
PORTIMÃO
GUIA
N125
LAGOS
FERRAGUDO
ALBUFEIRA
BURGAU
BENAGIL
ARMAÇÃO DE PÊRA
ATLANTIC OCEAN
SAGRES

ROUTE 21

Praia do Camilo, near Lagos

SAGRES TO ALBUFEIRA

CARNAGE AT THE CAVES

The Algarve is famous for its beaches. They are sublimely beautiful, and each one has its qualities, from the simple, wild perfection of Martinhal and the beaches of Sagres to the rugged, cliff-backed architecture of the caves, arches, stacks and cliffs of Benagil, Praia das Furnas and Camilo. We went searching for snorkelling, hoping for crystal-clear waters, multicoloured fish and exotic sights. What we ended up with was an unexpected supper and an adventure on the high seas.

BEST FOR: Snorkelling, walking, kayaking, SUPing

START: Sagres

END: Albufeira

MILEAGE: 103km (64 miles)

ALLOW: 4–5 days

MAP PAGES: 88, 89

The alarm goes off at 6 a.m. It's light already and the sun is up. We are still in bed. But we know we have to get up if we wish to complete today's mission. It's our final day on the Algarve and we are here, at Benagil, with the purpose of paddling our surfboards into its famous cave before anybody else does.

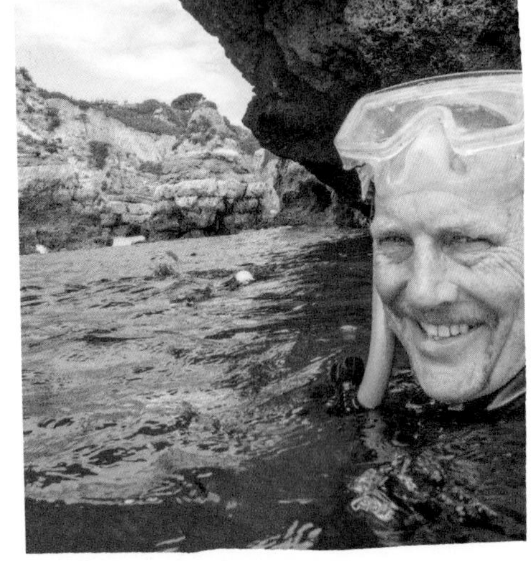

We slip out of bed, open the slider, and get ourselves ready for a morning on the water: boards are taken down off the roof, wetsuits turned inside out and faces smeared with waterproof sun cream.

Initially, we had wanted to snorkel our way along the Algarve, from Sagres to Albufeira, but somehow it didn't work out quite the way we'd hoped. A swell and south-westerly winds meant the sea was, in many places, too choppy to snorkel and the visibility was poor. Many of the more famous beaches – incredible for snorkelling on their day by all accounts – were no good for snorkelling by the time we got to them. When we arrived at Benagil and the bit that's famous for its hanging valleys, cliffs, caves and arches, the water was milky blue with churned-up silt. Still, when viewed in contrast with the sandy-coloured cliffs, it was very easy on the eye. It looked, if I may say, just like it did in the brochures. Even so, we had to change our plans slightly.

We sought shelter from the wind and swell in Sagres, on a tiny beach behind the harbour a couple of days after we arrived. It was hot and sunny and we jumped in wearing just our swimming stuff (no wetsuits) as we didn't expect too much from it. The day before, at Martinhal, a lovely crescent of white sand on the east side of Sagres, we had cruised over weed-covered boulders that hid octopus, starfish, blennies, parrotfish and wrasse for an hour or so. It was a good snorkel, but not as good as I had hoped. The beach at the harbour was the only place we could find where the wind wasn't causing chop.

As soon as I put my face in the water and sucked my first tube-full of air, I knew it would be good. The visibility was about 20m (66ft). I kicked out along the rocks at the side of the pier and floated into a shoal of thousands of glistening, twitchy, juvenile fish. As I swam through them, they parted like a murmuration chased by a hawk. I continued out along the rocks and to the stanchions of the pier. Here, where the water was 3–3.7m (10–12ft) deep, I saw wrasse, pollock and sea bream. I passed between the concrete pillars into the darkness. Below me, a small shoal of glinting mackerel chased the

smaller fish feverishly. Seen from above, their blotchy markings looked like waving weed in the shafts of sunlight. As they chased the sprats, the shoals parted and then regrouped. I watched the marauding mackerel for a few minutes. They harassed everything they came near to. I had never seen mackerel from under the water before. They seemed so voracious that I could understand why they are so easy to catch in September at home in Cornwall – they will eat anything. And that gave me an idea.

Lizzy and I got out of the water, dried off on the beach and rushed back to the van. I dived into a cupboard and pulled out the fishing gear. We have travelled with it for as long as I can remember and yet we have rarely used it. We have certainly never caught anything with it. I set up the reel, assembled the rod and tied a simple spinner to the line.

On the first cast, thanks to the clear water, I could see the shoal of mackerel chasing the lure: they circled it in a frenzy and grabbed at it until one of them was hooked. As the line went taught and I wound the reel – like an amateur – I lost the fish as I tried to lift it out of the water. It splashed into the water and swam off. I cast again and hooked and lost another. The next one that took the lure I let swim a little to tire it out before I tried to lift it out of the water – success!

After a few more casts, and no more than about 20 minutes of fishing, I caught another and we were able to call it a day – we had our supper. Eating it that night in a campsite just above Salema was heartily satisfying. There's something primal about eating fish you have caught yourself and cooked on the barbecue. The added bonus is being able to eat only what you catch instead of chomping on factory processed fish that's caught miles away and leaves a trail of pollution in its wake. We took all we wanted and needed.

Praia da Figueira

Over the next few days, we drove along the coast looking for places to snorkel, finding Zavial and Praia das Furnas, and walking down the steep-sided valley to Praia da Figueira, a tiny beach with no road access and a strip of beautiful white sands, plus lots of people sunbathing naked. We stopped at Salema, finding the dinosaur footprints in the rocks at the western end and enjoying an evening drink with the holidaying families made up largely of grandparents, parents and small children. Presumably, gramps was there to pay.

In Lagos, we attempted to snorkel at Camilo, a small cove of breathtaking beauty with a rock arch and stacks an easy swim from the shore. The visibility wasn't great, but the architecture was incredible. We jostled with the tourist boats for a chance to swim through the arch on the principle that they should wait for us – steam gives way to sail – because we were the more vulnerable. It was worth the ire of the boatmen to look up and see the hole in the rock above us, but sullied by having to bully my way in. The visibility was only a few metres so the snorkelling wasn't great but it was worth climbing down the set of steps (I stopped counting at 100) that led us down the crumbling cliffs.

Finally, we ended up at Benagil, with the new plan. Here, the water was milky, too, and the swell was crashing up against the cliffs, so snorkelling would have been pointless. Once we had decided we'd explore the caves, we headed down to the beach to do a recce. It was carnage.

The Benagil cave, the biggest and most spectacular in the area, is just a short paddle from the beach, which means that it's a magnet for tourists and the people who rent out sit-on-kayaks, SUPs and even boogie boards and flippers. On a calm day, I can imagine it's quite sedate, but with a swell it was entertaining. Groups of 10 or 15, plus individuals, were launching into the swell. Some made it past the heavily dumping breakers and some didn't. We watched as people with little or no experience set off into the surf and were beaten back, upturned, or drifted offshore. A man abandoned his SUP to swim out to his wife, who was having a meltdown about 100m (110 yards) offshore. They made it back, only to be upturned by a wave. When they finally hit land, she sat on the beach and sobbed. We enjoyed the *schadenfreude* but felt sorry for them. I couldn't understand why the operators were renting out equipment to people with no experience on a day that was challenging. Still, money talks.

The lure of the cave was too great for us, but as usual, we needed to do it our way. We walked to the cliff's edge to peer into the sinkhole, but it wasn't really enough to satisfy my curiosity. We needed to go into it. I wanted to photograph the cave and see it from the best seat in the house and to do that we needed to paddle into it when no one was around.

And that's how we come to be suiting up, at first light, in the car park above Benagil Beach. Even at 6.30 a.m. it's warm, so we pull our wetsuits up to our waists, pick up our surfboards and walk down to the beach. We are surprised to see other people arriving as we walk down. Operators are starting to set up, unloading kayaks from trailers and blowing up SUPs. We guess that they are offering tours to see the caves when they are less busy – exactly the reason we are up. Impatience gets the better of me and I chivvy Lizzy along, eager to be the first into the cave and to be able to photograph it empty.

We time our entry to the water and glide into the sea between sets of waves, paddling quickly to get ourselves into the safe zone beyond the

The cave at Benagil and Praia Marinha

dumping shore break. It takes us just a few minutes to get around to the cave, which is about 46m (50 yards) around the headland to the south. The sun is hitting the cliffs and making them glow orange, but the mouth of the cave is dark. The waves are crashing violently on to the beach within the cave, which is being lit by the hole in its roof. The sound reverberates around the mouth of the cave, an archway of about 46m (50 yards) wide and 27m (30 yards) tall. Lizzy holds back as I try to time my way onto the sand: I wait for a set to pass before paddling swiftly towards the beach. I dismount in the shallows, grab the board, and run up the sand with it, avoiding the next wave. It's a strategy that works well and gets me right into the cave.

I look around. It's huge, with two entrances, a wide beach, a deeper cave within and a circular hole in the ceiling that provides a bright patch of light on the sand. Immediately, I am gripped by it. I feel I am in a special place, at a time when I can have it to myself. I walk to the back of the cave and see that the rock-balancing Instagrammers have been here before me. About 20 stacks of stones sit like columns in a Hindu temple. I resist the urge to knock them all over (why can't people just leave nature alone? It's pretty enough as it is) and look out to where Lizzy is still sitting on her board. I can see why people want to come here, and in droves. And I am glad we decided to get up early to see it like this. After the experience of jostling with the boatmen to swim under an arch, the effort of getting up early is well worth it.

I paddle back to Lizzy and together we go back to the beach, aiming for the headland on the opposite side. A couple of SUPs appear, paddling into the cave as we leave.

We meet another group of SUPers as we reach the headland. We have a brief chat with the instructor, who tells us there is another cave about 400m (437 yards) further along.

We paddle around the huge cliffs and reach the cave – a narrow entrance where the waves are refracting off the cliffs, causing a lumpy, sinister-looking sea. The SUP group catches up with us and the instructor explains to me that the cave is calm inside, even if it looks rough outside. He tells me the best line to take and then leads his group inside. We wait at the mouth of the cave as the group paddles deep into the cave, and then head in ourselves when they come out. We paddle swiftly into the narrow gap between the cliffs and to the calm water inside the cave. The air and water there are warmer than outside and it feels to me as if I have walked out of an airconditioned building into blazing sunshine. We paddle through the rough water and to the interior of the cave, where it opens out into a huge, dark, echoing cavern. The swell, crashing into the back wall of the cave somewhere deeper inside, booms and resonates. Everything is amplified. I feel tiny and vulnerable here, trapped by swell and the echoing waves of sound. It's a little creepy and I don't stay long, paddling hard to make it out in one swift dash. The cool air engulfs me.

Lizzy and I sit on our boards a little way offshore. We can see a small flotilla of kayakers heading our way, while a small inflatable kayak carrying two people approaches from the opposite direction. As is inevitable, the spell is broken by the arrival of the day and its business as usual, so we make our way back to the shore, and to the van.

Our smug, early bird's breakfast awaits.

THE DRIVING

This journey, from Sagres on Portugal's southern tip, is all about finding beaches. There are so many of them that you could spend half a lifetime lazing on them all, so please, as usual, go ahead and meander. This is just a starting point. All beaches, as we know, display different characteristics and it's no different in the Algarve. The beaches around Sagres face different directions, which means they can have very different states depending on the swell and wind direction. Most likely, the Atlantic coast will have roaring rollers while the southern coast will be calmer. But it isn't always that way. We expected good snorkelling conditions – and found some – but the places where we expected to find still, clear water provided anything but.

We left Sagres on the N268. As you drive out of the strip that makes up this little town, you'll realise just how isolated and remote it is. With scrub either side and a few houses, it's on its own. First stop is Vila do Bispo, the turn off for western beaches. Here, the N268 meets the main Faro road, the N125. It's an OK road and runs down the spine of the peninsula so you'll come back to it time and time again as you explore offshoots. We took the M1257 to Praia da Ingrina and Praia do Zavial, two gorgeous beaches

Lagos

Lagos

that both have beach restaurants and limited parking. Zavial had great surf when we were there. The M1257 takes you on a loop back towards the N125, but you can continue around the coast by taking a right turn that's signposted to Tabual a couple of kilometres away from the beach. This will take you to Figueira and the N125. If you turn right just before the N125 roundabout (when you meet the road in Figueira), you'll come to a right turn after about 10m (33ft) that will take you to the fantastic beach at Figueira. It is marked with a brown sign. BIG MOHOS: DON'T TAKE THIS ROAD. It has a tight turn.

After visiting the beach, turn right on to the high street and continue on. This will bring you to the N125 and a roundabout. Go right here for Salema on the M537. The campsite is just down this road. On leaving Salema, turn right out of the campsite and follow the road to the beach. Turn left (it's actually straight on), on the bend before you get to the sea and follow this road through the hilly scrub to a T-junction, where you can turn left to continue or turn right to get to Praia da Boca do Rio, a big beach with a large parking lot.

When you leave the beach, turn right, following the signs for Burgau, up the cobbled road. Don't worry, it doesn't last but it will take you up the hill and around a sharp left-hand bend on the hill with great views back to the beach. Shortly after, you can take a right to Praia das Cabanas Velhas or continue on to the tiny fishing port-cum-tourist village of Burgau. Parking isn't easy here, but it's worth a stop as there are nice shops and restaurants. Don't take the road to the beach as it is narrow. Instead, continue on through the town, picking up the M537 towards Luz and Lagos. Go through Luz and out the other side until you meet the N125. Turn right on to it and follow signs for the beaches. This will take you into Lagos (you'll have to turn off to get to Camilo Beach at the fourth big roundabout).

The N125 will lead you into Lagos itself and along the harbourside, where there is lots of parking, and across the bridge when you turn right at the first roundabout after the straight section by the water. This is a shortcut and will take you on to the N125 again after the bridge.

From here, the N125 gets busier and busier as you start to hit the more built-up parts of the Algarve. However, it still passes through nice countryside, salt flats outside Portimão and scrubby hills and olive groves. Look out for storks in their gigantic nests on telegraph poles.

Praia do Camilo, near Lagos

Continue on the N125 until Lagoa, where you'll need to turn right at the roundabout signposted for Carvoeiro. This is the N124-1 and will take you into the town, almost to the beach and then out to Benagil and Marinha (M530, then M1273, then the M1154) and back to the N125 again.

The N125 starts to get busier the closer you get to Albufeira, with garden centres, potteries, car dealerships, shopping malls and supermarkets dominating. At Vale do Paraíso, the N395 takes you into Albufeira. The campsite is on this road.

WHERE TO STAY: CAMPING

Camping Orbitur, Sagres
Cerro das Moitas, 8650-998
Sagres, Portugal
Web: www.orbitur.pt
Tel: +351 282 624 371

A decent enough site that's a short cycle from Sagres and beaches. Free-for-all for pitches under the pines and very clean showers.

Salema Eco Camp, Budens
Praia da Salema, 8650-196 Budens, Portugal
Web: www.salemaecocamp.com
Tel: +351 282 695 201

A great campsite on a difficult site in a lovely valley that offers incredible views from the upper terraces for those brave enough to tackle the drive. Nice people. Nice site. Great ethics. Bravo!

Camping Albufeira
Estr. de Ferreiras N395, 8200-555
Albufeira, Portugal
Web: www.campingalbufeira.pt
Tel: +351 289 587 630

A huge campsite with no pitching rules, making it a bit of a free-for-all. However, there are great pools and it's very handy for Albufeira. Downside: they produce bespoke plastic cards for everyone who stays – wasteful.

WHERE TO STAY: *AIRES*

There are moho facilities at the Intermarché in Sagres, including emptying black waste. Wild campers who frequent Sagres and the area find this service useful.

There are a few private *aires* on this stretch of coast at Albufeira, Figueira and Parchal (among others). Check Park4Night for details.

IN THE AREA

Seven Hanging Valleys Walk (Percurso dos Sete Vales Suspensos) A 7km (4.3-mile) walk from Marinha to Vale de Centeanes Beach that will take you to the Algarve's most impressive natural scenery. Being a walk of hanging valleys, access to some beaches is impossible, but there are places along the way where it is possible to stop and swim or visit caves and sinkholes. The cliffs are an amazing range of colours, from ochre, gold and yellow to dusky browns and red. The sea is azure blue. The coastal architecture is incredible, with stacks, arches, caves and sinkholes along the way. Incredible. Parking is limited at Marinha so get there early. There's a big car park at Benagil.

Benagil cave tours There are lots of operators offering kayak, SUP and even boogie board rental to see the caves at Benagil. The group we met were taught by Bruno at Blue Xperiences, who offer SUP lessons, equipment and guided tours from Benagil Beach. Recommended. • **www.bluexperiences.pt**

Algarve beaches When conditions allow, the Algarve beaches are fantastic for snorkelling (and SUPing and kayaking). In general, they are fantastic anyway, with golden sands and blue seas, tall sandstone- and limestone-topped cliffs of all hues of ochre and yellow, and beach bars on almost every accessible one. We swam at most of those we visited.

Sagres beaches Some beaches in this region are remote, with possible wild camping nearby, although it is discouraged. If you do wild camp, tidy up!

Tonel is renowned for surf as it's on the western side of the town and therefore exposed to the Atlantic. It's a lovely beach with lots of parking and amazing water quality.

Martinhal is a beautiful stretch of sand with rocks at either end for snorkelling. The offshore island is popular with kayakers and SUPers.

Ingrina is a small beach with a restaurant, east of Martinhal.

surfing in Sagres

Sagres (and the area around it) is renowned for surfing and there is a lot of choice. Each beach faces a different direction, so offering protection from wind and waves, if needed.

Zavial is a surf beach east of Ingrina. There's a restaurant and beautiful white sand.

Figueira is a small beach that can only be accessed down a small track in a narrow valley. It's absolutely beautiful and kept quiet by the walk. Expect a bit of nudism. A-class campers and mohos, plus vans over 6m (20ft), will struggle with the corner on the access road to the car park. Park in town and walk.

Salema The beach here is lovely, with dinosaur footprints at the western end and restaurants and bars on the front. Small and well-heeled. Stay at the Eco Camp and cycle or take their transport.

Lagos and beaches The beaches of Lagos lie to the south of the old city, river and marina. They are famed for their stacks and arches. Boat tours leave from the river mouth by the castle. The old city has a lovely pedestrianised eating/shopping area with lots of beautiful buildings, eateries and shops.

On its day, Praia do Camilo is said to be one of the best snorkelling spots in the Algarve.

Albufeira This busy, built-up resort has some lovely beaches. We found Praia dos Aveiros, a small, quiet beach between the two larger beaches. It has sinkholes and caves and is recommended for snorkelling (although the water was too milky when we were there).

Benagil/Carvoeiro Lots of lovely stretches of sand on this section, including the beach at Carvalho, which can only be accessed through one of two tunnels cut into the cliffs.

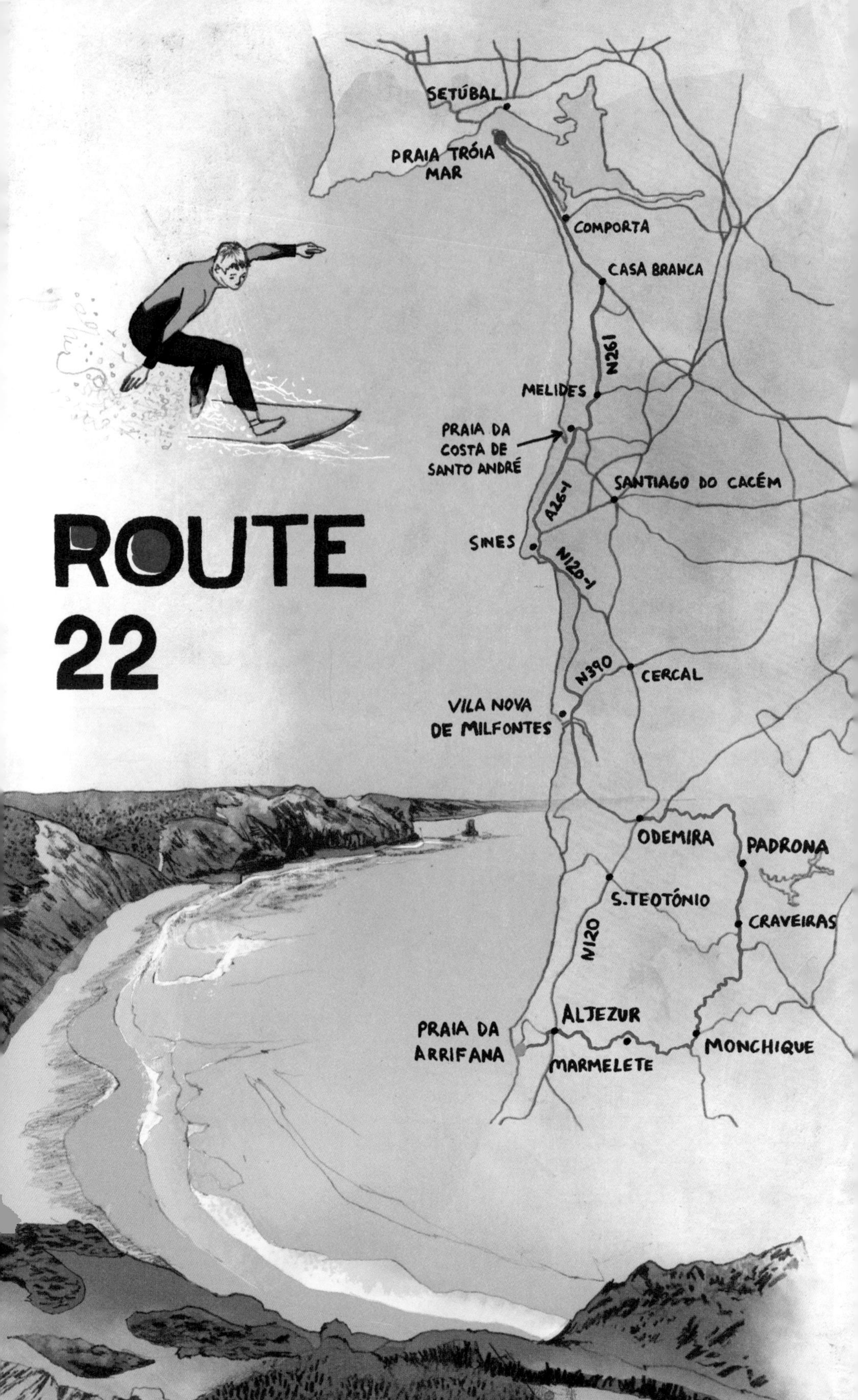
ROUTE
22
SETÚBAL
PRAIA TRÓIA MAR
COMPORTA
CASA BRANCA
N261
MELIDES
PRAIA DA COSTA DE SANTO ANDRÉ
SANTIAGO DO CACÉM
A26-1
SINES
N120-1
N390
CERCAL
VILA NOVA DE MILFONTES
ODEMIRA
PADRONA
S.TEOTÓNIO
CRAVEIRAS
N120
ALJEZUR
PRAIA DA ARRIFANA
MARMELETE
MONCHIQUE

ROUTE 22

PRAIA DA ARRIFANA TO TRÓIA

A MOUNTAIN OASIS

Starting 40km (25 miles) north of Sagres, in the coastal national park, this journey will take you from the lovely, whitewashed surf village of Arrifana into the mountains for some great driving on some interesting roads and amazing views of the Algarve. It will then take you back down to the coast, via an excellent reservoir for swimming, for a jaunt to resorts and beaches before ending up at the weird enclaved utopia of Tróia on the Peninsula de Tróia. From here, you can catch a ferry across the Rio Sado to Setúbal, your gateway to northern Portugal.

BEST FOR:
Views of the Algarve, beaches, winding roads

START:
Arrifana

END: Peninsula de Tróia

MILEAGE:
285km (177 miles)

ALLOW:
2–3 days

MAP PAGES:
76, 88, 64

We are in Arrifana out of curiosity. Years ago, I had a friend who went to live there and, legend has it, became a cave dweller for a while, waiting for the day when a spectacular wave would break in Arrifana's bay. Gary was a larger-than-life character and a surfboard shaper who spent long periods living in a van near me until he disappeared to Portugal. Whenever he returned, he would tell my surfing friends and me about Arrifana and how amazing its waves were. I wanted to see the place for myself.

We park on the cliff that leads from the beach access to the port. We open the slider and make a snack lunch. We sit on the step and eat, with the sun directly on us and the van sheltering us from the wind. It is incredibly hot, possibly over 35°C (95°F), and the van is beginning to heat up like an oven. I walk over to the edge of the cliff to cool off and look down at the port and at the point that's been made famous in my mind by Gary. It looks dangerous and difficult to surf and, it seems, everything Gary told us about it is true. I watch as a surfer takes off next to a huge rock that's creating a sucking, snarling boil. On the main beach, a little further to the south, there are hundreds of black dots in the water. The surf is crowded so I excuse myself and give it a miss.

We head back into the tiny village and up the coast on really rough, bumpy roads towards Praia de Monte Clérigo, a tiny, beautiful beach backed by a few shacks and villas at the end of the Aljezur valley. From here, we head into the

mountains of the Serra de Monchique to find somewhere to stay and to reach the highest point of the Algarve, at the Miradouro da Fóia at 902m (2,959ft). We need water and to drop our waste so we are searching for an *aire* with facilities rather than a wild spot. There are a couple we can try.

It's hot as we head into the mountains on a windy road that takes us through olive groves, stands of carob and cork oak, and small-scale agriculture. We drive with the windows open to keep cool, although Lizzy finds it hard to stay awake. She nods and dozes as I drive us further up into the mountains. The terraced hillsides are interspersed with meadows that are dry and yellowed, and occasional pines. At times, I can see down to the coast.

We arrive at a junction just short of the village of Monchique and I take a right towards the south coast of the Algarve and a small camping site that we have found on Park4Night.

While I have used the app to find places to stay, I have only recently begun to use it to actually find the places using the app's navigation function. Really, it's a game changer and allows us to rely on someone else to get us places instead of ourselves. Invariably, it's right and it makes for a much more peaceful atmosphere in the van. We have begun to read the reviews, too, and can always find something to laugh at. However, it is a good way to get a feel for a place. We ignore the reviews that say things like 'Phone was engaged. Zero stars.' and make our own judgements based on the overall vibe. This is usually spot on, although I always question why people give five stars to places that I drive away from.

I turn off towards the site a few miles later at the junction of a rough, unmade track where there is a small sign advertising the campsite. I follow the track into the yellow, featureless scrub, up a steep hill and around a sharp bend, following the contours of the land. I pass a donkey tied up to a post in a dry and dusty field. I jab Lizzy awake as we rise up further and arrive at the cobbled entranceway to the campsite. As soon as we pass through, it feels like we have arrived at a lush, green oasis. The trees are blooming and there are patches of grass, flowers in pots and shade from low trees. We are instantly struck. We step down from the van and are greeted by a short, tanned Portuguese woman wearing a sundress. She says hello and begins to speak to us in Portuguese. We apologise and say we can't speak Portuguese. She can't speak English and won't or can't speak Spanish, so we make do with pidgin Portugenglish (or something like that). She leads us off for a tour of the park. There are 18 pitches, black and grey waste,

showers and even a tiny pool with a view of the Algarve. All for €15 per night for the two of us.

We wander back to the office and hand over our passports so the woman can sign us in. We stand in silence looking at the books, maps and leaflets in the office until the woman has finished and we can choose a space. Only a couple of the pitches are occupied so we reverse into a space nearest the pool. We back in so that we can open the rear doors to enjoy the view of the mountains. Our space, like all the others, is made of compacted dirt with two runs of cobbles for the van to drive on to. There is an electricity point in a wooden box that's more like a bird box, and a tap. A fold-down table sits against rails that separate our plot from the next. The waste is a tiny pipe in the ground. We wonder how we will empty into it until we see, lined up against the opposite wall of the site, a collection of hoses with different ends. One end of each is identical and fits on to the hole in the ground while the other has different attachments that are designed to accommodate different types of grey water waste emptying. Ours is a tap so we choose one with a nozzle that fits snugly on to it. Others have dishes to push under the van or pans to collect waste from a dump valve. It's all rather ingenious and is something I have never seen before. Lizzy says, 'You can tell this site was designed by a woman.' She's probably right: It is neat, well-kept and cared for. Everything is as it should be and there is paper in the toilets. If only men would stay out of running campsites!

It's still really hot so we change into our swimmers and amble over for a swim in the small kidney-shaped pool. The shower is hot from the sun, but the pool is deliciously cool and clear. We lounge about in it for half an hour or so, chatting, enjoying the view of the mountains and, in the distance, the Atlantic on the Algarve coast.

That night, we sit outside until the sun goes down, watching bats fly by and listening to the cicadas in the olive groves in the valley below us. We sleep with the doors open because we feel safe and it's still hot. It is just perfect.

We set off in the morning to continue our journey and realise as we leave the compound that the site really is an oasis. As soon as we drive through the entrance we are back in a dry landscape, heading down a dusty track to the main road.

Later that day, we check into a campsite that's part of a big group, the Camping Orbitur Sitava Milfontes at Praia do Malhão. It couldn't be more different. The reception is polite and to the point but officious and there are rules to follow. It also costs us around €30. The site sprawls over a huge area of pine forest and has large areas devoted to seasonal pitches. These are common in Spain and Portugal and often comprise a caravan with an awning plus extra bits that have been added to over the years, such as sundecks, flower beds or picket fencing. Invariably, they end up looking neglected and like a camping jumble sale, and are really high-density.

Despite all this, the site is OK and we pass a quiet night, but really, we know where we'd rather be.

THE DRIVING

Arrifana is nice. It has a few surfy bars and eateries and a fantastic restaurant on the point by the old fort. The roads, however, aren't so good and are potholed and tricky, especially in the urbanisation of Arrifana. They do improve, though, so hang in there.

Leave Arrifana by following signs for Praia de Monte Clérigo. This will take you over a few roundabouts and on to the road heading for Vale da Telha. This will bring you to the lovely little beachside hamlet of Monte Clérigo. Follow the road along the back of the beach and up the hill past the shacks and villas – there are great views looking back. Follow this road (M1003-1) as it heads up the valley towards the N120 road. Take a left towards Aljezur, then another left at the N120 towards the village. You'll pass shops and bars before turning right and crossing the river. At the first roundabout, turn right on to the N267 following signs for Monchique and head out of town on the slow rise into the mountains. This road will take you into the Serra de Monchique, the diminutive mountain range that acts as the spine for the south and west coasts of the Algarve. It's a wonderful road

that twists and turns as it starts to rise more steeply through *dehesa*, olive and cork and offers great views towards Lagos and Portimão to the south.

When you reach the junction with the N266, turn right for the motorhome stopover or left to continue into Monchique. Once you get to the village, you'll have to follow the one-way system through the narrow streets. Follow signs for Fóia (N226-3) to drive up to the top of the mountain for fabulous views over the Algarve or follow signs for Lisbon to carry on along the N266. Monchique is great, with lots of cafes and bars and a nice square.

It's worth a drive up to Mount Fóia for the views, and tourist shops selling jumpers (in Portugal? What?). It's the highest point in southern Portugal at 902m (2,959ft) and offers stunning views down to the coast. There are cafes and restaurants and a street food van. The road is spectacular, winding its way around the mountain to give views all around as you climb.

Back in Monchique, follow the one-way system and signs for Lisbon on the N266. This is where it starts to get interesting. The road is … well, interesting, and suffers at times from subsidence, especially on tight bends. So, expect to be thrown about a bit. In fact, in my notes I wrote that the road is 'like a bucking bronco trying to chuck you off'. To help you feel extra safe, the roadside barriers are old and often rusted out. Don't drive off the edge as you probably won't be saved by the barrier and there's not much down below except steep mountainside, cork oaks and olive groves on rough, ancient terraces. It's dusty and dry and altogether beautiful, although if you have someone like Lizzy with you who hates eucalyptus trees (because they are an invasive, non-native cash crop) you might hear some grumbling from the passenger seat. At least if you are in a right-hand drive van, they won't be grumbling about the drop... That's for you to worry about.

Make no mistake, this is a wonderful road, with lots to keep you awake and it'll be almost a shame when you reach Nave Redonda and it goes a bit straight and less mountainous but still hilly with cork oaks, ash and some grasslands. It's still the N266.

Follow signs for the Barragem de Santa Clara on the N393 if you get hot and fancy a swim as there is a lovely reservoir beach just over the dam.

Carry on towards Odemira on the N266 and then at Milharadas, take a sharp left (follow the road around the bend) on to the N123 towards Odemira. It's a great road, with sweeping bends, lots of cork oak plantations and the occasional landslip to keep you on your toes. Turn left at the N263 to take you into Odemira.

At Odemira, take the left turn on to the N120. This will take you back towards Lagos, along the banks of the River Mira and then over it on a red-painted steel bridge.

A little way out of Odemira, take a right at a roundabout on to the N393 towards Vila Nova de Milfontes. This road will lead you back to the coast to head north and follows the rough course of the River Mira to its lovely estuary at Vila Nova de Milfontes. You'll cross over the river and come to a roundabout. Turn left for the town, turn right to carry on along the N390. It's a lovely town but unfortunately has little in the way of motorhome parking near the beach and estuary – big shame – but there are a couple of campsites. To carry on, leave town on the N390 and then turn left at the third roundabout out of town (second if you turned right at the first!) on to the CM1072 in the direction of Porto Covo. This will take you along the coast north and eventually back on to the N120 heading towards Sines. There are a few stop-offs along this road that are worth making. Praia do Malhão is lovely but is down a rough, dusty 5km (3.2-mile) track. Some vans stay overnight here. If you stay at the Camping Orbitur Sitava Milfontes you can cut off the corner by taking the back entrance to the beach – very handy!

Continue along the CM1072 until it meets the M554 outside Porto Covo. Turn left for the town – it's really nice, with lots of shops and cafes, villas and holiday developments, plus pleasant beaches and some great smells emanating from restaurants and houses. On leaving Porto Covo, take the M1109 north, a road that will carry you along the coast towards Sines.

Here, outside Porto Covo, there are a number of lovely beaches where lots of vans converge and – presumably – park overnight. Moho parking is difficult in Porto Covo, but the beaches to the north are fabulous.

The M1109 meets the N120-1 just south of Sines. Turn left here and follow the road into the city, following the A26-1 around the headland below the castle and old city, past the marina and port and the oil terminals. At the roundabout junction with the A26, take the A26-1 north along the coast. This is the longest stretch of beach in Europe, with sandy cliffs, the occasional lagoon, a few developments and some well-heeled resorts between here and Setúbal.

The A26-1 turns into the R261-5 and will take you north to the junction with the M544 outside Lagoas de Santo André e da Sancha Nature Reserve.

WHERE TO STAY: CAMPING

There are lots of campsites along this stretch, although we only stayed at one.

Parque de Campismo Orbitur Sitava Milfontes, Vila Nova de Milfontes
Brejo da, 7645-017 Vila Nova de Milfontes, Portugal
Tel: +351 283 89 01 00
Web: www.orbitur.pt/pt/destinos/alentejo/orbitur-sitava-milfontes

A large campsite that's close to the beach at Praia do Malhão. Good location, lovely beach.

WHERE TO STAY: *AIRES*

There are lots of *aires* along this stretch, notably at **Carvalhal**, **Comporta**, **Alentejo Litoral**, **Quinta do Rossi** and of course, **Monchique**.
Vale de Carrasqueira: This is easily the nicest *aire* I have ever stay at and well worth a stop. www.campingvaledacarrasqueira.com

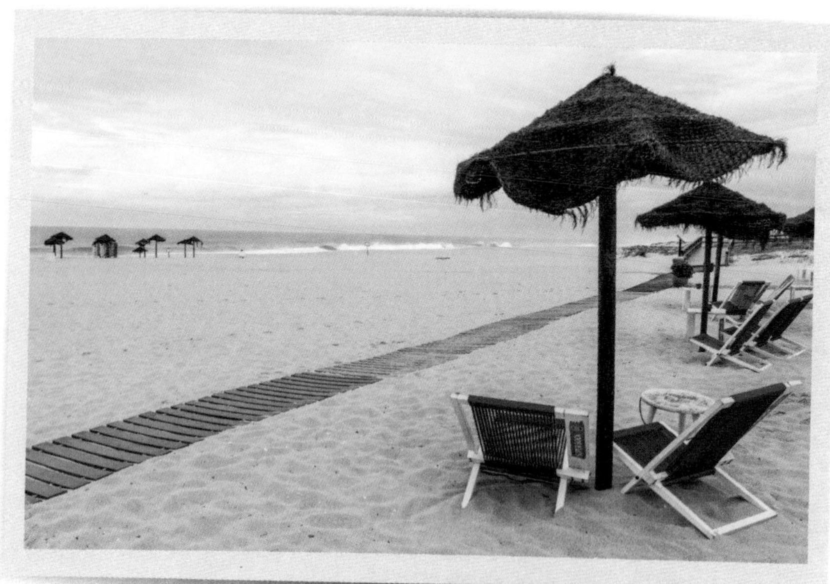

Turn left for the reserve and beach or right to carry on towards the N261. The beach is lovely here and there are opportunities to twitch on the lagoon.

At the junction of the N261, turn left and continue north along the coast. It's a flat, sandy coastal landscape with littoral forest on both sides, with smallholdings and forest taking turns to dominate. There is a campsite at Praia da Galé that has exclusive access to the beach and bar (but take a right and find the locals' way down) at the end of a long road through some incredible development for a golf course and holiday village – lovely coastal planting.

Continue north until you get to the junction at Comporta. The N261 changes to the N253-1, but it's really just a straight on. This road will take you on to the sand spit that separates the Atlantic from the Rio Sado and will take you all the way to Tróia at the end of the peninsula.

Tróia is a strange place. It's a holiday/business development with three high-rises, conference facilities and villas, plus golf courses and a marina sitting at the very tip of the peninsula. Along the well-paved and cared-for road there are a number of exclusive holiday developments with (we presume) exclusive beach access. Parking is difficult, especially because of the sand on either side of the main road. The main reason to be here really is to take the ferry across to Setúbal, which goes from the port on the eastern side of the peninsula before you get to Tróia (the ferry in Tróia is just a passenger ferry).

From Setúbal, you can continue north to Lisbon or east towards Évora and Spain.

IN THE AREA

Beaches From Arrifana to Setúbal there is around 150km (93 miles) of coastline to explore and hundreds of beaches.

Monchique A pretty mountain town that sits below Monte Fóia, with narrow streets, bars and cafes. A little down the hill there is a spa, Caldo de Monchique (• **www.monchiquetermalresort.com**), where, for a price, you can enjoy the spa, although you can just take a look at it and visit the lovely square, with restaurant and craft shops, for nothing.

Sines This ancient town has a fort and old town, although it's rather dominated by the fire-breathing oil industry these days. Even so, it's worth a stop and a wander. In the 1460s, Portugal's legendary explorer Vasco da Gama was born in the castle here.

Ferry Tróia/Setúbal There's a regular service from the tip of the Tróia Peninsula to Setúbal. You can book tickets and get the timetable at: • **www.atlanticferries.pt**

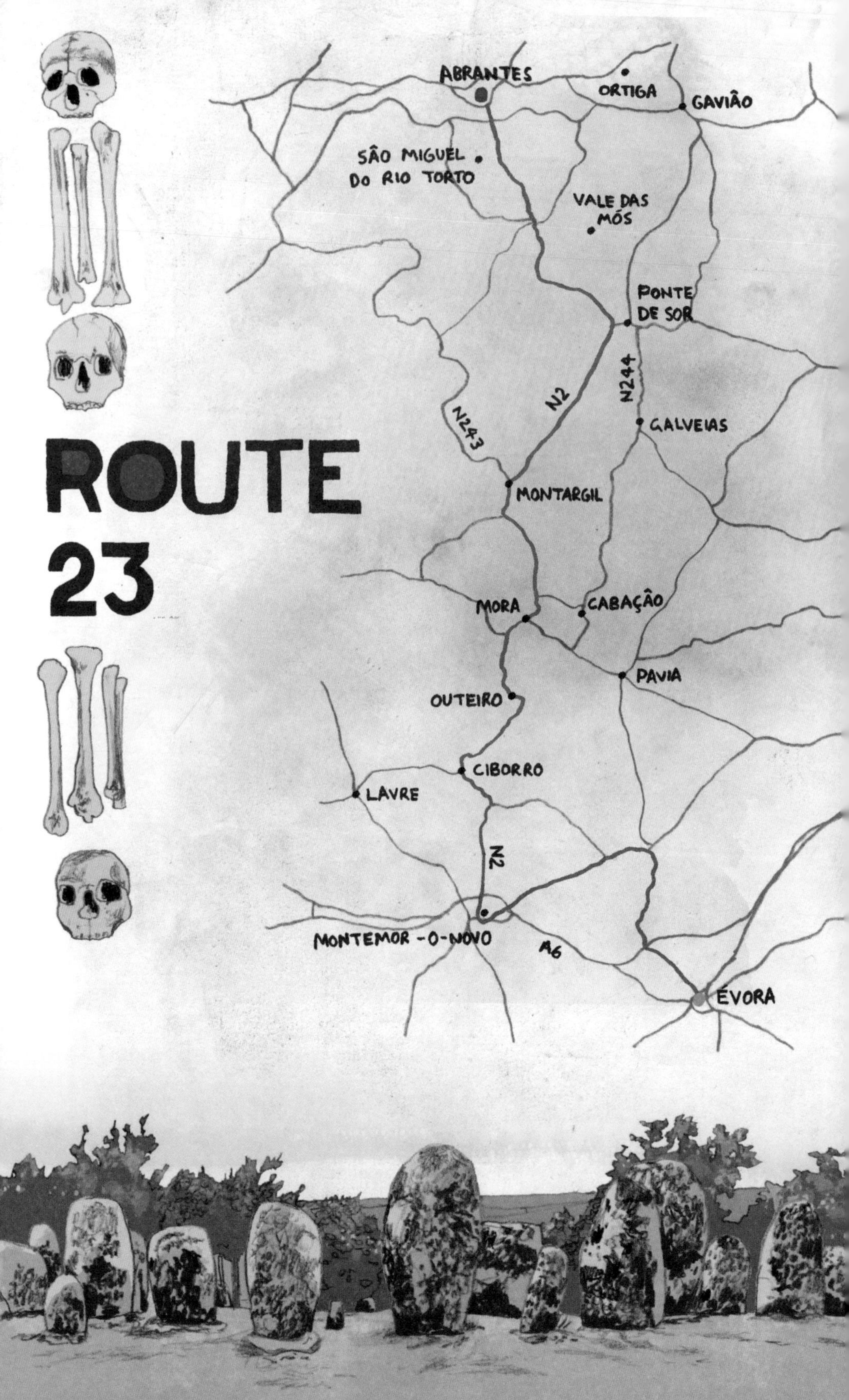
ROUTE
23
ABRANTES
ORTIGA
GAVIÃO
SÃO MIGUEL
DO RIO TORTO
VALE DAS
MÓS
PONTE
DE SOR
N2
N244
N243
GALVEIAS
MONTARGIL
MORA
CABAÇÃO
PAVIA
OUTEIRO
CIBORRO
LAVRE
N2
MONTEMOR-O-NOVO
A6
ÉVORA

ÉVORA TO ABRANTES

BIRTH, DEATH AND RAIN IN ÉVORA

This journey will take you through the centre of Portugal, from UNESCO World Heritage Site *Évora* to the city of Abrantes, an ancient Celtic settlement on the banks of the Tagus, along the middle section of the N2, Portugal's Route 66. If you want to get a feel for inland Portugal, this is one way to do it. Along the way, you'll pass through the Portuguese *dehesa* grasslands, through dusty olive groves and cork plantations, and villages and towns, with an opportunity to see remarkable treasures and ancient sites.

BEST FOR: Exploring inland Portugal, sightseeing, bones

START: Évora

END: Abrantes

MILEAGE: 150km (93 miles)

ALLOW: 2–3 days

MAP PAGES: 53, 65

We are hungry. We have little food in the van because we have a ferry to catch in the next few days and still want to see Évora, so getting here has been a priority over stopping to buy groceries. So, although we have got here late, we need to venture out to find a restaurant.

We are here because of a Dutch man, Wim, whom we encountered in Spain a few months ago. He is one of those characters who talks to everyone he meets. Lizzy met him while washing up and ended up chatting to him for an hour. He wandered back with her to our pitch to introduce himself to me and we got talking about where we'd been and where we were going. He told us about the Chapel of the Bones, a small side-chapel of the Church of St Francis in Évora, which is decorated with the bones of around 5,000 people.

In the ensuing months, the more we read about Évora, the more we decided to make it a part of our plans. Its city centre, the old city, is a UNESCO World Heritage Site because of its walls, gardens, basilica, churches, Roman theatre and the Chapel of Bones. We had to go. All we had to do was to work it into a route somehow. When we found out about the N2, things panned out, as they have a habit of doing, so we decided to begin this route in Évora, follow the aqueduct out of town on the R114 and then pick up the N2 at Montemor-o-Novo to take it as far as Abrantes, where we could pick up the A23 to head back to Santander.

One thing we had read about Évora was that it is Portugal's hottest place in summer because of its position at the centre of the country. Temperatures often reach into the 30s and sometimes into the 40s. Today, though, while it is still in the late 20s, there are dark clouds over the city, a brisk wind from the west and dampness hangs in the air like a mouldy dishcloth. The threat of rain has been with us all day and, although we have driven through spray and drizzle to get here, it has yet to truly pour down.

Lizzy and I grab jackets and set off for the city centre, which is just a ten-minute walk from the free motorhome parking. As we leave, it starts to drizzle a little. We continue walking, to a restaurant that serves local specialities and has great reviews, deciding to take a route that differs from the one being offered by Google so we can begin to get a feel for the city. We pass the city walls and turn right into the public gardens. The rain gets heavier and we walk, more quickly, trying to outrun it.

We pass part of a ruin that's preserved in a corner of the garden. Sitting on top of the ruined window frames and columns are six peacocks. They look down at us miserably as we pass, their feathers dripping. Silhouetted against the sky, sitting on top of the Gothic arches, they look like symbols of bad things to come. Lizzy and I discuss the peacock's place in mythology as we dash to the next available shelter beneath the columns of the Royal Palace of Évora, a building that was begun in 1648. For us, the eyes on a peacock's feathers are portents of calamitous happenings. A dash of pathetic fallacy to see us on our slippery, sodden way.

The rain gets heavier. It runs in sheets from the gutters of the palace, creating a wall of water that we have to run through to get out from under the columns. It soaks us more. We press on, leaving the gardens and coming to a long, empty street that is awash with running water. My denim jacket is just about holding the water off my skin, but I know it won't last long, so I shelter in a doorway and get out my phone to update directions. There is no

one about, except for a few cars, and the town is quiet. All we can hear is the hissing, dripping, plopping and sizzling of the rain as it falls on the cobbled street. Then the thunder rumbles and the rain takes on a new intensity. It crashes in fat, dive-bombing blobs like an angry waterfall, the gaps between the drops filled with more water. It runs in the gutters, shines on the cobbles, wets windows and splashes from the cars as they pass by.

We reach the restaurant, although it feels pointless to me. The water has seeped in through my jacket, through my shirt and to the skin. My feet are squelching in my shoes and my hair is dripping down my neck. Water falls from my eyebrows, off the end of my nose and down my face. I don't think I have ever been so wet when I haven't been in a bath, shower, river or the sea.

We wait in the entrance to the restaurant, hoping they have a table, although I can see why they might not have. Suddenly, I lose the will to eat. I don't want to sit among dry people dripping, causing puddles on the floor and wetting the chair, so I am quietly relieved when a waiter comes over and tells us they are full. We turn around, wait for a few moments in the foyer for a respite that never comes and then head out again. We get lost on the way

back to the van. By the time we reach it we are cold, miserable and very, very wet. We strip on the mat, dry off with towels and dump our wet stuff in the shower.

We eat a tin of tuna with rice. It rains all night, hammering on the skylight above our heads.

The next day, it is still raining, but not as heavily. We eat breakfast slowly until there is a glimpse of sun between the clouds and we feel we can venture out. We wander the city, finding the Roman baths at the town hall, the Roman theatre, the cathedral and the Chapel of Bones.

The Chapel of Bones is remarkable. The walls are lined with the remains of an estimated 5,000 people – dug up by Franciscan monks. A novel way perhaps to solve an overcrowding crisis in the city's cemeteries. Walking into the chapel is quite surreal because death is all around and yet I don't feel the weight of it like I expect to. I don't find it macabre or terrifying or

distasteful or even shocking, even though I rarely see human bones and have never seen them on this scale. The thing I find strangest is the way the monks have used different bones to decorate different parts of the chapel. Walls are lined with tibias and fibulas in one part, while the coccyx has its own section above the columns. Skulls adorn pillars and the arches of the vaulted ceiling. Each bone has a value, seemingly for its ability to decorate.

Instead of making contact with the ideas behind the chapel, I am annoyed with a guide for talking loudly to his German tour group while we are there. We wait until they leave and find ourselves alone in the company of the ghosts. We read the interpretation boards around the chapel. The message, translated into English from Portuguese poems, is that we should remember what we are and will become, with the implications that your time on earth is limited so it should be made good use of. I couldn't agree more, although I'm not necessarily in complete agreement with the next part of this, which is to spend time in the service of God. That's beyond me. But I get the bit about leading a useful life. Vanity, the poems tell us, is pointless when you are gone.

We leave the chapel and follow a sign to an exhibition of nativity scenes that is housed in a small corridor in the roof of the church. It seems a little incongruous so close to the chapel of the bones, but it makes both sense and a point by celebrating life. So much life!

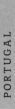

In the exhibition, there are nativities from all over the world. Each is made differently, using different techniques and representing the key figures in their own way. There must be a couple of hundred of them for us to pore over, as if we need an antidote to bring us back from the brink of the death downstairs. There are black Jesuses, Asian Marys and Russian Josephs. I love it and am enthralled by many of them, although many of the European versions – with their classic Catholic style – leave me cold. It is the folk art that inspires me: the Russian dolls, the colourful Mexican scenes, the simple African carvings. They are all beautiful in their own way. The exhibition, Lizzy and I agree, is fabulously curated. She likes the glass; I like the tiny scenes in a matchbox. The story of the nativity might be the same, but it is interpreted and represented differently across cultures. As a result, the mood improves as the light comes back. Time goes on.

We do something useful with the rest of our day, which is to find the best coffee and cake in Évora, at a cafe called Do Largo, a lucky find if ever there was one. Life-affirming brownies, nurturing coffees and a lovely atmosphere make us forget last night's dinner in a single mouthful.

But as we leave to go back to the van, it starts to rain again.

THE DRIVING

It is worth driving around Évora's ring road as it passes through the aqueduct and also follows the course of the city walls (on the outside). The *aire* is just off the N380.

Leave Évora at the ring road on the R114-4, following the aqueduct out of town to the north-west. It is a reasonably straight road through *dehesa* and scrub with holm oaks, which passes by the Convento da Cartuxa and goes under the A6 *autovía*. Shortly after the A6, when the road meets the N370 (it looks like you just carry on, but that is the N370), take a left turn towards Escoural on to the N370, then sharp right almost immediately to get on to the M529. Follow the M529 through fields of boulders, cattle, *dehesa* and cork oaks. It's a landscape that feels ancient, and it is – there are lots of ancient monuments nearby.

When the M529 meets the N4, turn left towards Montemor-o-Novo and head into the town through the

WHERE TO STAY: CAMPING

Parque de Campismo do Gameiro, Cabeção
Cabeção, Portugal
Tel: +351 926 10 07 68
Web: www.cm-mora.pt/locais/parque-de-campismo-do-gameiro

This is a small campsite by the Fluviário de Mora with access to the lake. It offers watersports and great swimming in an out-of-the-way location. There is an aire *here, too.*

WHERE TO STAY: *AIRES*

Évora: The *aire* in the city is free and has grey and black waste as well as fresh water.
Abrantes: There are a couple of *aires* in the town with a few free spaces (no services) close to the old city.

lovely *dehesa* and cork oaks, plus the occasional vineyard. Go under the motorway and then take the second turn-off at the first roundabout in the direction of Lisbon. Shortly after, take a right on to the N2 signed for Ponte de Sor/Mora (it's about the sixth right turn) and head out of town. You will join the N2 at the 522km (324-mile) mark of its 700km (435-mile) length and go backwards counting down. This road will be your guide and home for the next hundred kilometres so look out for the Casas dos Canonteiros roadhouses, the original petrol stations and milestones.

Follow the N2 through Brotas and Mora. After Mora, you'll enter a big plain with maize and pines, distant hills and a river to your left. You'll cross the river. The next turn will take you to the Fluviário de Mora (aquarium), where you can swim in the reservoir or camp if you need to stop. Follow the signs.

Back on the N2, keep going! You'll pass over the Barragem de Montargil (a reservoir dam) and then follow the west side of the reservoir past holiday encampments, a few campsites and exclusive apartment blocks. There is also a huge aerodrome just outside Ponte de Sor.

Keep on the N2 as you approach Ponte de Sor (take the first left at the roundabout towards Abrantes) and carry on towards Abrantes. As you approach the city, you'll pass through Rossio ao Sul do Tejo, a run-down suburb of Abrantes with lots of empty houses and industry, plus a railway crossing. It will bring you to the bridge over the Tagus. A quick detour to the right before the bridge will take you to a park by the river, which is a great place to see the city and river.

Over the river, follow the N2, then take a left after about 1.2km (¾ mile) towards the castle. The *aire* is next to the municipal buildings. Parking for motorhomes is available there too (time is limited on the spaces to the front – at the rear, you can overnight).

IN THE AREA

Capela dos Ossos (Chapel of Bones), Évora A remarkable place and Évora's best-known sight. It is situated in the St Francis Church. Pay on the door for entry. Very atmospheric. • **www.igrejadesaofrancisco.pt**

Évora Cathedral, Évora Dating back to around 1200, this cathedral is remarkable for its cloisters and the views from the roof, which can be accessed from the nave and give you a 360-degree view of the city. Excellent! Pay on entry. • **www.evoracathedral.com**

Roman temple and baths, Évora The Temple of Diana sits at the edge of the Diana Gardens and is incomplete, but still very impressive. The baths are harder to find, being inside the local council offices, but are free to see.

Another original Roman bath house is now a pricey private spa at • **www.inacquaveritas.com**

Aqueduto da Água de Prata, Évora This is a huge, almost intact mediaeval aqueduct that heads out of the city for 8km (5 miles). In the city, it has become part of life, and houses and workshops have been built into the arches. • **www.visitevora.net/en/agua-prata-aqueduct-evora**

Do Largo, Évora Coffee and cake. Delicious food and great coffees in Évora. A rare find. • **www.dolargo.pt**

Abrantes castle, gardens and old city The old city of Abrantes sits on a promontory overlooking the Tagus. The castle, which has origins back in Roman times (130 BC), sits overlooking it all. Impressive views all round, with a lovely garden below it on the city side. The old city centre is great to wander. • **www.turismo.cm-abrantes.pt**

Cromeleque dos Almendres, Almendres An impressive and very friendly oval of standing stones that is one of Europe's largest (there are just under 100 stones here). The road to get to it will have the crockery falling off the shelves but it's worth it for a chance to hang out with 7,000-year-old stones. Take the N114 out of Évora, then the CM1075. • **www.visitevora.net/en/almendres-cromlech-portugal**

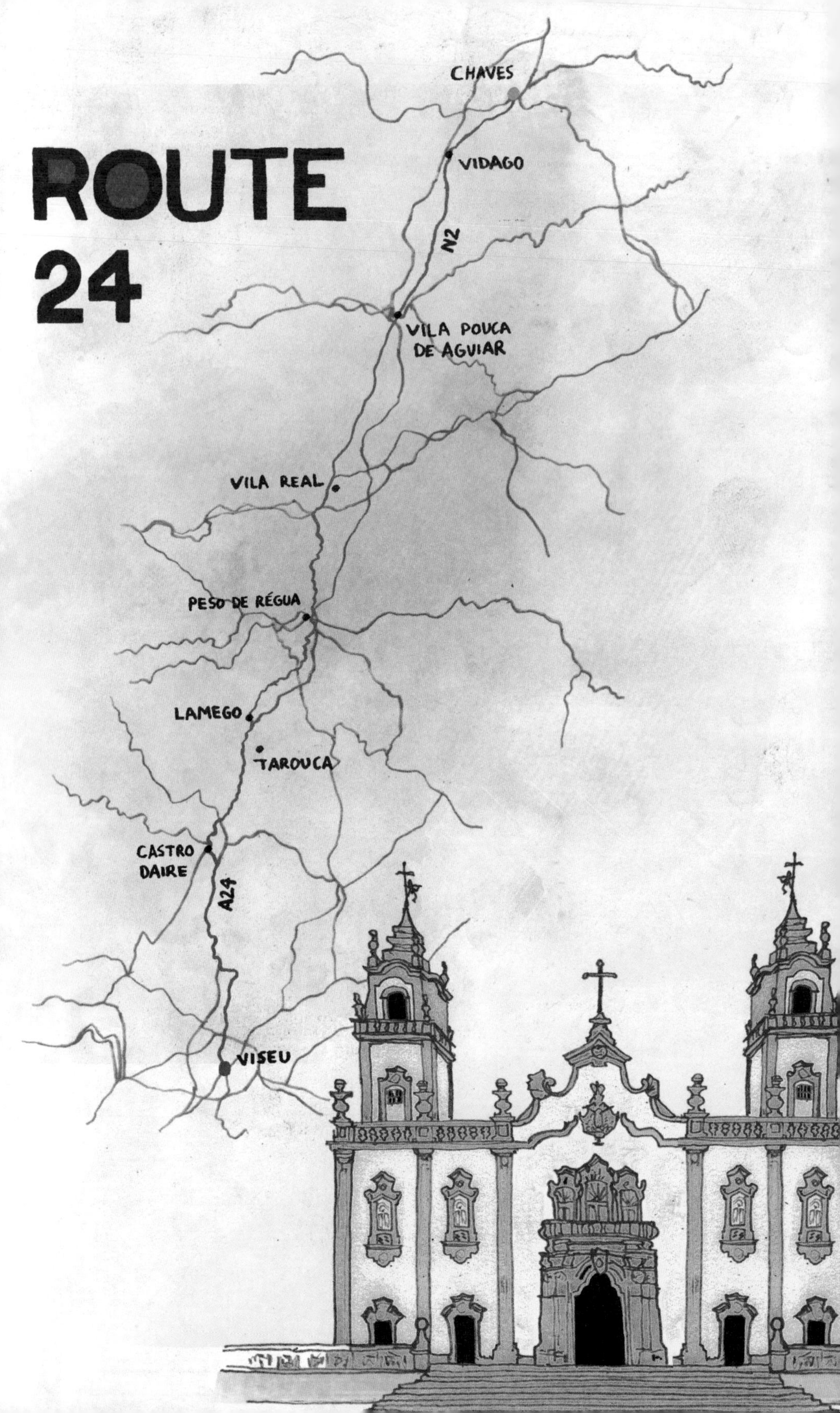
ROUTE
24
CHAVES
VIDAGO
N2
VILA POUCA
DE AGUIAR
VILA REAL
PESO DE RÉGUA
LAMEGO
TAROUCA
CASTRO
DAIRE
A24
VISEU

ROUTE 24

CHAVES TO VISEU

ROUTE 66 AND THE LANGUAGE BARRIER

The N2 is Portugal's 'Route 66', stretching from north to south and passing through the centre of the country. This journey will take you from near the Spanish border, almost directly south, across the Douro Valley and on to the cathedral city of Viseu. This area is famous for the quality of its hot springs, which have been enjoyed since Roman times.

BEST FOR: Spa treatments, exploring Portugal's interior

START: Chaves

END: Viseu

MILEAGE: 160km (100 miles)

ALLOW: 2–3 days

MAP PAGES: 27, 41

We arrive in Chaves late after a long drive from the north coast. We find a Park4Night spot on the river next to a little park and just below the town's main bridge. We are so tired that we bed down early and are barely disturbed by the comings and goings in the car park. I say barely, but they are enough to remember that they go on, seemingly all night.

We wake early to explore the city, walking up the river to the impressive Roman bridge through a part of the town that's a little grubby and run-down. It feels very real, as if we've stepped into a part of Portugal we weren't meant to see. Shopkeepers are setting up their small shops, selling religious icons, hardware and hair products.

The bridge is fabulous. It is known as Trajan's Bridge and was constructed in the 1st century AD. It once had 18 arches but now has only 12, the remaining six having been assimilated into the banks. To the south of the bridge, around 100m (109 yards) away, on the middle of a roundabout, we find the zero marker for the N2 road. This will be the start point for our journey as we follow the road to the south to Viseu. We aren't the first: the marker is covered in stickers from motorcycle and cycling clubs.

We wander across the bridge to find the Museum of the Roman Baths, a remarkable site that was uncovered in 2015 while developers were digging out an underground car park. Created in around 70AD, the baths were what made Chaves famous in the Roman world and gave the town its name of Aquae Flaviae. Unlike most Roman baths, which were used for washing and hygiene, these were used for healing and ran with the hot spring waters that bubble up here. The museum is free so we go in and walk to the edge of the balcony that surrounds the site, looking down at the pools and remains of the walls that were lost for almost 1,700 years following an earthquake. The water still flows through the baths and the atmosphere inside is hot and moist. Seeing it gives me one of those genuine 'wow' moments. Hardly surprising: the baths are the biggest in the Iberian Peninsula, possibly in Europe.

Our next stop is the Termas de Chaves, a modern-day version of the Roman baths that's housed in an austere, white-rendered modern building in the middle of a park on the riverside. In the square in front of the entrance we find a sunken spring where hot thermal water gushes from a pipe.

We enter the spa and find out how we can enjoy the healing properties of the water. The best option for us, it would seem, is an Aquae Duo 'treatment' that consists of a sauna, immersion in a bath of thermal water and then a massage. I'm keen. We book in for the next day, unsure of what to expect from the experience.

We arrive at the spa on time and are invited to wait for the nurse. He greets us in English, invites us to enter his office and asks us to sign a health form. He then tells us to head off down a corridor, which looks and feels like a sanitorium, and take a set of stairs to the first floor. When we get there, we are greeted by a woman in uniform behind a desk in a stark reception

space, who speaks in Portuguese to us. We have no idea what she has said. While we have been learning Spanish, Portuguese is impenetrable to us, even now we've spent weeks in the country. It sounds like Russian, despite it being similar to Spanish, because of the s sounds. I find it so difficult to understand even simple words

The nurse repeats what she said and then realises we don't speak Portuguese. We say we are sorry (in Spanish) and ask if she speaks English. She doesn't. Two more women, who have been behind the desk too, come round and hand us each a towelling robe. They mime taking off our clothes, give us a robe each and a key and usher us off to changing rooms. They open the door and point, through the changing room, to another door, which I assume means we get changed and then go through the other door.

We head into separate changing rooms. I strip off, change into my swim shorts and flip-flops and pull on the bathrobe. When I emerge from the changing room through the other door, the two masked women are waiting for me. I smile behind my mask and stand there awkwardly while no one speaks. It would be pointless, anyway, we realise.

When Lizzy emerges from her changing room, they lead us off down a corridor and into a side room. One of them says 'Sauna' and then '*Diez minutos*', points to a hook where we should hang our robes and our masks and then ushers us into the sauna, shutting the door after us. We sit down in the heat and try to relax, although it's a little unsettling to be bossed

about in a language we don't understand. When ten minutes is up, the two women appear again and tell us to shower (or at least that's what we assume they are telling us) and then send us back into the sauna for another ten minutes. When that is up, they come back and collect us, pointing to our robes to indicate that we should put them back on and then to their faces to remind us we must wear masks. We are led across the corridor to a brightly lit, clinical-looking room with two huge, white, body-shaped plastic bathtubs with head and footrests. The women start to fill the tubs – one each – and then point to hooks on the walls where our robes must go. Once the tubs are full, they indicate for us to get in. They check the temperature is OK for us. We nod and say '*si*' and then they push a button in some kind of control panel. It sounds as if a pump is starting, then the bath starts vibrating, sending jets of water into my back and making a loud mechanical noise. The women leave us, saying '*vinte minutos*'. Twenty minutes.

The noise from the tubs is so loud that I sink down into the bath so my ears are covered. Now all I can hear are the bubbles and jets of water. The frequency changes as the jets change, running a sequence that starts with tinkly, tiny bubbles on the soles of my feet and works its way up my body, gaining in depth and strength until it reaches my back with a powerful jet of water either side of my spine that rumbles like old men arguing in the next room. I close my eyes.

After about five minutes, I hear one of the women open the door slightly. She pops her head around the door briefly, looks at me and then switches off the light. The room is now in semi-darkness except for a green light that comes from underneath me somewhere in the bath. I close my eyes and concentrate on the bubbles, listening and feeling as the sequence runs. In what seems like a few minutes, the women return, turn on the lights and urge us to get out of the tubs. They hold towels behind us for us to wrap ourselves in, as if we are children. The woman assigned to me holds mine up at a height where it goes under my armpits so I have to roll it and secure it as if I were covering my boobs. She then holds the bathrobe in the same way. I reach behind me to find the arm holes and struggle a little, adding to my embarrassment at being helped into a towel.

Once we are dressed, we are led away again to another room, in which there are two massage tables. Some plinky piano music is being piped in and there are two candles on a table. One of the women leaves and the other indicates that we should now remove our robes. She points to a small white package in a clear plastic bag on top of a towel that sits on the bench Lizzy is standing next to. Lizzy picks it up and looks at the woman, who says '*si*' and mimes opening it. Lizzy obliges and pulls out a pair of very small disposable pants. She holds them up and laughs.

'Oh my god!' I say, also laughing. The woman then points to similar, but blue, package on my massage table. I open it and pull out a pair of blue disposable pants that are nothing more than two small triangles joined up with elastic. 'Oh!' I say.

The woman disappears and leaves us alone with our pants. I pull off my shorts and try mine on, assuming that the smaller paper triangle goes at the front. It barely covers my genitals. Lizzy says, 'I think you've got them on the wrong way round', but before I can take them off there is a knock at the door and it opens. We both lie quickly down like naughty kids, me on my front, and Lizzy on her back. Two different women come in, dressed similarly with uniforms, masks and hats. We can barely make out their faces, but I can see that one of them is older and wears glasses. The other has dark eyebrows and is much younger. The older woman goes to Lizzy and covers her with a towel. The younger woman comes to me, holds a towel over me and tells me to turn over, in English, then places the towel on to me. I can feel myself falling out of my pants but can't say anything. I guess she's seen it all before. She picks up my right hand and starts to massage it.

The massage is good and I am gently and kindly instructed when to turn over. Nothing else is said, which feels strange as I'd usually jabber away nervously whenever I am receiving any kind of intimate treatment like this.

But the language barrier keeps me quiet, which is probably for the best. I feel constantly on the verge of my comfort zone, especially when the massage gets close to the regions I'd consider to be intimate. I doze and enjoy being pushed and pulled, pressed and jabbed.

I assume Lizzy is receiving the same as she is quiet, too, and all I can hear is the piano music and the sound of oil being rubbed into soft, supple skin.

The massages come to a close – in perfect synchronicity – and the women leave us and the room. They are like masseur ninjas, stepping in, masked and unnamed, without introduction or niceties, to do a job and then leaving. It feels strange and impersonal and I jokingly complain to Lizzy that I never got to find out her name.

We take off our pants and bin them, then pull on our swimming costumes and robes again. One of the first women comes in again and leads us back to the changing rooms. I shower and get dressed and walk out to find Lizzy waiting for me. We say '*obrigado*' to the receptionist and leave.

I feel lighter as we walk into the sunshine outside, as if I have passed through some faceless rebirthing process. It's confusing but not unpleasant and I feel different but the same, perhaps a little less burdened with the stiffness I get in my back after a long drive.

We head back to the van and get ready to head south on the N2, the road that will lead us into the centre of Portugal.

THE DRIVING

The N2 starts at a roundabout around 100m (109 yards) from the Roman bridge in Chaves, and then heads almost straight south to Faro on the Algarve some 739km (459 miles) later. This section, the first 150km (93 miles), will take you into the mountains in Portugal's north and then down into the Douro, across the river and on to Viseu via Lamego.

So, this route is easy to follow – just stay on the N2!

We went around the roundabout a few times to make sure we got the feel for it, then we whipped off down the N2 to the south, following the straight road out of Chaves through a sea of out-of-town hypermarkets, DIY stores and fast-food chains that soon changed to an avenue of young acers before heading up hill into the pine-clad mountains

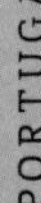

that encircle Chaves. The N2 heads into the hills, while the motorway that roughly follows its course stays in the valley until they cross over at Vila Pouca. At Vidago, there is another spa and it is possible to visit an old bottling plant just outside the village.

Continue through Vila Pouca amid the olive groves and sections of ancient woodland and towards Vila Real. Just outside Escariz, we stopped to take photos of a weird landscape of rounded tors of granite and heather.

Vila Real is a big town at the top of a gorge that marks a change in the landscape. After passing through town, you enter the Douro region, a UNESCO World Heritage Site. The N2 gets really curly here as it makes its way around the hillsides, offering great views of the huge viaduct that carries the A4 motorway. As you crest the hill, you see, for the first time, the terraced hillsides of the Douro that are covered with vines, olives and fruit trees. It seems as if most of the land has been given over to agriculture, with just a few patches of forest remaining. It's stunning.

At Santa Marta, there is a new motorhome *aire* with great views over the valleys. Then it's on to Peso da Régua, where there is a motorhome *aire* below the three bridges. You'll cross the Douro here on the smaller road bridge that carries the N2 and then continue on through the terraces up a tributary, the Varosa River. Then it's on to Lamego, where there is a huge set of steps leading to the Church of Our Lady of the Remedies above a square with statues of the four seasons. It's really pretty but a little confusing as you'll need to go around the square and back the way you came to stay on the N2.

The road leads out of Lamego, winding through villages, following the motorway, then on to a high plateau of granite and gorse, brush and heather, going over and under the motorway. Head through the cobbled streets of Castro Daire and on to Viseu, where the *aire* awaits at the point where the N2 meets the ring road.

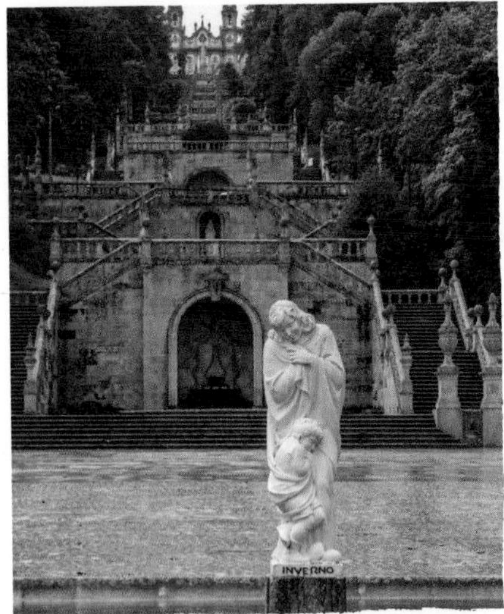

WHERE TO STAY: CAMPING

Parque de Campismo Quinta do Rebentão, Chaves
Vila Nova de Veiga, 5400-764 Chaves, Portugal
Web: www.campismochaves.pt
Tel: +351 276 32 27 33

A really lovely site in a wooded valley, adjacent to the outdoor pools, about ten minutes outside Chaves.

Camping Lamego Douro Valley, Lamego
EN2 - Lugar da Raposeira, 5100-027, Lamego, Portugal
Web: https://campinglamego.wixsite.com/webpage
Tel: +351 962 00 54 90

This is a really great overnight stopover with toilets and showers in the car park of a hotel that the owners are renovating. Very friendly and amazing views of Lamego.

WHERE TO STAY: *AIRES*

Guest House Chaves: A guest house that has spaces for motorhomes in the garden. It's situated very close to the Roman bridge and town centre. www.guesthousechaves.com
Viseu: Dedicated parking spaces in a car park on the edge of the town.
Peso da Régua: A fantastic *aire*, with electricity and all facilities, on the side of the Douro, below the three bridges.
Santa Marta: A new *aire* on the outskirts of this pretty hill town just to the north of Régua. Great views over the vineyards and valleys.

IN THE AREA

Thermal baths, Chaves It's as much a clinic as a spa, although you can pay to use the thermal baths. • www.termasdechaves.com

Museum of the Thermal Baths, Chaves Iberia's most important Roman baths – lost for 1,700 years – are housed in a new museum in the centre of Chaves. Remarkable.

Church of Misericórdia, Chaves A beautiful yet quite humble baroque church in Chaves with a wonky gilded altar and hand-painted tile walls.

Museu de Arte Contemporânea Nadir Afonso, Chaves A brutalist concrete marvel housing the work of local geometric abstractionist painter, one of Portugal's finest, Nadir Afonso. • https://macna.chaves.pt

Sanctuary of Our Lady of the Remedies, Lamego A rococo chapel at the top of a very long but picturesque staircase from the town square.

Sé Cathedral of Viseu This 12th-century cathedral is located in a large square. • www.visitportugal.com/pt-pt/content/se-catedral-de-viseu

ROUTE 25

PORTO
PESO DE RÉGUA
PINHÃO
TORRE DE MONCORVO
VILA NOVA DE FOZ CÔA
SÃU JOÃO DA PESQUEIRA
FREIXO DE ESPADA A CINTA
N-108
LAMEGO
DOURO RIVER
TAROUCA
N-222
FIGUEIRA DE CASTELO RODRIGO
PINHEL
N-221
VISEU
CELORICO DA BEIRA
GUARDA

ROUTE 25

GUARDA TO PORTO

SWIMMING TO SPAIN

The Douro is Portugal's great river, stretching from the border with Spain to the Atlantic at Porto. Its upper reaches are hard to get to as they form a series of gorges often referred to as the Grand Canyon of Portugal. The scenery – UNESCO designated with World Heritage Site status – is man-made but incredible. From Guarda, you'll have a gentle easing in to the glory to come as you wind around hilltop villages and through deep valleys before arriving at the Douro proper. That's when the real magic begins.

BEST FOR: Winding mountain roads, port, swimming, kayaking

START: Guarda

END: Porto

MILEAGE: 172km (107 miles)

ALLOW: 4–5 days

MAP PAGES: 26, 27, 42

We receive a text message from Annie and Graham, friends from home, when we are about to leave Guarda. We are walking into the city centre when my phone pings in my pocket. They have seen a post on Instagram about us heading for the Douro and wondered when we were likely to get there. They are there already, parked up in their motorhome at a *praia fluvial* (river beach) near Freixo de Espada à Cinta. I look at the map. After Guarda, our plan is to head north until we reach the Douro gorges (they have been compared to the Grand Canyon) and then follow the river downstream to Porto. Freixo de Espada à Cinta is very near to the point where the road from Guarda meets the Douro. We make plans to meet up at the river beach.

The road down to the beach is very steep, with a couple of hairpins and no safety barriers. All around, the hillsides have been terraced and are planted with vines and olives. We pass a few shacks with clay tile roofs on the way down, but by the time we almost get down to the level of the

reservoir, we feel as if we are somewhere remote and isolated. At the bottom of the road we reach a park with a pool complex. Above it, and with grass rooftops, are rooms with glass fronts belonging to a hotel. The hills above are steep and terraced and the reservoir – made by the dam downstream – is dark. A floating pool sits in a little inlet off the main body of water where a couple of people fish. No one is swimming. We pass the park and a pontoon where a tourist boat is moored, to find a gravel area beyond where there is a solitary motorhome.

We pull up beside it. The door opens and Annie and Graham leap out to greet us, full of excitement and chat. Lizzy jumps out of the van to hug them both while I park up. We are inches from the waterside, almost at water level. Backing on to the gravel area is a grove of orange trees that are ripe with small oranges. A huge fish jumps out of the water a good cast away from the edge where I park. I get out of the van to greet our friends.

We settle in and join the couple in their van while Graham cooks dinner. They have been to an Ironman event in Lisbon and have been making their way slowly home, training all the time. They tell us they have been in the floating pool and done 60 lengths during the day. At some point, somewhere between the second and third glass of wine, someone (I forget who) comes up with the idea of swimming across the reservoir in the morning. Lizzy, as always, is up for it, whereas I err on the side of caution and offer to do safety cover by paddling a surfboard as they swim. I am afraid of deep, open water, and especially that which is dark black, even though it is very clear. Annie, who was unsure she'd like it, is reassured by the idea of having an escape route if she loses her confidence halfway across.

Let me say, at this point, that no one has any idea how far it is across the reservoir. However, what excites the three of them so much is the idea that by swimming across they would swim to Spain. The Douro marks the border at this point between Spain and Portugal so any swim would be a foray into international waters. A crossing would be to truly traverse the geographical divide between the two countries.

In the morning, there is light cloud and no wind, which means the conditions are perfect, so all three swimmers are still keen.

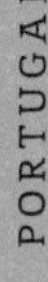

Me, not so, although I am happy to paddle a board. As mentioned, there is something inside me that fears deep and dark water. I think it comes from my family. They were never great swimmers and were frightened of reservoirs and gravel pits, the sea and rivers, possibly as a result of public information films that warned us, as kids, to never go near water. Maybe it was something to do with my sister nearly drowning when she was young that filtered down to me through my parents' anxiety?

Anyhow, the fear of deep water, combined with a lack of confidence in my own ability, allows me to pursue the idea of providing safety cover, so I climb up the ladder to the top of the van and get our kayaks and a surfboard down while the three swimmers get into their wetsuits. I paddle one of the kayaks out into the water, about 200m (218 yards) offshore, and stop. The kayak doesn't move, proving there is no current and reassuring Annie that it's safe to swim. I then switch to the board.

The three of them faff about with hats and goggles while I take photos and contemplate the distance and the reservoir. The water is still and clear. At the shore, the bottom is visible, but then it drops away so sharply that it soon becomes dark and impenetrable. When I jump in, I am out of my depth within 1.8m (2 yards) of the shore.

We begin to cross. It looks to be less than a kilometre (620m) across to the boat that's anchored by a shack on the opposite bank, but it's had to tell. I paddle and take photos, while the three of them swim. The water is smooth and flat, like a sheet of gently undulating glass. The olive grove-covered hillsides are reflected in the water in perfect spurs sticking out into the reservoir. As the swimmers splash through the water, the reflections are shattered into fragments of sky, rock and the darkness of the water below. When we get to the middle, we stop and celebrate passing into Spanish waters. They swim on. We arrive, after 15 minutes, at the other side, where there is a little concrete pontoon adjacent to where the boat is moored. Lizzy, Annie and Graham sit on it catching their breath.

Annie offers to paddle the board for a bit so I can swim a little. The reassurance of having the board emboldens me so I set off towards the vans. I can see the bottom for a few metres and then it's gone. All I can spy in the dark-green water are my own arms and the bubbles they create as I swim. It's lovely water and I begin to settle in and enjoy it. When we stop for a breath, Annie wants to swim again so Lizzy takes a turn on the board. I continue to swim, feeling slightly foolish for not being brave enough to do so in the first place. I offer to paddle the board, but Lizzy (reluctantly) lets me swim on. Before long, we have crossed into Portugal again and the vans, silent on the lakeshore, are within a few hundred metres. I swim on, determined now to at least complete one half of the swim.

I wade ashore and drip on the grass by the van, breathless but very happy.

As the day progresses, the clouds lift to reveal a stunning blue sky and bright sunshine. Lizzy and I set off to kayak up the river, waving goodbye to Annie and Graham as we go. The water is clear and still as we slice through the water, hugging the banks to watch kingfishers dart away from us and to look at the shacks and, on the Spanish side, smallholdings on the banks. We paddle for an hour, enjoying this incredible landscape of scrub and terraces, rocky outcrops and feeling the warmth of the sun on our arms. Eventually, when the sun drops below the hilltops and the shade creeps across the water, we paddle back to the van. Annie and Graham have gone and we are alone on the waterside. We open the back doors of the van and sit watching the fish rise as the light fades on another stunning day on the Douro.

THE DRIVING

Guarda sits on the top of a big hill, giving it great views of the countryside all around. So it's worth a visit. The town is lovely, with plenty of old narrow streets to get lost in. We started at the campsite and made our way out of town to the north on the N16, finding the N221 on a roundabout next to the junction between the A25 and the A23. The road starts out wooded and gentle, passing through small fields and small villages. Gradually, the views open out and the countryside becomes more open until Pinhel, when the road runs alongside a river valley, passing terraced hillsides in tributaries. At this point, it starts to get really good as the road begins to bend and curve around the hills, becoming narrower and heading into what feels like a wild landscape of granite tors and boulders with small meadows and more granite in the form of walls and houses. As the road continues,

it heads downwards into a larger version of the same landscape, with broom, cork oaks and olives as well as a few big trees, including eucalyptus, umbrella pines and birch. It is really stunning. You cross the Rio Côa, and the landscape changes from granite to red-layered sandstone with more terraces and brings you out on to a plateau with Castelo Rodrigo in front of you. It's worth a stop to see the castle and the views (plus there are some nice local shops selling PASTEL DE NATA LIQUEUR – do I need to say it again?).

Keep on the N221 and follow it through Figueira de Castelo Rodrigo and on to Escalhão and then into the Douro valley. The road starts its bendy

course again, taking you into the man-made landscape that has gained it UNESCO World Heritage Site status. The road curves around the steep hillsides offering views that change all the time and eventually brings you down to river level at Barca de Alva, where you'll see some of the huge river cruise boats that ply their trade up the river. Cross over the bridge, staying on the N221, and follow the road towards Freixo de Espada à Cinta. This section follows the river quite closely, but also high above it, so you'll get incredible views of the olive groves, vineyards and terraces that make the area so special. After a few miles, you'll head inland and the road will loop back to the north, taking you to a plateau with pines and agriculture.

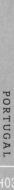

Turn left at the junction with the N220 and then turn left towards Torre de Moncorvo. This will take you through the plateau of rocky grasslands, agriculture, some industry, scrub, chestnut and pines. Eventually you'll get to Torre de Moncorvo (where there is an *aire*) and begin to descend again. Follow the N220 to the junction with the IP2–E802 and then head south until junction 12 and the N222. If you want to visit the Côa Museum, this is the junction to take for Vila Nova de Foz Côa.

At the roundabout coming off the motorway, take the first exit signed towards Régua. This is the N222. It will take you on another very bendy course and up into the hillsides of steep terraces, with far-reaching views of the Douro, though small isolated villages and past vineyards and wineries. When you reach the river level again, at the junction with the N323, you can

turn right and drive for a short way into the lovely town of Pinhão, where there are restaurants and bars, plus a nice river front (we stayed there). If you are big, take a right directly after the steel bridge.

Continuing on the N222 will lead you on one of the easiest and best stretches. It follows the river closely and passes one of the dams at Régua before landing you in Peso da Régua. You'll go under the motorway bridge and then the metal bridge before arriving at a junction. Turn left on to the N2 and then, at the roundabout, take the second exit across the big bridge on the N2. This will take you over the Douro. At the other side, you can either follow the signs for the *aire* to park (last exit before the bridge) or take the second exit on to the N108.

This will take you through the town and out the other side, alongside the river and then up into the hills of the Douro. After Régua, there are more houses and buildings and it feels busier, but still just as exciting in terms of driving. The views are amazing and the bends are continuous. It's not a quick road by any standards, even mine.

Follow the N108 but beware that it's easy to go wrong as you'll need to keep making left turns to stay on it, at Ribadouro and later on at Alpendurada, where you turn left at the roundabout, and at Torrao, where you turn left after going over the bridge. Keep following the signs to Porto.

You'll notice fewer vines along this section because you have passed out of the upper Douro wine region and into the hinterland of Porto. The terrain is still difficult and tortuous but offers excellent views at most points. There are more houses the closer you get to Porto but still wild areas. You'll go under the A41–IC24 and then eventually come to the end of the road at the junction with the A43 and A20. Follow the A20 over the Ponte de Freixo if you are camping at Vila Nova da Gaia (see below).

WHERE TO STAY: CAMPING

Camping Municipal de Guarda, Guarda
Avenida do Estádio Municipal, 6300-705 Guarda, Portugal
Web: https://portugal-campings.com/pt/places/camping-municipal-da-guarda
Tel: +351 271 22 12 00

A nice municipal site not far from the city centre and adjacent to the park.

Parque de Campismo Orbitur Canidelo, Vila Nova da Gaia
Praia de Salgueiros, Av. da Beira-Mar 441, 4400-382 Vila Nova de Gaia, Portugal
Web: www.orbitur.pt/pt/destinos/regiao-norte/orbitur-canidelo
Tel: +351 227 81 47 30

Being part of the Orbitur group means this campsite is well used and in a good spot. It is high-density but in a great location on the seafront near a selection of restaurants. Great beach.

WHERE TO STAY: *AIRES*

Peso da Régua: One of the best *aires* we have come across, with individual drainage, EHU and taps. Overlooks the Douro and is just a short walk from the town. Good place to launch a kayak.
Pinhão: There are a few places where it is possible to park on the quayside in Pinhão. Access is tricky for big mohos.
Praia fluvial: This Park4Night spot is right on the river below Freixo de Espada à Cinta. May get busy in summer. Treat with care.

IN THE AREA

Museum of Douro, Peso da Régua This lovely museum, which lies on the banks of the Douro at Peso da Régua, tells the story of the river, its wine-growing tradition and the port trade. It includes a free tasting of a lovely ten-year-old tawny port at the end. Just a short walk from the *aire*.
• **www.museudodouro.pt**

Archaeological Park and Museum of the Rio Côa, Vila Nova Foz Côa In 1998, a dam threatened to engulf thousands of pieces of 'newly discovered' rock art in the Côa valley. Having been dated to over 10,000 years old, the carvings were hastily given UNESCO World Heritage Site status and saved from the developers, mainly thanks to the passion of local schoolchildren. The museum that was built to celebrate the carvings is huge and sits above the valley. • **https://arte-coa.pt**

Boat trips Boat trips are available from most places on the Douro. Tours will take you on a seven bridges tour of Porto or on day trips out of Régua and Pinhão. Luxury cruises run out of Porto.

Kayak hire Kayaks are available to hire at Régua and Pinhão in the summer and some companies will take you on guided kayak tours of the gorges.

Vineyard tours Quinta do Vallado, established in 1716, is one of the oldest and most famous '*quintas*' (wine-producing estates) in the Douro Valley. It lies on both banks of the Corgo River, a tributary of the Douro River, right near to its mouth. They run tours and tastings in English (£25 per head) most days at 11.00am, 2.30pm and 4.30pm. Email to book.

• **www.quintadovallado.com**

Porto Porto is a fascinating city and I wish we could have stayed longer and explored more. However, we saw enough to get a flavour of this beguiling place and travelled

The waterfront in Porto

on the cable car from Gaia to the top of the huge Dom Luís I Bridge, mooched about on both sides of the harbour, wandered about in Foz, and enjoyed a glass or two of port looking at the city from outside one of the old port warehouses in Gaia. We rode in from the Orbitur campsite in Gaia – an easy cycle, mostly on cycle lanes.

Serralves Contemporary Art Museum, Porto A stunning art museum with world-class exhibitions. Well worth a visit if you like art spaces, exhibitions and gardens. The gardens have a fantastic tree canopy walk. • **www.serralves.pt**

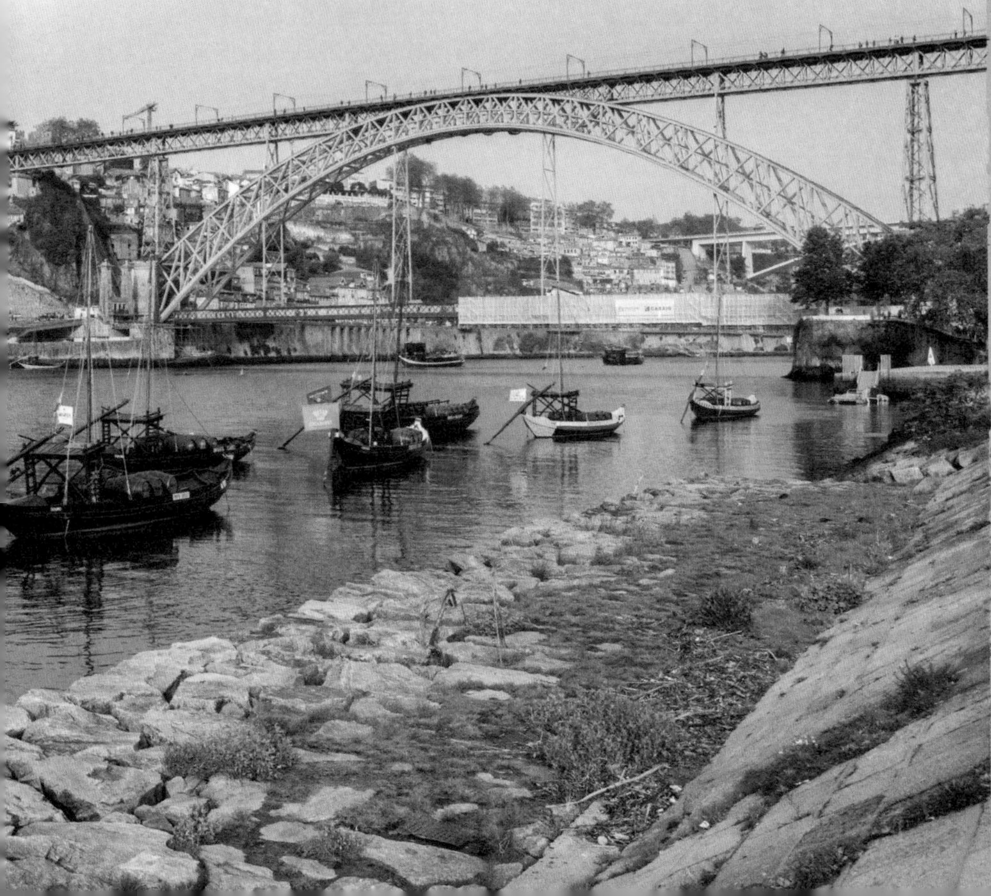

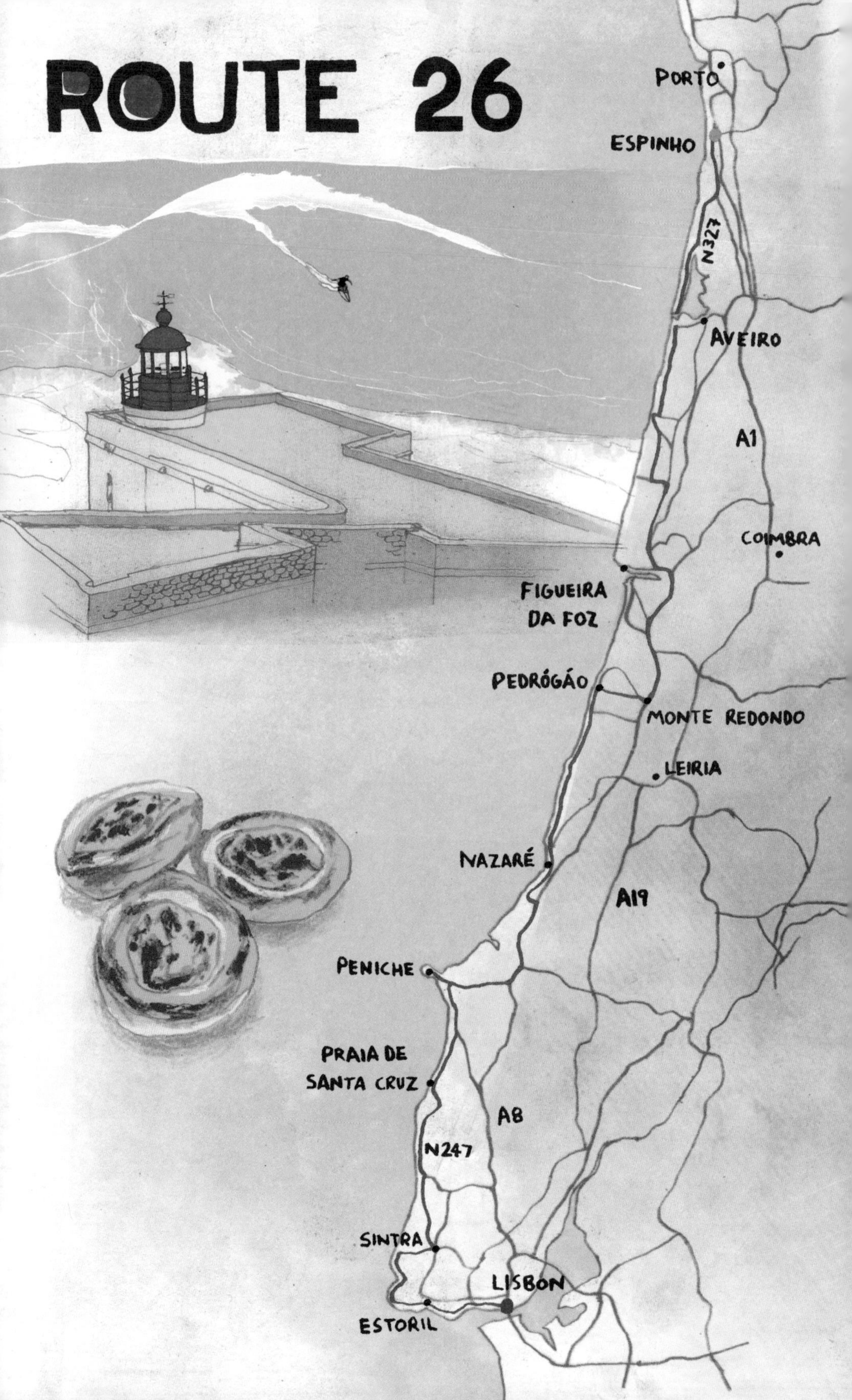
ROUTE 26
PORTO
ESPINHO
N327
AVEIRO
A1
COIMBRA
FIGUEIRA
DA FOZ
PEDRÓGÃO
MONTE REDONDO
LEIRIA
NAZARÉ
A19
PENICHE
PRAIA DE
SANTA CRUZ
A8
N247
SINTRA
LISBON
ESTORIL

ROUTE 26

ESPINHO TO LISBON

THE GIANTS OF NAZARÉ

The west coast of Portugal takes the full force of the Atlantic and, thanks to a unique geography, can produce surfing waves of world-beating magnitude. While summer brings surf that the average Joe might be able to manage, it is winter that brings the world's best to ride the waves at Nazaré. A journey out of season will take you to beach towns and through miles and miles of beautiful littoral landscapes. If you time it right, you may get a chance to witness the terror and beauty of the oceans' most powerful manifestation. Plus, it's a really great drive!

BEST FOR: Watching huge surf, exploring the coast, beaches, surfing.

START: Espinho

END: Lisbon

MILEAGE: 400km (249 miles)

ALLOW: at least 7 days, with at least 2 days in Lisbon (depending on the surf forecast)

MAP PAGES: 40, 52, 64

When we leave Porto and head south for Espinho and Lisbon I am itching to get going. This is the part of the writing of this book that I have been looking forward to the most. It has long been a dream to drive the coast of Portugal looking for surf, and this route gives me the opportunity, finally, to do exactly that.

As we drive along, the surf is huge. There has been a massive storm in the North Atlantic and it's sending waves with size and ferocity towards the coast of Portugal. We stop at a number of beaches along the way to check the size of the waves, following the coast road to the end of the spit at São Jacinto. There, we take the ferry across the estuary and watch the waves at Barra. The surf is still big, even though there are a few people surfing

in the shelter of the sea wall. We drive through Costa Nova and stop to take photos of the beautiful, candy-striped houses. Our next stop is Poço da Cruz, a tiny, quiet beach with a jetty making nicely shaped, if big, waves along a sandbar behind the breakwater. We spend the night at Gafanha da Boa Hora (Vagueira), a great *aire* right next to the beach run by a lovely family and with a fantastic beach bar. As the sun goes down, we watch the waves crash on to the sand.

I check my surfing app for the state of the storm. Tomorrow, it looks as if there might be a break in the size of the waves before the main swell hits the day after. Looking at the map, I can see that our journey will coincide with the main body of the swell – and the biggest predicted waves – arriving at Nazaré, about 180km (112 miles) down the coast. The Praia do Norte at Nazaré has become world famous in the last 20 years as the place where the world's biggest waves have been surfed. The world record, held by Sebastian Steudtner, was made at Praia do Norte in 2020 with a wave that was calculated by Guinness to be 26.2m (86ft). Some waves ridden at Nazaré are estimated to have been over 30.5m (100ft) tall but have never officially been ratified.

It seems as if we will be in the right place at the right time to see some extraordinary surfing. Our sights are set on Nazaré.

The next day, we arrive at Figueira da Foz, about 90km (56 miles) from Nazaré, and drive up to the Cabo Mondego to look for surf. The swell looks small enough for me to surf on a point break that's close to the road, so I

suit up and jump in. I catch two waves before the tide turns what looked like an easy point into a shallow, dumping mess. I guess that's why no one else was surfing. We park up for the night on an *aire* next to the breakwater. The next morning, we go for a run to the end of the breakwater at first light. Apart from the fishermen who line the sea wall, we are the first up. The tide is low and we can see that the swell is now three of four times the size it had been the day before. We swim in a sheltered cove out of the way of the waves and then return to the van to have breakfast. An hour or so later, we look again at the breakwater and notice the police have cordoned off the end. Huge waves are now smashing into the sea wall and crashing over it. The place we had run a little earlier is now awash with water from each wave as it hits the sea defences and spills over into the mouth of the harbour. The point I surfed yesterday is now huge, with waves running for miles from Cabo Montego almost to the main beach at Figueira da Foz.

We head to Nazaré, taking the N109, a little road that runs close to the coast. The light is ethereal as we drive alongside the waves. The sea spray makes a fine, salty mist that is being backlit by the sun. It makes everything look dreamy and surreal, as if a scene from a scary film or after a fire. The countryside seems to smoulder as the mist catches the light and the sun's rays are split by the branches of trees. The more the day wears on, the better it gets, until we find ourselves stopping every few miles to take photos and admire the surf and wildness of the land behind the dunes. It's an empty landscape of dunes and sandy scrub punctuated by beach towns that changes subtly to low cliffs the further we go.

We arrive at Nazaré just before dark and pitch up at the Orbitur campsite just outside town. The next morning, we are awake before dawn. We dress, eat and get ready to head to the fort, the vantage point from which it is possible to watch the waves at Praia do Norte. We cycle through the town, wondering which way to go, until we see people all heading in the same direction, as if some Pied Piper is calling them. It's the surf. We weave between the people and follow the road to the bluff overlooking the beach. The red-painted lighthouse that tops the fort is unmistakeable as we crest the hill and head sharply down towards the headland. We can see people lining the cliff edge, standing on top of the fort and, looming large behind, monstrous waves peaking up into tepees then breaking in an explosion of white water and spray, mist rising into the gloomy early morning light.

We lock the bikes and then settle down to watch what's unfolding before us. There are about 20 jetskis in the water. Some of them are towing surfers, some there for safety.

They zoom around in circles looking for the biggest waves to ride as they march in from open ocean. Some sets come in further to the north, while others build and then crash nearer to the lighthouse. At any given time, there is a moment of drama happening in the water: Someone is riding a wave, someone else is being rescued, someone else is trying to outrun the white water. We know that some of the safety drivers and surfers are among the most famous names in the surfing world and yet it's impossible to identify any of them as they are specks in the ocean among the huge waves, buzzing around the biggest peaks like surfing flies.

The waves at Nazaré are amplified by a deep underwater canyon directly off the end of the point. The bathymetry makes the waves more than double in size compared with beaches to the north and south, and rideable. Nazaré has become a part of the folklore of surfing and has been featured many times on social media, in the media and on TV. A film about chasing the biggest – the elusive 30.5m (100ft) wave – has been airing on HBO in the USA. The shape of the wave, the fort and the cliff are so very familiar to me and yet being here is overwhelming. What you don't get from a photograph or a film is the sound of the waves booming as they break, the wind blowing against our backs as we watch, the spray drifting over us as the waves crash against the base of the cliff and the chatter from the hundreds of people watching. I hear all kinds of languages and accents, including German, French, Dutch, Spanish and Portuguese. I also hear British, American,

South African and Australian accents. There are people from every walk of life, drawn by the promise of seeing the world's biggest waves in a natural arena – a headland in Portugal.

A surfer – I don't know who – is towed into a wave and rides down the mountain of water. He is chased by the avalanche of white water as it crumbles and explodes behind him and the chatter stops. When they complete the ride – and by that, I mean they don't fall and have to be rescued – the crowd claps and cheers.

As the sets of waves roll in and the mist rises, the wind blows and the jetskis in the water dodge the white water, I think what a privilege it is to be able to come here and watch. I would normally prefer to surf rather than watch but, this time, on this occasion and in this place, there is no question I would ever enter the water. The surfers here put in a lifetime's worth of training, breath holding, ski driving and surfing to prepare for what I am looking at and I am beyond grateful to them for it. This is the Olympics and Everest of surfing and anyone can simply turn up and witness it for themselves.

It's incredible. I am humbled and appreciative.

Another surfer drops to the bottom of a huge wave and the crowd claps and cheers the Giants of Nazaré.

NB. Praia do Norte, Nazaré only works in the winter when huge Atlantic storms send waves to the west coast of Portugal, so don't expect to turn up in the summer and see big waves. The season runs from late October to about April. If you want to see the world's best surf here you can check the wave sizes on www.magicseaweed.com to see if it's worth going.

THE DRIVING

If ever there was a route to take slowly in this book, it is this one. The west coast of Portugal is beautiful and ever-changing. It has vast empty beaches, cliffs, wetlands, beach towns and villages, tiny stops and big holiday towns. Espinho is one of them. After visiting Porto, we left the city and drove south to Espinho on the A1 and the A41 to pick up the N109, the road that would begin our trip south.

Heading south on the N109 took us through the busy centre of Espinho. We then took a right-hand turn to cross the railway in Maceda to reach Praia do São Pedro de Maceda. This enabled us to drive along the coast through pine forest and into the small beach town of Praia do Furadouro, where there is a campsite close to the beach.

On leaving Furadouro, take the Avenida do Emigrante and then turn right on to the N327 at the big roundabout outside the town. This will carry you along the eastern side of a finger of land that is separated from the mainland by the Ria de Aveiro. The road follows the river so there are great views of the tidal wetlands (look out for flamingos), while the Atlantic lies just over the dunes to the west. A number of tiny roads will take you to quiet beaches along this stretch. Take your time and explore. Torreira has a beach front but also a marina that's filled with colourful traditional Portuguese fishing boats.

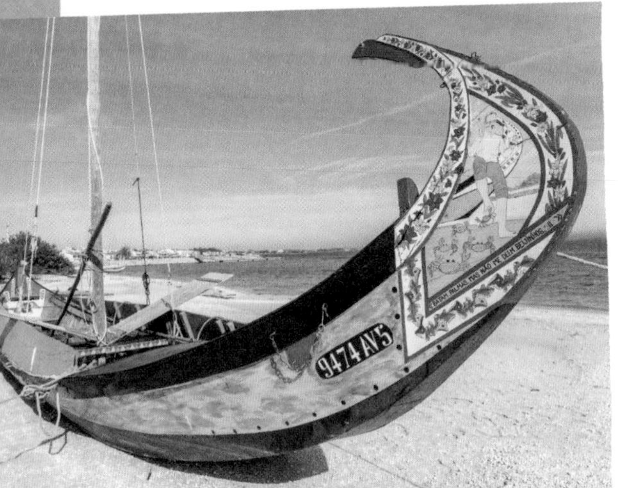

Follow the N327 to the end of the peninsula – it's a very quiet, straight and great road – to São Jacinto, another tiny beach town with a huge expanse of sand on the Atlantic side. In town, you can take the tiny ferry (OK for mohos – costs around €14 for a van plus extra passenger) across the river estuary to Aveiro. You'll come off in the port. Follow the signs for the A25 Praia da Barra. This will take you on to a very brief stretch of motorway over another part of the river to Barra. At the end of the motorway, turn right for Barra or turn left for Costa Nova. Barra is worth a look as it has a fabulous beach, shops, restaurants and lighthouse, with some motorhome parking on the river side to the north.

Heading south again, follow signs for Costa Nova. This will take you past the motorway junction (there is an *aire* here) and down the M592, still following the estuary. Your first major stop is Costa Nova – a town that's famous for its candy-striped houses that front the wetlands. It's a picture-perfect place that attracts a lot of tourists. We wondered where they all came from as we saw very few other people before or after the town!

After Costa Nova, it gets quieter. The road follows the river to Vagueira, a pretty beach town. Here, you can turn left on to the M591-2 to cross to the inland or you can follow the signs for the motorhome parking and Parque Aquático Vaga Splash and take the rough road to Praia de Duna Alta, where we found the nicest motorhome stopover we have ever been to. Run by a family with a visually impaired son, they are delightfully chirpy people and speak great English. The *aire* is fabulous, with amazing facilities (in summer, you can use the pool) and has direct access to the beach, where there is a brilliant and beautiful bar. Perfect for a sundowner.

Continue south from the *aire* and you'll come to Praia do Areão, which is effectively the end of the road. Turn right for the beach or turn left to cross the lagoon and continue through the cultivated wetlands as far as the CM591. It's not signposted, but it's on a cross-roads with a green-tiled

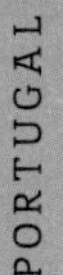

house opposite (caveat: at the time of researching). Turn right and head towards Praia de Mira. This will take you to a T-junction, where you'll need to turn right for the beach. This road will take you to a tiny roundabout in the town that's next to the lagoon on your left. Turn left here and follow the road around the lagoon, through the town, past the Orbitur campsite and through the pine forest to a roundabout in the middle of nowhere. Take the second exit, which has a sign saying the road is in bad condition (it isn't) and head south through the forest. This road is long and straight and continues for a few miles through the scrub and forest (some of it being cleared of eucalyptus). Where it rises to the top of a dune, the views are fantastic. After 11.3km (7 miles) you will come to another roundabout, at the junction with the N335-1. You can go straight if you want but, at the time of writing the surface had yet to be improved, so we turned left towards Tocha, a small town with a huge square. The N335-1 brought us back to the N109. Turn right here towards Figueira da Foz. This is a busy main road and will bring you to Figueira da Foz and a confusing junction with the bridge and the A14 motorway, which starts at the same junction. We followed the N109-8 into the city along the river and camped up at the *aire* by the jetty.

NB: It is a nice drive to continue on the N109-8 along the beach and out to the *mirador* (viewpoint) at Cabo Mondego. There are good restaurants in Figueira, plus a great antiques market on Saturdays on the quayside.

When you leave Figueira da Foz, head south over the bridge on the N109 and stay on it until you reach Monte Redondo (about 30km/18.6 miles). It's not a great bit of road and passes through small villages, aquaculture and farms. Turn right (it's the second right in the village) on to the N109-9 towards the coast and Aroeira. Continue on until you reach Praia do Pedrogão and then turn left at the roundabout to the campsite and the Estrada Forestale, the forest road. This will take you out

WHERE TO STAY: CAMPING

There are plenty of campsites in western Portugal to choose from: most towns have them. I can happily recommend the following:

Parque de Campismo do Furadouro, Ovar 3880-366 Ovar, Portugal **Web:** https://ccsjm.pt/categoria/parque-do-furadouro **Tel:** +351 256 59 60 10	*A large campsite about 500m (547 yards) from the beach at this pleasant beach town. Campers park near the entrance, while much of the site is given to seasonal pitches.*
Campsite Orbitur Valado (Nazaré), Nazaré Rua dos Combatentes do Ultramar 2, 2450-148 Nazaré, Portugal **Web:** www.orbitur.pt/pt/destinos/regiao-centro/orbitur-valado **Tel:** +351 262 56 11 11	*A good site with decent facilities outside Nazaré. It's cyclable to the town, but a little way out of town. Lots of surfers stay at Praia do Norte or at the Aquatic Park above the Far, where there is lots of tarmac.*
Ericeira Camping, Ericeira Estrada Nacional 247, Km 49,4, 2655-319 Ericeira, Portugal **Web:** www.ericeiracamping.com **Tel:** +351 261 86 27 06	*A site to the north of the town, opposite the beach.*
Peniche Praia Camping, Peniche Estr. Marginal Norte, 2520-605 Peniche, Portugal **Web:** www.penichepraia.pt **Tel:** +351 262 78 34 60	*Highly recommended site on the headland at Peniche. Close to beaches and surf. Spa on site.*
Lisboa Camping and Bungalows Estr. da Circunvalação, 1400-061 Lisboa, Portugal **Web:** https://lisboacamping.com **Tel:** +351 217 62 82 00	*A huge site in Monsanto Park with lots of pitches, a big pool, and a bar and restaurant. A little way from the city centre, but one of your only options to see the city. Book in advance in summer. More details on page 425.*

of town through littoral landscapes of pine, scrub and eucalyptus, and on to Praia da Vieira. There is a big *aire* here just after the river.

After Vieira, the Estrada Forestale becomes the Estrada Atlântico as it runs along the coast all the way into Nazaré. At Praia de São Pedro de Moel, the landscape begins to change a little, with dunes giving way to rocky cliffs. It is a spectacular bit of road that follows the coast closely and with a few access points to fabulous beaches and pounding surf. Eventually you will come to Nazaré and Praia do Norte. The Orbitur campsite is on the N8-5 a little way from both the town and Praia do Norte.

Leaving Nazaré, take the N242 through the wetlands at the back of Nazaré, around the lagoon at Praia de São Martinho do Porto and on to the N8 to go south to Caldas da Rainha. To negotiate Caldas, you'll need to follow the ring road to the west, which is the N360, and then re-join the N8 south of the city. This will take you on to Óbidos. Follow the N8 through the town and the turn right on to the N114 towards Peniche, taking the turn in Serra d'El-Rei for Baleal. This will take you to Baleal beaches, from where you can head south on the Avenue de Praia into Peniche. At the end of the beach road (by the Rip Curl shop), turn right at the roundabout to follow the N114 around the headland and back out of town again (you'll pass the turn-off to 'Supertubos' here) and on to the IP6 for one junction. Leave the IP6 and join the N247 south.

Stay on the N247 as it will take you along the coast through Ribamar, Praia da Santa Cruz, Barril and on to Ericeira. Stay on the N247 south of Ericeira and follow it all the way to Sintra. Here, it will follow a railway line around the city on a great bendy road and head up into the Parque Natural

WHERE TO STAY: *AIRES*

Vagueira: A really fantastic site next to the water park and right behind the dunes. Run by a lovely family. The grown-up son is well-travelled despite being sight impaired. As a result, he's great company and speaks good English. www.vagasplash.com/autocaravanas
Praia da Barra: There's a handy *aire* at the end of the A25 from Aveiro.
Óbidos: The *aire* is outside the city walls, just off the N114 and adjacent to the 3km (1.9 mile)-long aqueduct.
Figueira da Foz: A huge part of the car park adjacent to the breakwater is given over to *autocaravanas*. Fees apply during the week but not on Saturdays. Great location for exploring the city. Small beach next door.

de Sintra-Cascais, passing the Farol de Cabo Raso (worth a look) and then around the headland into Cascais. When you reach the junction with the N6 at Cascais, continue straight on as it will lead you towards the fortress, around the harbour and marina and then on to the N6 behind the beaches.

The N6 will take you all along the coast into Lisbon on a really great coastal cruise. Check out the beaches. Park up, have a swim! Enjoy. You are in one of Europe's most exciting cities!

IN THE AREA

Forte de São Miguel Arcanjo (Museum of Surf), Nazaré In the building under the lighthouse at the Promontório de Nazaré there is an exhibition of boards donated by the elite surfers who have surfed at Nazaré. It's a fascinating exhibition and entry (€2) gets you a ring-side seat on top of the lighthouse for viewing the surf.

Peniche A gritty but pretty town that's one of the hubs of Portuguese surfing. It is home to 'Supertubos' – a powerful, hollow beach break that's often a world contest site, as well as Baleal, a huge sweep of beach with shelter for beginners in huge swells. Go for a drive around the headland to Cabo Carvoeiro to find weird limestone shapes and views of the wild Atlantic. There is a campsite on the headland. • **www.penichepraia.pt**

Óbidos A medieval city in the mountains just east of Peniche. You will drive through it as you round the Lagoa de Óbidos. The city is one of the best-preserved in Portugal and also boats a 3km (1.9 mile)-long aqueduct, below which is an *aire*.

Caldas da Rainha A city with hot thermal springs that give it its name. Queen Leonora set up a hospital here, the first of its kind in the world. Caldas is also a UNESCO Creative City with a strong background in the arts and plenty of museums.

Ericeira A pretty port with great beaches that's a Save the Waves Coalition World Surfing Reserve due to the quality of the surf here. The town is pretty but groovy, with surf shops and narrow lanes. On first glance, there were lots of height barriers on car parks – a sure sign that there have been issues in the past. There is a campsite to the north of the town. • **www.ericeiracamping.com**

Lisbon A lively and funky capital city with a truly cosmopolitan vibe and great tourism infrastructure. Restaurants, bars, museums, viewpoints and, of course, the ever-present *pastel de nata*, the Portuguese speciality pastry. It also has a useable and city-wide tram system, many of which are older and very photographic.

The only place to stay that's anywhere near the city centre is the Lisboa municipal site, Lisboa Camping & Bungalows in the Parque Florestal de Monsanto to the west of the city centre. The 714 bus goes from right outside, costs €2 each way and takes you to Praça da Figueira (the town square) in about 40 minutes. • **https://lisboacamping.com**

We visited the Bairro Alto neighbourhood (narrow streets and old buildings) and the Chiado area (posh shopping) as well as the Alfama district (narrow streets and restaurants). We ate at the Time Out Market, a huge food court and events centre near to the river with lots of local specialities. • **www.timeoutmarket.com/lisboa**

The National Museum of Contemporary Art, Lisbon For culture vultures, this is worth a look, but it is by no means the only museum. There are museums to just about anything you could ever want, from Pharmacy to Money. • **www.museuartecontemporanea.gov.pt**

L. CAMÕES
24

INDEX

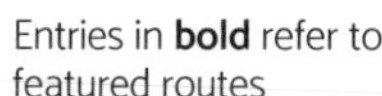

Entries in **bold** refer to featured routes

A

B

C

L

M

N

O

P

ACKNOWLEDGEMENTS

Lizzy, the chief navigator, route planner and camper van companion.
Tim and the team at **PFD** for all their encouragement and support.
Liz, Kate, Clara, Austin, Lucy, David and all the team at **Bloomsbury.**
Wim for the tips and recommendations.
Annie and **Graham** for swimming with us.
Grace, Maggie, Charlie, Lyle, Raef and **Lucy** for sharing their time with us.
Brittany Ferries' customer service staff, for being brilliant in very trying times.
The Cowboys of **Fort Bravo.**
The percebes collectors of Galicia.
Howie at **Roadpro** for his on call patience.